Johann Joseph Ignaz von Döllinger

Fables Respecting the Popes of the Middle Ages

A Contribution to Ecclesiastical History

Johann Joseph Ignaz von Döllinger

Fables Respecting the Popes of the Middle Ages
A Contribution to Ecclesiastical History

ISBN/EAN: 9783744794763

Printed in Europe, USA, Canada, Australia, Japan

Cover: Foto ©Lupo / pixelio.de

More available books at **www.hansebooks.com**

FABLES

RESPECTING THE

POPES OF THE MIDDLE AGES

RIVINGTONS

London .. .. *Waterloo Place*
Oxford .. .. *High Street*
Cambridge .. .. *Trinity Street*

FABLES

RESPECTING THE

POPES OF THE MIDDLE AGES

A Contribution to Ecclesiastical History

BY

JOHN J. IGN. VON DÖLLINGER

TRANSLATED, WITH INTRODUCTION AND APPENDICES

BY

ALFRED PLUMMER

FELLOW AND TUTOR OF TRINITY COLLEGE OXFORD

RIVINGTONS
London, Oxford, and Cambridge
1871

TO THE

PÈRE HYACINTHE

IN MEMORY OF

EVENTFUL DAYS SPENT WITH HIM

IN ROME AND IN PARIS

WHILE THIS WORK WAS IN PREPARATION

THIS VOLUME

IS AFFECTIONATELY DEDICATED

INTRODUCTION

INTRODUCTION

WHEN the translator was in Munich last year, he had the advantage of attending Dr. Döllinger's lectures on ecclesiastical history, and also the privilege of seeing something of him in private. It was then, with his sanction, and after consultation with him, that the present translation was undertaken. Several others of his still untranslated works were discussed, some of which it is hoped will before long appear in an English dress; but it was thought that, on the whole, the *Papstfabeln des Mittelalters* was the one likely to be interesting to the largest number of English readers.

<small>Occasion of undertaking this translation.</small>

There are certain problems in history which remain still unsolved, in spite of very frequent and very thorough discussion. Possibly they will always continue to be discussed, and will always remain unsolved. If, as seems to be the case in many of these instances, all existing evidence has been already discovered and brought to bear, and if even experts continue to interpret the evidence in as

<small>Unsolved, and apparently insoluble, historical problems.</small>

many different ways as the characters in Mr. Browning's *Ring and the Book* interpret the facts of the story told there,—what are non-experts to do but give up the question as hopeless, and as incapable of settlement as the dispute between Protagoras and his pupil? Among such unsolved historical problems we perhaps might mention these;—By what pass did Hannibal enter Italy?— Was the battle of Cannæ fought on the north or the south bank of the Aufidus?—Was S. Peter ever in Rome?—Who wrote the *Epistle to the Hebrews?*—Was Perkin Warbeck an impostor?— Are the Casket Letters genuine?—Was the Earl of Somerset guilty of the death of Sir Thomas Overbury?—Who was the man in the Iron Mask? —Who was Junius?—And lastly—thanks to the hideous disclosures of Mrs. Beecher Stowe—What is the "true story" of Lady Byron's separation from her husband? Others might be added to the list, but these will suffice. Perhaps no one, who reads through the list as it stands, but will object to one or more of these questions, as having, in the judgment of all candid and competent inquirers, been settled beyond appeal. And yet the very fact of their thus objecting might be but additional proof that an appeal is still possible. Mr. Law would consider that there is no reasonable doubt that the "Alps of Hannibal" are those which form the pass of the Little S. Bernard, and many scholars agree with him. But then

<small>The Alps of Hannibal.</small>

INTRODUCTION xi

Mr. Ellis is scarcely less confident that Hannibal's 8,000 horse, 40,000 foot, and 37 elephants, went over Mont Cenis. Dr. Arnold assumes it as certain that the battle of Cannæ was fought on the right bank of the river. His admirer, Professor Ihne, considers that the narratives of Livy and Polybius "prove conclusively that the field of battle was "on the left bank." Many students of ecclesiastical history will admit that "it is not so much a spirit "of sound criticism as a religious prejudice which "has led some Protestant writers to deny that the "Apostle [S. Peter] was ever in Rome."[1] And yet

<small>Cannæ.</small>

<small>St. Peter Rome.</small>

---

[1] These words, borrowed from Canon Robertson, were scarcely written, when some one, who is pleased to call himself "a follower "of Döllinger in Rome," wrote to the *Times* of May 30, 1871, to complain of Murray's *Handbook of Rome*, because it continually repeats the statement that S. Peter resided for some time in Rome; "whereas no sufficiently-informed person can now seriously hold "that S. Peter himself was ever in Rome; still less that he resided "there." This letter has called forth various letters in the *Times* and other journals, almost all of them in opposition to the self-styled "follower of Döllinger." It will be sufficient to notice the following points: (1) that in Murray's *Handbook* we find that localities with which S. Peter's name is connected are spoken of in this sort of way; "where S. Peter is *supposed* to have suffered martyr-"dom," &c.; (2) that Bassage, Le Clerc, Pearson, Hammond, Neander, Barrow, Thiersch, Alford, and many others, must be regarded as ill-informed persons, inasmuch as they "seriously hold" that S. Peter was, at least in the last year of his life, in Rome; (3) that Dr. Döllinger himself maintains that S. Peter founded the Church in Rome, and, after a long interval, died there. The theory that the apostle was never in Rome is condemned by him as monstrous. During the absurd attempt at a Jubilee, which was made in Rome June 16th and 17th of the present year, in honour of Pius IX., "qui Petri annos in Pontificatu Romano unus æquavit," it was curious to notice some of the local papers choosing this very question as a subject for leading articles, and endeavouring to show, with the writer to the *Times*, that S. Peter was never in Rome.

a Bampton Lecturer has recently declared from the University pulpit, that the positive evidence for S. Peter's ever having been in Rome is of comparatively late date and weak, while the negative evidence against it is very strong. Some critics will scarcely allow it to be called in question that *The Epistle to the Hebrews.* S. Paul is the author of the *Epistle to the Hebrews;* while a formidable number attribute it to Apollos, others to S. Barnabas or S. Luke. Are we not safe then in returning to the humble admission of Origen, that "Who wrote the Epistle, God alone knows with certainty?" Most people would give *Perkin Warbeck.* up the case of Perkin Warbeck. But it is easier to give him up than to prove that he was not the duke of York. Hume says somewhere, that the Whig who believes in the Popish Plot, and the *Guilt of Mary Queen of Scots.* Tory who believes in Mary queen of Scots, are beyond the reach of argument. There certainly are persons who, in spite of Hume, still believe in the innocence of Mary Stuart; and to believe in the innocence of Mary is to deny the authenticity of the damning Casket Letters. Yet Mr. Froude probably believes that he has established their genuineness beyond a doubt; and many other historians would be disposed to say that, though the fact is doubted, it is by no means doubtful. *Guilt of the Earl of Somerset.* His peers condemned the earl of Somerset on evidence which to the present generation seems inconclusive; but then it should be remembered that we have only the depositions of the witnesses, whereas the court not only read the depositions but saw the persons. Manner weighs much, and rightly, with a jury. Still, after admitting that Sir Thomas Overbury certainly was murdered, and in the way stated, and that the countess beyond a doubt compassed his death, perhaps no more can be said against the earl of Somerset than that there is no reason for believing him to be innocent, and much for believing him to be guilty. The Masque de Fer is the very Proteus of history, ever leading inquirers on to fancy that they have secured him in some definite form, and then—just when the chain of evidence which is to bind him to that form for ever seems all but complete—the mysterious prisoner shakes himself free, and reappears as a totally different person. No sooner has the complicated evidence, which promises to *prove* to us that the Iron Mask was Mattioli, been laboriously mastered, than we find ourselves compelled to reconsider whether he was not the comte de Vermandois, or a twin brother of Louis XIV. Much such another ambiguous personage is Junius. Mr. John Taylor showed that there was good reason for suspecting Sir Philip Francis of being Junius. Lord Brougham was convinced of it. Lord Macaulay claims to have all but proved it. And the elaborate work lately produced by the Hon. Edward Twisleton, and M. Charles Chabot, seems to be intended as a complete proof. But there are still persons who return a verdict of

_{The Iron Mask.}

_{Junius.}

"not proven," and think that Mr. Twisleton's book, with its numerous fac-similes of handwritings, itself furnishes evidence which goes far to show that Sir Philip Francis was *not* the author of the famous letters.

<small>Lord Byron.</small>

The amount of criticism which Mrs. Beecher Stow's "true story" called forth, not only as to her motive for publishing it, but also as to her facts, shows that the scandal about Lord Byron's private life is likely to remain one of the *dark* pages of biography in more senses of the word than one.

<small>The story of Pope Joan not one of these.</small>

This list of unsolved and apparently insoluble historical puzzles might, as has been said, be enlarged, and that almost indefinitely. Those selected are of very various importance, but they are, for the most part, popularly known as disputed questions; and they are purposely taken from very different periods in history. Many people have thought that the story of Pope Joan, which is the first of the "fables" discussed in this work, belongs to this class of historical riddles. Such appears to have been the opinion of Mosheim; such, as will be seen, was the avowed opinion of Kurtz. That there are still persons, and persons not altogether ignorant of history, who think the story of a female pope not incredible, the translator knows from experience. And perhaps it is not too much to say that most of those who gather round the

INTRODUCTION

card-table on winter evenings, to play or watch the round game which immortalizes the memory of the papess, would feel some hesitation in saying whether it had ever seriously been maintained that a woman had been pope, and still more hesitation in saying what grounds there are for believing or disbelieving the story. So long as such a state of haziness and uncertainty exists, even among educated persons, with regard to a fable so monstrous and so famous, a discussion of the birth, growth, and death of the story of Pope Joan—for, in spite of the efforts of Professor Kist, let us hope that the ghost of the papess *is* now laid for ever—will always be useful as well as interesting. There are some who can remember a somewhat similar case in the present century. Those who find it difficult to imagine how a fiction so preposterous as that of a female pope should ever have gained *any* serious belief, to say nothing of general acceptance, should remember the case of the famous Chevalier D'Eon. He was born in 1728, and after playing the parts of equerry to Louis XV., doctor of civil law, parliamentary advocate, officer in the army, ambassador, and royal censor, for some reason or other contrived to create first a doubt as to his sex, and then a general belief that he was a woman. The incredibility of the supposition that a woman could live thus long as a man, and in such very different characters, did not prevent it from being believed.

The case of the Chevalier d'Eon.

When he was about fifty years of age, he assumed female dress (being paid, it is said, by Louis XVI. to do so), and continued to wear it till the day of his death, when the question of his sex was decided. It had at times been the subject of heavy wagers; and from an article on female diplomatists, which appeared in a magazine some years ago, and in which he was mentioned, it would seem as if there were still persons who believed that the Chevalier may after all have been a woman. He died, in great indigence, in 1810.

<small>A fictitious pope.</small>

All who are familiar with the legend of S. Ursula and her ten thousand maidens, especially those who know the exquisite Chasse de Sainte Ursule, painted by Hans Memling, now in the Hospital of S. John at Bruges, are familiar with the name of Pope Cyriacus. But, possibly, not all are aware that the existence of any such pope is as great a fiction as the rest of the legend.

<small>A fictitious council invented.</small>

The Council of Sinuessa has long been famous in ecclesiastical history as a fiction, invented in the first instance by the Donatists, and amplified afterwards in order to serve as evidence in support of the claims of Rome. This is not the only case in which the Donatists have tried to falsify history in the matter of synods. While on the one hand,

INTRODUCTION

they attempted to foist on the Church a synod which never took place, wishing to show that pope Marcellinus had delivered up the Holy Scriptures and offered sacrifice to idols, on the other hand they attempted to deny the reality of a synod which certainly *did* take place in A.D. 305, at Cirta, in Numidia, and which seems mainly to have been composed of bishops who really had delivered up the Scriptures during the persecution under Diocletian, but who afterwards became most rigorous Donatists, frantically zealous against *traditores*. A real council denied, by the Donatists.

Other fables in connection with synods might be mentioned; but only those which are also *Fables respecting the Popes of the Middle Ages* are within the limits of the present subject. One such is far too considerable a fiction to be passed unnoticed. The object with which it has been invented is equally patent as in the case of the pretended Council of Sinuessa. In that case the object was to establish the principle—" prima sedes non judi-" catur a quoquam." In this the endeavour is to show that the decrees of an œcumenical council require the approbation of the pope. It is pretended that the Nicene fathers sent to pope Silvester, and asked him to give a formal sanction to the decrees of the council of Nicæa. The legend goes on to say that upon the decrees being forwarded to Rome, pope Silvester, with the emperor's consent, summoned another council of 275 bishops, Another fictitious council invented in support of papal claims.

in which the decrees of the Nicene fathers were approved, ratified, and supplemented with a number of regulations about the privileges and dress of the clergy, &c., questions quite foreign to that primitive age. The evidence for this fictitious synod is, as usual, a number of spurious documents. 1. A pretended letter from Hosius, bishop of Cordova, the reputed president at the council of Nicæa, Macarius, bishop of Jerusalem, and the two Roman priests Victor and Vicentius, who represented the see of Rome at the council in the absence of the aged Silvester. This letter is addressed to pope Silvester in the name of the whole council, and says that the pope ought to summon a Roman synod, in order to confirm the decisions of the council of Nicæa. 2. The pope's answer to this letter, together with his confirmation of the decrees. 3. A second letter from pope Silvester, very similar to the first. 4. The Acts of the pretended synod of 275 bishops mentioned above. 5. The so-called *Constitutio Silvestri*, of which some account is given elsewhere, is almost identical with these Acts, excepting that they do, and it does not, speak of giving approval to the decrees of the council of Nicæa. " These five documents," says bishop HEFELE, " have been preserved in several manu-" scripts, at Rome, Cologne, or elsewhere; they " have been reproduced in almost all the collec-" tions of the councils; but now all are unanimous " in considering them as spurious, as they evidently

marginal note: The evidence for it spurious documents.

INTRODUCTION

" are. They betray an age, a mode of thought,
" and circumstances, later than the fourth century.
" The barbarous, almost unintelligible, Latin of
" these documents specially points to a later cen-
" tury, and to a decay in the Latin language, which
" had not taken place at the time of the council of
" Nicæa."

The reasons for suspecting and condemning the first three of these documents need not detain us. They will be found in Hefele's *Conciliengeschichte*, t. bk. ii. ch. ii. § 44 (p. 443 of Clarke's translation). The reasons for considering the Acts of this Roman council as another instance of a *Fable respecting the Popes of the Middle Ages*, are the following. (*a*) It is incredible that all ancient authorities should be silent on the subject of so important a synod as one of 275 bishops summoned to confirm the decrees of Nicæa. Athanasius and Hilary professedly treat of the synods of this period, and neither of them even hints at this great synod at Rome. (β) The words " præsento 'Constantino " in the superscription cannot but mean that the supposed council was held in the presence of the emperor; whereas Constantine was not once in Rome during the whole of the year 325. But allowing that, as has been argued, these words of the superscription have been erroneously transferred from another passage, still (γ) the decree passed by these 275 bishops that Easter shall be celebrated between the 14th and 21st Nisan is

Reasons for regarding this council as a fiction.

anti-Nicene and absurd. (δ) So, again, the rule that the clergy are not to be tried before a secular tribunal is an anachronism. No such privilege was thought of in the Nicene period. (ε) Lastly, we have the crowning absurdity that this synod is represented as having decreed that a cleric who purposed becoming a presbyter must serve as an ostiarius for a year, as lector twenty years, as exorcist ten years, as acolyte five years, as sub-deacon five years, and as deacon five years. That is to say, a man must be well on for seventy years before taking priest's orders. An elder indeed!

Bishop Hefele condemns the documents as spurious, but would save the papal claims.

After bishop Hefele's letter to his clergy (April 23rd, 1871), one must cease to expect that historical learning will always baffle an authority which sets history at defiance. Otherwise one might have felt some astonishment that the learned historian of councils, after summing up to the effect that "all " these documents are, therefore, without doubt " apocryphal," should go on to plead, that " though " they are apocryphal, we must not conclude from " this that all their contents are false, that is to " say, that the council of Nicæa never asked " pope Silvester to give his approval to the " decrees."

Other fictions respecting early bishops of Rome.

Another fictitious synod may be mentioned in connection with early bishops of Rome, viz., the one which is said to have been held at Rome under pope Anicetus upon the Paschal question, at the time when Polycarp, bishop of Smyrna, visited

Rome. The meeting of these two bishops has been exaggerated into a council.

The legend that Marcellus, the successor of pope Marcellinus, was reduced to the servile office of a groom, rests on no better authority than these pretended Councils of Rome and Sinuessa. "Had "it any claim to truth," Dean MILMAN remarks, "the successors of Marcellus had full and ample "revenge, when kings and emperors submitted to "the same menial service, and held the stirrup "for the popes to mount their horses."

The fable of the baptism of Constantine by pope Silvester is the subject of the fourth of these essays. Truth, it is often said, is bolder and stranger than fiction. Truth in this case was *so much* stranger than fiction, that fiction was easily accepted in defiance of the authoritative evidence which supported the apparently incredible truth. And the truth which was discarded as incredible by an uncritical age, remains a subject for astonishment even to this day.[1] "He who had, five-and-twenty "years ago, been convinced of the Christian faith; "he who had opened the first General Council of "the Church; he who had called himself a Bishop "of Bishops; he who had joined in the deepest "discussions of theology; he who had preached to "rapt audiences; he who had established Chris-"tianity as the religion of the empire; he who

The baptism of Constantine.

[1] STANLEY, *Lectures on the Eastern Church.*

"had been considered by Christian bishops an in-
"spired oracle and apostle of Christian wisdom,
"was himself not yet received into the Christian
"Church. He was not yet baptized; he had not
"even been received as a catechumen. A death-
"bed baptism was to the half-converted Christians
"of that age, what a death-bed communion is to
"those of our own. In later ages, as we have seen,
"it was endeavoured to antedate the baptism of
"the emperor by ten or twenty years. But at
"that time it was too common to attract any
"special notice. Good and bad motives alike con-
"duced to the same end, and of all these Constan-
"tine was a complete example. He, like many of
"his countrymen, united, after his conversion, a
"sincere belief in Christianity with a lingering
"attachment to Paganism. He, like some even of
"the noblest characters in the Christian Church,
"regarded baptism much as the Pagans regarded
"the lustrations and purifications of their own
"religion, as a complete obliteration and expiation
"of all former sins; and, therefore, partly from a
"superstitious dread, partly from the prudential
"desire, not peculiar to that or any age, 'of making
"'the best of both worlds,' he would naturally
"defer the ceremony to the moment when it would
"include the largest amount of the past, and leave
"the smallest amount of the future."

The Donation. On the monstrous fiction of the Donation of

Constantine there is no need to add to what will be found in the fifth essay, either in the way of introduction or comment. The more that one considers the subject, the more one wonders at the ignorance and audacity of those who perpetrated the forgery, the credulity of those who through so many centuries accepted it as historical, and (it is surely not unfair to add) the dishonest and short-sighted policy of those, who, knowing it to be false, were either too avaricious to forego claims for which it was the chief or sole foundation, or too timid to confess that Rome had countenanced and profited by a lie.[1]

The obscurity of the early bishops of Rome has been noticed as one great element in the foundation of that enormous dominion over the minds and bodies of men which their successors enjoyed. " Rome had no Origen, no Athanasius, no Ambrose, " no Augustine, no Jerome. . . . . . This more " cautious and retired dignity was no less favour- " able to their earlier power, than to their later " claim to infallibility. If more stirring and am- " bitious men, they might have betrayed to the

Liberius no obscure person like the early popes.

---

[1] The Donation of Constantine has these two elements of truth in it; (1) " in as far as that document aimed at proving the possession " of property by the popes before the arrival of the Franks in Italy, " it was substantially correct."—(REICHEL'S *See of Rome in the Middle Ages*, p. 58); (2) " it is the most unimpeachable evidence of " the thoughts and beliefs of the priesthood which framed it, some " time between the middle of the eighth and the middle of the tenth " century."—BRYCE'S *Holy Roman Empire.* London, 1866, p. 108.

"civil power the secret of their aspiring hopes; if they had been voluminous writers, in the more speculative times, before the Christian creed had assumed its definite and coherent form, it might have been [still] more difficult to assert their unimpeachable orthodoxy."

Parallel between Liberius and Boniface VIII.

With the pontificate of Liberius we feel that this period of primitive obscurity has altogether passed away. The bishops of Rome are no longer unknown unimportant personages, attracting little or no attention beyond the limits of their small and humble congregation, except when the policy or fanaticism of an emperor singled them out as objects of persecution. There is already much that is prophetic of Gregory VII. and Boniface VIII. Liberius is no Telesphorus or Hyginus, far less known to the Romans of the time than the current imperial favourite or the latest successful gladiator. He is no Pontianus, Fabianus, or Xystus, going forth quietly to exile or to death in submission to the will of a tyrant. Rather we find in him, along with much weakness, vacillation, and time-serving, the haughtiness of his successors eight or ten centuries later. He is already the influential and popular ecclesiastic, who can answer the demands of a heterodox emperor with a flat refusal, flinging back his presents and disdaining his threats. In his contest with Constantius there is something that reminds us of that between Gregory and Henry, and between Innocent and Frederick, still more of that between Boniface and Philip the Fair. The violent seizure of Liberius by the imperial emissaries, and the still more violent seizure of Boniface by William of Nogaret and Sciarra Colonna, have much in common; as also the triumphant returns of both pontiffs to Rome. But the triumph of Boniface was the result of momentary enthusiasm, succeeded by a general and lasting revolt against him; and this, as has been very justly remarked, is his severest condemnation. The triumph of Liberius was an earnest of the enduring affection of his people; an affection which had remained true to him during his exile, and which he seems to have retained until his death. The real greatness of Boniface was lost sight of in the presence of his avarice, his haughtiness, and his tyranny. The guilty compromise by means of which Liberius purchased his return was forgotten in the general amiability of his character. It is a coincidence worth noting that, while Liberius thus prominently steps forward from the obscurity which envelopes most of his predecessors, he at the same time loses the character of unfailing orthodoxy, with which (in the absence of evidence to the contrary) it is not difficult to invest them. Zephyrinus, it is true, during his long pontificate, had held and taught heterodox and contradictory doctrines respecting the Godhead, sometimes following Noetus, sometimes Sabellius. But his errors were the errors of a confused and ignorant man,

With their obscurity the popes lose the character of inerrancy.

ruled by the powerful and subtle mind of Callistus; and Zephyrinus left behind him no formal statement of his beliefs to discredit his office. It was reserved for Liberius to commence his pontificate by excommunicating Athanasius, and to regain it by signing the semi-Arian creed of Sirmium,[1] and once more renouncing communion with the great champion of the creed of Nicæa.

It is only just to his memory to add that in his last days he was the means of winning over a large number of Oriental bishops to accept the creed to which he had once himself been so lamentably untrue.

Felix II. and Felix V. If Liberius is the forerunner of those haughty and time-serving pontiffs who, contending as equals with emperors and kings, were alternately opposed and flattered by them, Felix is the forerunner of those anti-popes who were set up by Ghibelline princes for purposes of their own,—Guibert of Ravenna, Maurice "the Barbarian," cardinal Octavian of S. Cecilia.[2] Like his namesake, the last of the anti-popes, Felix gave way before the indisputable success of his rival, and retired to end his days in peaceful seclusion. Felix II., living on his estate near the road to Portus, anticipates by nearly

---

[1] It is a little doubtful which of the three Sirmian creeds Liberius signed. The first was far the least Arian of the three. But in any case he abandoned the Nicene creed. See a very thorough discussion of this question in the appendix to Dr. NEWMAN's *Arians of the Fourth Century*. Note III., pp. 433–440 of the third edition.

[2] Clement III., Gregory VIII., Victor IV., according to their assumed titles.

eleven centuries Felix V., once more Amadeus of Savoy, in his quiet retreat at Ripaille.

Wie der Geschichtschreiber ein rückwärts gekehrter Prophet, so ist der Prophet häufig nur ein rückwärts gekehrter Geschichtschreiber, und verkündet als künftig bereits geschehene Dinge. So writes DR. DÖLLINGER in his essay in the current number of Raumer's (now Riehl's) *Historisches Taschenbuch*, on *Der Weissagungs-glaube und das Prophetenthum in der christlichen Zeit*. History is inverted prophecy; prophecy is often only inverted history. The historian may write the future in the past; the prophet, his whole soul full of the glories or miseries of the past, sees them (or their opposite) again in front. How much of the history of pope Anastasius II. is a prophecy of events with which the author of the above-mentioned essay is now most intimately connected, we are not yet in a position to say. The memory of pope Anastasius has been blasted, because he ventured to doubt the damnation of one who had been excommunicated by the bishop of Rome. After centuries of infamy, his name has been rescued from calumny and restored to honour, as that of one who knew how to be generous even in theological controversy, and to be tolerant in an age when toleration was more than rare. Between the violence of Felix III. and Gelasius, and the troubled election and reign of Symmachus, the

Two cases of unjust excommunication.

brief pontificate of Anastasius is an oasis, on which the eye rests with pleasure, in the midst of an age in which religious controversy everywhere was at fever-heat, and in which the unity of the Church was shattered to a degree which seemed to threaten the very existence of Christianity itself. And at the present time, while most of the piety and much of the learning in the Roman Church has bound its own eyes and hands and feet, and bowed in unreasoning submission before an all but deified pope, there is still one to whom the bewildered student of ecclesiastical history can look with confidence; one who after a long life of rare activity, devoted to the defence of authority, still dares to teach that Truth is supreme;—ἀμφοῖν γὰρ ὄντοιν φίλοιν ὅσιον προτιμᾶν τὴν ἀλήθειαν. History has done tardy justice to the memory of the "heretic" Anastasius. The "heretics" of our own day, who have again ventured to doubt the efficacy of an unjust anathema, can afford to look forward with calmness to the verdict of posterity. They have been nobly loyal to history, and history will not be unfaithful to them.

Attempts to defend Honofarious to succeed.

On the vexed question of Honorius a few words will be found in an Appendix. It must ever remain the great, though by no means the only historical obstacle in the way of infallibilists. If they would but agree on some *one* method of attempting to surmount the difficulty, they might have a better prospect of convincing those, who have no interest in the question beyond a desire to arrive at the truth. But seeing that so many varying, and often conflicting hypotheses are put forward, and that some of them are so violent that any historical fact whatever might be discredited by such means, only those are likely to be convinced, who approach the question with a determination, or at least a strong desire to be so. " Comme leur cause est " mauvaise," dit Bossuet, " ils ne peuvent tenir bon " sur aucun point; n'ayant aucun moyen solide, ils " en cherchent toujours de nouveaux; ils passent " d'une argumentation à l'autre, sentant bien que " chacune leur échappe." Mais tous ces défenseurs ensemble oublient ce conseil de bons sens:

> " Le trop d' expédients peut gater une affaire . . . .
> N' en ayons qu'un, mais qu'il soit bon."

Thus far our course has been clear enough. The question with regard to nearly all the fables discussed up to this point will be considered by most impartial historians as closed. Few who have examined the subject will still venture to maintain that Pope Joan and Pope Cyriacus may have been real personages, or that the Council of Sinuessa, and the baptism of Constantine by Silvester in Rome, may have been historical facts. The question which is still open with respect to such stories is not—" are they true?" but—" how and when " did they arise?" The case of pope Gregory II.

<small>Difficulty of determining the policy of Gregory II.</small>

and the emperor Leo the Isaurian, is somewhat more difficult. To say that Gregory stirred up the Italian revolt against Leo is untrue, as is argued in the essay on the subject which follows. To say that the pope had nothing whatever to do with hastening the rupture between Rome and the East, seems to be an erroneous statement on the other hand. Gregory no doubt shared the belief, common in his age, that the empire was the necessary complement of the Church, and that the welfare of Christendom depended upon the preservation and union of both. Hence his unwillingness to break with the Byzantine court, even though the prince at the head of it was, from Gregory's point of view, a heretic who, if not demented, was scarcely a Christian. But the attitude was a difficult one to maintain. It was difficult outside the Church to persuade men to remain loyal to a prince, whom inside the Church he was openly denouncing as an impious and sacrilegious renegade. The long absence of the emperors from Rome, and the unpopular conduct of their representatives in Ravenna, had done much to destroy all respect for the imperial authority in Italy; and Gregory's exhortations to loyalty fell on unwilling ears. His denunciations of the heretic and persecutor, who was making a clean sweep of their most cherished religious objects, found an echo in the heart of every one, whether priest or layman, soldier or peasant. "To your tents, O Israel!" was everywhere the cry; and the proposal seems to have been seriously entertained of electing a new emperor, and conducting him to Constantinople to displace the apostate. But Byzantine rule in Italy, though doomed, was not yet dead. It lingered on for fifteen, or perhaps we may say five-and-twenty years longer,[1] the shadow of its former self. The idea of Rome as an independent state, perhaps scarcely occurred to Gregory; or, if it did, he knew that such a state would have but a poor chance of making a stand against the hated Lombards. What the Gauls had been to old Rome, and the Saracens became to Europe in general at a later age, the Lombards were to Italy in the eighth century. Horror of these northern barbarians was perhaps the leading motive in Gregory's policy. In the empire, as an institution, he was probably disposed to believe as necessary and divine. Towards Leo, personally, his feeling could scarcely have been other than one of the deepest repugnance. But the one paramount fact, outweighing every other consideration, was the necessity of keeping the Lombards in check, and the inability of Rome to do this single-handed.

[1] The insurrection at Ravenna, in consequence of the publication of Leo's iconoclastic edict, took place in A.D. 727. Rome remained subject to the Byzantine emperors till 741, when, at the election of pope Zachary, the asking of the exarch's consent was for the first time omitted, never again to be renewed. When the exarchate became extinct in 752, the last tie, for long a very fragile one, which had connected Italy with the Eastern empire, was hopelessly severed. The independent dukedom of Rome followed, to be succeeded half a century later by the new-born empire of the West.

The pontificate of Silvester II.[1] is the first streak of dawn in that black night which settled down on the papacy soon after the death of John VIII., and which did not finally clear away till a German was elevated to the papal throne, in the person of Clement II., and the great mind of Hildebrand had begun to make itself felt in Rome. Both the first gleam and the break of lasting day were due to appointments made by German emperors. It was, thanks to the chivalrous and enthusiastic Otho III., "the wonder of the world," that his tutor, the learned Gerbert, was raised to the chair of S. Peter; just as it was Henry III. to whom the perplexed synod of Sutri owed and owned its obligations for the appointment of Clement II. The learning and science with which Gerbert adorned an office, which for more than a century had been distinguished chiefly by the ignorance and wickedness of those

Good popes appointed by German emperors.

---

[1] "As to a real free election of a pope, there was neither thought "nor mention of it. ... In Rome, as well as out of it, there was "nothing on which the pope could rest for support. Without the "emperor he was a mere ball tossed about by the hands of the "audacious factions of the nobles. Emperors, acting under the "advice of their bishops and spiritual councillors, had given more "worthy popes to the Church than the Roman chiefs, who had no "motive in selection beyond the gratification of their own ambition; "and they sometimes preferred the most unworthy candidate, "because they hoped to find in such a more pliant tool. ... The "popes were elevated sometimes by the one, sometimes by the other "party; but, after a brief period of time, were deposed again, and "either ended their days in dungeons, or were murdered. It was "not until Otho III. appointed his cousin Bruno, and afterwards the "celebrated Gerbert, as popes, and protected them by an armed "force, that the papacy could once more obtain and exercise its "influence and authority in ecclesiastical affairs."—DÖLLINGER. *Kirche und Kirchen*, II., i. English translation, pp. 341, 342.

who held it,[1] seemed to his contemporaries to be
marvellous. By the eleventh, twelfth, and thirteenth centuries it was believed to be something
more. From the marvellous to the supernatural is
an easy leap with the vulgar of all ages. It is one
which most persons in those times were ever ready
to take. They could see but one probable explanation of knowledge so extraordinary—a compact
with the devil. "Homagium diabolo fecit et male
finivit," is the startlingly brief note on him in the
lives of the archbishops of Ravenna.[2] It is not difficult to see why the supernatural assistance was
supposed to be diabolical rather than divine. As
an imperial nominee, "the new Silvester of the
new Constantine" was regarded with suspicion

---

[1] "There is not one at Rome, it is notorious, who knows enough
"of letters to qualify him for a door-keeper. With what face shall
"he presume to teach, who has never learned.... To such monsters,
"full of all infamy, devoid of all knowledge, human and divine, are
"all the priests of God to submit?" Speech of Arnulph, bishop
of Orleans, at the council of Rheims, a speech in which there is
good reason to believe that Gerbert himself, not yet archbishop of
Rheims, is the real speaker.—MILMAN, *Lat. Christ.* book v., chap. xiii.

July, A.D. 991.

[2] MILMAN, l. c., note x.
Walther von der Vogelweide makes use of Gerbert as a very vul-
nerable spot in the history of the papacy.
"Der stuol ze Rôme ist allerêrst berihtet rehte,
Als hie vor bî einem zouberære Gêrbrehte.
Der selbe gap ze valle wan sîn eines leben:
Sô wil sich dirre und al die kristenheit ze valle geben.
Alle zungen sulu ze Gote schrien wâfen,
Und riiefen ime, wie lange er welle slâfen,
Si widerwürkent sîniu werc und felschent sîniu wort.
Sîn kamerære stilt im sînen himelhort,
Sîn süener mordet hie und roubet dort,
Sîn hirte ist zeinem wolve im worden under sînen schâfen."

by the turbulent nobles, who soon after his election broke out into open rebellion. In the decree for the election of Gerbert, Otho speaks of these feudatory princes as the scum of the earth, an expression not likely to conciliate them to the pontiff thus introduced to them. And the Roman historians of a later age knew that Gerbert had given utterance to such damnable doctrines as these: "Rome "cannot make lawful that which God condemns, "nor condemn that which God has made lawful.

Silvester's liberalism a probable cause of the calumnies against him.

"Rome cannot expel from her communion him who "is convicted of no crime. The papal decrees are "only of force when they concur with the Evan- "gelists, the Apostles, the Prophets, and the "genuine canons of the Church." This was as archbishop of Rheims in a letter to the archbishop

A.D. 996.

of Sens. The Middle Ages accused him of magical arts, and of intercourse with Satan. It seems to have been reserved for a historian[1] of the present age to suspect him of having compassed the death of his predecessor, Gregory V.!

Silvester II. did not long survive his patron. Otho died Jan. 22nd, 1002; Silvester, May 12th, 1003; both, it is said, of poison, administered by the revengeful hand of Stephania. Both left many grand projects unfulfilled.[2] The temporary gleam

---

[1] GFRÖRER, who calls him "die Schlange zu Ravenna," p. 1507. —MILMAN, bk. v., chap. xii., note 9.

[2] The year A.D. 1000 was to be the commencement of a new golden age both in Church and State. The various expectations

of light passed away, and the darkness which followed seemed all the deeper in consequence.

> "Plangat mundus, plangat Roma,
> Lugeat Ecclesia."

Thus much on the subjects of these essays. Of the author of them it is difficult to write with calmness, at a time when his name has become a watchword with the one, and a byword with the other, of the two great parties into which the whole of Germany—one might almost say the whole of Europe—is at the present moment divided. It is difficult to be temperate in one's language, when one thinks that the very severest of all ecclesiastical punishments—a punishment usually reserved for priests who have been guilty of the grossest immorality—has been inflicted on the most learned and the most honest of living theologians, and by the hand of one who a few months ago was contending for the same truth for which he is now making his brother-priest suffer. Be the miseries of the greater excommunication what they may, who would not prefer them to the position of the present archbishop of Munich? If anything could increase the shame of a judge who had pronounced such a sentence, it would be to become the hero of such journals as the *Volksbote* and the *Vaterland*.

which were formed with respect to that year in the time immediately preceding might be made the subject of another essay on mediæval fables.

To do the archbishop justice, it is only fair to say that he has spoken to his Chapter with disapprobation of some of the indecent articles which the Ultramontane press has of late been pouring forth against the "heretic," "Herr Reichsrath "Döllinger."

It seems almost an impertinence to offer to tell who Dr. Döllinger is. Yet there are some Englishmen to whom he was not even a name until he was excommunicated, and to whom even now he is little more than a name. For the sake of those who may chance to become acquainted with him as an author first in the present volume, I venture to add the following particulars respecting him and his works, mainly from the biographical notice of him in Mr. Maccabe's translation of *Kirche und Kirchen*.

<small>Biographical sketch of Dr. Döllinger as an author.</small> John Joseph Ignatius von Döllinger was born at Bamberg on the 28th of February, 1799, and was educated at Würtzburg. He was ordained priest April 15th, 1822, and began life as a parish priest in Franconia; he then became professor in the Ecclesiastical Seminary of Aschaffenberg, and, in 1826, was appointed one of the Faculty of Theology in the new University of Munich. The results of the French revolution were then everywhere felt. Rationalism was everywhere predominant; and there was no master-mind among the Roman Catholics of Germany. The student

was thrown upon his own resources, and compelled to rely on his own independent research for the acquisition of knowledge and the formation of his judgment. The results of such a course are everywhere apparent in the works of Dr. Döllinger. Profound and extensive learning, a judgment ever seeking to free itself from personal and partial influences, the habit of going direct to original sources, a critical method to which patristic, scholastic, and modern authorities are alike subjected, are among the characteristics which distinguish his writings.

Dr. Döllinger's earliest work was on *The Doctrine of the Eucharist in the first three Centuries*,[1] 1826. Two years later appeared a *History of the Reformation*, forming the third volume of "Hortig's Ecclesiastical History." He then undertook to rewrite the whole work, and in 1833 and 1835, published the first and second volumes of the *Church History*,[2] by which his name first became widely known for the learned and able defence of Catholicism, and for the confidence and courage with which many views, repeated until they had become regarded as unquestionable, were abandoned as unwarranted. *The History, Character, and Influence of Islamism*[3] appeared in 1838; and

---

[1] *Die Lehre der Eucharistie in den ersten drei Jahrhunderten.*
[2] *Kirchengeschichte.*
[3] *Mohammed's Religion nach ihrer innern Entwickelung und ihrem Einflusse auf das Leben der Völker. Eine historische Betrachtung.* Regensburg, 1838.

a compendium of the History of the Church down to the Reformation was published in 1836–1843. The history of the first centuries is given with extreme brevity; but that of the Middle Ages, though much compressed, displays even more erudition than the larger work on the earlier period. In the English translation these two histories have been unskilfully combined in one. Between 1846 and 1848 Dr. Döllinger published three large volumes on the history of German Lutheranism—*The Reformation, its internal Development and Effects*.[1] It is, as Dr. Döllinger himself remarked to the present writer, a one-sided book, written with the definite object of disproving the theory that the German reformers revived pure apostolic Christianity in the presbytery. It contains large quotations from the writers of the reformation period in their own language. This fact, while giving the work a value for the student which it can never lose, renders it uninviting to the more general reader, and scarcely capable of translation. A whole volume is devoted to the history of the development of the doctrine of Justification by Faith only. The research exhibited is immense.

During this period Dr. Döllinger delivered courses of lectures on several other branches of Divinity,

---

[1] *Die Reformation, ihre innere Entwickelung und ihre Wirkungen im Umfange des luther. Bekenntnisses.* Regensburg, 1848-1851.

besides those which specially belonged to his chair; on "the Philosophy of Religion," "Canon Law," "Symbolism," and "the Literature of the Patristic "Age." He céded his professorship of ecclesiastical history for some years to Möhler, whose lesser writings he afterwards collected, taking meanwhile the professorship of dogmatic theology, which in his hands became a history of revelation and of the development of doctrine. He did not print his lectures, but published from time to time a number of occasional writings. Among the earliest were *An Essay on the Religion of Shakespeare*, and a lecture *On the Introduction of Christianity among the Germans*. *A Commentary on the Paradise of Dante*, accompanied by the designs of Cornelius, appeared in 1830; *Mixed Marriages*[1] in 1838, during the conflict between the Prussian Government and the archbishop of Cologne. Articles on the Tractarian movement, on John Huss and the council of Constance, and on the Albigenses, appeared at various times in the *Historisch-politische Blätter*, a periodical over which Dr. Döllinger (though rarely a contributor) presided for many years. A dissertation on *the position*[2] *of the Church towards those who die out of her Communion* was written in 1842, on the occasion of the death of the dowager queen of Bavaria.

---

[1] *Ueber gemischte Ehen*.
[2] *Pflicht und Recht der Kirche gegen Verstorbene eines fremden Bekenntnisses*. A reprint from the *Histor. polit. Blätter*, 1852.

A lecture on *Error, Doubt, and Truth*,[1] was delivered to the students of the University of Munich on January 11th, 1845, and afterwards published. A speech on *the Freedom of the Church*,[2] one of the most admirable of his smaller works, was delivered on October 3rd, 1849, before a meeting of the Catholic Union of Germany at Ratisbon. *Martin Luther, a Sketch*, was reprinted, in 1852, from a theological encyclopædia, to which he also contributed articles on Bossuet and Duns Scotus. A pamphlet on *Coronation by the Pope* was put out in 1853, when it was feared that Pius IX. would be induced to crown Napoleon as emperor of the French. The pamphlet discussed the different occasions on which coronations by the pope had taken place, and the error which had been committed in the latest instance.

From 1845 to 1847 Dr. Döllinger represented the University of Munich in the Bavarian Chamber. Several of his speeches have been published.[3] In 1847 he was deprived of his professorship, and consequently of his seat in the Chamber, where the ministers who had been raised to power by Lola Montez dreaded the influence of his eloquence and character. Having been elected a deputy to the national parliament in 1848, he

---

[1] *Irrthum, Zweifel, Wahrheit, eine Rede u. s. w.*

[2] *Die Freiheit der Kirche.*

[3] *Drei Reden, gehalten auf dem bayerischen Landtage,* 1846. 1. *Die kirchlichen Anträge des Reichrathes.* 2. *Die protestantischen Beschwerden.* 3. *Die Judenfrage.*

spoke and wrote with great effect in favour of religious liberty; and the definition of the relations between Church and State, which was passed at Frankfort, and afterwards nominally adopted both at Vienna and Berlin, is said to have been his work. The same spirit and the same principles, which made him in religion the most thorough of controversial writers, and the most earnest advocate of reforms, guided him also in politics, and inspired him in society, making him at once the exponent of the highest catholicism, and the champion of religious freedom. Tyranny in the Church was condemned as one great support of absolutism in the State, and the faults and shortcomings of Catholics were rebuked as one fruitful source of Christendom's divisions. In adjudicating between religion and society, Protestantism and Rome, Dr. Döllinger admitted no compromise, but, acknowledging the just claims and real progress of the modern world, and the evils which afflict the Roman Church, he sought to distinguish that which is essential and true from those things with which ignorance or interest, superstition or scepticism, have overlaid and obscured it.

In the spring of 1849 he returned to Munich, and was restored to his professorship, and also to his seat in the Chamber, which, however, he resigned two years later, in order to devote himself to the completion of his literary plans. Since that time several great works have been published by him. The appearance of the *Philosophumena*, by Miller, 1851, gave rise to a prolonged discussion, in which many Catholics sought to weaken the testimony of the author, whilst Protestant writers endeavoured to use his authority for the purpose of throwing discredit on the Church of Rome. In answer to both parties—especially to Giesler, Baur, Bunsen, Wordsworth, and Lenormant—Dr. Döllinger published, in 1853, *Hippolytus and Callistus: the Roman Church in the Third Century*,[1] perhaps of all his writings, the one in which his ingenuity of combination, his skill as a logician, and his lofty tone in handling the interests of his Church, are most conspicuous. The classical learning shown in this work was more abundantly displayed in the introduction to the history of Christianity, which appeared under the title of *Paganism and Judaism*,[2] better known in England by the title which its translator, the Rev. N. Darnell, of New College, has given to it, *The Gentile and the Jew*. In 1860 appeared a volume entitled *Christianity and the Church in the period of their Foundation*,[3] which some consider to be the author's masterpiece. In October, 1861, Dr.

---

[1] *Hippolytus und Kallistus, oder die römische Kirche in der ersten Hälfte des dritten Jahrhunderts; mit Rücksicht auf die Schriften und Abhandlungen HH. Bunsen, Wordsworth, Baur, und Giesler.* Regensburg, 1853.

[2] *Heidenthum und Judenthum.*

[3] *Christenthum und Kirche in der Zeit der Grundlegung.* Regensburg, 1860. Translated by the Rev. H. N. Oxenham, *The First Age of Christianity and the Church*.

Döllinger published his celebrated work on the papacy and the temporal power, well known in England from Mr. W. B. Maccabe's translation, with the title of *The Church and the Churches*.[1] The present work, *Fables respecting the Popes in the Middle Ages*,[2] appeared in May, 1863. The latest writing published by Dr. Döllinger, not reckoning the famous *Declarations*[3] which have appeared in the *Allgemeine Zeitung*, is a most interesting essay on *Belief in Soothsaying and Prophecy in Christian Times*[4] in Raumer's *Historisches Taschenbuch*. In this he has collected together the most remarkable of the prophecies which have been current in various parts of Europe since the opening of the Christian era, and classified them according to their origin, subject matter, and object. The number is truly astonishing. Dr. Döllinger purposes to continue the subject with an essay on Dante, in his character as a *prophet*, in both senses of the word—i. e., as a great and inspired teacher, and as a seer, or foreteller of future events; aspects of the great mediæval poet which have hitherto been comparatively lost sight of. He is also engaged on a work treating of the constitution and internal government of the Church. The pressing need

[1] *Kirche und Kircle, Papstthum and Kirchenstaat.* München, 1861.
[2] *Die Papstfabeln des Mittelalters.* München, 1863.
[3] Especially those which appeared March 29th and June 13th, 1871.
[4] *Der Weissagungsglaube und das Prophetenthum in der Christlichen Zeit.*

which exists at the present time for a thorough and dispassionate investigation of this intricate subject, can scarcely be over-stated. Those who are best acquainted with Dr. Döllinger's works will feel the greatest confidence that, as far as fairness and thoroughness are concerned, the forthcoming work will leave little to be desired. The two qualities which have distinguished the leading spirits in the great religious movement of the present time are their fearless appeal to first principles and antiquity, and their moderation.

It would be no unpleasing task to endeavour to express all that one knows and feels of admiration, gratitude, and respect for the great theologian who is the centre and pivot of the whole movement. But the words of another great man, who, under circumstances still more difficult and trying, has been to France what Dr. Döllinger has been to Germany, will carry far more weight than any words of the present writer.

In the touching discourse on *France and Germany*, which PÈRE HYACINTHE delivered in London in December last, occurs the following striking passage :—[1]

" C'est en Allemagne que le Protestantisme s'est
" développé le plus complètement peut-être dans les
" deux directions nécessaires à tout mouvement reli-

---

[1] *France et Allemagne.* Discours prononcé à Londres, le 20 Décembre, 1870, par le R. P. Hyacinthe. London, Macmillan and Co., 1871, pp. 30, 31.

" gieux, et qui, souvent opposées dans leur marche,
" finissent toujours par se réconcilier, je veux parler
" de la science et de la piété. Oui, la science sous
" sa forme la plus progressive, téméraire, égarée
" quelque-fois, mais honnête, profonde et féconde,
" la science a eu son foyer dans ces universités sans
" rivales, je peux le dire, même en Angleterre ; et
" la piété, sous sa forme la plus pratique et la plus
" touchante, a eu son sanctuaire dans le cœur de
" ces populations instruites et naïves qui se repo-
" sent de leurs travaux dans la paix en lisant la
" Bible et Schiller, et qui vont au combat, comme
" dans cette guerre, en chantant les versets de leurs
" vieux psaumes sous les sapins de leurs vieilles
" forêts !

" Mais a côté de ce Protestantisme, auquel j'ai *Père Hyacinthe's estimate of him.*
" voulu rendre hommage, l'Allemagne n'a pas cessé
" de nourrir un Catholicisme non moins éclairé, non
" moins honnête, et non moins libéral. Il s'est
" manifesté au Concile du Vatican par cette oppo-
" sition triomphante dans son apparente défaite, à
" laquelle il avait donné quelques uns de ses plus
" fermes soutiens. Toutefois ce n'est pas dans un
" évêque, mais dans un simple prêtre qu'il se per-
" sonnifie, vieillard demeuré jeune par l'esprit et le
" cœur sous le poids des années et de l'expérience,
" patriarche de la science allemande, comme on l'a
" si bien dit, mais patriarche de la conscience
" aussi, et qui, grand par le caractère autant
" que par l'intelligence, impose le respect à

"ceux qui ne savent pas l'aimer. J'ai nommé Döllinger."

"Toutefois ce n'est pas dans un évêque, mais "dans un simple prêtre qu'il personnifie,"—a fact which churchmen contemplate with mingled sorrow and pride. But this is not the first time that the Church has had such an experience. The history of the first great council shows us results strikingly similar. The bishops, so valiant for the truth at the council of Nicæa, afterwards, one by one, group by group, fell away and signed confessions, which, like the recent definitions of the Vatican, *might be explained to mean* the truth, which in word and intent they contradicted, and left the faith to be preserved by the lower clergy and the laity. Once more is the saying of S. Hilary most true, "Sanctiores sunt aures plebis quàm corda sacer-"dotum." The fact is very striking; and it has a moral, which will best be pointed out in the words of one, whose history of those troubled times would alone have made him famous, had he written nothing else. In one of the Appendices[1] to his history of the Arians, Dr. NEWMAN writes as follows :—

"The episcopate, whose action was so prompt

Marginal note: Parallel between the Arianizing bishops and the minority of the Vatican council.

---

[1] *The Arians of the Fourth Century*, Appendix, note v., pp. 454, 455 of the third edition. At p. 368 he remarks:—"The question of "the Arianizing bishops was one of much difficulty. They were in "possession of the churches; and could not be deposed, if at all, "without the risk of a permanent schism." Here, again, we have a state of things remarkably similar to that which exists at the present day.

" and concordant at Nicæa on the rise of Arianism,
" did not, as a class or order of men, play a good
" part in the troubles consequent upon the council;
" and the laity did. The Catholic people, in the
" length and breadth of Christendom, were the
" obstinate champions of Catholic truth, *and the
" bishops were not.* Of course there were great and
" illustrious exceptions: first, Athanasius, Hilary,
" the Latin Eusebius, and Phœbadius; and after
" them, Basil, the two Gregories, and Ambrose;
" there are others, too, who suffered, if they did
" nothing else, as Eustathius, Paulus, Paulinus,
" and Dionysius; and the Egyptian bishops, whose
" weight was small in the Church in proportion to
" the great power of their Patriarch. And, on
" the other hand, as I shall say presently, there
" were exceptions to the Christian heroism of the
" laity, especially in some of the great towns. And
" again, in speaking of the laity, I speak inclu-
" sively of their parish-priests (so to call them), at
" least in many places; but on the whole, taking a
" wide view of the history, we are obliged to say
" *that the governing body of the church came short,
" and the governed were pre-eminent in faith, zeal,
" courage, and constancy.*

" This is a very remarkable fact; but there is a
" moral in it. Perhaps it was permitted in order
" to impress upon the Church, at that very time
" passing out of her state of persecution to her
" long temporal ascendancy, the great evangelical

"lesson, that, not the wise and powerful, but the
"obscure, the unlearned, and the weak constitute
"her real strength. It was mainly by the faithful
"people that Paganism was overthrown; it was
"by the faithful people, under the lead of Atha-
"nasius and the Egyptian bishops, and in some
"places supported by their bishops or priests, that
"the worst of heresies was withstood and stamped
"out of the sacred territory."

This fact is of the more importance, because it has of late been argued (Père Gratry himself insisted on the point in a recent conversation with the translator), that for nearly the whole of the episcopate to accept error, while the truth remained with priests and laymen, is without a parallel in the history of the Church. Of course the conclusion which many would draw from this is, that the truth is on the side of the bishops, and not on the side of the protesting clergy and laity. The above remarks, however, tend to show that the premise, from which this conclusion is drawn, is false.

One other testimony to the merits of our author, one who voted with the majority in the Convocation of the University of Oxford on June 6th of the current year, may be allowed the pleasure of quoting.

The Oxford Diploma.

"Quoniam satis cognitum et perspectum habeat
"Universitas, virum admodum reverendum Jo-
"hannem Josephum Ignatium von Döllinger, Doc-
"torem in sacrâ Theologiâ, Capituli Regii Præpo-

" situm, Professorem Historiæ Ecclesiasticæ in
" Universitate Monacensi, senatorem superioris
" ordinis in Parliamento Bavariæ, Prælectoris His-
" toriæ munus per multos olim annos gerentem
" inter suos ingenii et eruditionis famâ, gratiâ
" insuper et honoribus floruisse: necnon inde usque
" personâ Scriptoris Historici indutâ, ecclesiæ mili-
" tantis tempora et vicissitudines copiose et lucu-
" lenter explicuisse; adhibitâ semper in veritate
" investigandâ singulari sagacitate, industriâ, et
" sedulitate indefessâ; *immo etiam in controversiis*
" *tractandis (quod difficillimum est) arbitrum se potius*
" *quam litigatorem præstitisse;* totam denique rerum
" gestarum, sententiarum, consiliorum narrationem
" *ita expossuisse, ut nullus fere recentiorum modera-*
" *tius vel sapientius scripsisse judicandus sit,*—nos
" Cancellarius, magistri et scholares Universitatis
" Oxoniensis, in frequenti Convocatione magistro-
" rum Regentium et non Regentium, pro more
" nostro pios et doctos undequâque oriundos colendi
" et (quoad licuerit) decorandi, vi et virtute præ-
" sentis hujusce diplomatis prædictum Johannem
" Josephum Ignatium creamus et constituimus
" Doctorem in Jure Civili, cumque omnibus juribus
" et privilegiis quæ ad talem gradum spectant frui
" et gaudere volumus.

" In cujus rei testimonium sigillum Universitatis
" Oxoniensis commune, quo hac in parte utimur,
" præsentibus apponi fecimus."

INTRODUCTION

Aim and object of the present translation.

A few words may be added in conclusion, with reference to the present translation. The ideal aimed at has been, faithfully to reproduce the full meaning of the original, and yet at the same time to use only such words and phrases as an English author, writing at first hand, would employ; in short, to avoid, if possible, all such forms of expression as would at once proclaim that the work was a translation and not original. If this ideal has been in any degree approached, it is in a great measure owing to the peculiarly lucid style of the author. In freedom from difficult constructions, from long and hopelessly involved sentences, from ponderous and untranslateable compound-words, Dr. Döllinger's writing stands in marked contrast to only too many German authors of the present day. For the most part his sentences admit of being translated literally and verbatim.

The object of the translation is twofold. The first and main object, to make one more of Dr. Döllinger's works accessible to that large number of the English public, who are debarred from reading them in the original. It is hoped that persons who are not professed students, nor in any special way interested in ecclesiastical history, will be induced to read these essays. And for this reason a few simple notes, in the way of explanation and supplement, have been added, in order to make the text as clear as possible to those whose knowledge of the historical facts under consideration may chance to be somewhat superficial. For a similar reason passages have been cited in extenso in many places, where the original at most gives only a reference. Labbe, Harduin, &c., are not rare works, it is true; but they are not accessible to every one; and many who could have access to them, would be unable or unwilling to spend time in consulting them, and yet would be glad to know the exact words of the passage to which reference is made. The indulgence of students of history is asked in both these cases. They are begged to tolerate notes stating facts, which to them seem elementary or obvious, and containing quotations from books, which "are in every library."[1] For the appendices much the same apology must be made as for the additional notes. Only one of them belongs to the original work, viz., Appendix B, containing the story of the papess as given in the Tegernsee MS. in the Munich Library. In the original it stands as a lengthy foot-note. It seemed more convenient to place it with the other appendices at the end of the volume. The Table of Contents has been very greatly enlarged.

The other object of the translation is secondary, having reference only to one or two of the essays, which have a bearing, more or less direct, upon the present crisis in the Roman Catholic Church. No one nowadays needs to have it proved to him

Evil results of the fictions remain after the fictions have been exposed.

---

[1] The notes added by the translator are distinguished from those of the original work by being enclosed in square brackets.

that the council of Sinuessa and the Donation of Constantine are as mythical as the Trial of Orestes or the Garment of Nessus. One examines and studies the details of the stories for various reasons, but scarcely in order to test their truth. That question has been long since closed. But what it *is* of importance still to consider is this:—that though these legends have been abandoned, the claims which have been made on the strength of the legends have *not* been abandoned. The self-condemnation and self-deposition of Marcellinus is consigned to the regions of fable; but the principle *Prima sedes non judicabitur a quoquam* is maintained. The grant made to Silvester is allowed to be apocryphal; but the authority and territory, which the popes acquired or retained on the strength of that supposed grant, are still either possessed or claimed. It would not be too much to say that the bulk of what is now claimed or re-claimed by the Roman See, in the way of supremacy, infallibility, and temporal dominion, is demanded, either directly or indirectly, in virtue of documents which have been either forged or falsified. The invalidity of the title-deeds has been exposed again and again, but possession (or vehement claim to possession), through a most unhappy prescription, still continues. "C'est une question " totalement gangrenée par la fraude."

Nor is this all. These lamentable impostures have left behind them a far worse legacy than that

of ill-gotten possessions or ill-founded claims.
Offspring of a spirit of falsehood, they have
begotten a spirit like unto their parent. It is
impossible to live long among those who are
devoted to the interests of the Vatican, or to read
much of the literature which is written in support
of those interests, without feeling that the concep-
tion of truth entertained by these advocates is a
saddening travesty of the sacred reality. In some
cases the sense of truth, the love of truth for
its own sake, nay even the very power of discriminating between truth and falsehood, seems
almost lost. PÈRE GRATRY has published some
mournful proofs which he has had of this fact in
examining ecclesiastical candidates at the Sor-
bonne.[1] The noble words in which he condemns

---

[1] *Première Lettre à Mgr. Dechamps*, pp. 67-70. To which we may add the fact that Alfonso de Liguori, the unconscious dupe of the grossest forgeries, the conscious author of a system of casuistry, which may shortly be described as "lying made easy," has lately been made a Doctor of the Roman Church. Because, forsooth, "plurimos Libros conscripsit, sacrâ eruditione et pietate refertos, "sive, inter implexas Theologorum tum laxiores, tum rigidiores "sententias, ad tutam muniendam viam, per quam Christifidelium "animarum Moderatores inoffenso pede incedere possent; sive ad "Klerum informandum, instituendum; sive ad Catholicæ Fidei "veritatem confirmandam, et contra cujuscunque generis aut nomi- "nis Hæreticos defendendam; sive ad asserenda hujus Apostolicæ "Sedis jura; sive ad Fidelium animos ad pietatem excitandos. Hoc "porro prædicari verissime potest, nullum esse vel nostrorum tem- "porum, qui, maximâ saltem ex parte, non sit ab Alphonso refu- "tatus. Quid quod ea, quæ, tum de Immaculatâ Sanctæ Dei "Genetricis Conceptione, *tum de Romani Pontificis ex Cathedrâ* "*docentis Infallibilitate*, plaudente christiano populo, et frequent- "issimo universi catholici orbis Antistitum concessu approbante, a "Nobis sancita sunt, in Alphonsi Operibus reperiuntur et nitidissime

such "pious frauds" will serve as an apt conclusion to these introductory remarks.[1]

"En présence de ces faits, monseigneur, il faut
"d'abord, si nous sommes des enfants de lumière,
"si nous sommes les disciples de celui qui dit : 'Je
"'suis venu pour rendre témoinage à la vérité,' il
"faut, si seulement nous sommes des hommes
"d'honneur, il faut rejeter loin de nous avec
"d goût, avec horreur, avec indignation, ce travail
"des faussaires. Il faut le rejeter avec éclat, avec
"solennité, de telle sorte que, dans le monde entier,
"aucun homme ne puisse soupçonner dans aucun
"de nous la moindre arrièrepensée de maintenir
"*aucun résultat de ces impostures misérables.*"

"exposita, et validissimis argumentis demonstrata?"—*Papal Brief.* Rome, July 7, 1871.

[1] *Deuxième Lettre à Mgr. Dechamps*, pp. 23, 24.

A. P.

HEWORTH,
    September, 1871.

THIS translation has been undertaken with the express sanction of the author.

The translator is responsible for all that appears between square brackets, thus [　], and for all the appendices, excepting Appendix B., as also for the italics and the insertions in the margin.

AUTHOR'S PREFACE

THE present publication is the fruit of a course of reading and study, which I undertook with a view to a more considerable work, intended to embrace the history of the papacy. It seemed to me, however, that the results of my researches, which are here given to the public, combine to this extent as a connected whole, that all these fables and inventions—however different may have been the occasions which gave them birth, and however intentional or unintentional may have been their production—have, nevertheless, had at times a marked influence on the whole aspect of the Middle Ages, on the history and poetry of the time, on its theology, and its jurisprudence. For this reason I may, perhaps, venture to hope that not only theologians and ecclesiastical historians, but lovers and students of mediæval history and mediæval literature in general, will find this book not altogether devoid of interest.

J. V. DÖLLINGER.

MUNICH, *May* 24*th*, 1863.

TABLE OF CONTENTS

PAGE

I. POPE JOAN.

Not yet sufficiently proved to be a myth 3
Not an inexplicable riddle 6
Eight explanations stated 7
All eight assume that the story is older than the 13th
    century 9
The Papess not mentioned by Marianus Scotus 10
             nor by Sigebert of Gemblours .. 11
             nor by Otto of Freysingen .. 11
Stephan de Bourbon the first chronicler who mentions
    her 13
Martinus Polonus the chief means of spreading the story 15
Even in his case the story is an interpolation 16
Various ways of interpolating 18
In "Anastasius" also the story is a later addition .. 21
Reasons for inserting the Papess between Leo IV. and
    Benedict III. 23
Writers who copy Martinus Polonus 26
Writers of the 14th century who mention her 27
The Dominicans and Minorites spread the story .. 29
Used as an argument at the council of Constance .. 31
The Dominicans might easily have exposed the story .. 33
Not known to the Greeks till 1450-1500 34
Aventin and Onufrio Panvinio the first to deny it .. 36

ANALYSIS OF THE STORY.

Discrepancies about the name of the Papess 37
             the date of her Pontificate 38
             her previous abode 38
             the mode of the catastrophe .. 39
Boccacio's version probably the popular one 41

Origin of the Story.

	PAGE
Four elements of production.—1. A statue	43
2. An inscription	44
3. A seat of unusual shape	47
4. A custom	53

Examples of similar Stories.

The two wives of the Count of Gleichen	54
The Püstrich at Sondershausen	55
Archbishop Hatto and the mice	56
Figure on the Riesenthor of Vienna Cathedral	58
The origin of the house of Colonna	59

Abode of the Papess.

Why represented as coming from England	60
Mayence	61
Athens	65

II. POPE CYRIACUS.

This fiction had a definite object	71
Visions of the nun Elizabeth of Schönau	71
S. Ursula and her maidens	72
Abdication of Cyriacus	73
Martinus Polonus the chief means of spreading the story	73
The story brought to bear on the abdication of Cœlestine V.	75

III. MARCELLINUS.

The story of his abdication very ancient	79
The whole story a tissue of absurdities	81
Its object, to prove that popes are above all tribunals	82
Probable date of its fabrication	83
Use made of it by Nicolas I., Gerson, and Gerbert	84

IV. CONSTANTINE AND SILVESTER.

Multitude of writers who mention the baptism of Constantine by Silvester at Rome	89
The true account seemed incredible in the Middle Ages	90
The story certainly originated in Rome	91
Probable date of its fabrication	93
Not generally accepted at first	94
Influence of the *Liber Pontificalis*	95
Attempt of Ekkehard to reconcile the two accounts	96
Theory of Bonizo of Sutri	97

	PAGE
Italian chroniclers who follow him	98
The story appealed to by Hadrian I., Nicolas I., and Leo IX.	99
Johannes Malalas the first Greek who accepts it	100
The true account seemed incredible to the Greeks also	101
Æneas Sylvius and Nicolas of Cusa knew the truth	102
The truth spreads slowly	102
Its final triumph due to French theologians	102
The story a favourite subject for poems	103

V. THE DONATION OF CONSTANTINE.

Account of the Donation in the *Liber Pontificalis* suspicious	107
Evidence of Hadrian I.	108
No traces of the Donation till about 750	108
Theory that it was a Greek fabrication disproved by the language of the document	110
The Greek text an evident translation	111
Why the Greeks so readily believed in the Donation	114
Accepted in the West before even known to the Greeks	116
The work of a Roman ecclesiastic	117
Probable date of the forgery	118
Roman horror of the Lombards	118
Not ungrounded	121
Scheme of Gregory II. to make Rome independent	121
The Donation gave an historic basis to this scheme	122
Not fabricated by the pseudo-Isidore	123
Contents of the document	124
The momentous ninth clause	126
Change of " or " into " and "	127
The senate, patriciate, and consulate in the 8th century	128
Papal officials an imitation of imperial officials	130
Stated object of the Donation	132
Certainly known in Rome before 850	133
Æneas of Paris treats it as authentic	133
Hincmar and Ado are more reserved	134
Leo IX. shows full belief in it	134
Remarkable silence of Gregory VII.	134
Urban II. claims Corsica on the strength of it	135
Hadrian IV. gives Ireland to Henry II. on the strength of it	136
Neapolitan clergy fabricate a Donation	139
The Donation disputed in Rome when found inconvenient	140
by monks	140
by followers of Arnold of Brescia	141

	PAGE
But, though disputed, still largely used	143
Claims of the popes to the imperial insignia and homage	144
Dissatisfaction in Germany at such claims	147
Historians, more cautious than the clergy, limit without denying the Donation	147
From the 12th to 14th century its authority increases	150
Innocent IV's statement of papal supremacy	151
Lawyers allowed the Donation only the right of prescription	154
Uncertainty as to its extent	157
Extension given to it by German law-books	162
Two opposite views respecting it:—	
1. That it and similar endowments were admirable	163
2. That the wealth of the Church was a source of infinite evil	163
Hence the story of the angel's lament	168
Mediæval sects adopted the second view	170
The fiction exposed by Æneas Sylvius	173
Also by bishop Pecock, cardinal Cusa, and Lorenzo Valla	174
Its last defenders	176

VI. LIBERIUS AND FELIX.

The true account	181
Felix an antipope	182
Liberius an apostate	183
He is fairly called heretical	184
He re-establishes his orthodoxy	186
Felix more culpable, and without excuse	187
The fable	189
Object of it to whitewash the party of Felix	189
Not older than the 6th century	189
Version of the *Liber Pontificalis* and of the *Acts of Felix*	191
Version of the *Acts of Eusebius*	193
Name of Felix inserted into martyrologies, calendars, &c.	194
He is confounded with the African martyr Felix	196
The fable originated in the *Liber Pontificalis*	198
Difficulties when the truth became known in the 16th century	201
A forged inscription	202
Paoli's monstrous hypothesis	203
The fable finally abandoned	204

VII. ANASTASIUS II.—HONORIUS I.

	PAGE
Anastasius II.	209
Dante selects him as an instance of an heretical pope	209
Was he a heretic?	211
Dante's error the common belief of the time	215
This erroneous belief created mainly by Gratian	217
Opposite fate of Honorius I.	220
Monothelitism an attempted compromise between monophysitism and orthodoxy	221
Honorius confessedly a monothelite	222
Anathematized by the VIth general council	226
For actual heresy, not for mere negligence	227
The papal legates vote for the anathema	228
Pope Agatho's vain attempt to avert the anathema	229
Leo II. confirms the anathema	230
The *Liber Diurnus* requires every pope to confirm the anathema	232
Marked silence of the *Liber Pontificalis*	232
The anathema treated in the East as a matter of course	235
Hincmar of Rheims assents to it	236
Silence of the *Liber Pontificalis* followed by historians	236
The anathema on a pope is thus forgotten	237
Leo IX. shows utter ignorance of it	238
A Greek first reminds the West of the fact	241
Torquemada sacrifices the council to save Honorius	241
The question not seriously debated till the 16th century	242

VARIOUS HYPOTHESES.

1. That the *Acts of the council* have been interpolated	242
2. That they are really the Acts of another synod	243
3. That the letters of Honorius are forgeries	243
4. That Honorius was condemned for negligence only	244
5. That the letters of Sergius are forgeries	247
6. That the letters of Leo II. are also forgeries	248
7. That Honorius was condemned by the Greeks only	248
8. That Honorius wrote, not as pope, but as a private teacher	249
The Monothelitism of Honorius would never have been questioned, had he not been pope	250

VIII. POPE GREGORY II. AND THE EMPEROR LEO III.

Gregory II. represented as heading a revolt against Leo III.	253
Martinus Polonus once more the spreader of error	253

	PAGE
Theophanes the source of the statement	254
Gregory headed no revolt, but helped to quash one	255
View of Gregorovius inconsistent with facts and itself	258
Difficult position of Gregory II.	259

IX. SILVESTER II.

Gradual defamation of his memory	265
1. That he was too fond of profane arts and sciences	265
2. That his election at Ravenna was due to sinister arts	266
3. That he was addicted to magic and black art	266
4. That he sold himself to the devil	267
The fable of Roman origin	267
Its object	268
The Dominicans spread the fable	269
The truth recognised in the 14th century	273

APPENDICES.

A. Further particulars respecting Pope Joan	273
B. The story of the Papess in the Tegernsee MS.	280
C. Further illustrations of similar growth of myths	283
D. Letter of pope Hadrian to Henry II. of England	289
E. Decisions " ex cathedrâ."	292
F. The latest defenders of Honorius	298

POPE JOAN

POPE JOAN

THE subject of Pope Joan has not yet lost the interest which belongs to it as a fact in the province of historical criticism. The literature respecting her reaches down to the very latest times. As recently as 1843 and 1845 two works on this question have appeared from the pens of two Dutch scholars; the one by Professor KIST,[1] to prove the existence of Pope Joan, the other, a very voluminous one, by Professor WENSING, of Warmond, to disprove Kist's position. In Italy BIANCHI-GIOVINI has written a book on the subject in the same year, 1845, without being aware of the works of the two Dutch writers. In Germany no one—at any rate of those who know anything of history—will easily be induced to entertain a serious belief

The story of Pope Joan not yet sufficiently proved to be a fable.

---

[1] [*A woman in the chair of S. Peter.* Another edition of this has lately appeared; Gütersloh, 1866. Professor KIST thinks that Pope Joan was possibly the widow of Leo IV.]

in the existence of the female pope. To do so, one must do violence to every principle of historical criticism. But the banishment of the subject to the realm of fable has not yet been completely accomplished. The riddle—how this extraordinary myth originated—remains still to be solved.

<small>That an author like Luden should treat it as probable is sufficient evidence of this.</small>

Nothing but the insufficiency and misdirection of all previous attempts at an explanation can account for the fact that a man like LUDEN, in his *History of the German People*,[1] does all he can to make the reality of the well-known myth at any rate probable. "It is inconceivable," says he, "how it could ever enter into any man's head to "invent such an insane falsehood. He must either "have invented his lie out of sheer wantonness in "order to scoff at the papacy, or he must have "intended to gain some other object by means of "it. But of all the dozens of writers who mention "Pope Joan and her mishap, there is not a single "one who can be called an enemy of the papacy. "They are clergy, monks, guileless people, who "notice this phenomenon in the same dry way in "which they mention other things, which seem to "them to be strange, wonderful, laudable, abomin-"able, or in any way worth mentioning." "And "one cannot imagine," says Luden further on, "an object which could seem to any one to be "attainable by means of such a falsehood. More-"over, it is inconceivable how people in general

---

[1] *Geschichte des deutschen Volkes*, VI., 513-517.

"could have believed in the story, and that without the slightest doubt, for nearly 500 years from the eleventh century onwards, if it had not been true."

It is marvellous enough that Luden should make the myth of Pope Joan a matter of general belief from the *eleventh* century onwards. It would be very much nearer the truth to say that it did not find general belief till the middle of the *fourteenth* century. The author, however, of the article on Pope Joan in the *Nouvelle Biographie Générale*, published at Paris by Dr. Hofer, as lately as 1858, goes very much greater lengths.[1] "Cette croyance a donc régné dans le monde chrétien depuis le *neuvième* siècle jusqu'après la renaissance." And to crown it all, HASE thinks it, at any rate, credible that the Church, not content with creating facts, annihilated them, also, whenever the knowledge of them seemed critical for the already tottering papacy.[2] According to Hase and Kist, then, we must state the matter thus: that soon after the year 855 an edict issued from Rome to this effect, " Let no one presume to say a word about the fact of a female pope," for at that time Rome did not feel her position to be as yet very secure. About the middle of the thirteenth century, however, a counter order issued from the same place; "Henceforth it is lawful to discuss history; we now

Erroneous views as to the time and mode in which the story won general belief.

---

[1] Vol. XXVI., p. 569.
[2] *Kirchengeschichte*, 7. Aufl. s. 213.

"consider our position safe, and can venture to let the narrative appear in historical works."

<small>Some consider the question to be insoluble.</small>

The judgment of KURTZ is, at any rate, more sober and free from prejudice.[1] "The evidence before us," he says, "forbids us to assign to the myth any historical value whatever. We must, however (quite apart from the falsification of the acts, which, in some cases, is manifest, in others is a matter of suspicion,) characterise the myth as a riddle, which criticism has as yet not solved, and *probably never will.*"

<small>The present essay is offered as a solution.</small>

That the riddle has not yet been solved, that all attempts at explanation which have been made up to the present time, must be held to have miscarried, is true enough; that a solution which may satisfy the historian is, nevertheless, possible, it will be the object of the following pages to show.

<small>Previous explanations:
1. That it was a satire on John VIII.</small>

Let us first glance for a moment at the explanations which have been set forth up to this time. BARONIUS considers the myth to be a satire on John VIII., "ob nimiam ejus animi facilitatem et mollitudinem," qualities which he exhibited more especially in the affair of Photius. Others,

<small>2. A satire on the rule of the infamous Theodora and Marozia.</small>

Aventine to begin with, and after him Heumann and Schröck, prefer to reckon the supposed satire as one on the period of female rule in Rome, the reign

---

[1] *Handbuch der Kirchengeschichte,* 1856, II. Band, 1. Abtheilung, s. 225.

of Theodora and Marozia under certain popes, some of whom were called John; in which case, however, it would have to be transferred from the middle of the ninth century to the tenth. The supposition to which the Jesuit SECCHI in Rome has given publicity, that it is a calumny originating with the Greeks, namely with Photius, is equally inadmissible. The first Greek who mentions the circumstance is the monk Barlaam in the fourteenth century. PAGI's assertion also, which ECKHART supports, that the myth was an invention of the Waldenses, is pure imagination. The myth evidently originated in Rome itself, and the first to give it circulation were not the Waldenses, but their most deadly enemies—the Dominicans and Minorites.

<small>3. A Greek calumny.</small>

<small>4. A fiction of the Waldenses.</small>

LEO ALLATIUS thought that it was a false prophetess called Thiota, in the ninth century, who gave occasion for the birth of the myth. And the explanation invented by LEIBNITZ[1] is a forced attempt to meet the exigencies of the case. It might very well, he thinks, have been a foreign *bishop* (pontifex episcopus), really a woman in disguise, who gave birth to a child during a procession at Rome, and thus occasion to the story.

<small>5. A perverted account of Thiota the prophetess.</small>

<small>6. A female bishop.</small>

BLASCO and HENKE supposed that the myth about the female pope was a satirical allegory on the origin and circulation of the false decretals

<small>7. An allegorical satire on the False Decretals.</small>

---

[1] *Flores sparsi in tumulum Papissæ*, ap. SCHEID, biblioth. hist. Goetting., p. 367.

of Isidore. An idea which, to begin with, is at variance with the spirit of that century, an age in which men had no notion of satirical allegories; and, in the next place, contradicts itself, for the story of Pope Joan originated at a time when no one doubted the genuineness of the false decretals of Isidore. Nevertheless, GFRÖRER has lately taken up this idea, and worked it out in a still more artistic manner.[1] "The whole force of the fable," he says, "resides in these two points, that the "woman was a native of Mayence, and that she "came from Greece (Athens), and ascended the "papal chair. In the first particular I recognise "a condemnation directed against the canons of "the pseudo-Isidore, in the second an allegorical "censure of the alliance which Leo IV. wished "to make with the Byzantines. . . It is said that "in the later days of Leo IV. the papal power "in Mayence and Greece was abused, or to make "use of a metaphor, of which the Italians are very "fond in such cases, was at that time *prostituted*." Side by side with this explanation, which can scarcely fail to provoke the smiles of nearly every one who is acquainted with the Middle Ages, stands the extraordinary circumstance, that for this attempt of Leo IV. to compromise himself more than was right with the Byzantines, there is no authority whatever. It is purely an hypothesis of Gfrörer's. But his rendering of

[1] *Kirchengeschichte*, III., III., 978.

the myth about Pope Joan is now made to do further service as a proof of the correctness of this hypothesis, as well as for his assumption that the false decretals originated in Mayence.

In short, all the attempts at explanation, which have hitherto been made, split on this rock—that the myth had its origin in a much later age; when the remembrance of the events and circumstances of the ninth and tenth centuries had long ago faded away, or at most existed only in the case of individual scholars, and, therefore, could not form material for the construction of a myth. I believe, that is to say, that I can without difficulty produce convincing evidence, that the myth about the woman-pope, though it may possibly have had somewhat earlier circulation in the mouth of the people, was not definitively put into writing before the middle of the thirteenth century. This evidence could not have been given with anything like certainty before the present time. For it is only during the last forty[1] years that all the stores of mediæval manuscripts in the whole of Europe have been hunted through with a care such as was never known before. Every library corner has been searched, and an astounding quantity of historical documents, hitherto unknown (what a mass of new material exists in the Pertz collection alone, for instance!), has been brought to light. Neverthe-

But all these explanations assume that the story originated in a much earlier age than was really the fact.

It is not older than the thirteenth century; a fact impossible to prove before the present century.

---

[1] [This was written in 1863.]

less, not a single notice of the myth about Pope Joan has been discovered, which is earlier than the close, or, at the very most, the middle of the thirteenth century. We can now say quite positively, that in the collected literature, whether western or Byzantine, of the four centuries between 850 and 1250, there is not the faintest reference to the circumstance of a female pope.

<small>Erroneous belief that Pope Joan is mentioned in the eleventh and twelfth centuries:
1. By Marianus Scotus.</small>

For a long time it was supposed that the myth, though certainly not to be found in any author of the ninth or tenth century, appeared as already in existence in the eleventh and twelfth centuries. MARIANUS SCOTUS[1] is said to have been the first to mention the female pope, and he certainly does mention her in the text as given by Pistorius. Now, however, that the text in the great Pertz collection has been edited by Waitz[2] according to the most ancient manuscripts, the fact has come to light, that Marianus knew nothing whatever of Pope Joan. In his case, as in the case of so many other authors, the short mention of the female

<small>2. By Sigebert of Gemblours.</small>

---

[1] [Born, probably in Ireland, about 1028; died at Mayence, 1086; not to be confounded with Marianus, the Franciscan, a Florentine writer of the fifteenth century. In 1056 Marianus Scotus entered the abbey of S. Martin at Cologne; in 1059 he moved to the abbey of Fulda, and thence in 1069 to Mayence. He passed for the most learned man of his age, being a mathematician and theologian as well as historian. His *Chronicon Universale* is based on Cassiodorus, augmented from Eusebius and Bede, and the chronicles of Hildesheim and Wurzburg, and extends down to the year 1083; published at Basle by Hérold, 1559.]

[2] *Monumenta*, VIII., 550.

pope has been interpolated at a later period. In the chronicle of Sigebert of Gemblours, and the supplements of the monks of Orcamp (*Auctarium Ursicampinum*), the notice of the papess is wanting in all original manuscripts. She was first inserted by the first editor in the year 1513.¹ Kurtz has lately appealed again to the supposed evidence of Otto of Freysingen.² In the list of the popes, continued down to the year 1513, which is printed with his historical works,³ Pope John VII. (in the year 705) is marked as a woman, without one single word of explanation. And in the edition of the *Pantheon*, as given by Pistorius, we find in

3. By Otto of Freysingen.

---

¹ "In nullo quem noverimus Sigeberti codice occurrit locus "famosus de Johanna papissa, quem hoc loco editio princeps "exhibet," says the latest editor, BETHMANN, ap. Pertz, VIII., 340. Compare the remark, p. 470, where Bethmann says decisively, "nemo igitur restat (as interpolater of the passage) nisi primus "editor, sive is Antonius Rufus fuerit, sive Henricus Stephanus." It is a mistake when KURTZ elsewhere (p. 228) says with regard to Siegbert and Marianus: "The oldest editors would scarcely have "added the passages in question out of their own heads; and there-"fore it is probable that the passages were purposely omitted in the "codices which they had before them." There are no signs whatever of anything being intentionally omitted or effaced; in many of the manuscripts, on the other hand, there are plenty of signs of subsequent insertions and additions in the margin. [Sigebert was born about 1030, and died 1112. His chronicle extends from 381, where Eusebius ended, to 1112.]

² *Kirchengeschichte*, II., 226.

³ [OTTO, BISHOP OF FREYSINGEN, went with his brother, Conrad III., on his crusade to the Holy Land, resuming his diocese on his return. He died in September 1158, having held the see twenty years. His chronicle in seven books extends down to 1146. The first four books are a mere compilation from Orosius, Eusebius, Isidore, Bede, &c.; the last three are of great value. He also wrote two books *De gestis Friderici I. Ænobarbi*, which come down to the year 1157.]

the list of the popes these words, "the Papess "Johanna is not reckoned."

In all three cases the notice of the Papess is an interpolation. The oldest MSS. do not contain it.

Meanwhile a close investigation of the oldest and best manuscripts of Gottfried's *Pantheon* and of Otto's chronicle have brought it to light, that originally neither the word "fœmina" was placed in Otto's chronicle against the name of John VII., nor the gloss "Johanna Papissa non numeratur" in the *Pantheon* between Leo IV. and Benedict III.; both of which insertions are given in the printed editions.[1]

In the chronicle of Otto the addition to the name of John VII. is manifestly the work of a later copyist or reader, who inserted the word quite at random, because he was bound to have a female John somewhere among the popes. The fact that this John comes as early as the year 705 was the less likely to puzzle him, because the list of popes in this chronicle does not give the dates.[2]

---

[1] [That confusion prevailed in some of the lists of the popes precisely at this point is shown by an annalist, who apparently wrote in Halberstadt 854: "Benedictus papa, ut quidam volunt, hoc anno "factus est, et post hunc Paulus (!), post cum Stephanus per annos "quatuor sedisse inveniuntur."—BAXMANN, *Politik der Päpste*, I., p. 361, note.]

[2] In the good original manuscripts of the *Pantheon* in the royal library at Munich the addition about Pope Joan is wanting. These are:—Cod. Lat. 43 (from Hartmann Schedel's collection) f. 1181, b. Cod. Windberg. 37, or Cod. Lat. 22,237, f. 168 b. Similarly in the oldest manuscripts of the chronicle of Otto in the Munich library the addition to the name of John VII. does not appear. These are Cod. Weihensteph. 61, or Lat. 21,561, which is of about the same date. Cod. Frising. 177, or Lat. 6,517. Cod. Scheftlarn. Lat. 17,121, in which the list of popes comes to an end with Hadrian IV., and therefore is also of the same date.

First appearance of the fable

The first who has really taken up the myth is the author of a chronicle, to which STEPHAN DE BOURBON appeals without giving any more exact quotation.[1] That is to say, Stephen, a French Dominican, born towards the close of the twelfth century, died in the year 1261, in his work on the seven gifts of the Holy Spirit,[2] which was written just about the middle of the thirteenth century, makes the first mention of Pope Joan, whom he assetrs he has discovered in a chronicle. Now seeing that he quotes with exactness all the sources from which he has gathered together the collection of passages which contribute to his practical homily, we can, at least with great probability, show from what chronicle he has obtained this mention of Pope Joan. Among chroniclers he names Eusebius, Jerome, Bede, Odo, Hugo of S. Victor, the "Roman Cardinal," and John de Mailly, a Dominican. We may set aside all but the two last. The "Roman Cardinal" (or Cardinal Romanus (?)—there were several of this name, but none of them wrote a chronicle) is probably none other than the author of the

<small>Stephan de Bourbon, who died A.D. 1261, is the first chronicler who mentions her.</small>

---

[1] [He merely says] "dicitur in chronicis." He means no more than *one* chronicle; Chronica is constantly used in the plural as a title. Otherwise Stephan would naturally have added "variis" or "pluribus."

[2] It has never been printed. The whole, or portions of it, exist in the French libraries, one portion of it in the Munich library. ECHARD was the first to cite it at great length in his work, *Sancti Thomæ Summa suo auctori vindicata*, Paris, 1708; and again in the *Scriptores Ordinis Prædicatorum*, pt. I.

Historia Miscella, or continuation of Eutropius, whom the Dominican, Tolomeo of Lucca, also quotes later on among his authorities as Paulus Diaconus Cardinalis;[1] but he cannot be distinguished with certainty. It remains then that the lost, or as yet undiscovered, chronicle of the Dominican Jean de Mailly,[2] who, moreover, must have been a contemporary of Stephen's, is the only source to which the latter can have been indebted for his account of Pope Joan. And Jean de Mailly, we may be tolerably certain, got it from popular report.

<small>Stephan de Bourbon probably received the story from his contemporary, Jean de Mailly.</small>

We can, therefore, consider it as established—that not until the year 1240 or 1250, was the myth about the woman-pope put into writing and transferred to works of history. Several decades more passed, however, before it came actually into circulation and became really wide-spread. The chronicle of Jean de Mailly seems to have remained in obscurity, for no one, with the exception of his brother-Dominican, Stephen, notices it; and even Stephen's large work—great as was its value, especially to preachers, on account of the quantity of examples which it contained, was not possessed by very many, as the scarcity of existing manuscripts of it proves. The *Speculum Morale*, which bears the name of Vincent of Beauvais, was the chief cause of this. For this work appropriated

<small>About A.D. 1240 or 1250 the story found its way into historical works, but did not become widely known till about A.D. 1290 or 1300.</small>

---

[1] Cf. Quetif et Echard *Scriptores Ordinis Prædicatorum*, I. 544.
[2] On him see the *Histoire littéraire de la France*, XVIII., 582.

most of the examples and instances given by Stephen, but was superior to Stephen's book both in convenience of arrangement and fullness of matter, and eclipsed it so completely, that the narrative about Pope Joan, in the form in which it appears in Stephen's work, is to be found nowhere else.

The chronicle of MARTINUS POLONUS has been the principal means of giving circulation to the myth. This book, which gives a contemporary history of the popes and emperors in the form of a dry, mechanical, and utterly uncritical collection of biographical notes, exercised a most extraordinary influence on the chroniclers and historians from the beginning of the fourteenth century onwards, especially on their ways of thinking in the later Middle Ages. Wattenbach's[1] statement, that Martinus Polonus became almost the exclusive historical instructor of the catholic world, is not an exaggeration. Of no other historical book is there such an inexhaustible number of manuscripts in existence as of this. All volumes of the *Archiv für deutsche Geschichtskunde* show this. And indeed the book was held in estimation in almost all countries alike, was translated into all languages, was continued over and over again, and still more frequently copied by later chroniclers. That the effect of a book, which was utterly unhistorical and stuffed

<small>The popular but worthless chronicle of Martinus Polonus chiefly instrumental in spreading the fable.</small>

[1] *Deutschlands Geschichtsquellen*, s. 426.

with fables, was to the last degree mischievous, that (as Wattenbach says) the careful, thorough, and critical investigation of the history of the early Middle Ages, which was prosecuted with so much zeal during the twelfth century, was completely choked, or nearly so, by Martin's chronicle, cannot be denied.

<small>The influence of Martinus Polonus due to his connection with the papal court.</small>

The position of the author could not fail to win for his history of the popes an amount of authority such as no other similar writing obtained. Troppau was his birth-place, the Dominican order his profession. He was for long the chaplain and penitentiary of the popes; as such lived naturally at the papal court, followed the Curia, which was then constantly on the move, everywhere, and died [A.D. 1278] as archbishop designate of Gnesen. His book, therefore, was considered to a certain extent to be the official history of the popes, issuing from the Curia itself. And hence people accepted the history of Pope Joan also, which they found in Martinus Polonus, all the more readily and unsuspectingly. The form in which he gives the myth became the prevailing one; and most authors have contented themselves with copying the passage from his chronicle word for word.

<small>But the mention of Pope Joan is an interpolation in this case also.</small>

Nevertheless, Martin himself, as can be proved, knew nothing about Pope Joan, or, at any rate, said nothing about her. Not until several years after his death did attempts begin to be made to insert the myth into his book. It is no doubt correct that Martin himself prepared a second and later edition of his work, which reaches down to Nicolas III., 1277, while the first edition only goes down to Clement IV. (died 1268). But the second is exactly like the first in arrangement. Each pope, and each emperor on the opposite page, had as many lines assigned to him as he reigned years, and each page contained fifty lines, that is, embraced half a century. Hence, in the copies which kept to the original arrangement of the author, additions or insertions could only be made in those places where the account of a pope or emperor did not fill all the lines assigned to him, owing to the short period of his reign. But the insertion of a pope had been rendered impossible by Martin himself and all the copyists who kept to the plan of the book, by means of the detailed chronology, according to which every line had a date, and in the case of each pope and emperor the length of his reign was exactly stated. But for this same reason Pope Joan also, if she had originally had a place in his book, could not have been *effaced*, nor have been omitted from the copies which held fast to the arrangement of the original.

<small>The plan of Martinus' chronicle such as to render the detection of an interpolation very easy.</small>

Pope Joan, therefore, does not occur in the oldest manuscripts of Martinus. She is wanting especially in those which have kept to the exact chronological method of the author. Nor is the idea, that Martinus inserted her in the latest

<small>Even in his latest edition Martinus is silent about the Papess.</small>

edition of his book prepared by himself, tenable. That theory is contradicted by manuscripts, which come down to the time of Nicolas III., and, nevertheless, contain no trace of Pope Joan. Echard[1] has already noticed several such manuscripts. The exquisite Aldersbach[2] manuscript, now in the Royal Library at Munich, gives the same evidence. There are, however, plenty of manuscripts in which her history is written in the margin at the bottom of the sheet, or as a gloss at the side.[3] It was thence gradually, and one may add very violently, thrust into the text. This was done in various ways: either Benedict III., the successor of Leo, was struck out, and Pope Joan put in his place, as is the case in a Hamburg[4] codex reaching down to the year 1302. Or she is placed, usually by some later hand, without any date being given, as an addition or mere story in the vacant space left after Leo IV. Or, lastly—merely in order to gain the necessary two years and a half for her reign—the whole chronological reckoning of the author is thrown into confusion; either by assigning an earlier date than is correct to several of Leo's predecessors, and that as far back as the year 800; or by giving to individual

Various ways in which the interpolation has been accomplished.

---

[1] On this point see QUETIF et ECHARD. *Scriptores Ordinis Prædicatorum*, l. 367; and Lequien *Or. Chr.* III., 385.

[2] Aldersp. 161, fol. Pergam.

[3] In the *Archiv für ältere deutsche Geschichtskunde* quotations from several of these are given, e. g. VII., 657.

[4] Archiv VI., 230.

popes fewer years than belong to them. This eagerness to interpolate the female pope in the book at all hazards—so to speak,—without shrinking from the most arbitrary alterations in the chronology in order to attain this object, is certainly somewhat astounding. Just the very circumstance which above all others conferred on Martin's book a certain amount of value, viz. the painstaking and continuous chronological reckoning line by line, has been sacrificed in several manuscripts,[1] merely in order to make the insertion of Pope Joan possible; or else only one year has been placed against the name of each pope, either in the margin or in the text, in order to conceal the disagreement between the insertion of Pope Joan and the chronological plan of the author.

Some of them astonishingly violent.

It was in the period between 1278 and 1312 that the interpolation took place; for TOLOMEO OF LUCCA, who completed his historical work in the year 1312, remarks[2] that all the authorities which he had read placed Benedict III. next after Leo IV.; Martinus Polonus was the only one who put Johannes Anglicus in between. By this means two facts are established; first, the industrious collector Tolomeo knew of no writing in which a mention of Pope Joan was to be found,

The interpolation was made between A.D. 1278 and 1312.

---

[1] "Nulla chronologia, sed adest fabula," says ECHARD of several manuscripts of Martinus which he had seen, p. 369.
[2] *Hist. Eccles.*, 16, 8.

except the chronicle of Martinus; secondly, the copy of Martinus with which he was acquainted was one which had her *already* inserted, and that in the *text*. Had the account of her merely been written alongside in the margin, this would undoubtedly have aroused Tolomeo's suspicions, and he would have noticed the fact in his own work.

<small>The chronicle *Flores Temporum* instrumental in spreading the fable in Germany.</small>

Another main vehicle for circulating the myth about the papess was the chronicle *Flores Temporum*, which exists in numerous manuscripts under the names of MARTINUS MINORITA, HERRMANNUS JANUENSIS, and HERRMANNUS GIGAS. It was printed by Eccard, and, in another form, by Menschen; and after that of Martinus Polonus was the most widely circulated of all the later chronicles. Unlike Martinus Polonus, however, it appears to have come into general use in Germany only. It reaches down to 1290, and is in the main not much more than a compilation from the chronicle of Martinus Polonus, as the author himself states. According to the conjecture of Eccard and others, Martinus Minorita is the original author,[1] and Herrmannus Januensis or Gigas the continuer[2] of the chronicle down to the year 1349. Pertz,[3] on the other hand, is of opinion that what is printed under the name of Martinus Minorita is only a bad extract from the

---

[1] *Archiv der Gesellschaft für deutsche Geschichtskunde*, VIII. 835.
[2] Archiv I., 402 ff.
[3] Achiv VII., 115.

work of Herrmannus Gigas, who brought his chronicle down to the year 1290, and died in 1336.

The relation between the Minorite Martin and the Wilhelmite Herrmann of Genoa appears meanwhile to be this :—that the latter has copied the Minorite, with [1] many omissions and additions, but without mentioning him. Martin the Penitentiary —that is Martinus Polonus—is given as the main authority. It was from him, then, beyond all doubt, that the story about Pope Joan passed (embellished with additions) into chronicles of considerably later date ; for manuscripts in which it is wanting have not come within my knowledge.

This chronicle no doubt derived the story from the interpolated Martinus Polonus.

The story of Pope Joan has also been inserted in the so-called ANASTASIUS [2] (the most ancient collection known of biographies of the popes), and in precisely the same form as that in which it exists in Martinus Polonus. The run of the wording does not allow one to suppose for one moment that the story really formed any part of

In the lives of the popes, commonly known as "Anastasius," the story of Pope Joan is again a later addition ;

---

[1] Bruns, in Gabler's *Journal für theolog. Lit.* 1811, vol. VI., p. 88, &c. Bruns had a manuscript before him in Helmstädt, which was marked as a work of Herrmannus Minorita. But at the end of the document the author was correctly styled Herrmannus Ordius S. Wilhelmi.

[2] [ANASTASIUS, THE LIBRARIAN of the Vatican, took part in A.D. 869 in the eighth General Council at Constantinople, where his learning and knowledge of Latin and Greek were of great service to the papal legates. His celebrated *Liber Pontificalis* is a compilation of lives of the popes from S. Peter down to Nicolas I., first printed at Mayence in 1602. Only the lives of some of the popes of his own times can be regarded as his own composition.]

the original text. The interpolation must have been made with the most foolish wantonness, or just as has been done in the Heidelberg manuscript, by striking out Benedict III., and then inserting Joan in his place. In other copies she has been added by a later hand in the margin, at the side, or quite at the bottom of the page.

Possibly copied from Martinus Polonus: The most natural supposition, and the one which Gabler[1] also follows, seems then to be, that the account of her passed from Martinus Polonus into the few, and very much later, manuscripts of Anastasius which contain it. Nevertheless, I am driven to the conjecture that the myth was in the first instance added at the end of some copy of the collection of biographies of the popes which bears the name of Anastasius. *More probably added to "Anastasius" first, and thence transferred to Martinus.* It has, that is to say, long ago been remarked[2] that the life of Benedict III. in this collection is the work of a different author from that of the lives immediately preceding it, especially of the very detailed life of Leo IV. There must, therefore, beyond all doubt, have been copies which came to an end with Leo IV., whose biographer was obviously a contemporary. The notice of Pope Joan might then have been added at the end by a later hand, and from thence have passed into the manuscripts of Martinus Polonus.

[1] Gabler's *Kleinere theolog. Schriften*, vol. i., p. 416.
[2] See Bähr, *Geschichte der Röm. Literatur im Karoling. Zeitalter*, p. 269.

One sees this from the catalogue of manuscripts which Vignoli gives at the beginning of his edition. The Cod. Vatic., 3764 reaches down to Hadrian II., the Cod. Vatic. 5869 only down to Gregory II.; the Cod. 629 to Hadrian I.; others to John VIII., Nicolas I., Leo III., and so forth. In Cod. 3762, which comes down to the year 1142, the fable of the papess is added in later and smaller handwriting underneath in the margin.

The MSS. given in Vignoli's catalogue show this.

This conjecture, one must allow, is by no means easy to prove. But supposing it correct, we have then the simplest of all explanations for the interpolation of Pope Joan between Leo IV. and Benedict III., where she certainly has not the[1] slightest connection with the history of the time. Meanwhile, I find in Martinus himself reasons for this place being assigned to her, and the following two reasons in particular. The first is a mere matter of chance, arising out of the mechanical arrangement; for Martinus did not know how to fill up the eight lines which he was obliged to devote to the eight years of Leo's pontificate, so that the first lines of the page which contained the second half of the ninth century remained empty. Here, therefore, the interpolation could be managed

This conjecture explains why Pope Joan was inserted between Leo IV. and Benedict III.

1. There was a blank space in that part of Martinus' chronicle.

---

[1] Leo IV. died July 11th, 855. Benedict was forthwith [the same month] elected; and, after the emperor had given his consent, was consecrated on 29th of September in the same year, the very day after the Emperor Lothair died. It is notorious that contemporaries, such as Prudentius and Hincmar, notice that Benedict was Leo's immediate successor, and a diploma of Benedict's dated as early as October 7th, 855 (Mansi *Concill.* xv., 113) is still extant.

without the slightest trouble. But there was a further reason in the nature of the story itself. For the extreme improbability that a woman should be promoted to the highest ecclesiastical office, and be chosen by all as pope, was explained in the myth by her great intellectual attainments. She surpassed every one in Rome, so it was said, in learning. Naturally then, as soon as a definite historical place had to be assigned to her (the *popular* form of the myth had not troubled itself with fixed dates), a tolerably early period—at any rate, one anterior to the time of Gregory VII.— had to be chosen for her. For this, however, they were obliged to fall back on a period in which there was only a single instance known of a man being elected to the papacy on account of his transcendent knowledge. Since Gregory the Great there had been no pope who was really very remarkable for learning. In the four centuries between John VI., 701, and Gregory VII., this very Leo IV. is the only one whom Martinus notices in particular as a man who "divinarum " scripturarum extitit ferventissimus scrutator," one who already, in the monastery [of S. Martin] to which his parents had sent him for purposes of study, became remarkable for his learning no less than for his mode of life, and on this account also was unanimously[1] elected pope by the Romans

marginalia: 2. Pope Joan was supposed to have been elected, like Leo IV., for her learning.

marginalia: 1073-1085.

---

[1] [Sergius died Jan. 27th. Leo IV. was forthwith elected, and consecrated on April 10th, without waiting even for the leave of the

after the death of Sergius. On that occasion, then, it was intellectual attainment which influenced the votes of the Romans; and therefore it might happen that a woman, whose sex was not known, might be chosen as pope by the Romans, because of her intellectual superiority. Now the interpolated Martinus speaks of Joan in much the same terms as of Leo; "in diversis scientiis ita profecit, "ut nullus sibi par inveniretur," and "quum in "urbe vita et scientia magnæ opinionis esset, in "papam concorditer eligitur." And hence in Martinus Polonus, who speaks in this manner of no other[1] pope in that century, the place assigned to Pope Joan was that immediately after Leo IV., whom she resembled in this particular. And since every one took the work of Martinus as their authority, she retained this position.

It is at the stage when the myth was just beginning to gain circulation, and was still received with suspicion on many sides, that the passages on the subject in the *Historical Mirror* of VAN MAERLANT and in TOLOMEO OF LUCCA come in. Maerlant's Dutch chronicle is in verse, and is mainly taken from Vincent of Beauvais, but with

847.

By Van Maerlant, and Tolomeo of Lucca, the story was still received with suspicion.

999-1003.

---

sovereign, not as denying his authority, but because of the pressing fear of the Saracens, who had ventured up the Tiber, and plundered the Basilica of S. Peter at the end of 846. See BAXMANN, *Politik der Päpste*, vol. i., p. 352. This fear of the Saracens may have had something to do with the unanimity of the electors.]

[1] For Gerbert (Silvester II.) owed his promotion, according to Martinus, not to his great learning, but to the devil.

additions from other sources. Maerlant says moreover (about the year 1283), "I do not[1] feel clear or certain whether it is fable or fact; but in the chronicles of the popes it is not usually found." So also a manuscript list of the popes down to John XXII. (13). "Et[2] in paucis chronicis invenitur."

<small>The interpolated Martinus Polonus is copied by Geoffroi de Courlon;</small>

One of the first who has taken the story of Pope Joan from the interpolated Martinus Polonus is GEOFFROI DE COURLON, a Benedictine of the Abbey of S. Pierre le Vif at Sens, whose chronicle,[3] a somewhat rough compilation, reaches down to 1295.

<small>By Bernard Guidonis;</small>

Next comes the Dominican BERNARD GUIDONIS, in his unprinted *Flores Chronicorum*, and also (in the year 1311) in his now printed history[4] of the popes. He inserts Johannes Teutonicus (not Anglicus, therefore, according to him) natione Maguntinus, together with the whole fable about Pope Joan, keeping faithfully to his authority Martinus Polonus.

<small>By Leo of Orvieto.</small>

About the same period another Dominican, LEO OF ORVIETO, contributed to the circulation of the fable, by receiving it into his history of the popes

---

[1] *Spiegel Historical*, uitgeg. door de Maatschappij der nederl. letterk. Leyden, 1857, III., 220.

[2] This is inferior to the manuscript of the *Otia imperialia* by Gervasius in Leyden. WENSING, *de Paussin Johanna*, p. 9.

[3] *Notices et extraits*, II., 16. He adds, moreover, "Unde dicitur quod Romani in consuetudinem traxerunt probare sexus electi per foramen cathedræ lapideæ."—S. *Hist. lit. de France*, XXI., 10.

[4] MAII *Spicil*. Rom. VI., 202.

and emperors, which reached down to Clement V. [1305]. In his case also Martinus Polonus is the source from which he draws in this particular, as also in his whole book.[1]

Now follow in the first half of the fourteenth century the Dominican JOHN OF PARIS, SIFFRID IN MEISSEN, OCCAM the Minorite (who turned the story of Pope Joan to account in his controversy with John XXII.), the Greek BARLAAM, the English Benedictine RANULPH HIGDEN, the Augustine AMALRICH AUGERII, BOCCACCIO, and PETRARC.[2] *Writers between A.D. 1300 and 1350.*

A chronicle of the popes by AIMERY OF PEYRAT, Abbot of Moissac, written in the year 1399, has Johannes Anglicus in the list of popes, with the remark, "Some[3] say that this pope was a woman." *Writers between A.D. 1350 and 1400.*

The Dominican JACOBO DE ACQUI,[4] who wrote about the year 1370, inserts him without this remark, but with the extraordinary statement that his pontificate lasted *nineteen years*.

Of course people in general regarded the circumstance as to the last degree disgraceful to the

---

[1] In the third volume of LAMI's *Deliciæ Eruditorum*, Florent., 1737, p. 113.
[2] *Chronice delle vite de' Pontefici*, &c., Venetia, 1507, f. LV. He is here called Giovanni d'Anglia, and the dates are advanced two years, so that Benedict III. is placed in the year 857 (instead of 855), and Nicolas I. in 859 (instead of 858). [Benedict III. died early in 858—April 7th; so that the difference between that and the end of 859 would not be far short of two years.]
[3] *Notices et extraits*, VI., 82.
[4] *Monum. hist. patriæ, Scriptores*, III., 1524.

Roman See, and, indeed, to the whole Church. The woman-pope had reigned for two years and a half, had performed a vast number of functions, all of which were now null and void; and, added to all this, there was the scandal of giving birth to a child in the open street. It was scarcely possible to conceive anything more to the dishonour of the chair of the Apostle, or, indeed, of the whole of Christendom. What mockery must not this story excite among the Mohammedans!

As early as the close of the thirteenth, or beginning of the fourteenth century, GEOFFROI DE COURLON introduces the story with the heading *Deceptio Ecclesiæ Romanæ.*

MAERLANT[1] says sorrowfully :—

> "Alse die paves Leo vas doot—
> Ghesciede der Kerken grote scame."

"Johanne la Papesse," says[2] Jean le Maire, in the year 1511, "fist un grand esclandre à la "Papalité."

All state that since that time the popes always avoid that street, so as not to look upon the scene of the scandal.

At the close of the thirteenth century the story spreads with astounding rapidity.

Now, when we consider that, according to the declaration of the Dominican Tolomeo of Lucca,

---

[1] ["Als der Papst Leo war todt—
Geschah der Kirche grosso Schame—"
After Pope Leo was dead
A great scandal rose in the church.]

[2] In the *Traité de la différence des Schismes et des Conciles de l'Eglise,* part III., f. 2.

down to the year 1312, the story was extant nowhere, except in certain copies of Martinus Polonus, that already innumerable lists of the popes, in their chronological order, were in existence, in none of which was there any trace of the female pope to be found,—the eagerness, which suddenly meets us at the close of the thirteenth century, to make the fable pass muster as history, and to smuggle it into the manuscripts, is certainly very astonishing. The author of the *Histoire lit. de France* has good reason for saying, " Nous[1] ne " saurions nos expliquer comment il se fait que ce " soit précisément dans les rangs de cette fidèle " milice du saint-siège que se rencontrent les pro- " pagateurs les plus naïfs, et peut-être les inven- " teurs, d'une histoire si injurieuse à la papauté." Undoubtedly the thing emanated principally from those otherwise most devoted servants of the Roman See, the Dominicans[2] and the Minorites. It was certainly they, especially the former of the two, who were the first to multiply the copies of Martinus Polonus to such an extent, and thus spread the fable everywhere. The time at which

This was due mainly to the Dominicans and Minorites, especially the former.

[1] XXI., p. 10.
[2] [A serious rupture between Rome and the friars took place under Innocent IV. The University of Paris, alarmed at the hold which the monks were getting, especially on the professorship, decreed that no religious order should hold more than one of the theological chairs. The Dominicans appealed to the pope. Innocent decided against them, and within a few days died. His death was openly attributed to their prayers—" quia impossibile erat " multorum preces non audiri." Hence the well-known saying, " From the litanies of the friars, good Lord, deliver us."]

It was done mainly during the reign of Boniface VIII., the enemy of these two orders.

this took place meanwhile solves the enigma. It was in the time of Boniface VIII., who was not favourably disposed to the two orders, and whose whole policy[1] they abhorred. We see this in the unfavourable judgments which the Dominican historians formed respecting him, and in the attitude which they assumed at the outbreak of the strife between him and Philip the Fair. We notice that from the time of this crisis, which was especially a crisis for the waning power of the popes, historians among the monastic orders mention and describe with a sort of relish scandals in the history of the popes.

In the fifteenth century the story was accepted without question.

In the fifteenth century hardly any more doubt about her shows itself. Quite at the beginning of the century the bust of Pope Joan was placed in the cathedral at Sienna along with the busts of the other popes, and no one took offence at it. The church of Sienna in the time that followed gave three popes to the Roman See,—Pius II., Pius III.,

The bust of Joan in the Cathedral of Sienna among the popes till A.D. 1600.

---

[1] [His treatment of the English Franciscans made this not unnatural. The Franciscans, in direct contradiction of their vow of mendicancy, had gradually become very wealthy. The pope alone could free them from their rule. The English Minorites offered to deposit forty thousand ducats with certain bankers, as the price of permission to hold property. Boniface played with the monks till the money was paid, then absolved the bankers from their obligation to pay back money which mendicants ought never to have owned, and appropriated it as "res nullius" to his own uses. He thus made implacable enemies of the most popular and intellectual order in Europe. When Philip appealed severally to all the monastic orders in France, all the Franciscans, and with them the Dominicans, Hospitallers, and Templars, took their stand by him against the pope.]

and Marcellus II. Not one of them ever thought of having the scandal removed. It was not till two centuries later that, at the pressing demand of pope Clement VIII., Joan was metamorphosed into pope Zacharias.[1] When Hus at the council of Constance supported[2] his doctrine by appealing to the case of Agnes, who became Pope Joan, he met with no contradiction from either side. Even the Chancellor GERSON himself availed himself of the circumstance of the woman-pope as a proof that the Church could err[3] in matters of fact. On the other hand the Minorite JOHANN DE ROCHA, in a treatise written at the council of Constance, uses the case of Johannes Maguntinus to show how dangerous it is to make the duty of obedience to the Church depend upon the personal character of the pope.[4]

1592-1605. Her pontificate used as an argument at the Council of Constance: 1. By John Hus; 2. By Gerson; 3. By Johann de Rocha; and no one questioned the fact.

HEINRICH KORNER, a Dominican of Lubeck, 1402 to 1437, not only himself received the story about the woman-pope in its usual form into his

Heinrich Korner of Lubeck.

---

[1] LEQUIEN, *Oriens Christianus*, III., 392.

[2] That is to say, he tried to prove that the Church could get on very well for a long time without any pope at all, because during the whole of the reign of Agnes, namely, two years and a half, it had had no real pope.—L'ENFANT, *Histoire du Concile de Constance*, II., 334. In his work *De Ecclesia* also, Huss comes back with delight to the woman-pope, whose name was Agnes, and who was called Johannes Anglicus. She is to him a striking proof that the Roman Church has in no way remained spotless: " Quomodo ergo illa Romana " Ecclesia, illa Agnes, Johannes Papa cum collegio semper immacu- " lata permansit, qui peperit ?"

[3] In the speech which he made at Tarascon before Benedict XIII. in the year 1403. Opera, ed. DUPIN, II., 71.

[4] In DUPIN's edition of the writings of Gerson, v. 456.

chronicle, but stated in addition that his predecessor, the Dominican Henry of Herford (about 1350), whom he had often copied, had purposely concealed the circumstance, in order that the laity might not be scandalised by reading that such an error had taken place in the Church, which assuredly, as the clergy taught, was guided by the Holy Spirit.[1]

Scholastic theologians accepted the fiction, and adapted their systems to it.

The matter was now generally set forth as an indubitable fact, and the scholastic theologians endeavoured to accommodate themselves to it, and to arrange their church system and the position of the popes in the Church in accordance with it.

Æneas Sylvius thought it might be a fiction.

Æneas Sylvius, afterwards pope Pius II., had however replied to the Taborites, that the story was nevertheless not certain. But his contemporary, the great upholder of papal despotism,

Theory of Torrecremata;

cardinal Torrecremata,[2] accepts it as notorious, that a woman was once regarded by all Catholics as pope, and thence draws the following conclusion; that, whereas God had allowed this to happen, without the whole constitution of the Church being thrown into confusion, so it might also come to pass, that an heretic or an infidel should be recognised as pope; and, in comparison with the fact of a female pope, that would be the smaller difficulty of the two.

---

[1] Ap. Eccard., II., 442.
[2] "Quum ergo constet quod aliquando mulier a cunctis Catholicis "putabatur Papa, non est incredibile quod aliquando hæreticus "habeatur pro Papa, licet verus Papa non sit."—*Summa de Ecclesia,* edit. Venet., p. 391.

S. Antoninus, belonging like Torrecremata to the middle of the fifteenth century, and like him a Dominican,[1] avails himself of the Apostle's words respecting the inscrutability of the divine counsels in connection with the supposed fact of a female pope, and declares that the Church was even then not without a Head, namely Christ, but that bishops and priests ordained by the woman must certainly be re-ordained. *Of S. Antoninus.*

The Dominican order, whose members have contributed more than any one else to spread the fable everywhere, possessed in their strict organisation and their numerous libraries the means of discovering the truth. The General of the order had merely to command that the copies of Martinus Polonus, and the more ancient lists of the popes, of which there were quantities in existence in the monasteries of the order, should once for all be examined and compared together. But people preferred to believe what was most incredible and most monstrous. Not one of these men, of course, had ever seen, or heard, that a woman had for years been public teacher, priest, and bishop, without being detected, or that the birth of a child had ever taken place in the public street. But that in Rome these two things once took place *together*, in order to disgrace the papal dignity—this people believed with readiness. *The Dominicans might easily have exposed the fiction.*

Martin le Franc, provost of Lausanne, about

---

[1] *Summa hist.*, lib. 16, p. 2, c. 1, § 7.

Poem of Martin le Franc, A.D. 1450.

1450, and secretary to the popes Felix V. and Nicolas V., in his great French poem, *Le Champion des Dames*, celebrated Pope Joan at great length. First we have his astonishment, that such a thing should have been permitted to take place.

> " Comment endura Dieu, comment
> Que femme ribaulde et prestresse
> Eut l'Eglise en gouvernement ?"

It would have been no wonder had God come down to judgment, when a woman ruled the world. But now the defender steps forward and makes apology—

> " Or laissons les péchés, disans,
> Qu'elle étoit clergesse lettrée,
> Quand devant les plus souffisants
> De Rome eut l'issue et l'entrée.
> Encore te peut être montrée.
> Mainte Préface que dicta,
> Bien et saintement accoustrée
> Où en la foy point n'hésita." [1]

She had, therefore, composed many quite orthodox prefaces for the mass.

The Greeks did not learn the story till A.D. 1450–1500.

It was not until the second half of the fifteenth century that the story came into the hands of the Greeks. Welcome as the occurrence of such a thing would have been to a Cerularius and like-minded opponents of the papal chair in Constantinople, no one had as yet mentioned it, until Chalcocondylas, in the history of his time, in which he describes the mode of electing a pope, mentions

---

[1] Ap. OUDIN, *Comme de Scr. eccl.*, III. 2466.

also the fiction of an examination as to sex, and
apropos of that relates the catastrophe of Pope
Joan; an occurrence which, as he remarks, could
only have taken place in the West, where the
clergy do not allow their beards to grow.[1] It is
in him that we get the outrageous feature added
to the story, that the child was born just as the
woman was celebrating High Mass, and was seen
by the assembled congregation.[2]

In the fifteenth and sixteenth century, says the
Roman writer CANCELLIERI, the romance about
Pope Joan circulated widely in all chronicles which
were written and copied in Italy, and even under
the very eyes of Rome.[3] Thus it appears in print in
RICOBALDO's Italian chronicle of the popes, which
Filippo de Lignamine dedicated to pope Sixtus IV.
in 1474. So also in the history of the popes by
the Venetian priest Stella.[4] For long, and even
as late as 1548 and 1550, it found a place in
numerous Roman editions of the *Mirabilia Urbis
Romæ*,[5] which was a sort of guide for pilgrims and
strangers.

The story universally appealed to in Italy, A.D. 1400 to 1600.

---

[1] *De rebus Turcicis*, ed. Bekker, Bonn, 1843, p. 303.

[2] Ὡς εἰς τὴν θυσίαν ἀφίκετο, γεννῆσαί τε τὸ παιδίον κατὰ τὴν θυσίαν καὶ ὀφθῆναι ὑπὸ τοῦ λαοῦ.

The cleric, who examines the sex of the newly-elected, cries out with a loud voice: ἄρρην ἡμῖν ἐστιν ὁ δεσπότης, l. c., p. 303. Barlaam, who had mentioned the fable as early as the fourteenth century, lived in Italy.

[3] *Storia de' solenni possessi*. Rome, 1802, p. 238.

[4] *Vita paparum*, R. Basil, 1507, f. E. 2.

[5] Other old editions of this strangers' guide to Rome have the title—*Indulgentiæ ecclesiarum urbis Romæ*. The circumstance about

Felix Hemmerlin, Trithemius, Nauclerus, Albert Krantz, Coccius Sabellicus, Raphael of Volterra, Joh. Fr. Pico di Mirandola, the Augustine Foresti of Bergamo, Cardinal Domenico Jacobazzi, Hadrian of Utrecht, afterwards pope Hadrian VI.,— Germans, French, Italians, Spaniards, all appeal to the story, and interweave it with their theological disquisitions; or, like Heinrich Cornelius Agrippa, rejoice that the tenets of the canonists about the inerrancy of the Church had come to such glaring shame in the deception of the woman-pope, and that this woman, in the two years and a half of her reign, had ordained priests and bishops, administered sacraments, and performed all the other functions of a pope; and that all this had, nevertheless, remained as valid in the Church. Even JOHN, BISHOP OF CHIEMSEE, introduces Agnes and her catastrophe as a proof that the popes were sometimes under the influence of evil spirits.[1] PLATINA, who thought the story rather suspicious, nevertheless would not omit it from his history of the popes (about 1460), because nearly every one maintained its truth.[2] AVENTIN in Germany, and ONUFRIO PANVINIO in Italy, were

the woman-pope is found in all of them; and for well-nigh eighty years no one in Rome ever thought of having the scandal expurgated from a work, which was constantly being reprinted, and was put into the hands of every new-comer. [A reprint has lately been published at Berlin, 1869, edited by Parthey.]

[1] *Onus Ecclesiæ*, 1531, cap. 19, § 4.

[2] "Ne obstinate nimium et pertinaciter omisisse videar, quod fere omnes affirmant"

the first to shake the general infatuation. But still in the year 1575 the Minorite RIOCHE, in his chronicle, opposes the certainty of the collected Church to the hesitating statements of Platina and Carranza.[1]

Aventin and Onufrio Panvinio the first to deny it.

In order to arrive at the causes of the origin and development of the myth, let us now proceed to dissect it.

Analysis of the story.

Originally the woman-pope was nameless. The first accounts of her, in Stephan de Bourbon, and in the *Compilatio Chronologica* in Pistorius' collection, know nothing as yet of a Joan. In the latter authority we read: "fuit et alius pseudo- "papa, cujus nomen et anni ignorantur, nam "mulier erat." Her *own* name was not discovered till somewhat late—about the end of the fourteenth century. She was called Agnes, under which name she was a very important and useful personage, especially with John Hus; or Gilberta[2], as other's would have it. For the *pope* a name was found at an early stage; people took the most common one—John. There had already been seven of this name before 855, and in the period during which the myth was spreading, the number reached one and twenty.

Discrepancies:
1. About the name of the Papess.

Much the ame thing happened with the *time* at

---

[1] *Chronique.* Paris, 1576, f. 230.
[2] [Besides Agnes, Gilberta, or Gerberta and Joanna, she is also called in various authors Margaret, Isabel, Dorothy, and Jutta.]

2. About the date of her pontificate.

which she was supposed to have lived. The myth while still in its popular form of course did not touch upon this question. But the first authority who relates it at once gives it a date also. The event, says Stephan de Bourbon, took place about the year 1100. He places it therefore (and this is very remarkable) at the very time in which we have the first mention of the use of the pierced chair at the enthronement of the new pope. How people in general came afterwards to assign the year 855 as her date, has been already explained.

3. About her previous abode.

Stephan de Bourbon knows nothing up to his time of England, Mayence, or Athens. The woman is as yet no great scholar or public teacher, but only a clever scribe or secretary (artem notandi edocta), who thus becomes the notary of the Curia, then cardinal, and then pope. A century later in Amalricus Augerii[1] all this is enlarged upon and coloured according to fancy. At Athens she becomes by careful study a very subtle reasoner. While there she hears of the condition and fame of the city of Rome, goes thither and becomes, not a notary, as Stephan says, but a professor,[2] attracts many and noble pupils, lives at the same time in

---

[1] Ap. ECCARD, II., 1607.

[2] Even great teachers, says JAKOB VON KÖNIGSHOFEN (Chronicle, p. 179), were eager to become her pupils, for she had the chief of the schools in Rome. The papal secretary, DIETRICH VON NIEM (about A.D. 1413), professes to give the very school in which she taught, viz., that of the Greeks, in which St. Augustine also taught.

the greatest honour, is celebrated everywhere for her mode of life no less than for her learning, and hence is unanimously elected pope. She continued some time longer in her honourable and pious mode of life; but later on too much good living made her voluptuous, she yielded to the temptations of the Evil One, and was seduced by one of her confidants.

Particularly astonishing is the disagreement as to the way in which the catastrophe took place. Three or four versions of it exist. According to the first, as we find it in Stephan de Bourbon, it appears that she was with child at the time of her election to the papacy, and the dénouement took place during the procession as she was going up to the Lateran palace.[1] The Roman tribunal condemned her at once to be tied by the feet to the feet of a horse, and dragged out of the city, whereupon the populace stoned her to death. In this version of the story, however, Stephan stands quite alone. The usual narrative, as it has passed from the interpolated Martinus Polonus into later authors, makes her, after a quiet reign of more than two years, give birth to a child in the street during a procession, die at once, and forthwith be buried on the very spot. Boccaccio is quite different from this again. According to him all takes place

4. About the mode of the catastrophe.

---

[1] "Quum ascenderet," i..e, palatium, as we have it in the description of the coronation of Paschal II.;—"ascendensque palatium." Ap. Murator. *SS. Ital.* III., i. 354.

tolerably quietly; there is no death, the enthroned priestess merely sheds a few tears, and then retires into private life. "Ex apice pontificatus dejecta se in misellam evasisse mulierculum querebatur." And again: "A patribus in tenebras exteriores abjecta cum fletu misella abiit."[1]

<small>Boccacio's Zibaldone</small>

The attitude which BOCCACCIO assumed with regard to the episode of the female pope, which was just the kind of thing to please a man of his turn of mind, is particularly remarkable. In his *Zibaldone*, which he wrote about the year 1350, he included a short chronicle of the popes, which according to his own confession, was entirely borrowed from the *Chronica Martiniana*. In this the female pope is not mentioned; without doubt because he did not find her in his copy of Martinus Polonus. On the other hand, he has inserted her in two later writings,[2] *De casibus virorum et feminarum illustrium*, and *De mulieribus claris*, and has pictured the whole with the enjoyment which was to be expected from the author of the *Decamerone*. His narrative, however, differs essentially from the usual version according to Martinus; and seeing that it agrees with no other known version, it

[1] In the *Fragmentum hist. autoris incerti* in Urstis, P. II., p. 82, which says that King Theodoric killed "Johanna Papa" at Rome along with Boethius and Symmachus, Johanna is merely a mistake of some copyist for Johanne. [No version of the myth of Pope Joan places her as early as this—524, 525. John I. was pope precisely at this period 523 to 526.]

[2] To speak more exactly, he has related the story twice over in the same work, for the two writings mentioned really make up only one work.

would appear that Boccaccio has taken it directly from popular tradition (where it would naturally assume very various forms), and worked it up. He knows the length of her pontificate with the greatest exactitude: two years, seven months, and a day or two. Her original name he does not know: " Quod proprium fuerit nomen vix cognitum " est. Esto sunt, qui dicant fuisse Gilibertam." *His version seems to be the popular tradition.*

These fourteenth century witnesses are of no very great importance, for they one and all of them merely copied the interpolated passage in Martinus Polonus, often with scarcely the alteration of a word. On the other hand the recently published *Eulogium Historiarum* of a monk of Malmesbury, of the year 1366, has a peculiar form of the story to be found nowhere else, although the author in other places borrows freely from Martinus Polonus. The girl is born in Mayence, and sent by her parents to male teachers to receive instruction in the sciences. With one of these, who was a very learned man, she falls in love, and goes with him in man's attire to Rome. Here, because she surpassed every one in knowledge, she was made cardinal by pope Leo. When, as pope, she gives birth to a child during the procession, she is merely deposed. This version, therefore, would come nearest to the description given by Boccaccio. It knows nothing of the journey to Athens.[1]

---

[1] *Eulogium, Chronicon ab orbe condito usque ad annum* 1366; edited by Frank Scott Haydon. Lond. 1858, T. 1.

Variations in the finale.

The catastrophe appears somewhat further spun out in a manuscript chronicle of the abbots of Kempten. There we are told that "the Evil Spirit came to this Pope John, who was a woman, and afterwards was with child, and said, 'Thou pope, who wouldest be a Father with the other Fathers here, thou shalt show publicly when thou bringest forth that thou art a woman-pope; therefore will I take thee body and soul to myself and to my company.'"[1]

Another less severe and uncompromising finale was however attempted. By a revelation or an angel she was allowed to choose, whether she would suffer shame on earth or eternal damnation hereafter. She chose the former, and the birth of her child and her own death in the open street was the consequence.[2]

Embellishments.

The story of the female pope once believed, many other fables attached themselves to it. It was through the special aid of the devil, we are told, that she rose to the dignity of pope, and thereupon wrote moreover a book on necromancy.[3] Formerly there was a greater number of Prefaces in the missal. The reduction in number which took place afterwards with regard to those whose author and purpose were unknown, was explained

---

[1] Ap. Wolf, *Lection. Memorab.* ed. 1671, p. 177.

[2] So in the *Urbis Romæ Mirabilia*, a work frequently printed in Rome during the fifteenth and sixteenth centuries. Then in HEMMERLIN, opp. 1597, f. 99, and in a German chronicle of Cologne.

[3] TIRAQUELL. *de ley. matrim. et Basil.*, 1561, p. 298.

by the supposition, that Pope Joan had composed those which had been struck out.[1]

Now how is the first origin of the myth to be explained? Four circumstances have contributed to the production and elaboration of the fable:— 1. The use of a pierced seat at the institution of a newly elected pope. 2. A stone with an inscription on it, which people supposed to be a tombstone. 3. A statue found on the same spot, in long robes, which were supposed to be those of a woman. 4. The custom of making a circuit in processions, whereby a street which was directly in the way was avoided. *Origin of the story. Four elements of production:*

In a street in Rome stood two objects, which were very naturally supposed to be connected,—a statue with the figure of a child or small boy, and a monumental stone with an inscription. In addition to this came the circumstance, that solemn and state processions made a circuit round this street. The statue is said to have had masculine rather than feminine features; but certain information on this point is wanting, for Sixtus V. had it removed. The figure carried a palm-branch, and was supposed to represent a priest with a serving boy, or some heathen divinity. But the *1. A Statue.* *1585–1590.*

---

[1] Thus, in an Oxford manuscript of Martinus Polonus we read:— "Hic (Johannes Anglicus) primus post Ambrosium multas pre- "fationes missarum dicitur composuisse, quæ modo omnes sunt "interdictæ." Ap. MARESIUM, *Johanna Papissa restit.,* p. 17. So also the above-mentioned Martin le Franc.

long robes and the addition of the figure of the boy to the group, created a notion among the people that it was a mother with her child. The inscription was then made use of to explain the statue, and the statue to explain the inscription, the pierced chair and the avoiding of the street served to confirm the explanation. This piece of sculpture was not (as has been maintained) first mentioned by Dietrich von Niem in the fifteenth century; but Maerlant says, as early as 1283, i.e., at the time of the first circulation of the myth :—

> " En daer leget soe, als wyt lesen
> Noch also up ten Steen ghehouwen,
> Dat men ane daer mag scouwen."

2. A stone with a puzzling inscription.

The myth now sought, and soon found, further circumstances with which to connect itself. The enigmatical inscription on a monumental stone which stood on the spot, and which hitherto no one had been able to interpret, became all at once clear to the Romans. It referred to the female pope and the catastrophe of the dénouement.

The stone was set up by one of those priests of Mithras who bore the title "Pater Patrum," apparently as a memorial of some specially solemn sacrifice; for the worship of Mithras from the third century of the Christian era onwards was a very favourite one in Rome and very prevalent, until in the year 378 the worship was forbidden and the grotto of Mithras destroyed.

The earliest notice of the stone with the inscription, which was supposed to be the tombstone of the female pope, is to be found in Stephan de Bourbon. According to him the inscription ran thus,—

"Parce Pater Patrum papissæ prodere partum."

Now without doubt it did not stand so in as many words. But "Pap." or " Parc. Pater Patrum" followed by " P. P. P." was certainly the reading; an abbreviation for " propria pecunia posuit."

"Pater Patrum" appears constantly on monuments as the title of a priest of the Mithras[1]-mysteries. In this case, probably, the name of the priest of Mithras was Papirius.[2] The remaining letters may have become illegible.

<small>Attempts to interpret the inscription.</small>

The problem therefore now was to interpret the three " P's."

One reading was,

"Parce Pater Patrum papissæ prodere partum;"[3]

or, as others supposed,

"Papa Pater Patrum papissæ pandito partum;"

or, according to another explanation still better,

"Papa Pater Patrum peperit papissa papellum."

---

[1] Conf. ORELLI, *Inscriptionum latinarum ampl. coll.* 1818, 1933, 2343, 2344, 2352.

[2] For several inscriptions with the abbreviation PAP., see ORELLI, II., 25.

[3] This is the oldest interpretation as given by Stephan de Bourbon; see ECHARD, *S. Thomæ Summa suo Auctori vindicata*, p. 568.

Thus was the riddle of the inscription solved, and the myth confirmed in connection with the statue and the pierced chair. The stone had turned out to be the tombstone of the unhappy Pope Joan.[1]

The verse, however, especially in its first and second form, was altogether a most extraordinary one for an epitaph. There must be something more to account for it, and, accordingly, the myth was soon enlarged. It was reported that Satan, who of course knew the secret of the papess, had addressed her in the words of the verse in a full consistory.[2] That, however, did not seem a very satisfactory explanation; and so the supposed epitaph was altered and enlarged,—and the story at last ran thus:—that the papess, while exorcising a man possessed by a devil, had asked him, when the unclean spirit that dwelt in him would leave him, and it had mockingly answered—

"Papa Pater Patrum papissæ pandito partum,
Et tibi nunc edam (or dicam) de corpore quando recedam."[3]

Other instances have occurred of an unintelligible inscription being explained by a story[4] being

---

[1] Hence the most ancient witness, Stephan de Bourbon, says expressly:—"Ubi fuit mortua, ibi fuit sepulta, et super lapidem "super ea positum scriptus est versiculus, etc."—Ap. ECHARD., l. c., p. 568.

[2] So the *Chronica S. Ægidii*, ap. Leibnitz SS. Brunsvic., III., 580. The Chronicon of Engelhusius (Leibnitz, II., 1065) makes the evil spirit in the air shout out the verse at the birth of the child during the procession.

[3] So, for instance, the Chronicle of HERMANNUS GYGAS, p. 94.

[4] [Compare the famous verse about Pope Silvester II.:—"Scandit "ab R. Gerbertus in R, post papa viget R," p. 268.]

attached to it. Thus the chronicles, since the time of Beda, declare that an inscription had been found at Rome with the six letters:—

"R. R. R. F. F. F."

According to other instances of abbreviations in inscriptions this can at any rate mean—

"Ruderibus rejectis Rufus Festus fieri fecit."

But people constructed out of it the prophecy of an ancient Sibyl respecting the destruction of Rome, and interpreted—

"Roma Ruet Romuli Ferro Flammaque Fameque."

While the inscription on the stone occupied more especially the clergy and the more educated among the laity, and stimulated them to attempt explanations of it, the imaginative powers of the populace were chiefly excited by the seat which stood in a public place, and was always to be seen by every one, on which every newly-elected pope, in accordance with traditional custom, took his seat.

3. A seat of unusual shape,

From the time of Paschal II. in the year 1099 we find mention of the custom that, at the solemn procession to the Lateran palace, the new pope should sit down on two ancient pierced seats made of stone. They were called "*porphyreticæ*," because the stone of which they were made was of a bright red kind. They dated from the times of ancient Rome, and had formerly, it appears, stood in one of the public baths; and had thence come

On which each newly-elected pope sat.

into the oratory of S. Silvester near the Lateran.[1] Here then it was usual for the pope first to sit on the right-hand seat, while a girdle from which hung seven keys and seven seals was put round him.[2] At the same time a staff was placed in his hand, which he then, sitting on the left-hand seat, placed along with the keys in the hands of the prior of S. Lawrence. Hereupon another adornment, made after the pattern of the Jewish ephod, was placed on him. This sitting down was meant to symbolise taking possession; for Pandulf goes on to say,—" per cetera Palatii loca solis Ponti-" ficibus destinata, jam dominus vel sedens vel " transiens electionis modum implevit."

It was therefore a mere matter of accident that these stone seats were pierced. They had been selected on account of their antique form and the beautiful colour of the stone. Every stranger who visited Rome could not fail to be struck with their unusual shape. That they had formerly been intended to be used in a bath had passed out of every one's knowledge; and the idea of such a use would be one of the last to occur to people in the middle ages. They were aware that the new pope sat, and on this occasion only in his whole life, on

---

[1] MONTFAUCON, *diar. Ital.*, p. 137.

[2] " Ascendens palatium," we read in the Roman sub-deacon, PAN-DULFUS PISANUS, " ad duas curules devenit. Hic balthco suc-" cingitur, cum septem ex eo pendentibus clavibus septemque " sigillis. Et locatus in utrisque curulibus data sibi ferula in " manu, &c."—Ap. Murator, *SS. Ital.*, P. III., P. I., p. 354.

this seat, and this was the only use to which the seat was ever put. The symbolical meaning of the act and of the ceremonies connected with it was unknown and foreign to the popular mind. It invented for itself an explanation of its own, just such an explanation as popular fancy is wont to give. The seat is hollow and pierced, they said, because they wanted to make sure that the pope was a man. The further question, what need there was to make sure of this, produced the explanation;—because, in one instance certainly, a woman was made pope. Here at once a field was opened for the development of a myth. The deception, the catastrophe of the discovery; all that was forthwith sketched out in popular talk. Myth delights in the most glaring contrasts. Hence we have the highest sacerdotal office, and together with it its most shameful prostitution by sudden travail during a solemn procession, followed by childbirth in the open street. This done, the woman-pope has fulfilled her mission. The myth accordingly at once withdraws her from the scene. She dies in childbirth on the spot; or, according to another version, is stoned to death by the enraged populace. *(Monstrous story to explain this circumstance.)*

The story that the newly-elected pope sat down on the pierced seat in order to give a proof of his sex is first found in the Visions of the Dominican, ROBERT D'USEZ,[1] who died in Metz in the year *(This story occurs long before the English writer, William Brevin.)*

[1] *Hist. litt. de France*, xx. 501.

1296. He relates that in the year 1291, while he was staying at Orange, he was taken in the spirit to Rome, to the Lateran palace, and placed before the porphyry seat, "ubi dicitur probari papa au " sit homo."[1] After him JACOBO D'AGNOLO DI SCARPERIA in the year 1405 declares respecting it, in a letter to the celebrated Greek, Emanuel Chrysoloras, in which he describes the enthronisation of Gregory XII. as an eye-witness, that it is a senseless popular fable.[2] It is consequently not correct to say, what has been constantly maintained, that the English writer, William Brevin,[3] about 1470, was the first to make mention of the supposed investigation as to the sex of the pope.[4]

Of later witnesses it is worth mentioning, that

---

[1] *Liber trium virorum et trium spirit. virginum*, ed. Lefebvre, Paris, 1513, f. 25.

[2] Juxta hoc (sacellum Sylvestri) geminæ sunt fixæ sedes porphiretico incisæ lapide, in quibus, quod perforatæ sint, insanam loquitur vulgus fabulam, quod Pontifex attractetur, an vir sit. Ap. CANCELLIERI, p. 37.

[3] In a work *De septem principalibus ecclesiis urbis Romæ*.

[4] According to HEMMERLIN (*dialog. de nobil. et rusticis*), the investigation was made by two of the clergy: "et dum invenirentur " illæsi (testiculi), clamabant tangentes alta voce; testiculos habet. " Et reclamabant clerus et populus; Deo gratias." According to Chalcocondylas, the words were:—ἄρρην ἡμῖν ἐστιν ὁ δεσπότης. [De rebus Turcicis, ed. Bekker, Bonn., 1843, p. 303.] How readily the popular story was believed is shown by BERNARDINO CORIO, of Milan, who describes in his historical work the coronation of pope Alexander VI. in the year 1492, when Corio himself was in Rome. There we read, " Finalmente essendo finite le solite solemnitati in " SANCTA SANCTORUM et dimesticamente toccatogli li testicoli, ritorno al palacio." *Patria Historia*, P. VII., fol. Riv. Milano, 1503. In the later editions the passage is omitted. Corio, however, says himself, that he was not in the church where it took place, but was standing outside.

the Swede Lawrence Banck, who has minutely
described the solemnities which accompanied the
elevation of Innocent X. to the papacy [Sept.
1644], declares, with all earnestness, that it certainly
was the case, that an investigation into the
sex of the pope was the object of the ceremony.¹
At that time, however, the custom of sitting on
the two stone seats, along with several other ceremonies,
had disappeared long since, namely, since
the death of Leo X. And, moreover, Banck does
not state that he himself had seen the ceremony,²
but only that he had often seen the *seat*, and
by way of proof that it took place, and with this
particular object, *appeals to writers of the fifteenth
and sixteenth centuries*. Cancellieri, therefore, had
good reason for expressing astonishment at the
shamelessness of a man, who speaks on other
things as an eye-witness, and who had only to
inquire of a single educated Roman to learn that
the custom in question had been given up for more
than a hundred years.

But the strongest case of all is that of GIAM-PETRO VALERIANO BOLZANI, one of the literary courtiers of Leo X., and loaded with benefices,³ according to the immoral custom of the time. This man, in a speech addressed to cardinal Hippolytus

<small>Bolzani's account of the matter.</small>

---

¹ In the book *Roma Triumphans*, Franecker, 1645, Cancellieri has quoted his long account entire.
² CANCELLIERI, p. 236.
³ For the long list of his benefices, see MARINI, *Archiatri Pontificij*, I., 291.

de Medici, printed at Rome with papal privilege, did not scruple to decorate the fiction about the investigation into the sex of each newly-elected pope with new and fabulous circumstances. The ceremony takes place, he declares, quite openly in the gallery of the Lateran church before the eyes of the assembled multitude, and is then most unnecessarily proclaimed by one of the clergy and entered in the register.[1] Thus the wanton frivolity of Italian literati, and the stupid indifference of ecclesiastical dignitaries, worked together to spread this delusion, damaging as it was to the otherwise jealously guarded authority of the papal see, right through the whole mass of the populace. At the same time one could hardly have a more striking instance of the irresistible power which a universally-circulated story exercises over men, even over those of superior intellect. Any one could learn without trouble from a cardinal, or from one of the clergy taking part in the ceremony, what really took place there. But people never asked, or else imagined that the answer meant no more than a refusal to vouch for the fact. They heard this examination of the newly-elected pope spoken of everywhere, in the streets and in private houses, as a notorious fact.

Was it then that the meaning assigned to the

---

[1] Resque ipsa sacri præconis voce palam promulgata in acta mox refertur, legitimumque tum demum Pontificem nos habere arbitramur, quum habere illum quod habere decet oculata fide fuerit contestatum.

pierced seat influenced the explanation of the inscription and of the statue, or that contrariwise these two objects, gave occasion for the myth about the ceremony connected with the seat to arise? That point it is now of course out of our power to determine. We can only see that the explanation of the three objects is as old as the myth about the woman-pope.

A further confirmation of the whole was soon found in a circumstance of no importance in itself, and for which a perfectly natural explanation was ready at hand. It was remarked that the popes in processions between the Lateran and the Vatican did not enter a street which lay in the way, but made a circuit through other streets. The reason was simply the narrowness of the street. But in Rome, where the woman-pope was already haunting the imagination of the masses, it was now discovered that this was done to remind men how the woman had given birth to a child as she was going through this street, and to express horror at the catastrophe which had taken place just at that spot. In the first version of the fable, as we find it in the interpolated Martinus Polonus, it is said: "*creditur* omnino a *quibusdam*, quod ob de-testationem facti hoc faciat." With[1] later writers

4. The route taken by popes in processions between the Lateran and the Vatican.

---

[1] The chroniclers copy one from another to such a slavish extent in this narrative, that the incorrect expression of the interpolater, "Dominus Papa, quum vadit ad Lateranum, eandem viam semper *obliquat*" (instead of *declinat*) has been retained by all his followers. The avoided street was, moreover, pulled down by Sixtus V., *on account*

the thing is thoroughly established as a notorious fact.

Examples of similar growth of myths. It may now be worth while to show by a few examples, how easily a popular myth, or a mythical explanation, may be called into existence by a circumstance, so soon as anything is perceived in it, which seems in the eyes of the people to be astonishing, or which excites their imagination.

The two wives of the Count of Gleichen. The bigamy of the COUNT OF GLEICHEN plays an important part in our literature, and is still believed to be true by numberless people. A count of Gleichen is said to have gone to Palestine in the year 1227, in company with the Landgrave of Thuringia, and there to have been captured by the Saracens and thrown into prison. Through the daughter of the Sultan he obtained his liberty; and the story goes that, although his wife was living, he obtained a dispensation from pope Gregory IX. in the year 1240 or 1241, and married the princess; and the three lived together in undisturbed peace for many years afterwards. It is a well-known fact that the very bed itself (an unusually broad one) of the count and his two wives, was shown for a long time afterwards.

This story is told for the first time in the year

of its narrowness. [The spot where the catastrophe was said to have taken place is between the Colosseum and S. Clement's.]

1584, that is to say, three centuries and a half later.[1] But from that time onwards it is related in numerous writings, and in the next century became a matter of popular belief, so that henceforth it was printed in all histories of Thuringia, and is to be found in particular in JOVIUS, SAGITTARIUS, OLEARIUS, PACKENSTEIN, &c. In this case, also, it was a *tombstone* which gave occasion to the story. On it was represented a knight with two[2] female figures, one of whom had an extraordinary head dress decorated with a star. No sooner had the myth which fastened on to this figure begun to weave its web, than relics and proofs began to multiply. Not only was the bedstead shown, but a jewel which the pope had presented to the Turkish princess, and which she wore in her turban; a "Turk's road" was pointed out, leading to the castle, and a "Turk's room" within it. And not a word about all this until the seventeenth century. In earlier times no one had ever heard a syllable about the story or the relics.

Another instance is afforded by the PÜSTRICH AT SONDERSHAUSEN, a bronze figure, hollow inside, with an opening in the head. It was found in the year 1550, in a subterranean chapel of the castle of Rotenburg, near Nordhausen, and was brought to Sondershausen in the year 1576,

The Püstrich at Sondershausen.

---

[1] In DRESSERI *Rhetorica*, Lips., p. 76, squ.
[2] It is, as PLACIDUS MUTH, of Erfurt, has conjectured with much probability, the monument of a count of Gleichen, who died in 1194, and his two wives.

where it still exists in the cabinet of curiosities. Thirty or forty years had scarcely passed before a legend had grown up, which quite harmonised with a time immediately succeeding the great religious contest of the Reformation, and with a country in which the old religion was vanquished. The Püstrich was said to have stood in a niche in a pilgrimage church, and by monkish jugglery to have been filled with water, and made to vomit flames of fire, in order to terrify the people, and induce them to make large offerings. Frederick Succus, preacher in the cathedral of Magdeburg, from 1567 to 1576, relates all this, with many details as to the way in which the deception was managed, adding the remark, "that no one could "do the like now-a-days, so as to make the image "vomit flames, and that many thought it was per-"haps brought about by magic and witchcraft."[1]

Again, every one knows the story of ARCH-BISHOP HATTO, OF MAYENCE, who had a strong tower built in the middle of the Rhine, in order to protect himself from the mice; but in spite of that was devoured by them. This event, which would have fallen within the year 970, had it happened *at all,* is mentioned for the first time

Archbishop Hatto and the rats.

[1] RABE, *Der Püstrich zu Sondershausen*, Berlin, 1852, p. 58. He shows how absurd the story is, although repeated in the seventeenth century by WALTHER, TITUS, and RÖSER. Even in the year 1782 GALETTI, and in 1830 the preacher QUEHL related the ridiculous story. Rabe conjectures with probability that the Püstrich is nothing more than the support of a font. [Others have supposed it to be an idol of the Sorbic-Wends.]

at the beginning of the fourteenth century, in Siffrid's chronicle. Before that there is not a trace of it. The Mäusethurm, or Muusthurm[1] (that is, Arsenal), as BODMANN explains, was not built till the beginning of the thirteenth[2] century. Its name with the people slipped from Muusthurm to Mausthurm, and thus, according to all appearance, gave rise to the whole story. In all that is historically known of Hatto II. there is not a feature with which the legend could connect itself. The story of a prince or great man, who tried to save himself from the pursuit of mice in a tower surrounded by water, is to be found in several other places. It appears in the mountains of Bavaria; it occurs among the myths of primitive Polish history. In[3] the latter case King Popiel, his wife, and two sons, are followed and killed by mice in a tower in the Goplosee, which to this day bears the name of Mouse-tower. Wherever a tower on an island was to be seen, the object of which could no longer be explained, there sprang up the story of the blood-thirsty mice.[4]

[1] Ap. Pistor. SS., Germ., I., 10.

[2] [By a bishop named Siegfried, together with the opposite castle of Ehrenfels, as a watch tower and toll-house for collecting duties on all goods which passed up or down the river. Maus is possibly only another form of Mauth, toll or excise. Archbishop Hatto died in 970.]

[3] RÖPELL'S *Geschichte Polens*, I., 74. [See Appendix C.]

[4] LIEBRECHT's explanation in Wolf's *Zeitschrift für deutsche Mythologie*, II., 408, seems to be erroneous. He says, that "at the root of "legends on this subject lies the primitive custom of hanging the

If an unusual hollow was remarked in a stone, a hole of extraordinary shape, anything which the imagination could take for the impress of a hand or a foot, there at once a myth attached itself. A stone in the wall of a church at Schlottau in Saxony, which is thought to look like the face of a monk without ever having been carved by the hand of man, has given occasion to a legend of attempted sacrilege, and marvellous punishment.[1]

Figure on the Riesenthor of Vienna Cathedral.

On the RIESENTHOR (Giant-Porch) of S. STEPHEN's CATHEDRAL at Vienna, a youth is introduced in the carving of the upper part, who appears to rest a wounded foot on the other knee. A legend has been spun out of that. The architect, Pilgram,[2] is said to have thrown his pupil, Puchsprunn, from the scaffolding, out of jealousy, because the execution of the second spire

---

"chiefs of the nation as an offering to appease the gods, on the "occurrence of any national calamity, such as famine through the "ravages of mice, for instance." In the first place, human sacrifice by means of hanging is almost, if not quite, unknown; secondly, it is not usually a tree, but a tower on an island, to which the legend attaches itself; and, lastly, the legend places the event, as in the case of Hatto, very much later—quite in Christian times. [But may we not give up the hanging, and even the tree, and still retain the idea of propitiatory sacrifice?]

[1] See GRÄSSE's *Sagenschatz des Königreichs Sachsen*.

[2] [Pilgram was one of the later architects, successor of Jörg Œchsel about 1510. The church was founded in 1144. The Riesenthor seems to belong to a period subsequent to the fire of 1258; but it and the Heidenthürme are almost the oldest parts of the present building, and therefore existed long before Pilgram's time.]

had been transferred to the latter while still under Pilgram.[1]

The fable of the papess belongs to the local myths of Rome, of which a whole cycle existed in the Middle Ages. Hence it may be worth while to compare the birth of such a myth with a Roman example. The legend about the ORIGIN OF THE HOUSE OF COLONNA, whose power and greatness afforded material for the imagination of the people, is so far similar in the mode of its birth to that about Pope Joan, in that it was a piece of sculpture, viz., the arms of the house, which are a column, which the legend endeavoured to explain. Just as the lozenge of Saxony, the wheel of Mayence, and the virgin of the Osnabruck arms, have called forth legends of their own to explain them.

The origin of the house of Colonna.

A smith in Rome notices that his cow, every day, goes of her own accord in the same direction. He follows her, creeps after her through a narrow opening, and finds a meadow with a building in it. In the building stands a stone column, and on the top of it a brazen vessel full of money. He is about to take some of the money, when a voice calls out to him, " It is not thine ; take three " denarii, and thou wilt find on the Forum to " whom the money belongs." The smith does so, and flings the three pieces of money to three different parts of the Forum. A poor neglected lad finds them

[1] HORMAYR. *Wien, seine Geschicke, u. s. w.*, 27, 46.

all three, becomes the smith's son-in-law, buys great possessions with the money on the column, and so founds the house of Colonna.¹

> *But why was the Papess represented as coming from Mayence?*

This, perhaps, is sufficient illustration of the way in which the legend of Pope Joan arose. Two circumstances, however, require special discussion, the statement that the woman came from Mayence, and that she had studied in Athens.

The first mention that we find respecting the original home of the female pope, namely, in the passage interpolated into Martinus Polonus combines two contradictory statements. It makes her an Englishwoman, and, at the same time, a native of Mayence: "Johannes Anglus, natione Mogun-

> *And from England?*

"tinus." Probably two stories were extant, of which one made the impostor come from the British Isles, the other from Germany. The reason for one story making her a native of England may have been this. It was a most common thing for Englishwomen to go on pilgrimages to Rome: we find S. Boniface even in his day complaining of the number of them, and their dubious

> *Because the story was regarded a blow struck at papal authority, and England was looked upon as specially hostile to Rome.*

character. Or it may have been that the birth, and first spreading of the myth, fell just within that long period of the violent struggle between Innocent III. and king John, while England was accounted in Rome as the power which above

---

¹ Fr. JACOBI DE ACQUI *Chronicon imaginis mundi*, in the *Monumenta hist. patriæ*, Script., Vol. III., p. 1603.

all others was hostile to the Roman see. For, from the very beginning, the fictitious event was considered as a deep disgrace, a heavy blow struck at the authority of the Roman see; and the myth expressed that by making a country, which was considered as hostile to Rome, to be the home of a woman-pope. In like manner the mythical king Popiel, who was devoured by mice, on account of the wrong done to his father's brothers, is represented in the Polish myth as having married the daughter of a German prince, in order that the guilt of instigating him to the crime might fall on a woman of a foreign nation, and one always hostile to the Sclaves.[1]

It is not difficult to explain how the other version of the story, which became the prevalent one, came to assign MAYENCE as the native place of the papess.

The rise of the myth falls into the period of the great contest between the papacy and the empire, a time when the Germans often appeared in arms before Rome and in Rome, broke down the walls of the city, took the popes prisoners, or compelled them to take to flight. "Omne " malum ab Aquilone," was the feeling at that time in Rome. Germany had then no special capital; no recognised royal or imperial place of residence. No city but Mayence could be called the most important city in the realm. It was the

Germany was another special enemy of Rome; and Mayence was the leading city of Germany.

[1] RÖPELL, *Geschichte Polens*, p. 77.

seat of the first prince of the empire,[1] and the centre of government. "Moguntia, ubi maxima "vis regni esse noscitur," says Otto of Freysingen.[2] In the *Ligurinus* of the Pseudo-Gunther, it is said of Mayence:

"Pene fuit toto sedes notissima regno."

<small>Roman hatred of Mayence appears in other myths.</small> In the cycle of myths which cluster round Charles the Great, and which Italy also appropriated (e.g. in the *Reali di Francia*, which was extant as early as the fourteenth century, and in other productions which belong to the same cycle of myths), Roman aversion to the German metropolis, Mayence, is glaringly prominent. Mayence is the seat and home of the malicious scheme of treachery against Charles the Great and his house. Ganelo, the arch-traitor, is count of Mayence. All his party, and his associates in treachery, are called "MAGANZESI." They and Ganelo, or the men of Mayence, represent the treacherous usurpation of the empire by the Germans, in violation of the birthright of Rome.

So again in PULCI's *Morgante*, and in ARIOSTO's *cinque canti* or *Ganeloni*. The poem, *Doolin of Mayence*, is, to a certain extent, a German rejoinder

---

[1] [The electoral-archbishops of Mayence were the premier princes of the empire; they presided at diets, and at the election of the emperor. Even in Roman times the Castellum Moguntiacum was the most important of the chain of fortresses which Drusus built along the Rhine, and which in like manner became the germs of large towns.]

[2] *De gestis Frederici I.*, c. 12.

to the polemics of Rome, as shown in the Carolingian myths. Here Doolin, son of Guido, count of Mayence, steps forward as the rival of Charles the Great, first fights with him, then after an indecisive battle is reconciled to him, with him goes to Vauclere, the city of Aubigeant (Wittekind), king of Saxony, marries the daughter of the latter, Flandrine, and ends by joining with Charles in the subjugation of Saxony.

Ganelo of Mayence, the treacherous founder of the first German kingdom by separation from the Westfrankish kingdom, is supplemented in the Italian myth (which thus represents the great contest and opposition between Guelf and Ghibelline) by another native of Mayence, Ghibello. The story is to be found in BOGARDO's Italian version of the *Pomarium* of RICCOBALDO OF FERRARA. King Conrad II. (it is Conrad III. who is meant) nominates Gibello Maguntino to be administrator of the kingdom in Lombardy in opposition to Welfo, whom the Church had set up as regent of Lombardy. Gibello is of noble but poor family, had studied for awhile in Italy, acquires then great eminence in his native city, Mayence, becomes chancellor of Bohemia, but is publicly convicted of "baratteria," i.e., of political fraud or treason. He and Welfo now have a contest together, which ends in Gibello dying at Bergamo, and Welfo at Milan. Gibello of Maganza is, as one sees, a repetition of Gano or

Ganelo of Maganza. But one sees also at the same time why Johannes or Johanna must be made to come from Mayence, and why "Magun-"tinus" or "Magantinus" be called "Margan-"tinus."[1]

In later times the story, now romancing with an object, endeavoured to harmonise the two statements, that the female pope was "Anglicus," and also "natione Maguntinus." The parents of Joan were made to migrate from England to Mayence, or she was called "Anglicus," it was said, because an English monk in Fulda had been her paramour.[2]

German writers became ashamed of Pope Joan;

In Germany, however, people began now to be ashamed of the German origin of Pope Joan. She was thrown in the teeth of the Germans, we

---

[1] Both in manuscripts and printed copies we repeatedly find Margantinus instead of Marguntinus. It would appear that Margan, a famous abbey in Glamorganshire, is here indicated, where the *Annales de Margan*, with which the second volume of GALE's *Historiæ Anglic. Scriptores* commences, were composed. People could not reconcile the appellation Anglicus with the distinctive name Maguntinus, and accordingly changed the German birthplace into an English one. Bernard Guidonis came to the rescue in a different way; instead of Anglicus, he wrote Johannes Teutonicus natione Maguntinus. *Vitæ Pontificum*, ap. Maii *Spicil, Rom.* VI., 202. Among the amusing attempts which have been made to reconcile the two adjectives, Anglicus and Maguntinus, may be mentioned the version of Amalricus Augerii (*Historia Pontificum*, ap. Eccard, II., 1706). Here the woman-pope is called Johannes, Anglicus natione, dictus *Magnanimus* (instead of Maguntinus). The author would intimate that the boldness and strength of character, without which such a course of life, involving the concealment of her sex for so many years, would not have been possible, had won for her the distinctive title of "magnanimous."

[2] Compare MARESH *Johanna Papissa restituta*, p. 18.

are told in the chronicle of the bishops of Verden, because she is said to have come from Mayence.¹ Indeed some went so far as to say that this circumstance of the German woman-pope was the reason why no more Germans were elected popes, as WERNER ROLEVINK mentions, adding at the same time that this was not the true reason.² In order to conceal the circumstance, we find in the German manuscripts of Martinus Polonus " Mar-" gantinus" constantly instead of " Magantinus;" and the *Compilatio Chronica* in Leibnitz³ knows only of Johannes Anglicus. This feeling that the nationality of the woman-pope was a thing of which Germany must be ashamed has even produced a new romance, the object of which was manifestly nothing else than to transfer the home of the female pope and her paramour from Germany to Greece.⁴

And endeavoured to make her an Englishwoman.

The other feature in the myth, that the woman studied in Athens, and then came and turned her knowledge to account in Rome as a teacher of great repute, is thoroughly in accordance with the spirit of mediæval myths. As a matter of fact, no

And why was she represented as studying at Athens?

¹ Ap. LEIBNIT; *SS. Brunsvic.*, II., 212.
² *Fascic. temp. at.* VI., f. 66. So also in the Dutch *Divisiechronyk*, printed at Leyden in the year 1517. " Om dat dese Paeus " wt duytslant rus van ments opten ryn, so menen sommige, dat dit " die sake, is dat men genen geboren duytsche meer tat pacus " settet."
³ *SS. Brunsvic.*, II., 63.
⁴ It is to be found in a manuscript from Tegernsee, now in the royal library at Munich, of the fifteenth century, *Codex lat. Tegerns.*, 781. [See Appendix B.]

F

one for a thousand years had come from the West to Athens for purposes of study; for the very best of reasons, because there was nothing more to be had there. But that was no obstacle to the myth; according to which Athens in ancient times (that means perhaps before the rise of the University of Paris) was accounted as the one great seat of education and learning. For that there was, and ought to be, only one "Studium," just as there was, and ought to be, only one Empire and one Popedom, that was quite one of the sentiments of the age. "The Church has need of three powers or institu-"tions," we read in the *Chronica Jordanis*, "the "Priesthood, the Empire, and the University. "And as the Priesthood has only one seat, "namely Rome, so the University has and needs "only one seat, namely Paris. Of the three "leading nations each possesses one of these in-"stitutions. The Romans or Italians have the "Priesthood, the Germans have the Empire, and "the French have the University."[1]

Because there could be but one university, which was then at Athens.

This University was originally in Athens, thence it was transported to Rome, and from Rome Charles the Great (or his son) transplanted it to Paris. The very year of this transfer was stated. Thus we find in the *Chronicon Tielense*,[2] "Anno D.

---

[1] Ap. SCHARD *De jurisd. imperiali ac potest. eccles. variorum Authorum Scripta:* Basil., 1566, p. 307.

[2] Ed. van Leeuwen: Trajecti, 1789, p. 37. So also Gobelinus Persona. The anonymous writer in Vincent of Beauvais had previously stated, "Alcuinus studium de Roma Parisios transtulit, "quod illuc a Græcia translatum fuerat a Romanis."

" 830, Romanum studium, quod prius Athenis
" exstitit, est translatum Parisios."

Hence in ancient times, according to the prevailing notion, the University was at Athens; and whoever would rise to great eminence in the sphere of knowledge, must go there. There were only two ways in which a foreign adventurer could attain to the highest office in the Church—piety, or learning. The myth could not make the girl from Mayence become eminent through piety; this would not agree with her subsequent seduction and the birth of the child in the open street. Therefore it was through her learning that she won for herself universal admiration, and, at the election to the papacy, a unanimous vote. And this learning she could only have attained in Athens. For the University, as Amalricus Augerii says, was at that time in Greece.[1]

<small>Joan was elected for her learning, and, therefore, must have studied at the university.</small>

[1] Ap. Eccard., II., 1707.
[For additional matter on the general subject of the Papess, see Appendix A.]

POPE CYRIACUS

POPE CYRIACUS

POPE CYRIACUS was inserted into the Roman list of popes about the same time as Pope Joan, and like her maintained himself in his usurped position for a long time. Here interested imposture, visionary fancy, and groundless credulity, have conspired together to create a pope who is as unreal and as purely imaginary as Pope Joan. *The fiction of Pope Cyriacus an interested imposture.*

In the middle of the twelfth century the nun Elizabeth, in the monastery of Schönau, in the diocese of Trèves, stood wrapt in ecstasy. Her visions were inexhaustible; and as often as a grave was opened, and the bones and remains of some nameless corpse were found, the name and history of the unknown dead were revealed to her, as she said, by an angel or a saint. This worked with inspiriting effect on those who wanted new relics of saints for a church or a chapel, in order to attract the stream of population thither. Elizabeth had already been occupied with the myth of S. Ursula[1] and her maidens; and since 1155 *Visions of the nun Elizabeth of Schönau. S. Ursula and her maidens.*

---

[1] [They are said to have been martyred in 237; the sixteenth centenary of the event was celebrated in 1837. Yet it was the Huns returning from their defeat at Chalons, in 451, who put the

thousands of corpses had been dug up in the fields near Cologne, all of which were said to have belonged to S. Ursula's company. At last, however, the corpses of *men* also came to light. Tombstones with inscriptions were discovered there, or rather were forthwith invented. They spoke of an Archbishop Simplicius, of Ravenna; Marinus, bishop of Milan; Pantulus, of Basle; several cardinals and priests. There was, moreover, a stone with the inscription—" S. Cyriacus " Papa Romanus qui cum gaudio suscepit sacras " virgines et cum iisdem reversus martyrium sus- " cepit et S. Alina V." These epitaphs were sent by the abbot Gerlach to Elizabeth. By the visions which she saw in her states of magnetic clairvoyance she was to decide whether these tablets were to be believed.[1] For he himself, as he said, entertained a suspicion that the stones might have been quietly buried there with a view to gain. Her[2] unwillingness to act as judge was overcome,

---

maidens to death! S. Ursula's name appears in no martyrology earlier than the tenth century. Mr. BARING-GOULD considers her as " no other than the Swabian goddess Ursel or Hörsel transformed " into a saint of the Christian calendar."—*Curious Myths of the Middle Ages*, 1869, p. 331.]

[1] The inscriptions and the narration of S. Elizabeth are to be found, *Acta SS*. Octbr. IX., 86-88. The finding of the tombstones was arranged, it appears, in order to explain the appearance of so many bones of males in the field (ager Ursulanus), where people had been accustomed to expect only the bones of the pretended virgins, and in order to vindicate the honour of the maidens.

[2] "Diutina postulatione me multum resistentem compulerunt," are her words.

and now came the following history to light. At the time when Ursula and her maidens came to Rome, Cyriacus had already reigned a year and eleven weeks as the nineteenth pope. In the night he received the command of heaven to renounce his office, and go forth with the maidens, for a martyr's death awaited him and them. He accordingly resigned his authority into the hands of the cardinals, and caused Antherus to be raised to the papacy in his place. The Roman clergy, however, were so indignant at the abdication of Cyriacus that they struck his name out of the list of the popes. *[Cyriacus abdicates in order to accompany S. Ursula.]*

Accordingly, every objection created by previously existing authorities was forthwith quashed, and the chroniclers of the thirteenth century determined without further thought that the newly discovered pope must be inserted between Pontianus and Anteros (238). The first to do this was the Premonstratensian monk ROBERT ABOLANT AT AUXERRE, who in the first part of this century composed a general chronicle. The Dominicans, VINCENT OF BEAUVAIS and THOMAS OF CHANTINPRÉ, followed, and after them the Cistercian ALBERICH. MARTINUS POLONUS was in this case also the decisive authority and source of information for the times subsequent to himself. In him the reason why Cyriacus was not found in the *Catalogus Pontificum* is given with more particularity: "Credebant enim plerique eum non *[Martinus Polonus again the chief means of circulating the fiction.]*

"propter devotionem, sed propter oblectamenta
"virginum Papatum dimisisse." And on this
point Leo of Orvieto has followed him. Aimery
du Peyrat[1] also, and Bernard Guidonis[2] contend
for Cyriacus, while Amalrich Augerii passes him
over. The oldest chronicle in the German language (about 1330) says of him: "Want er lies
"daz babesthum und die würdikeit wider der
"Cardinal willen, und fur mit den XI. tüsing
"megden gen Colen, und wart gemartert. darumb
"tilketen die cardinal sinen namen abe der be-
"biste buche."[3] The *Eulogium historiarum*, compiled by a monk of Malmesbury about the year
1366, introduces him with the remark, "Hic cessit
"de papatu contra voluntatem cleri."[4] In the
fifteenth century Cyriacus, as was to be expected,
appeared in all the better known historical works;
in Antonius, Philip of Bergamo, Nauklerus, &c.,
and hence has passed even into the older editions
of the Roman breviary.[5]

But as early as the last year of the thirteenth

[1] *Notices et Extraits*, VI., 77.

[2] MAII *Spicil.*, VI., 29.

[3] *Oberrheinische Chronik*, edited by S. A. GRIESHABER, 1850, p. 5.

[4] Ed. SCOTT HAYDON, Lond., 1858, I., 180. [Huic successit SIRIACUS papa qui sedit anno uno, mensibus III.; hic cessit de papatu contra voluntatem cleri, sequendo XI.M. virgines quas baptizaverat, et substituendo ANACLERUM, et ideo non apponitur in catalogo paparum.]

[5] BERTI, in the *Raccolta di Dissertazion* of ZACCARIA, II., 10, remarks that he finds the fabulous acts of S. Ursula even in the breviary of 1526; and, according to LAUNOI, they are still in the breviary of 1550.

century the story of Cyriacus had become of no small practical importance, and the lawyers had appropriated it for their purposes.

The resignation of Cœlestine V., and the consequent elevation of Boniface VIII. to the papacy, created very great commotion. Many were of opinion that it was utterly impossible for a pope to resign, for he had no ecclesiastical superior who could release him from his sacred obligations, and no one can release himself. The numerous opponents of Boniface pounced upon this question, and it was now of importance to discover instances of popes resigning. Accordingly the author of the glossa ordinaria to the decree, in which Boniface VIII. affirmed the right of popes to resign, appealed to the undoubted instance of Cyriacus;[1] and thenceforward nearly all canonists availed themselves of the same pretended authority, and not only they but theologians also, as, for example, ÆGIDIUS COLONNA[2] and SYLVESTER PRIERIAS. It was usual to quote three popes in primitive times as instances of abdication, Clement, Marcellinus, and Cyriacus;[3] so that it really was a most

The fable acquired great importance in reference to the abdication of Cœlestine V.

Other fictitious abdications.

---

[1] "Datur autem certum exemplum de Cyriaco Papa, de quo "legitur, quod cum Ursula et undecim millibus virginum martyr- "izatus est." Then follows the narrative as given by MARTINUS POLONUS. Thus it stands in the older editions of the Lib: VI. *Decretal.*, cap. Renunciat. Lugdun., 1520, 1550, 1553. In the later editions the passage is omitted.

[2] *De renunciatione Papæ*, in Rocaberti *Biblioth. max. pontif.*, II., 61.

[3] So, for instance, AUGUSTINUS DE ANCONA, Summa quest. 4 art. 8: "Respondes dicendum, quod Canones et gesta Pontificum quatuor

strange misfortune that all three cases should be imaginary.

The supposed resignation of Clement was invented merely to harmonise the discrepancy between the statements, according to which he was sometimes said to have come immediately after S. Peter, sometimes not till after Linus and Anacletus.

[The case of Marcellinus is discussed in the next chapter.]

" Summos Pontifices narrant renunciasse Pontificatui, Clementem,
" Cyriacum, Marcellinum et Cœlestinum." So again, ALBERICUS DE ROSATE, DOMINICUS A S. GEMINIANO, JOHANNES TURRECREMATA, ANTONIUS CUCCHUS, BARTHOLOMÆUS FUMUS, and others.

MARCELLINUS

MARCELLINUS

THE fable about Pope Marcellinus is far more ancient than the fiction of Pope Cyriacus. For nearly a thousand years it passed for truth along with the equally imaginary synod of Sinuessa, and has been much used by theologians and lawyers in support of their theories.[1] *The abdication of Marcellinus a very ancient fiction*

At the beginning of the persecution under Diocletian (this is the fable in substance) the pontifex of the Capitol represented to Marcellinus, who was then pope, that he might without scruple offer incense to the gods, for the three wise men from the East had done so before Christ. Both agreed to let the point be decided by Diocletian, who was at that time in Persia, and he naturally ordered that the pope should offer incense. Accordingly Marcellinus is conducted to the temple of Vesta, *He offers sacrifice to the gods;*

---

[1] [It is well known that this fable has been admitted into the Roman breviary. The interpolation seems to have been made in the first half of the sixteenth century. "A la fête de Saint Marcellin, "le 16 Avril, l'ancien bréviaire romain de 1520 se borne au récit du "martyre de ce Pape. Mais voici un autre bréviaire romain de 1536 "(Bibl. Sainte Geneviève, No. BB 70), et un autre de 1542 (Ibid. "No. BB 67) ou l'on introduit la fable odieuse et ridicule du "prétendu concile de Sinuesse."—A. GRATRY, *Première lettre a M*^{gr.} *Deschamps,* p. 58.]

and offers there, in the presence of a crowd of Christian spectators, to Hercules, Jupiter, and Saturn. At the news of this three[1] hundred bishops leave their sees, and gather together to hold a council, first in a cavern near Sinuessa, but, as this would not hold more than fifty, afterwards in the town itself. Along with them were thirty Roman priests. Several priests and deacons are deposed, merely because they had gone away when they saw the pope enter the temple. Marcellinus, on the other hand, neither may nor can be judged, being supreme head of the church,—this conviction pervades the whole synod,—the[2] pope can only be judged by himself. At first he attempts to palliate his act; but seventy-two witnesses make accusation against him. Thereupon he[3] acknowledges his guilt, and himself pronounces his own deposition on the 23rd of August, 303. After this the bishops remain quietly together in Sinuessa, until Diocletian, upon receiving intelligence of this synod in Persia, sends an order for the execution of many of the three hundred, and this is carried into effect.

And is tried before the council of Sinuessa.

---

[1] [A number quite impossible for that country, especially in a time of persecution.]

[2] [The bishops say to him, " Tu eris judex; ex te enim damnaberis, " et ex te justificaberis, tamen in nostra præsentia. Prima Sedes " non judicabitur a quoquam."]

[3] [He denied his guilt the first two days; but on the third day, being adjured in God's name to speak the truth, he throws himself on the ground, covers his head with ashes, and repeatedly acknowledges his guilt, adding that he had been bribed to sacrifice.]

Since the time of Baronius not a single historian worth mentioning has renewed the attempt to maintain the authenticity of this synod of Sinuessa and its acts, meaning this clumsy structure of absurdities and impossibilities.[1] Whether any residuum of truth, any actual lapse on the part of Marcellinus in the persecution, lies at the bottom of the fabrication, cannot now be stated with certainty. Contemporary writers say nothing on the subject. Later on the Donatists alone, in the time of Augustine, professed to know that Marcellinus, and with him his successors, Melchiades, Marcellus, and Silvester, who were at that time priests, had [delivered up the Scriptures, and had] offered incense to the gods in the persecution. The bishop of Hippo treats it as a fabrication. Theodoret maintains that Marcellinus was conspicuous at the time of the persecution (of course for his constancy). However, it has lately come to light that a fiction, composed about the same time, and perhaps by the same hand, as that about the synod of Sinuessa, nevertheless was connected with events which really took place in Rome.

The whole story a tissue of absurdities.

---

[1] [HEFELE (*Conciliengeschichte*, III., iii., § 10, note 2) gives the main authorities against the fable. Augustine, *De unico Baptismo contra Petilianum*, c. 16; Theodoret, *Hist. Eccl.*, lib. i., c. 2. Among commentators, Pagi, *Crit. in Annales Baronii*, ad ann. 302, n. 18; Papebroch, in the *Acta Sanct. in Propyl. Mag.*, vol. VIII.; Natalis Alexander, *Hist. Eccl.* sæc. iii., diss. xx., vol. IV., p. 135, ed. Venet., 1778; Remi Coillier, *Hist. des auteurs sacrés*, vol. III., p. 681. Among Protestant authors, Bower, *Gesch. d. Päpste*, vol. I., p. 68 ff.; Walch, *Hist. d. Päpste*, p. 68 ff.; *Hist. der Kirchenvers.*, p. 126].⁕

This was the *Constitutum Silvestri*. And hence it is possible that a circumstance, at that time still known in Rome, may have afforded the first material for the fabrication respecting Marcellinus also.

<small>Object of the fiction to prove that the pope is superior to all tribunals.</small>

But however that may be, of a synod at Sinuessa at this time there is not a trace anywhere else to be found. The Acts of the pretended synod are evidently fabricated in order to manufacture an historical support for the principle, *that a pope can be judged by no man.* This incessantly-repeated sentence is the red thread which runs through the whole; the rest is mere appendage. By this means it is to be inculcated on the laity that they must not venture to come forward as accusers of the clergy, and on the inferior clergy that they must not do the like against their superiors. The date and occasion of the fabrication can be stated with tolerable certainty. The older list of the popes, which comes down to the death of Felix III. in 530, and can scarcely have been made later than the seventh century, has already taken up the fable about the apostacy of Marcellinus.

<small>Probable date of the fabrication of the story.</small>

On the other hand, the language of the document is so barbarous that it can hardly have been written before the close of the fifth century. And thus we are directed to those troubled sixteen years (498–514), in which the pontificate of Symmachus ran its course. At that time the two parties of Laurentius and Symmachus stood opposed to one another in Rome as foes. People, senate, and clergy were divided; they fought and murdered in the streets, and Laurentius maintained himself for several years in possession of part of the churches. Symmachus was accused by his opponents of grave offences. He must answer for himself before a synod, which King Theodoric had summoned; if he should be found guilty he must be deposed, cried the one party; while the other party maintained that for a pope there was no earthly tribunal.[1] This was the time at which Ennodius wrote his apology for Symmachus, and this accordingly was also the time at which the synod of Sinuessa, as well as the *Constitutum* of Silvester, was fabricated. The hostile party were numerous and influential, their opposition was tenacious and unremitting, their demand for an inquiry and examination of witnesses seemed natural and fair; and therefore the adherents of Symmachus caught at this means of showing that the inviolability of the pope had been long since recognised as a fact, and enounced as a principle.

A third fabrication, the *Gesta de Xysti pur*-

---

[1] "Hos (his, viz., nonnullis episcopis et senatoribus) palam pro "ejus defensione clamantibus, quod a nullo possit Romanus Ponti- "fex, etiamsi talis sit, qualis accusatur, audiri." *Vita Symmachi* in MURATORI, *SS. Ital.*, III., II. 46. [" In sacerdotibus cæteris potest si "quid forte nutaverit, reformari: at si papa urbis vocatur in " dubium, episcopatus videbitur, non jam episcopus, vacillare."— *Avitus ad Serrat.* apud LABBE, p. 1365.

He adds further on, "Non est gregis pastorem terrere, sed judicis".]

<small>Other fabrications with a similar object.</small> *gatione et Polychronii Jerosolymitani episcopi accusatione*, was produced by the same hand, and for the same purpose.[1] As in the Apology of Ennodius, so also in the *Constitutum* and the *Gesta*, the principle is inculcated that a pope has no earthly judge over him. If he lies under grave suspicion, or if charges are brought against him, he must himself declare his own guilt, himself pronounce his own deposition, as Marcellinus, or he must clear himself by the simple asseveration of his own innocence, as Xystus III., according to the *Gesta*, is said to have done, when a charge of unchastity was brought against him by Bassus. Besides all this, the prosecution of a bishop for anything whatever was rendered difficult or impossible according to the three fictitious documents; for seventy-two (or, according to the *Gesta*, at any rate forty) witnesses were to be required in such cases.

<small>Use made of the fiction:
1. By Nicolas I.</small> In later times the fable was made use of for altogether different purposes. Pope Nicolas I. quoted it in his letter to the Greek emperor[2] Michael [A.D. 862], because by it was shown how contrary to ecclesiastical discipline was the deposition of Ignatius, who had been sentenced by his inferiors.

<small>2. By Gerson;</small> Gerson[3] made use of it, on the other hand,

---

[1] They are all to be found in the Appendix to COUSTANT's edition of the *Epistolæ Pontificum Rom.*

[2] Ap. HARDUIN, *Conc. Coll.*, v., 155.

[3] *Serm. coram Alex.* v. II., 136, ed. Dupin.

together with the lapse of Liberius, in order, by means of these instances of *heresy* in popes (this word, as is well known, was specially used at that time in the wider sense of *a denial of the faith*), to prove the legitimacy of a council assembled either *without* or *against* the authority of the pope. Gerbert also appealed to it with a similar object. 3. By Gerbert.

CONSTANTINE AND SILVESTER

CONSTANTINE AND SILVESTER

If mere number of witnesses could make a statement credible, there would be no fact more certain or irrefutable than that the emperor Constantine, more than twenty years before his death, was baptized at Rome by pope Silvester, and at the same time cured of leprosy. For nearly eight hundred years the whole of western Europe had no other belief, and for just as long a period people laboured in vain to explain the fact how, nevertheless, the sources from which every one acquired his knowledge of the fourth century on other points, viz., the *Historia tripartita*, the chronicle of Jerome, and the chronicle of Isidore, could be unanimous in stating that Constantine was baptized not in Rome, but in a castle near Nicomedia, not by the pope, but by the Arian bishop Eusebius, not immediately on his conversion from heathenism, but only just before his death. *[margin: Overwhelming number of writers who mention the baptism of Constantine by Silvester at Rome. Although the chief authorities give the true account.]*

It cannot be denied that according to the mode of thought and historic sentiment of the Middle Ages, the real facts must have appeared incon- *[margin: But the true account seemed to the Middle Ages incredible.]*

ceivable, while the fabulous version, on the other hand, seemed perfectly natural and intelligible. The most important and decisive event of antiquity, the transition of the ruler of the world from heathenism to Christianity,—where else could this take place but in the capital of the world? It must have been the Head of the Church who opened the doors of the Church to the Head of earthly sovereigns. And that the pious Constantine, the son of the sainted Helena, the founder of the Christian empire of Rome, should of his own accord have remained all his life long unbaptized, denied the Sacraments, and in reality have had no claim even to the name of Christian,—that was a thing which it was utterly impossible to believe.

<small>The "baptistery of Constantine" may have helped to produce the fable.</small>

A baptistery which bore the name of Constantine at a very early period, possibly because it was really built by his order, and at his cost, may have given further occasion to the myth, in that people thought that it was called so because Constantine was baptized in it. For in later times it was considered as an irrefragable lasting witness to the truth of a circumstance which all were eager to believe.

The legend of Silvester, manifestly fabricated in order to attest the fact of Constantine's having been baptized in Rome, cannot have been composed later than the close of the fifth century. It is all of one casting, and bears no traces of later

A Roman fiction

additions. The Greek[1] text in which it is contained is evidently a translation from the Latin, which no doubt was written in Rome.[2] In the whole document there is not one historical trait to be found. Constantine is, to begin with, the enemy of the Christians, and causes many of them —among them his own wife—to be executed, because they will not offer sacrifice to idols, so that Silvester flies to Mount Soracte. The emperor, struck with leprosy, is told that to be cured he must bathe in a pool filled with boys' blood newly shed; but overcome by the tears of the mothers of these boys, he rejects the horrible remedy, and is directed in a heavenly vision to apply to Silvester. Silvester heals him of his disease by means of Christian baptism; whereupon the whole of Rome, senate and people, believe in Christ. Two episodes are interwoven with the story; the first respecting an enormous snake living under the Tarpeian Rock, and slaying thousands with its pestiferous breath, until Silvester closes the entrance of its hole; and secondly, a long disputation with the Jews (brought about by Helena), in which Silvester comes off victorious.

It no doubt originated in Rome.

Details of the story all false.

The author is acquainted with the ecclesiastical history of Eusebius. He intends (as he says at

---

[1] Edited by COMBEFIS in his *Illustr. chr. Martyrum tecti Triumphi*, Paris, 1660.

[2] This is shown by a passage quite at the beginning, in which it is said of Eusebius: τῇ ἑλληνικῇ συνεγράψατο γλώσσῃ. Of course no Greek would have made such a remark.

the outset) to complete Eusebius' narrative; but he either was not acquainted with the biography of Constantine, which gives an account of the baptism of the emperor, or at any rate he presupposed that his readers were not acquainted with it. And he actually did succeed in getting his fable admitted, in spite of the decisive and unanimous witnesses of the fourth century. Even the chronicle of Jerome, which people otherwise followed with unqualified assent in matters of history, was at last on this point superseded.

The legend of Silvester is mentioned for the first time in the decretal of pope Gelasius (492–496), *de libris recipiendis et non recipiendis*. There it is said, "the name of the author is indeed unknown,[1] " but one is told that it was read by many Catholics " in the city of Rome, and many churches imitated " this ancient custom."[2] It is manifest that these are not the words of Gelasius himself, and were not written in Rome, but elsewhere. The whole is a subsequent addition; one of the many which gradually crept into the document in the period between A.D. 500 and 800. Nevertheless, the invention of the legend must fall either within the time of Gelasius, or more probably soon after him,

---

[1] Cf. the double text in FONTANINI *de antiquitatibus Hortæ*, Rome, 1723, p. 322, and CREDNER's edition.

[2] "Pro antiquo usu," which means the ancient custom of introducing the writings used in Rome into other churches also. In another manuscript the reading is "et pro hoc quoque usu multæ " hæc imitantur ecclesiæ."— See CREDNER, *Zur Geschichte des Kanons*, 1847, p. 210.

within the time of Symmachus. For in the fictions which belong to the time of Symmachus, and which were called into existence by the circumstances relating to this pope, especially in the *Constitutum Silvestri* and the *Gesta Liberii Papæ*, the baptism of Constantine at Rome, and his cleansing from leprosy, are mentioned with unmistakeable reference to the legend. And, moreover, this is done with a designedness and violence which betrays the fact, that the legend of Silvester was a composition exciting the very gravest doubts, and therefore required to be supported and confirmed. Above all, it was wished to weaken the strength of such weighty evidence as that which Jerome, Ambrose, Prosper, and others afforded for the baptism of Constantine in the palace of Acyron, near Nicomedia; and therefore in the *Gesta Liberii* an emperor is invented, who is supposed to be the nephew of Constantine, and who is called in turn Constantine, Constantius, and Constans. Then, without any further occasion or any closer connection with the contents of the document, it is asserted of this personage that he was baptized by Eusebius of Nicomedia, in Nicomedia, at the Villa Aquilo. Here everything is accounted for; the change of name, as well as the transformation of the son into a nephew of Constantine. This nephew then takes it as a grievous affront that Liberius should say that his uncle was baptized by Silvester, and thereby cleansed from

margin: 498-514.

margin: Violence with which the fiction is introduced.

margin: A fictitious emperor.

his leprosy; and he threatens that when he comes to Rome he will give the flesh of Liberius to the birds and beasts of prey. Hence it is the more probable—nay, certain, that the legend of Silvester and the fiction of the baptism of Constantine at Rome became extant contemporaneously with the fables which were invented in the interests of Symmachus and the Roman clergy of that time, that is to say, in the first few years of the sixth century.

<small>Probable date of the fabrication of the story.</small>

There was, however, still a considerable interval before the story passed into the chronicles, and from them into ecclesiastical literature generally. ISIDORE adhered to the historical version of the matter, and FREDEGAR also (A.D. 658) remained still true to the genuine account. GREGORY[1] OF TOURS (died A.D. 598) already alludes to the fable; and BEDE (in the year 729) is, properly speaking, the first who, by means of his chronicle, prepared the way for the introduction of the story of Constantine's baptism in Rome into the annals of the

<small>Some time before the fiction was generally accepted.</small>

---

[1] [In two of his three accounts of the baptism of Clovis by S. Remigius, e.g.: "Procedit novus Constantinus ad lavacrum, dele-"turus lepræ veteris morbum," &c. In the magnificent new edition of the *Recueil des Historiens des Gaules et de la France* (PALMÉ, Paris, 1869) there is the following interesting note, *in loco*: "Colb. ad Marginem hæc habet, ab annis circ. 400 addita.; *Ecce* "*iste Historiographus concordat cum Historia S. Silvestri de lepra* "*Constantini mundata in fonte baptismi*. Et quidem certum videtur "ex hoc loco, ubi etiam Chlodoveus Constantino et sanctus Remi-"gius beato Silvestro comparantur, tunc temporis jam invaluisse "opinionem de baptizato Romæ Constantino per beatum Sil-"vestrum, lepraque ejus mundata." But in cod. Reg. this passage is left blank.]

West;[1] nevertheless he did not succeed for some time longer. FREKULF (about the year 840), who holds fast to good authorities in his *Universal History*, abides by a baptism in Nicomedia at the end of the emperor's life. Even the painstaking HERMNAN THE LAME OF REICHENAU (about A.D. 1050) seems to know nothing of the fable, and his contemporary, MARIANUS SCOTUS, who follows Jerome as an authority, has still the correct version.[2]

For the majority, however, the authority of the *Liber Pontificalis*, the Roman biographies of the popes, was irresistible. The fable of the baptism in Rome had already passed into the oldest list of the popes, one reaching back to the sixth century and in like manner into the enlarged collection which was based upon this one, the so-called Anastasius. In like manner Ado (died A.D. 875) inserts in his universal chronicle, which is based upon Bede, the fable of Constantine having been baptised in Rome, being misled by Bede, and by the *Liber Pontificalis*. He betrays the latter

Enormous influence of the Liber Pontificalis.

---

[1] Venerabilis BEDÆ opera historica minora, ed. Stephenson, London, 1841, p. 81. [Bede does not dwell on the supposed event; he mentions it merely in passing. "Constantinus fecit *Romæ, ubi* " *baptizatus est*, basilicam beati Joannis baptistæ, quæ appellata est " Constantiniana; item basilicam beato Petro in templo Apollinis, " nec non et beato Paulo, corpus utriusque ære Cyprio circumdans v " pedes grosso," &c.]

[2] The reading "rebaptizatus" instead of "baptizatus" in a manuscript of Gemblours, on which SCHELSTRATE lays great stress, is manifestly the correction of a copyist who believed in the baptism at Rome.

source by the long list of ecclesiastical donations and buildings, which Constantine is said to have ordered in Rome, and which Ado has borrowed from that Roman chronicle of the popes. On the other hand, ORDERICUS VITALIS (about A.D. 1107), and HUGO OF FLEURY (in the year 1109), who in their ecclesiastical works narrate the whole fable, —leprosy, bath of children's blood and all, have drawn directly or indirectly from the legend of Silvester; while OTTO OF FREYSING, though he declares these details to be apocryphal, nevertheless holds fast to the baptism in Rome by Silvester, "in accordance with the Roman tradi-"tion," as he says.

Ekkehard's attempt to reconcile the true and false accounts.

The first critical attempt to remove the contradiction between the old and new versions of the story was made about the year 1100 by EKKEHARD, a monk in the monastery of Michaelsberg, and from 1108 onwards, abbot of the monastery of Aurach. The means which he employed were these. He transferred the outrageous cruelty of Constantine, the execution of his nephew, of his son, his wife, and many friends, to the earlier part of the emperor's reign, after his victory over Licinius. Thereupon the Cæsar is struck by God with leprosy, but baptized by Silvester. He says, in conclusion: "Some persons maintain that Con-"stantine fell into the Arian heresy, and was re-"baptized by Eusebius of Nicomedia. The church "histories, however (that of Eusebius, namely, of "which Ekkehard made much use), do not state "this, but that he died in great sanctity." Ekkehard, therefore, understood the version of Jerome to relate to a second baptism, by means of which Constantine got himself received into the sect of the Arians,—a means of getting out of the difficulty at which many since Ekkehard have caught. Nevertheless the author of the MAGDEBURG[1] ANNALS (written in the year 1175), a monk in the monastery of Bergen, near Magdeburg, does not allow himself to be misled by the authority of Ekkehard, whom he otherwise uses as his basis. He remains true to the version of the *Ecclesiastical History* (the *Tripartita*), that Constantine put off his baptism till the end of his life.

Another variation is tried by the Italians, under the leadership of BONIZO, bishop of Sutri, and subsequently of Piacenza (died A.D. 1089), an authority not used by the Germans. In his history of the popes[2] Bonizo had to choose between three accounts of Constantine's baptism. That is to say, besides the two ordinary accounts, he had also before him the one contained in a spurious decretal of pope Eusebius, now no longer extant, stating that this pope (and therefore in the year 310[3]) had already instructed, and baptized the emperor.

Theory of Bonizo of Sutri.

---

[1] Formerly known as *Chronographus Saxo*; now as *Annales Magdeburg.*, in PERTZ' collection, XVI., p. 119.

[2] It is found in the fourth book of his *Libri Decreti*, whence MAI gives it in the *Nova Bibliotheca Patrum*, VII., P. 3, p. 39.

[3] [The papacy of Eusebius falls wholly within the year 310.]

The decretal was, of course, pure invention, in order that, by changing the Nicomedian into the Roman Eusebius, support might be got for the theory of Constantine's baptism in Rome, a theory of immense importance to the Romans. Bonizo will only allow the first half of the statement, considers the "baptizatum," as a vitium scriptorum, and gives it as his opinion, that after the instruction which he had received in Rome, Constantine postponed baptism on account of the distracting cares of government, receiving it at the hands of Silvester, and not before. But that it was altogether false what was stated in the *Tripartita Historia*, that he was not baptized until the end of his life, and then into the Arian faith. None but a maniac could believe that, after the council of Nicæa, and after the circumstances of Arius' death, of which the emperor had been a witness, he still could have lapsed into Arianism. Bonizo goes so far as to claim the authority of the whole Church in favour of his opinion. "That Constan-"tine was baptized by Silvester," he says, "is the "undoubting belief of the Catholic Church." And the Italian chroniclers of the twelfth and thir-

Italian chroniclers who follow Bonizó.

teenth centuries, SICARD,[1] bishop of Cremona, and Romuald,[2] of Salerno, have copied him in this, the latter word for word. On the other hand, GOTFRIED OF VITERBO, in his *Pantheon*, undismayed by the "mente captus" of Bonizo, avails

[1] MURATORI, SS., VII., 555.   [2] Ibid., VII., 78.

himself of the hypothesis of an Arian re-baptism in Nicomedia. In this bishop ANSELM OF HAVELBERG (about the year 1187) had already preceded him in his dialogues against the Greeks.[1] Anselm was misled by another apocryphal writing, viz., a spurious *History of Pope*[2] *Silvester*, forged under the name of Eusebius, of Cæsarea, and differing from the legend.

Of great influence in the matter was the additional fact, that the popes also themselves made use of the apocryphal legend of Silvester, and maintained Constantine's baptism at Rome as historical. Hadrian I., in the letter which was read at the second council of Nicæa, A.D. 787, quoted a long passage out of the legend as evidence of the primitive use of images.[3] Nicolas I. cited a supposed passage from a pseudo-Isidorian letter which bore the name of Silvester, with the

The popes themselves appeal to the fiction as true.

858 867.

---

[1] In D'ACHERY's *Spicilegium*, nov. edit., 1207.

[2] It exists in manuscript, according to D'ACHERY, in the library of S. Germain. Ratramnus (in D'ACHERY, l. c., p. 100) quotes a passage from it. It seems to have been forged, in order to defend Roman claims and customs against the objections of the Greeks.

[3] Ap. Harduin, IV., 82. [The gist of it is this. The apostles Peter and Paul appear to Constantine, and tell him to abandon the idea of the bath of blood, and seek out Silvester in his exile on M. Soracte; he will cure the emperor of his leprosy. Constantine goes to Silvester, who produces images of SS. Peter and Paul, in order to prove to the emperor that the two who appeared to him in the vision were not gods, but these two apostles. Constantine recognises the likeness, is convinced and baptized, and proceeds to build and restore churches, which he takes care to adorn with images. Compare the curious and very different version of the story given in the *Urbis Romæ Mirabilia*, reprinted from the Vatican manuscripts by GUSTAV PARTHEY, Berlin, 1869.]

distinctive title "Magni Constantini baptizator."[1] Leo IX., also, in controversy with the Patriarch Cærularius, laid stress on the fact that Constantine was the spiritual son of Silvester by baptism.

1048-1054.

Johannes Malalas the first Greek who accepted the fable.

Among the Greeks, JOHANNES MALALAS, at Antioch, is the first who has accepted the Roman baptism of Constantine. He lived at the end of the sixth century, and was certainly one of the least intelligent, and most prolific in fables, of all the Byzantine annalists. His authority may possibly have been the Greek translation of the legend of Silvester, which had recently been made. It is true that he did not accomplish much in the way of introducing the fable, because his own work was not very widely disseminated. But seeing that Constantine was honoured in the Greek Church as a saint, and his festival was yearly celebrated on the 21st of May, with the greatest[2] solemnity, especially in Constantinople, it gradually came to appear quite inconceivable[3] to the Greeks, that he should, of his own accord, have remained all his life outside the pale of the Church, and should not have received baptism till he was on his death-bed.

---

[1] Ibid., v., 144.
[2] Bolland, ad 21 Mai, p. 13, 14.
[3] [In Constantine's own age it was probably too common a case to provoke either surprise or censure. A century later we find S. Ambrose and S. Augustine postponing the reception of baptism till they were over thirty years of age, long after they were convinced of the truth of Christianity. STANLEY'S *Eastern Church*, Lect. VI., sub fin.]

Accordingly we find an author as early as the abbot Theophanes (died A.D. 817) setting the Anatolian theory of the baptism in Nicomedia, by Eusebius, in opposition to the Roman theory of the baptism of Silvester, but forthwith declaring that he considered the Roman account as the more correct; for, of course, Constantine, if unbaptized, could not have taken his seat with the fathers at Nicæa, and could not have taken part in the sacred mysteries: to assert or suppose that he could, was to the last degree absurd.[1] Accordingly, if even the Byzantines, as early as the ninth century, had become so unfamiliar with the circumstances and true history of the fourth century, it cannot excite wonder that the later Greek historians should have considered the incorrect account as an established fact. And this is the case with the lately published THEODOSIUS[2] MELITENUS, CEDRENUS, also ZONARAS, GEORGIUS HAMARTOLUS, GLYKAS, and NICEPHORUS KALLISTUS.

To the Greek also the true account seemed incredible.

Seeing, then, that all the chronicles of the popes subsequent to the *Liber Pontificalis*, and based upon it, relate the baptism of Constantine at Rome, and that MARTINUS POLONUS, with his predilection for what is fantastic and distorted, has imported the *Gesta Silvestri* with its whole tissue of fables into his original work, the fable main-

The Liber Pontificalis and Martinus Polonus paramount on this subject during the Middle Ages.

---

[1] Ed. Classen, I., 25.
[2] *Chronographia*, ed. TAFEL., Monachii, 1859, p. 61.

tained itself in unquestioned sovereignty throughout the Middle Ages; until, with the re-awakening of the knowledge of the Greek language and literature, and of the critical historic sense, the two most advanced spirits of their age, ÆNEAS SYLVIUS and NICOLAS OF CUSA recognised the truth.[1] Nevertheless it needed still two centuries and more, before the powerful authorities which gave support to the fable were demolished. All the canonists kept fast to the theory of a Roman baptism for some time longer, for in the collections of canons by ANSELM and DENSDEDIT, and, above all, in the *decretum* of GRATIAN (here certainly marked as "palea," that is, as later insertions), bits out of the *Gesta Silvestri* found a place, and these presupposed the truth of the statement respecting the emperor's baptism. Hence the Cardinals JACOBAZZI, REGINALD POLE, BARONIUS, BELLARMINE, and in later times even CIAMPINI himself, and SCHELSTRATE, still continued to defend the theory of a baptism in Rome, sometimes again taking refuge in the desperate resource of an Arian re-baptism. It was the profound erudition and historical criticism of French theologians, which first enabled truth to win a complete victory.

Besides all this, the legend of Silvester was welcome material for the poetry of the Middle Ages. The venomous dragon, the disputation

[1] Opera, Basil., 1551, p. 338.

with the Jews, the slain ox, the emperor's leprosy, and its healing—all this is picturesquely described in the *Kaiserchronik*, but with the greatest elaboration in the poem *Silvester*, by CONRAD OF WÜRZBURG. The *Laekenspieghel* of JAN DE CLERC, and the versified legends of the saints avail themselves of it in like manner; and even WOLFRAM OF ESCHENBACH alludes in the *Parzival* to the miracle of the ox raised to life again.

[The exploded falsehood still lives on in that museum of exploded falsehoods—Rome. On the base of the ancient obelisk which adorns the piazza of S. John Lateran, an inscription in large capitals, still states

CONSTANTINVS
PER CRVCEM VICTOR
A S· SILVESTRO HIC
BAPTIZATVS
CRVCIS GLORIAM
PROPAGAVIT;

and the *custode* of the Baptistery is still allowed to tell all visitors, that in that building pope Silvester baptized the emperor.]

<small>The legend still asserted as a fact in Rome.</small>

THE
DONATION OF CONSTANTINE

THE DONATION OF CONSTANTINE

The *Liber Pontificalis* enumerates a quantity of houses and pieces of land in various places, which Constantine is said to have given to the Church of Rome. The source alone renders these donations suspicious, one which has made such abundant use of the fictions of the age of Symmachus. And the suspicion increases when one remarks that so enormous a number of donations are attributed to Constantine alone, while the book does not mention a single other donation of any of the emperors who follow, until Justin and Justinian in the sixth century; and they are said to have given nothing more than cups and vessels. In addition to this there is the silence of all contemporary writers, and the circumstance that Constantine, liberal as he proved himself towards the Church, nevertheless, according to all accounts, never gave lands, but only made over to it rents or sums of money. Accordingly the author of the *Vita Silvestri* in the *Liber Pontificalis* appears to have attributed the whole amount of property, which had been gradually

The account of the Donation in the Liber Pontificalis suspicious in itself.

inherited or occupied, just as it existed in his own day (that is in the seventh or eighth century), exclusively to donations of Constantine. Indeed ASSEMANI says, that Hadrian I. certainly had documents of the donation of Constantine before him, for in his letter to Charles the Great in the year 775 he appeals to such as existing in the archives of the Vatican. However, if one looks closer, Hadrian is speaking of donations in Tuscany, Spoleto, &c., which various emperors, patricians, and other pious persons had made to S. Peter and the Roman Church, but which the Lombards had taken away from it; respecting these there are several documents[1] still extant. CHRISTIAN LUPUS has already remarked that Ammianus Marcellinus, up to the year 370, knows only of one source of papal property, viz., the offerings of matrons; and that accordingly, the Roman Church at that time was not yet in possession of large and rich patrimonies.[2]

Until the middle of the eighth century there is not a trace to be found of the Donation which has since become so famous, by virtue of which Constantine, immediately after his baptism, and to show his gratitude for the cure wrought by Sil-

---

[1] *Ital. Historiæ Scriptores illustr.*, III., 328. The statement of GFRÖRER is misleading (*Gregor VII.*, vol. v., p. 6). He says that Baronius has "published several documents, by means of which Constantine conferred houses, lands, &c., on the three chief basilicas of Rome." What Baronius did was merely to have printed the passages from the *Liber Pontificalis*.

[2] *Synodorum gener. Decreta*, &c., Bruxell, 1671, IV., 597.

vester, gave to this pope and his successors, a number of the most comprehensive ecclesiastical and civil rights, and to the Roman clergy many honourable privileges, and, morreove, made over Rome and Italy to the pope.

Here, then, at the outset we have these two questions to answer. *Where* and *when* was this document forged?

We have it both in Latin[1] and in Greek. It

---

[1] ["There is one old Latin text of it, but four Greek texts. See F. A. Biener *De collectionibus cann. Ecclesiæ Græcæ*, Berol., 1827. 8, p. 72, ss. The first alone is of historical importance, being found in the pseudo-Isidorian decretals under the title of *Edictum domini Constantini Imp.*, and extracts from it in the *Decret. Gratiani dist.*, XCVI., c. 13." GIESELER, *Eccles. Hist.*, II., i. 1, § 20. In the first letter of Hadrian I. to Charles the Great, A.D. 77 (*Cod. Carol.*, No. 49), occurs the following: "Et sicut temporibus b. Sylvestri Rom. Pont.
" a sanctæ recordationis piissimo Constantino M. Imperatore per
" ejus largitatem sancta Dei catholica et apostolica Romana ecclesia
" elevata atque exaltata est, et *potestatem in his Hesperiæ partibus*
" *largiri dignatus est*; ita et in his vestris felicissimis temporibus
" atque nostris S. Dei Ecclesia, i.e., b. Petri Apostoli, germinet
" atque exsultet: quia ecce novus christianissimus Dei Constantinus
" Imperator his temporibus surrexit, per quem omnia Deus sanctæ
" suæ Ecclesiæ bb. Apostolorum principis Petri largiri dignatus
" est. Sed et cuncta alia, quæ per diversos Imperatores Patricios
" etiam et alios Deum timentes, pro eorum animæ mercede et venia
" delictorum—b. Petro Apostolo—concessa sunt, et per nefandam
" gentem Langobardorum per annorum spatia, abstracta atque
" ablata sunt, vestris temporibus restituantur. Unde et plures
" donationes in sacro nostro scrinio Lateranensi reconditas habemus,"
&c. Some think that we have here an allusion to the donation of Constantine, e.g. DE MARCA (*de conc. Sac.*, III., 12), according to whom the Donation was forged, A.D. 767, "jussu Romanorum Pon-
" tiff: pia quadam industria." CENNI, on the contrary, shows (*monum. domin. Pontiff.*, I., 304) that Hadrian has in view only the Acta Sylvestri, to which he also refers in his letter to Constantine and Irene, and which in part suggested the later donation of Con-

does not exist in the more ancient manuscripts of the legend of Silvester, nor in the more ancient copies of the *Liber Pontificalis*; later on, however, it has been inserted into both. But it is certainly to be found as early as the most ancient manuscripts of the pseudo-Isidore collection, and was therefore at any rate composed before the year 850.

<small>Theory that the Donation was a Greek fabrication.</small>
That the Donation was a fiction of the Greeks, composed in Greek, and brought from the East to Rome, has indeed been long ago maintained by BARONIUS. Next BIANCHI[1] undertook to defend this view, on no better grounds, however, than the weak allegation, that it is to be found in Balsamon; and, lately, RICHTER[2] also has given as his opinion that it probably originated in Greece. But from the Greek text, as well as from the contents of the document itself, the very opposite of this can be demonstrated to a certainty.

<small>Disproved by the language of the document itself.</small>
At the very beginning of it Constantine speaks of his "satraps," whom he places before the senate and the "archons" (optimates). This expression does not occur in the Byzantines, but was of common use in Rome and with western writers; for instance in the letter of pope Paul I. to Pepin[3]

---

stantine. The words "potestatem in his Hesperiæ partibus largiri dignatus est" are especially remarkable in this connexion. Ibid., I. ii., 2, § 5.]

[1] *Della podestà e polizia della chiesa*, v., p. 1, 209.
[2] *Kirchenrecht*, fifth edition, p. 77.
[3] "Ducem Spoletinum cum ejus Satrapibus." Ap. CENNI, *Monumenta*, I., 154. In like manner King Luitprand sends, "Duces et

[A.D. 757], and in a document of king Ethelred, for Ealdorman. Moreover, the Greek translator has either read incorrectly or not understood the expression in the Latin, that "the emperor had "chosen S. Peter and his successors as sure 'pa-"'troni' before God;" that is to say, he turns "firmos apud Deum patronos" into "primos "apud Deum patres," for he absurdly translates "πρώτους πρὸς τὸν Θεὸν πατέρας."[1]

Again, if a Greek had composed the document, he would certainly, in mentioning the four oriental "Thrones," have placed Constantinople not last, but first. Nowhere but in Rome would Constantinople have been mentioned last, for there, down to the time of Innocent III., recognition was persistently refused to the canons of the second and fourth general councils which settle the order of precedence for the patriarchates. On the other hand, the Byzantine tendencies of the translator are shown in that, though he retains the expression about the Lateran *palace*, "that

The Greek text evidently a translation from the Latin.

"Satrapas suos." *Lib. Pontif.* ed. Vignoli, II., 63. [Not Paul's first letter to Pepin, in which he announces his election to the papacy as successor to his brother Stephen (for the election had been contested in favour of the Archdeacon Theophylact), but the second, in which he complains that the promised territory has not been ceded to the papal see. Ealdorman, i.e., governor of a county, later earl. The history of the word is a curious one, supplanted in its honourable meaning by the Danish "carl," living on itself as the less honourable "alderman."]

[1] From the addition καὶ δεφενσώρας we may be tolerably certain that, in the Latin original used by the translator, "patronos *et* "*defensores*" was the reading.

"it surpasses all palaces in the whole world," he nevertheless omits the distinction given to the Lateran *church*, that it is accounted "caput et "vertex omnium ecclesiarum in universo orbe ter-"rarum." Equally characteristically the passage about the possessions in Judæa, Asia, Greece, Africa, &c., which Constantine gives "pro con-"cinnatione luminarium" in the Roman churches, is left out in the Greek version, and the words "summus Pontifex et universalis urbis Romæ "Papa," are merely rendered "$\tau\hat{\wp}$ $\mu\epsilon\gamma\acute{\alpha}\lambda\wp$ $\dot{\epsilon}\pi\iota\sigma\kappa\acute{o}\pi\wp$ $\kappa\alpha\grave{\iota}$ $\kappa\alpha\theta o\lambda\iota\kappa\hat{\wp}$ $\pi\acute{\alpha}\pi\alpha$." Thus the title $o\grave{\iota}\kappa o\nu\mu\epsilon\nu\iota\kappa\acute{o}s$, which had been assumed by the patriarchs of Constantinople, and which would correspond far better than $\kappa\alpha\theta o\lambda\iota\kappa\acute{o}s$ to universalis, is avoided no doubt intentionally, so that the whole title, according to the language in use in the Oriental Church, might have been applied equally well to the bishop of Alexandria, who was also called $\pi\acute{\alpha}\pi\alpha$,[1] as to the bishop of Rome.

[1] [πaπas or πaπa, Papa, was originally a general name for all Greek presbyters and Latin bishops; but from an early age it was the special address which, long before the name of patriarch or archbishop, was given to the bishop of Alexandria. "Pope of Alex-"andria" was a well-known dignity centuries before the bishops of Rome claimed an exclusive right to the title of pope. This was first done by Gregory VII., in a Council held at Rome in 1076. STANLEY (*Eastern Church*, p. 113) gives the following curious explanation of the name: "Down to Heraclas (A.D. 230), the bishop of Alexandria, "being the sole Egyptian bishop, was called 'Abba' (father), and his "clergy 'Elders.' From his time more bishops were created, who "then received the name of 'Abba,' and consequently the name of "'Papa' (*ab-aba*, pater patrum grandfather) was appropriated to the "Primate. The Roman account (inconsistent with facts) is that

Further on we meet with a word never used by any Greek author with whom I am acquainted, κούνσουλοι for consuls, with the usual word ὕπατοι merely inserted alongside as an explanatory note. This can only be explained on the supposition of the text being a translation. And here the Greek text itself affords palpable evidence of a distorting of the original in a way which betrays the unlearned translator. The original ordains that the Roman clergy shall have the same privileges as the imperial senate, namely, that its members become patricians and consuls, and so can attain to the very highest honours which the Byzantine kingdom has to bestow. Instead of this object, which expresses a wish of the Roman clergy, quite natural and not unattainable under the circumstances of the time, the Greek text represents the emperor as making an enactment, the realisation of which no one could have seriously expected, namely, that to the Roman clergy generally should be attributed that pre-eminence and greatness, which the great senate, *or* the patricians, consuls, and other dignitaries possessed. Last of all comes

The Greek text contains absurd mistranslations.

" the name was first given to Cyril, as representing the bishop of " Rome in the council of Ephesus (Suicer, *in voce*)." He then adds other fantastic explanations: " 1. *Poppæa*, from the short life ' of each pope; 2. *Pa*, for Pater; 3. *Pap*, suck; 4. *Pap*, breast; 5. *Pa* " (Paul) *Pe* (Peter); 6. παπαῖ! (admiration); 7. *Papos*, keeper " (Oscan); 8. *Pappas*, chief slave; 9. *Pa*(ter) *Pa*(triæ); 10. *Pa*, " sound of a father's kiss. See ABRAHAM ECHELLENSIS, *De Origine* " *Nom. Papæ*, 60." It is a little difficult to believe that all of these are serious.]

the story that Constantine, holding the reins of Silvester's horse, had performed the office of groom to Silvester (στράτωρος ὀφφίκιον ἐποιήσαμεν), a story which, both in its wording and circumstance, is unmistakeably of western growth, alike foreign to oriental customs and oriental sentiment. The circumstance occurs for the first time in the year 754, when Pepin showed this mark of respect to Stephen III., who had come to visit him.[1] This act caused such great satisfaction in Rome, that it was forthwith transferred to Constantine and made into a pattern and rule for kings and emperors.

The chief passage in the document, the cession of Rome and Italy *or* of the western regions to the pope, is correctly rendered in the text as given by BALSAMON. On the other hand, it is wanting in other Greek recensions, especially in the one by MATTHEW BLASTARES[2] (about 1335), and in others given by BOULANGER and FABRICIUS,[3] from a Parisian manuscript.

Reason why the Greeks were so ready to believe in this Donation to old Rome.

This is not hard to explain. The fictitious Donation has acquired a high canonical authority among the Greeks. Since Balsamon's time it has taken its place among a mass of manuscripts

---

[1] "Vice stratoris usque in aliquantum loci juxta ejus sellarem "properavit."—*Vita Steph.* in VIGNOLI, II., 104.

[2] BEVERIDGE, *Pandectæ Canonum*, I., p. 2, p. 117. But the Latin translator has made a laughable mess of the sense, making the emperor say, "Placuit ut Papa ab urbe Roma et occidentalibus "omnibus provinciis et urbibus exiret."

[3] *Biblioth. Gr.* ed. nov. VI., 699.

respecting Greek ecclesiastical rights;[1] and Greek eyes, usually so keensighted for the discovery of Latin forgeries, were in this case so blinded, that they readily accepted the palpable forgery, and set to work to make capital out of it in practice. BLASTARES quite goes into raptures over it. "Nothing more pious or more worthy of reverence "is to be seen anywhere," he says, "nothing "which better deserves to be proclaimed far and "wide." This satisfaction rested on a very simple calculation. The canon of the second œcumenical synod of 381, that palladium of the Byzantine Church, enacts that the bishop of Constantinople shall have all the privileges of the bishop of Rome, and (as was further concluded) that the clergy of new Rome shall have, in like manner, all the rights of the clergy of old Rome. Therefore, says Balsamon, and this was the opinion of the clergy of the capital, all in the way of honours, dignity, and privileges, which Constantine had showered on the clergy of old Rome with so prodigal a hand, holds good also for the clergy and patriarch of new Rome. Another and later imperial enactment, also cited by Balsamon,[2] serves to confirm this,

Because of the famous canon which gave the clergy of new Rome all the privileges of old Rome.

---

[1] They are for the most part enumerated in BIENER *De collectionibus Canonum Eccles. Græcæ*, 1827, p. 79. In the Vienna Codex, which LAMBECIUS describes *Comment.*, lib. VIII., p. 1019, nov. ed., the remark is added "παρεξεβλήθη ἀπὸ τοῦ ἁγιωτάτου πατριάρχου Κωνσταντινουπόλεως κυροῦ Φωτίου ταῦτα. A man so well read as Photius was in literature and history, of course perceived not only the unauthenticity of the document, but also the object of the fiction.

[2] Cf. tit. 1, c. 36, p. 38, then tit. 8, c. 1, pp. 85, 89, ed. Paris, 1620.

viz., that Constantinople shall enjoy, not merely the privileges of Italy, but those of Rome itself. The emperors themselves accepted the objects at which this document was aimed, at any rate those which had reference to the relations between ecclesiastical and civil dignities. Thus MICHAEL PALŒOLOGUS, in the year 1270, wrote to direct the patriarch, that whereas he, the emperor, had appointed the deacon Theodore Skutariotes to the office of Dikæophylax (supreme judge or custos justitiæ), the said deacon should also be invested with an equivalent ecclesiastical dignity, namely, that of an exokatakoilos (that is an assessor of the patriarch with the right of precedence of the bishops), according to the terms of Constantine's rescript to Silvester.[1]

The Donation was accepted in the West long before it was even known by the Greeks.

Moreover, the Donation was acknowledged in the West centuries before it was known and noticed by the Greeks. The lately-published GEORGIUS HAMARTOLUS[2] (about the year 842) recounts the fables connected with the legend of Silvester in considerable detail, but does not say a single word about the Donation. On the contrary, he represents the emperor as giving up the West to his sons Constantius and Constans and to his nephew, Dalmatius, intending to make Byzantium his own place of residence. The first Byzantine who

---

[1] *Novellæ Constitutiones Imperatorum post Justinianum*, ed. ZACHARIE, 1857, p. 592.

[2] *Chronicon*, ed. E. de MURALTO, Petropoli, 1859, p. 399.

mentions and makes use of the Donation is BAL- *The Donation was certainly the work of a Roman ecclesiastic.*
SAMON, who died patriarch of Antioch in the year
1180, that is at a period when the Greeks had long
since lost every foot of territory in Italy, and the
giving away of Italy to the papal chair was a
matter perfectly harmless so far as they at least
were concerned. But at that time the Latins had
for long been paramount in Syria, and it was from
them probably that Balsamon got the document.

The Donation of Constantine, therefore, beyond
all doubt was composed in the West,[1] in Italy, in
Rome, and by a Roman ecclesiastic. The time of
its appearance points to the same conclusion.

[1] [The author of *Der Papst und das Concil* entirely concurs in this conclusion, placing the date of it a little before 754, it having been obviously composed with a view to being shown to Pepin. "There can be no doubt as to the Roman origin of the 'Donation.' The Jesuit Cantel has rightly recognised this in his *Hist. Metrop. Urb.*, p. 195. He thinks that a Roman subdeacon, John, was the author. The document had a threefold object—against the Lombards, who were threatening Rome, against the Greeks, who would acknowledge no imperium of the Roman see over their church, and also with a view to the Franks. The attempt of the Jesuits in the Civiltà to make a Frank the author, merely because Æneas of Paris and Ado of Vienne mention the Donation in the ninth century, is scarcely worth serious discussion; it condemns itself. The closest agreement in style and thought exists between the Donation and contemporary Roman documents, especially the *Constitutum Pauli*, I. (HARDUIN *Concil.*, III., 1999 ff.), and the *Epistola, S. Petri*, composed in 753 or 754, about the same time as the Donation. The expression 'Concinnatio luminarium,' which occurs in papal letters of that age, in the *Constitutum Pauli* and the *Donatio*, and nowhere else, betrays at once a Roman hand. So do the form of imprecation and threat of hell-torments, exactly as in the *Constitutum* and the *Epistola S. Petri*; and the term 'Satrapæ' wholly foreign to the West, and occurring only in the Donation and contemporary papal letters. See Cenni, *Monum. Domin. t. Pontif.*, I., 154." JANUS, III., note 103.]

The date at which the Donation of Constantine was composed may be placed with overwhelming probability in those years which extend from the time when the power of the Lombard kingdom began to decline, i. e., from about A.D. 752,[1] to the year 777, in which pope Hadrian first makes mention of the gift of Constantine. Earlier than that the author could not well expect any result from his invention. What he aimed at was a great kingdom embracing the whole of Italy under the rule of the pope, instead of an Italy divided between the Lombards and the Greeks, in which Rome was perpetually exposed to the attacks of the one and the maltreatment of the other. In Rome the rule of the Greeks, however oppressive it might be at times, was always preferred to that of the Lombards. The latter dominion was considered as the greatest of all evils, while the emperor and exarch of Ravenna received, on the whole, willing obedience in Rome. The popes were far from wishing to overthrow the Byzantine dominion in Italy, even when its yoke seemed intolerable, as, for example, under the two iconoclasts Leo and Constantine Copronymus. Even when the opportunity presented itself, they still did not wish to overthrow it. At any rate, between 685 and 741, we see ten popes follow one another, all of whom,

The date of the forgery lies probably between A.D. 752 and 777.

Roman horror of the Lombards.

---

[1] [The year of Pepin's accession; in 755 he was besieging the Lombards in their own capital. Astolph yielded at once, and ceded the whole of the contested territory to Pepin and the pope. Cf. MILMAN, *Latin Christianity*, bk. IV., chap. XI.]

with one exception, were either Syrians (John V., Sergius, Sisinius, Constantine, and Gregory III.), or Greeks (Conon, John VI., John VII., and Zacharias). This fact alone is sufficient to show that Byzantine influence in Rome was still quite predominant.[1] And the one Roman amongst them, Gregory II., did all that lay in his power to keep down the Italians (who were embittered by Leo's tyrannical persecution of image-worship, and had already begun to think of electing a Roman emperor of their own), under the yoke of subjection. He caused a rebellion which had broken out against Byzantium to be put down by Roman troops, and

---

[1] ["Noch völlig überwiegend war." Some might think this expression rather too strong of the period between 716 and 741. Gregory II. (716-731) begins a new era in the papacy. His immediate predecessor Constantine "was the last pope who was the humble subject of "the Eastern emperor." Gregory's opposition to Leo the Isaurian on the subject of iconoclasm is quite uncompromising. His letters to the emperor on the question are arrogant and defiant, almost brutal in tone. "Neque judicium Dei reformidasti, quum scandala in "hominum corda, non fidelium modo, sed et infidelium, ingruo- "rent." "Tu mundum totum scandalizasti, ut qui mortem nolis "subire, et infelicem rationem reddere." "Ingredere rursum ad "veritatem, unde exivisti; excute spiritus elatos, et pertinaciam "tolle; atque ad omnes scribe quoquoversum; eosque quibus "offendiculo fuisti, erige, quosque excæcasti; tametsi præ nimiâ "tuâ stupiditate illud pro nihilo habes." "Scripsisti ut concilium "universale cogeretur; et nobis inutilis ea res visa est. Tu persecu- "tor es imaginum, et hostis contumeliosus et eversor. Cessa, nobis "hoc largire ut taceas: tum mundus pace perfructur, et scandala "cessabunt." Gregory concludes this long and offensive letter with a prayer that God will drive out from the emperor's heart the evil beings which dwell there. HARDUIN *Acta Concil.*, IV., 1. The second letter is also strong in language. Gregory III. during his briefer pontificate (731-741) maintained the inflexible opposition of his predecessor.]

had the head of the ringleader of the rebels sent to Constantinople. The popes always regarded as a calamity every conquest which the Lombards made in Italy at the expense of Greek dominion; a calamity which they zealously strove to avert by prayers and remonstrances, as well as by personal intercession with the Lombard kings. They had clearly and fully recognised the fact, that when the possession of the exarchate should have strengthened Lombard power and Lombard craving for the possession of the whole peninsular, then the decree for their own subjection, and that of Rome, under this detested dominion, would be already sealed.

Even Byzantine dominion was preferred to Lombard.

How powerful the fear of the Lombards and the aversion to them must have been in Rome, may be seen from the fact that Byzantine dominion was always considered preferable there; although, assuredly, neither the popes nor the Roman clergy had had so much to endure at the hands of the Lombards as at the hands of the Greeks. True that they had to bear heavy exactions, owing to the avarice of the exarchs, to one of whom even the sacred vessels belonging to St. Peter's had to be given as pledges (about the year 700). True, that, if ever the emperor's suspicions were excited in Byzantium, the popes must submit to be summoned thither to answer for themselves; as Sergius is said to have been brought thither at the command of Justinian II., and pope Constantine, in the year 709, was compelled to obey the summons of the emperor to Nicomedia in Asia, while the exarch John caused four leading ecclesiastics to be executed[1] in Rome. For all that the antipathy to the Lombards was paramount. The reason for this hatred was, as it seems, mainly the Lombards'[2] barbarous mode of warfare, the perpetual ravaging, firing, and burning, which threatened to change the beautiful peninsular at last into an unproductive uninhabited wilderness. Not until the incapacity or disinclination of the Greeks to protect the provinces of Italy against the Lombards compelled the Italians to renounce the hopes and wishes which they had hitherto entertained, did they throw themselves into the strong arms of the Franks. But even as late as 752 Stephen IV. had made another appeal to the Greek emperor, imploring him to appear with an army for the defence of Italy against the Lombards.

This horror not ungrounded.

After the year 728 Gregory II. made an attempt to form a confederation of states, which was to maintain itself independently alike of the Greeks and of the Lombards; the head and central point of it was to be the papal chair.[3] The plan came

Scheme of Gregory II. to make Rome an independent power.

---

[1] *Vita Constantini*, ed. VIGNOLI, II., p. 9.

[2] [The Lombard host contained various wild Teutonic or Sclavonian hordes. Their wars with the Franks kept them somewhat in check, otherwise they might have devastated Italy still more. Compare the story of Alboin pledging his adulterous queen Rosmunda in a cup made of her father's skull, and the tragical end of both.]

[3] [This statement somewhat qualifies what is said in Essay VIII. of Gregory being well aware that Italian states could *not* stand without Byzantine support; and, least of all, the Roman. See p. 260.]

The Donation was an attempt to give a historic basis to such a scheme.

to nothing. In Rome, however, the idea ripened more and more, that the power of the pope might come forward in Italy and take the place of the decaying power of the Greeks, and the reluctantly tolerated power of the Lombards; and hence this document of the Donation was forged, to represent this as the normal condition of things, planned long ago by the first Christian emperor. Whether this was before the donation of Pepin or after it, can now no more be decided; but at any rate it was before the founding of the Frankish kingdom of Italy, and therefore before 774. For after this was established all prospect of realising a union of Italian states fell to the ground, and then the fiction of the Donation would have ceased to have any object. But it may very well have been composed soon after the giving up of the exarchate through Pepin, in order to prepare the way for claims to the whole of Italy, and to give them an historical basis against the day when the internal weakness of the Lombard kingdom should end in complete disintegration. And so, not long after this, in the time of Charles the Great,[1] a document was forged, in which, in very wild, and in some places scarcely intelligible Latin, a detailed narrative is put into the mouth of king Pepin of all that had taken place between him, the Greeks, the Lombards, and pope Stephen; and it then makes Pepin give nearly the whole of Italy (Venetia and

---

[1] In FANTUZZI; *Documenti Ravennati*, VI., 265.

Istria included) to the pope, either there and then, or (as in the case of Beneventum and Neaples) by promising them when they should be conquered.[1]

The pseudo-Isidore, as has been noticed already, incorporated the Donation of Constantine into his collection as an ancient document; and it certainly is found in all known manuscripts. The pseudo-Isidore, undoubtedly, did not compose it himself, although this has lately been supposed by GREGOROVIUS.[2] The contents and purpose of the fiction were altogether alien to the West-Frankish author of the False Decretals. The language also is different from his. But it is equally untenable, on the other hand, that it did not come into existence till the tenth century, as the Oratorian MORIN attempted to show. His main argument is, that Otho III., in his deed of gift of the year 999, mentions a deacon John with the sobriquet

The Donation was not fabricated by the pseudo-Isidore.

---

[1] Instead of the emperor Constantine, Pepin talks of the emperor Leo (the Isaurian is intended), saying that Leo's ambassador, Marinus, had come to him. Here there is a confusion of the presbyter, Marinus, sent from Rome to Pepin, and that Spatharius Marinus, whom Leo had sent to Italy with the commission to put pope Gregory II. out of the way. The document, moreover, makes the Greek emperor give the pope formal leave to choose out a protector, with whom he could then decide as seemed best respecting the Roman duchy and the exarchate. It is manifestly invented with a double object, first, by supplying the consent of the Byzantine court to do away with a legal objection; and, secondly, to bring about an enlargement of the donation of Charles the Great.

[2] *Geschichte der Stadt Rom.*, III., 400. Cenni had anticipated him in maintaining this, and that "plaudentibus nostri ævi cruditis," as he thinks. *Monum.*, I., 305.

"Digitorum mutius," (i. e., mutilus, *mozzo*,) as the man who wrote the document in golden letters in Constantine's name. This John the deacon, Morin supposes, is the man whom John XII. first used as his tool, and then, in the year 974, caused his right hand to be cut off.[1] A mistaken idea; for a man who had lost his right hand would not have been called "with mutilated fingers," as a sobriquet. Moreover, the Donation of Constantine may very well have been extant at an earlier period, before John the deacon, of whom the draughtsman of Otho's document makes mention, wrote it out in golden letters, in order to invest it with greater dignity.

The supposed evidence of this has been quite misunderstood

An analysis and closer consideration of the contents of the document will give a still higher degree of certainty to the supposition, that it originated in Rome between 750 and 774.

The contents of the document argue a Roman origin between 750 and 774.

The following are among the grants made in the Donation to the popes and the Roman clergy:—

> 1. Constantine desires to promote the Chair of Peter over the empire and its seat on earth, by bestowing on it imperial power and honour.
>
> 2. The Chair of Peter shall have supreme authority over the patriarchal Chairs of Alexandria, Antioch, Jerusalem, and Con-

---

[1] According to LUITPRAND, *Hist. Ottonis*, in Pertz, v., 316, and *Contin. Reginon.*, ad a., 964.

stantinople, and over all churches in the world.¹

3. It shall be judge in all that concerns the service of God and the Christian Faith.²

4. Instead of the diadem, which the emperor wished to place on the pope's head, but which the pope refused, Constantine has given to him and to his successors the phrygium³ (that is the tiara) and the lorum which adorned the emperor's neck, as well as the other gorgeous robes and insignia of the imperial dignity.

5. The Roman clergy shall enjoy the high privileges of the imperial senate, being eligible to the dignity of patrician or consul, and having the right to wear the decoration worn

---

¹ [" Ut principatum teneat tam super quatuor sedes, Alexandri-" nam, Antiochenam, Hierosolymitanam ac Constantinopolitanam, " quamque etiam super omnes in universo orbe terrarum ecclesias." As cited by Leo IX., Harduin, VI., 935.] The Greeks have omitted this article in the recension in Blastares, and in that of the Parisian manuscript.

² This article also is wanting in both the above-mentioned texts. [Leo IX., of course, retains it, " et ejus judicio quæque ad cultum " Dei vel fidei Christianorum stabilitatem procuranda fuerint, " disponantur."]

³ [Leo IX. says, at first, *both* the diadem and the phrygium : " deinde " diadema, videlicet coronam capitis nostri, simulque phrygium, " necnon et superhumerale, videlicet lorum quod imperiale cir-".cumdare assolet collum." But later on, after mentioning Silvester's refusal of the gold crown, " phrygium autem candido nitore, " splendidam resurrectionem Dominicam designans, ejus sacrat-" issimo vertici manibus nostris imposuimus, et tenentes frenum " equi ipsius, pro reverentia beati Petri, &c."]

by the (optimates or) nobles in office under the empire.[1]

6. The offices of cubicularii, ostiarii, and excubitæ, shall belong to the Roman Church.

7. The Roman clergy shall ride on horses decked with white coverlets, and, like the senate, wear white sandals.

8. If a member of the senate shall wish to take orders, and the pope consents, no one shall hinder him.[2]

9. Constantine gives up the remaining sovereignty over Rome, the provinces, cities, and towns of the whole of Italy *or* of the western regions, to pope Silvester and his successors.

The momentous ninth clause was evidently of very secondary importance in the eyes of the composer.

Judging from the detailed and careful manner in which each single clause is treated, we may conclude that the author, who beyond all doubt was a Roman ecclesiastic, had the articles and colour of the dress proper to the pope and clergy, with their titles and insignia of rank, far more at heart than the ninth clause which, tacked on at the end and expressed in few words, was so preg-

---

[1] Imperialis militia, στρατία, which MÜNCH (*On the Donation of Constantine*, p. 22) translates as "the imperial army," remarking that the Roman clergy had been desirous of wearing military decorations. A glance at DUCANGE's *Glossary* would have told him what "militia" or "στρατία" meant at that time [viz., court officials.]

[2] So the Greek text. The Latin reading "nullus ex omnibus "præsumat superbe agere" makes no kind of sense with the context just preceding.

nant with consequences, *the donation of Rome and Italy.* And here one must at the same time remember, that the composer intended Italy alone, and not pretty nearly the whole of the West which belonged to the kingdom of Rome at the time of Constantine, that is to say, Gaul, Spain, Britain, &c., to be comprehended in the Donation as well as Italy. In all probability he knew nothing of the real extent of the empire at the time of Constantine, but had only the circumstances of the eighth century before his eyes; for he says "Italy *or* the western regions," doubtless merely to define more closely the geographical expression "Italy," and to include Istria, Corsica, and Sardinia. Not until a later age was the "*or*" changed into "*and.*" And for long the matter was so understood. The popes[1] Hadrian I. and Leo IX., the emperor Otho III. and cardinal Peter Damiani found in the document merely the donation of Italy.

He merely contemplated Italy and the islands.

Change of "or" into "and."

If one considers the remaining clauses, that is to say the demands and wishes of Roman ecclesiastics clad in the form of supposed concessions, one sees that they altogether have reference to the state of affairs in Rome and Italy about the middle of the eighth century. The author naturally has not so

The other clauses have reference to Roman, not Byzantine, distinctions of rank.

---

[1] ["Et sicut temporibus beati Silvestri Romani Pontificis, a "sanctæ recordationis piisimo Constantino Imperatore, per ejus "largitatem sancta Dei Catholica et Apostolica Romana Ecclesia "elevata atque exaltata est, et potestatem in his Hesperiæ partibus "largiri dignatus est, &c., &c." Letter of Hadrian I. to Charles the Great.—*Recueil des Historiens des Gaules et de la France,* ap., PALMÉ, Paris, 1869, v., 550, c.]

much the arrangements and relations of rank in Constantinople before his eyes, as those of that part of Italy which at that time was still Byzantine. The *senate*, with which the clergy in Rome wished to be placed on an equality in certain privileges, was no longer the old Roman senate. That had perished in the sixth century, during the wars with the Goths and the Lombards. The senate is never mentioned[1] in the period from the end of the sixth to the middle of the eighth century, but reappears first in the year 757 as the collective body of the Roman optimates.[2] After that time we have mention made of a special place for the senators [senatorium] in the two chief churches in Rome. Those who sat there received the Holy Communion from the hands of the pope himself.[3] It was, in fact, a new official nobility which was formed, partly out of the military aristocracy of citizens, partly out of ecclesiastical dignitaries; and the latter were also to have their share—this was one of the objects which the author of the fiction had in view—in the highest titles of honour which the emperors granted to certain pre-eminent members of the civil, or rather military aristocracy.

<small>The senate in the eighth century.</small>

---

[1] SAVIGNY's assertions (*Geschichte des Röm. Rechts*, I., 367) are on this point too strong; that in all centuries, as he says, are to be found undeniable traces of the real continuance of the Roman senate is, at any rate, without foundation as regards the period between 660 and 750.

[2] " Salutant vos et cunctus procerum senatus, atque diversi " populi congregatio." CENNI, II., 146.

[3] MABILLON, *Mus. Ital.*, II., XLIV., LIX., 10.

The ranks of *patrician* and *consul*, for instance, which were to be made accessible to the Roman clergy, were at that time the highest at which ambition[1] could aim. A patrician,[2] or member of the imperial Privy Council, was promoted to his rank by being solemnly invested with an embroidered robe of state; and even governors of provinces felt themselves raised in dignity by the addition of this title, the highest in the empire. From the year 754 onwards the pope, in the name of the Roman republic (which still continued to be considered as always virtually existing), and with the acquiescence of the Roman people, claimed to have the power of conferring the title of "patrician of Rome;" and gave it, as is well known, in the first instance to king Pepin and king Carloman.[3]

<small>The patriciate in the eighth century.</small>

---

[1] In the *Vita Agathonis*, Vignoli, I., 279, we have the high dignitaries thus reckoned: "Patricii, Hypati cum omni Syncleto." In the year 701 Theophylact was Cubicularius, Patricius, Exarchus Italiæ, ibid., I., 315.

[2] [This new rank of patrician was created at Constantinople, and was not conferred on old Roman families. It was a personal, not an hereditary dignity, and became extinct with the death of the holder. A patrician family at this period merely meant one, of which the head was a patrician. The patricians were the highest of the *illustres*; consuls alone ranked higher. A patrician was distinguished by such titles as Magnificentia, Celsitudo, Eminentia, and Magnitudo. The new dignity was not confined to subjects of the empire, but was sometimes given to foreigners, such as Odoacer. Other sovereigns imitated the emperors and popes in conferring this title on eminent subjects, but such patricians ranked far below Roman patricians. Smith's *Dictionary of Antiquities*, "Patricii," sub fin.]

[3] ["In the meantime the right of conquest, and the indefinite title of patrician, assigned by the pope (Stephen), acting in behalf, and with the consent of the Roman republic, to Pepin—a title which might be merely honorary, or might justify any authority which he

Thus the highest temporal dignity in Rome, after that of emperor or a Cæsar, was to be in the pope's gift, and that without any theoretical infringement of the imperial prerogative. When the Greek dominion perished in north and central Italy, the patriciate, as a dignity conferred on particular governors, vanished along with it, and there remained only the one Roman patriciate, the chief dignity among the inhabitants of the city of Rome.

The consulate in the eighth century. The consuls also, as Savigny[1] has remarked, were first mentioned in the middle of the eighth century, and constituted the rank next to the patricians. The chief city magistrates bore this title, one, however, which thenceforward occurs merely as a title of honour. One such consul (and dux) was Theodatus, the tutor of Hadrian I., and afterwards primicerius of the Roman Church. His contemporary Leoninus, in like manner, was at the same time both consul and dux, afterwards a monk.[2]

Papal officials of the household in imitation of the imperial officials. Further use of Constantine's name was made to obtain for the popes the right of having gentlemen of the bed-chamber, door-keepers, and a body-guard (cubicularii, ostiarii, excubitores). Here again the date fits exactly. Formerly in Italy there were only *imperial* cubicularii. Not until the time of

---

might have power to exercise—gave a kind of supremacy to the king of the Franks in Rome."—MILMAN, *Lat. Chr.*, IV., c. XI.]

[1] A., a., O., p. 370. He quotes FANTUZZI, *Mon. Rav.*, I., 15.
[2] *Vita Hadr.*, in VIGNOLI, II., 162, 210.

Stephen IV. and Hadrian I. do we find an instance of a *papal* cubicularius, viz., Paul Afiarta,[1] who at the same time was superista, that is, overseer of the palace. In[2] the first *Ordo Romanus* in MABILLON, who describes the Roman ceremonial at the end of the eighth and beginning of the ninth century, the cubicularius tonsuratus, who had to carry the papal robes, is mentioned for the first time.

In the Roman *Ordo* of Cencius (twelfth century) the portarii or ostiarii pro custodiendo palatio were placed in the second rank under the Roman scholæ or guilds of the papal court servants, and described according to their duties.[3] Lastly, the excubitores are unmistakeably the so-called adextratores of a later age, a guard of honour,[4] which escorted the pope in processions and visits to churches.

The author of the Donation manifestly attached great importance to the point, that the Roman clergy should have the privilege of decking their horses with white coverings. Altogether in harmony with the spirit of the time and place, where this was considered as a thing of extraordinary importance, and as a precious privilege of the Roman clergy surpassing all others. Hence Gregory the Great had before this notified to the

The right of using white horse-coverlets.

---

[1] That he was cubicularius of the pope, and not of the emperor, is plain from the *Vita Hadr.*, in VIGNOLI, II., 164 and 166; for in other instances the *Liber Pontificalis* adds imperialis, as in the case of Theodore Pellarius, ib. I., 263.

[2] *Mus. Ital.*, II., 6.

[3] l. c., p. 194, 96.

[4] l. c., p. 196.

archbishop of Ravenna, that the Roman clergy would on no account concede that the use of horse-coverlets (mappulæ) should be allowed to the clergy of Ravenna.¹ The Roman biographer finds great fault with pope Conon, because (about A.D. 687) he had allowed the deacon Constantine of Syracuse, whom he had nominated rector of the patrimony there, to make use of such a coverlet.²

Stated object of the Donation; to light the tombs of SS. Peter and Paul.

Lastly, the object attributed to Constantine is altogether in accordance with the sentiments of the eighth century; viz., that he endowed the Roman Church with possessions in the East and West, in order that the lamps and tapers which burnt in the churches and at the tombs of the Apostles S. Peter and S. Paul might be kept up by the revenues. And thus pope Paul I. writes to Pepin, in the year 761, saying that the contest which the king had undertaken against the Lombards was waged by him for the restoration of the lamps of S. Peter.³

Both internal and external evidence, therefore, conducts us to the period between 750 and 775 as the time when the Donation of Constantine came into existence. The supposition of NATALIS ALEXANDER and of his follower CENNI,⁴ that it was

---

¹ GREG. M. *Opera*, II., 668, ed. Paris, cf. Gratian. *Decre.*, dist. 93, c. 22.

² *Vit. Conon.* ap. VIGNOLI, I., 301.

³ CENNI, I., 185: "Pro cujus restituendis luminariis decertatis." So also the pseudo-Constantine, "Quibus pro concinnatione lumina-" "rium possessiones contulimus."

⁴ *Monum.*, I., 304.

not known in Rome before the middle of the ninth century, is certainly incorrect. Hadrian I. undeniably alludes to it in the words that Constantine had "given the dominion in these regions of the West" to the Romish Church. These are the "occidentalium regionum provinciæ (ἑσμῶν χωρῶν ἐπαρχίαι)" of which the Donation speaks. Nevertheless, it is quite certain that at first no pains were taken to make it generally known. From Hadrian I. to Leo IX. (776 to 1053) there is no trace of it to be found in the letters of popes; in the older manuscripts of the *Liber Pontificalis* there is no mention of it; but by means of the pseudo-Isidore (that is from 840 onwards), it began to be known outside Italy, and indeed perhaps more in France than in Italy itself. For though LUITPRAND, bishop of Cremona, as imperial ambassador at Byzantium boasted of the large donations which Constantine had given to the Roman Church, in Persia, Mesopotamia, and Babylonia; yet he knew nothing of the contents of the forged document, or at any rate, gave no hint of it; while, on the other hand, two men who for their age were so learned and so well read in ecclesiastical history and literature as ÆNEAS, bishop of Paris, and HINCMAR, bishop of Rheims, readily accepted it. The former of them (about the year 868) represents to the Greeks that Constantine had declared that two emperors, the one of the realm, the other of the Church, could not rule in common in one city.

The Donation certainly known in Rome before A.D. 850.

No pains taken at first to make it well known.

Æneas of Paris treats it as authentic.

He had therefore removed his residence to Byzantium, but had placed the Roman territory, "and a "vast number of various provinces," under the rule of the Apostolic chair, and had conferred royal power[1] on the pope. Hincmar, expresses himself with more reserve. He and his contemporary bishop ADO, of Vienne, in his chronicle (about 860), know only of Constantine's having given up the city of Rome to the pope.[2]

So also Hincmar and Ado, but with some reserve.

Pope LEO IX. recounted nearly the whole text of the Donation to the patriarch Michael Cerularius in the year 1054, openly and confidently, without having (as it would seem) a single misgiving as to the weakness of his document. He wished the patriarch to convince himself "of the earthly and "heavenly imperium, of the royal priesthood of the "Roman Chair," and retain no trace of the suspicion "that this chair "wished to usurp power by the "help of foolish[3] and old wives' fables." He is, however, the only one of all the popes who has brought the document expressly before the eyes of the world, and formally challenged criticism. In remarkable contrast to him, his guide and adviser and successor, Gregory VII., never made use of it, in not one of his numerous letters even mentions

Leo IX. seems to have the fullest belief in it.

Remarkable silence of Gregory VII.

---

[1] *Liber adversus Græcos*, in D'ACHERY, *Spicil.*, VII., III.
[2] Epist. 3, c. 13.
[3] HARDUIN, *Conc.*, VI., 934. ["Sed ne forte adhuc de terrena ipsius "dominatione aliquis vobis dubietatis supersit scrupulus, neve "leviter suspicemini ineptis et anilibus fabulis sanctam Romanam "sedem velle sibi inconcussum honorem vindicare et defensare "aliquatenus," &c., &c.]

it,—a most expressive silence, when one considers how strong the temptation must have been to him, to avail himself of this weapon against his numerous and overpowering enemies. Not so his friend, cardinal PETER DAMIANI. He holds up the privilege granted by Constantine as an impenetrable shield against the Greeks, who supported the cause of the imperial anti-pope Cadalous, and does not forget to add that the emperor had also given over the kingdom of Italy to the rule of the popes.[1]

Peter Damiani's argument.

The use and meaning of the forged Donation entered, to a certain extent, a new stage when Urban II., in the year 1091, used it to support the claim of the Roman Church to the possession of Corsica. He deduced the right of Constantine to give away islands from the strange principle, that all islands were legally *juris publici*, and therefore state domain. It cannot but excite surprise that Urban did not prefer to appeal to the donation of Charles the Great, or rather does not once mention it. For not only is Corsica enumerated among the donations which Charles is said to have made, but Leo III. says this distinctly in a letter to Charles in the year 808.[2] The Church at that time, how-

Urban II. claims Corsica on the strength of the Donation.

---

[1] HARDUIN, l. c., 1122. [As "defensor Romanæ ecclesiæ," he argues that Constantine had abdicated, as regards Rome and Italy, in favour of the pope. If, then, the emperor had no authority in Rome, how could he have a voice in the election of pope?]

[2] CENNI, II., 60.

<small>Yet Corsica had really been given to Rome by Charles the Great.</small>

ever, having no fleet, was not in a position to maintain a possession which was perpetually threatened by the Saracens; and so Leo was obliged to beg the emperor to take the island to himself, and protect it with his "strong arm;" and (as the Corsican historian LIMPERANI[1] remarks) the Roman Chair for 189 years abstained from exercising any dominion in Corsica. Not until the year 1077 do we find Gregory VII.[2] saying, that the Corsicans are ready to return under the supremacy of the pope; and from the letter of Urban II. to bishop Daibert, of Pisa, it appears that this actually took place at that time, or not long afterwards.

<small>Claim of Hadrian IV. to Ireland.</small>

On this notion, that it was the islands especially that Constantine had given to the popes, they proceeded to build, although nothing had been said about them in the original document; and with a bold leap the Donation of Constantine was transferred from Corsica to the farthest West, viz., to Ireland; and the Papal Chair claimed possession of an island, which the Romans themselves had never possessed, and had scarcely known.

<small>1154-1159.</small> This was done by Hadrian IV.,[3] an Englishman

---

[1] *Istoria della Corsica*, Roma, 1780, II., 2.

[2] Lib. 6, epist. 12.

[3] [Nicolas Breakspeare, the poor English scholar, yielded to none of his predecessors, Hildebrand not excepted, in the assertion of the papal authority. "He was surpassed by few in the boldness and "courage with which he maintained it. English pride might "mingle with sacerdotal ambition in his boon of a new kingdom to "his native sovereign. The language of the grant developed

by birth; "Anglicana affectione," as the Irish chieftains declared somewhat later (1316) in a letter to John XXII.[1] At the desire of the English king, Henry II., the pope conferred on him the dominion over the island of Ireland (1155), which, "like all Christian islands, un-"doubtedly belonged of right to S. Peter and the "Roman Church." The king thus received a dominion which, it must be owned, he had first to win with the sword; and, indeed, it was not till after a contest of five hundred years, and for the most part only by colonization from outside, that it was completely won. It did not help the English much to say to the Irish, "Your island "belonged in former times to the pope, and since "he has given it to king Henry, it is your duty "to submit yourselves to English rule." The Irish, who were not altogether ignorant of the history of their native land, knew quite well that neither the Roman emperors nor the popes had

The Irish contest the validity of the gift.

"principles as yet unheard of in Christendom. The popes had "assumed the feudal sovereignty of Naples and Sicily, as in some "vague way the successors to the power of Imperial Rome. But "Hadrian declared that Ireland, and all islands converted to Chris-"tianity, belonged to the special jurisdiction of S. Peter. The pro-"phetic ambition of Hadrian might seem to have anticipated the "time, when on such principles the popes should assume the power "of granting away new worlds." — MILMAN, *Lat. Christ.*, VIII., c. VII.]

[1] In M'GEOGHEGAN'S *Histoire de l'Irlande*, II., 106 sq. They state that up to 1170 they had sixty-one kings, "nullum in temporalibus "recognoscentes superiorem." Hadrian had acted "indebite, ordine "juris omisso omnino." [For this famous letter of Hadrian to Henry II., see Appendix D.]

ever possessed a foot's breadth of their country, and could not therefore exactly understand how pope Hadrian had the power to make a present of it to England.

Hadrian does not mention the Donation of Constantine in his Bull; but his friend and confidant, JOHN OF SALISBURY, the one who,[1] according to his own confession, induced him to take this step so pregnant with consequences, quotes the Donation of the first believing emperor as the ground of this "right of S. Peter" over all islands.[2]

---

[1] "Ad preces meas illustri regi Anglorum, Henrico II., concessit "et dedit Hiberniam jure hæreditario possidendam, sicut literæ "ipsius testantur in hodiernum diem. Nam omnes insulæ, de jure "antiquo, ex donatione Constantini, qui eam fundavit et dotavit, "dicuntur ad Romanam Ecclesiam pertinere."—*Metalog.* 4, 42, opp. ed. GILES, v., 206. The embarrassment of Irish writers in later times, as regards the Bull was, as one might expect, considerable. STEPHEN WHITE (*Apologia pro Hibernia*, ed. Kelly, Dublin, 1849, p. 184), and LYNCH, or GRATIANUS LUCIUS (*Cambrensis eversus*, Dubl., 1856, II., 434 sq),. struggle in vain to prove it a bungling forgery. LANIGAN, on the other hand (*Eccles. History of Ireland*, IV., 160), admits its genuineness, and gives vent to some sharp criticisms on the pope and his Bull. M'GEOGHEHAN (*Histoire de l'Irlande*, Paris, 1758, I., 462) foregoes the appeal to the Donation of Constantine, and contents himself with saying, "Le Pape qui étoit "né son sujet, lui accorda sans peine sa demande; et la liberté d'une "nation entière fut sacrifiée à l'ambition de l'un par la complaisance "de l'autre."

[2] The ABBE GOSSELIN (*Pouvoir du Pape sur les Souverains*, II., 247, ed. de Louvain) has attempted to show that pope Hadrian, properly speaking, did not in the least intend to dispose of Ireland in his Bull; that he claimed nothing but a purely spiritual jurisdiction in Ireland, merely the right to demand the payment of Peter's pence. His reasons for this view are very weak, and he omits to notice evidence which is quite decisive. He omits to notice that Hadrian says, "that the people of Ireland are to accept and honour the

The Roman clergy with their Donation of Constantine had, on the whole, obtained their object very successfully; attempts were now made in Naples to advance the interests of the clergy there by similar means. In a chronicle of the church of S. MARIA DEL PRINCIPIO, it is stated that Constantine gave the whole of the kingdom of Sicily on both sides of the straits, along with other possessions, to pope Silvester; the town of Naples was the only thing which he reserved as imperial property. Accordingly the two, Constantine and Silvester, came to Naples together, and, seeing that Constantine very often heard mass here in the Episcopal Church, he attached fourteen prebendaries to it, and endowed these with landed and other property, and founded the dignity of a cimeliarch.[1]

The clergy of Naples fabricate a Donation.

Meanwhile, in Italy at this time the Roman

"king (who up to this time had not had the most remote right to the island) as their lord and master (sicut Dominum veneretur)." He omits all notice of the statement of John of Salisbury, who was better informed than any other man respecting the whole circumstance, and respecting the meaning of the Bull, which had been introduced by himself. Lastly, he omits to notice the fact that Hadrian formally invested king Henry with the rights of a suzerain by means of a ring which he sent him. The words, that all islands belong "ad jus beati Petri et SS. Rom. Ecclesiæ," Gosselin persists in understanding of the spiritual jurisdiction of the pope, quite in defiance of the use of words in the language of that time.

[1] PARASCANDOLO, *Memorie stor. crit diplomatiche della chiesa di Napoli*, 1807, p. 212. The chronicle appears to belong to the end of the twelfth or beginning of the thirteenth century. [Cimeliarch, κειμηλιαρχης, treasurer.]

story of Constantine's Donation was rejected without scruple, so soon as it clashed with maintained rights or with political plans. In Rome, in the year 1105, the monks of the monastery Farfa, which had been endowed with great privileges by the emperors, contended with some of the Roman nobility for the possession of a certain castle. The latter upheld the title of the Roman Church (on which their own title was supposed to depend) to the disputed property, and traced back this title to the Donation of Constantine. Thereupon the monks, without directly denying the genuineness of the document, brought forward a detailed historical proof that the document could not possibly mean a Donation of Italy, for the emperors who had succeeded Constantine had always possessed and exercised in full their dominion over Italy. Accordingly, Constantine could only have given spiritual rights to the popes in Italy.¹ In Rome itself at that time (under Paschal II.) the pope was so far from being recognised as the temporal sovereign of a distinct territory, that the monks with their abbot felt able, without contradiction, to state before the Roman judges as a recognised fact—that temporal power and government did not befit the pope, for it was not the keys of an earthly kingdom, but only the keys of the kingdom of Heaven that he had received from God.

About forty years later commenced the great

---

² *Historiæ Farfenses*, in PERTZ *Monum.*, XIII., 571.

political and religious movements in Italy generally, and the efforts of the Arnoldists, in Rome in particular, which aimed[1] at placing the control of the imperial dignity in the hands of a rabble in Rome—a town populace constantly augmented by the influx of people from the country, but which was supposed to represent the true Romans and heirs of the old Roman empire. Thence began the first misunderstandings between the Hohenstaufen, Frederick I., and the Papal Chair. It was inevitable that the Donation of Constantine should again play an important part. When a Roman faction, stirred up by Arnold of Brescia, was purposing to arrogate to itself the control of the city, the papal party in Rome had appealed to the Donation, according to which it appeared that Rome belonged to the pope. In opposition to this Wetzel, an Arnoldist, maintained in his letter to Frederick, in the year 1152, that "that lie and "heretical fable of Constantine's having conceded "the imperial rights in the city to pope Silvester, "was now so thoroughly exposed, that even day "labourers and women were able to confute the "most learned on the point, and the pope and his "cardinals would not venture to show themselves "for shame."[2] And in fact, Eugenius III. had

In the movement headed by Arnold of Brescia.

The Donation again plays a part.

---

[1] [That to Arnold of Brescia himself much higher aims, and a much nobler policy, must be attributed than are here allowed to his followers, would perhaps scarcely be denied.]

[2] Ap. MARTENE, *ampl. coll.*, II., 556.

been obliged to leave Rome[1] (for the second time) in the beginning of the year 1150, and remained until the December of 1152 in Segni and Ferentino. It is, however, remarkable that the arguments, with which the Arnoldist and his Roman day labourers and housewives knew so well how to demolish the lie about the Donation of Constantine, themselves in their turn rested upon errors and fictions. Constantine, says Wetzel, was a Christian already, and therefore had been baptized before the time of Silvester, consequently the whole story of the Donation to Silvester is untrue. As proof of this a passage is quoted out of an apocryphal[2] letter of pope Melchiades, which is found in the pseudo-Isidorian collection, and is also made use of by Gratian; and it is proved from the *Historia tripertita* (of Cassiodore) that Constantine was a Christian before his entry into Rome.[3]

In spite of this contradiction in Rome itself, the Donation was made the basis of higher and con-

---

[1] [On the first occasion (March 1146) Eugenius retired first to Viterbo, and thence to Sienna; then, after a year's delay, to France, where he became little more than the mouthpiece of S. Bernard. He returned to Italy towards the end of 1148, but to Viterbo and Tusculum, not to Rome. It was not till the end of 1149 that he once more entered the capital, and then only as its bishop, not as its sovereign.]

[2] A document much used, sometimes under the title *Libellus de munificentia Constantini*.

[3] Wetzel does not appeal, as one would have expected him to have done, to the baptism in Nicomedia at the end of the emperor's life, as related in the Tripertita from Eusebius. No doubt the idea of the baptism in Rome was too deeply rooted in the minds of the Romans to allow him to make such an appeal.

stantly increasing claims at this time, and, indeed, as early as the close of the eleventh century. Already in the time of Gregory VII., or immediately after him under Urban II., the inclusion of the Donation in the new collection of rights and title-deeds showed clearly an intention of making an extensive use of it. This was now done by ANSELM OF LUCCA, cardinal DEUSDEDIT, and the compiler of the collection which is known under the name of IVO OF CHARTRES.[1] On the other hand, BURCHARD OF WORMS, in his collection, which was made between 1012 and 1023, has not yet included it. Specially surprising is the change which is made in Anselm's work of the "*or*" into a most significant and comprehensive "*and.*" He has, "quod Const. Imp. Papæ concessit coronam "et omnem regiam dignitatem in urbe Romana, "et Italia, *et in partibus occidentalibus.*" What practical meaning Roman ecclesiastics intended to give to these last words, appears from a statement made by OTTO OF FREISINGEN. In his chronicle, which was composed between 1143 and 1146, he asserts the authenticity[2] of the Donation, and relates how Constantine, after conferring the imperial insignia on the pope, went to Byzantium, adding that, "for this reason the Roman Church "maintains that the western kingdoms have been

But although disputed, the Donation is still largely used;

By Anselm of Lucca;

By Otto of Freisingen.

---

[1] More exact references in ANTONIUS AUGUSTINUS, *de Emend. Grat. Opp.*, ed. Lucens, III., 41, in the notes.
[2] Chron. 3, 3 ap., URSTIS, I., 80.

"given over to her possession by Constantine, "and demands tribute from them to this day, with "the exception of the two kingdoms of the "Franks" (that is, the French and the German one). The defenders of the empire, however, objected, "that in each transaction Constantine "had not conferred the empire on the popes, but "had merely chosen them as spiritual fathers."

<small>Tribute rarely demanded of a nation on the strength of the Donation.</small>

To the best of my knowledge there are no papal documents extant, with the exception of the one about Ireland, in which the payment of tribute is demanded of the whole realm on the strength of the Donation of Constantine. Just the very pope who went the greatest lengths in such demands, Gregory VII., never appealed to the Donation in making them, but to feudal rights of the Roman see dating from an earlier period; and he attempted[1] (without result, however) to exact tribute from France. And yet, as appears from his letters,[2] Gregory had had the archives thoroughly searched, in order to discover documents, from which a feudal dependence of the several kingdoms and countries upon the Roman Chair might be claimed.

<small>Claim of the popes to the imperial insignia and homage.</small>

· However, the ninth canon in the Dictates, which, though not proceeding from Hildebrand himself, are, nevertheless, the work of his time, is unmistakeably borrowed from the Donation; "the

---

[1] Cf. MURATORI, *Antichità Ital.*, Firenze, 1833, x. 126 sq.
[2] *Epist.* 23. lib. 8.

"pope alone may make use of the imperial in-
"signia." Serious stress was never laid on this
point. The popes did not assume the sceptre,
sword, and ball. Boniface VIII. is the only pope
who, according to one account, is said to have
done so at once at the celebration of the Jubilee
in the year 1300. But if Constantine had really
ceded Italy and the West to the pope, it appeared
to follow naturally and fairly that the empire in
its whole extent of territory was a present, a free
gift of the popes, and therefore (according to the
then prevalent ideas and dispositions) a fief of the
Roman Chair, the emperor being vassal and the
pope suzerain. And then, if not the kingdom of
Germany, at any rate that of Italy with the
Lombard crown would be reckoned as a papal fief.
Certainly, since A.D. 800, since the first founding
of the Western empire, a broad way had been
made towards this end. At that time the pope
prostrated himself to the ground before the newly-
crowned emperor, and did obeisance to him in the
form of homage paid to the old emperors.[1] Now,
however, a picture had been placed in the Lateran
palace which represented the emperor Lothair
doing homage to the pope,[2] with verses, in which

[1] *Annales Laurissenses*, in PERTZ, I., 138: "Et post laudes ab "Apostolico more antiquorum principum adoratus est."
[2] {Compare the gross misrepresentations of the circumstances of the council of Florence in the bassi relievi on the gates of S. Peter's at Rome.—MARRIOTT'S *Testimony of the Catacombs*, London, 1870, p. 104, &c.]

it was stated in so many words that the king had first confirmed the rights of the city before the gates of Rome, and had then become the vassal (homo) of the pope, whereupon he had received the crown as a gift[1] from the latter. At the same time many Romans had declared that the German kings had possessed the Roman empire,[2] no less than the Italian kingdom, merely as a present from the popes. From this arose that storm of dissatisfaction which broke out in Germany in the year 1157, when a letter from Hadrian to Frederick Barbarossa spoke of "beneficia" which he had granted to the emperor, or could still grant, and expressly called the imperial crown itself such a beneficium, i. e., a feod, as it was understood at the imperial court. Hadrian could easily justify himself, by saying that he had used the word in its ordinary, not in its technical and political sense, that he had intended to say nothing more than

[1] RADEVIC., I., 10; MURAT., VI., 748.

[2] Imperium Urbis. The imperial dignity itself the pope could not confer on the strength of the Donation of Constantine, which contained nothing about it, but only (as the Romans said) as the organ of the Roman republic and in their name, for they considered themselves as the heirs of the old populus Romanus; or else, as the defenders of the Donation supposed, as the supreme Head of the city of Rome, to which the right of electing the emperor, originally inherent in the Roman republic, came as a matter of course. Hence, although the *empire* itself was no fief of the Roman Chair (for which reason it was never actually given away), nevertheless it was possible to maintain in Rome, that the *imperium urbis* and the *kingdom of Italy* belonged to the pope alone to confer, seeing that he had received both from Constantine, and that he would confer them only as fiefs, reserving his own supremacy; but that without these two things there was no empire.

that it was he who had placed the crown on the emperor's head.[1] But, in Germany, men mistrusted the Roman clergy, and the bitter feeling remained, as we find provost GERHOH OF REIGERSBURG expressing it at the time in sharp words, a man otherwise thoroughly devoted to the Papal See. He says, that the custom (which of course rested for support on the Donation of Constantine) of the emperor holding the pope's stirrup had prompted the Romans to paint these offensive pictures, in which kings or emperors were represented as vassals of the popes; from which they gained nothing, excepting the embittered feelings and hard words of temporal princes.[2] If the popes by allowing such pictures claimed to be emperors and lords of emperors, making the emperors their vassals, this was nothing else than to destroy the power ordained of God and to go against the divine order. *Dissatisfaction in Germany at such claims.*

However, whatever meaning and extent of application the Roman clergy might give to the supposed Donation; whatever new collections of laws might contain on the subject; the historians of this and the following period are wont, when they mention the Donation at all, cautiously to confine it within tolerably narrow limits. SICARD OF CREMONA gives a very detailed account of the fabulous baptism of Constantine,[3] but quotes nothing more *Historians more cautious than the clergy. They limit, without denying, the Donation.*

---

[1] "Per hoc vocabulum 'contulimus' nil aliud intelleximus quam 'imposuimus.'"

[2] Treatise of the provost GERHOH OF REIGERSBURG, *De investigatione Antichristi*, edited by STULZ, Vienna, 1858, pp. 54, 56.

[3] In MURATORI, VII., 554.

than this from the Donation, that the emperor gave Silvester regal privileges, and ordained that all bishops should be subject to the pope; but he does not go on to explain the nature of these regal privileges. ROMUALD OF SALERNO knows and mentions merely this ecclesiastical supremacy.[1] ROBERT ABOLANT confines himself to mentioning a privilege bequeathed by Constantine to the popes, without any farther statement.[2] A hundred years later, an historian so entirely devoted to papal interests as TOLOMEO OF LUCCA quotes nothing beyond this from the Donation, that the emperor had conferred on certain Roman ecclesiastics (the cardinals of a later age) the rights and prerogatives of the Roman senate.[3] And while of the papal biographers BERNARD GUIDONIS is entirely silent about the Donation; the dominion over the city of Rome, and the conferring of the imperial insignia, is all that AMALRICH AUGERII quotes from it.[4] On the other hand the Spaniard, LUCAS B. OF TUY (about A.D. 1236), represents the dominion over Italy (regnum Italiæ) as having been conferred on the pope.[5] His contemporary, the Belgian BALDUIN, monk in the monastery Ninnove, restricts Constantine's gift once more to the dominion over Rome.[6]

[1] MURATORI, VII., 79.
[2] *Chronologia*, Trecis, 1609, p. 49.
[3] *Hist. Eccl.*, 5, 3, 4, in MURATORI, XI., 825.
[4] Ap. ECCARD., II., 1665.
[5] *Corpus chronicorum Flandriæ*, ed. DE SMET, II., 613.
[6] *Chronicon mundi*, ap. SCHOTTI, *Hisp. illustr.*, IV., 36.

All the more remarkable on this account is the discussion in which, at the close of the twelfth century, a man who, in a certain sense, belonged to both nations, engaged. GOTTFRIED, a German, educated in Bamberg, chaplain and secretary to the three Hohenstaufen sovereigns—Conrad, Frederick, and Henry VI.—who ended his days as a canon at Viterbo, states in his *Pantheon*,[1] which he dedicated to pope Urban III., A.D. 1186, that, in order to secure greater peace to the Church, Constantine had withdrawn with all his pomp to the Greeks, to Byzantium, and had given the pope regal privileges, and, on the strength of them, as it would appear, Rome, Italy, and Gaul. (This is the first time that *Gaul* is expressly mentioned as being included in the Donation.) Thereupon he makes the "supporters of the empire," and the "defenders " of the Church," state their *pros* and *cons*. The former point to the historical fact, that Constantine divided his kingdom between his sons, and to the well-known texts in the Bible. The latter, however, answer, that the will of God is declared in the very fact of the Donation; that God would allow His Church to have fallen into the error of a possession to which it had no right, was not to be supposed. Gottfried himself, however, does not venture to decide; he leaves the solution of this question to the powers that be.

Godfrey of Viterbo leaves the question open.

In the *Otia imperiala* (leisure hours), which

Gervasius of Tilbury makes a compromise.

[1] Ap. PISTORI, II., 268.

GERVASIUS OF TILBURY wrote for the emperor Otho IV. about the year 1211, it is stated, that Constantine had conferred royal power over the countries of the West on Silvester, without intending to transfer to him along with it either the kingdom itself or the empire, which he reserved for himself. But the giver is superior to the receiver, and the royal and imperial power is derived immediately from God. God, he says, is the creator of the empire, but the emperor is the creator of the papal supremacy.[1]

<small>From the twelfth to the fourteenth century the Donation gains ground.</small>

On the whole, however, the authority of the Donation from the close of the twelfth century onwards was in the ascendant; and belief in it, and in the wide extent of territory which Constantine included in it, grew stronger. Gratian himself did not include it, but it was soon inserted as "palea,"[2] and thus found an entry into all schools of canonical jurisprudence, so that from this time forth the lawyers were the most influential publishers and defenders of the fiction. The language of the popes also was henceforward more confident. "Omne regnum Occidentis ei (Silvestro) tradidit et dimisit,"[3] says Innocent III. Gregory IX. followed this out to its consequences in a way surpassing anything that had been done

<small>1198-1216.</small>
<small>1214-1227.</small>

---

[1] Ap. LEIBNIT, *SS. Brunsvic.*, I., 882.
[2] But with the more moderate expression, "Italiam *seu* occi-"dentales regiones," not with the unlimited "*et*" of Anselm.
[3] *Sermo de S. Sylvestro, Opera*, Venetiis, 1578, I., 97.

before, when he represented to the emperor Frederick II., the ablest and most formidable opponent who had yet sustained the lists against the Roman See, that Constantine had, along with the imperial insignia, given over Rome with the duchy *and the imperium* to the care of the popes for ever. Whereupon the popes, without diminishing in any degree whatever the substance of their jurisdiction, established the tribunal of the empire, transferred it to the Germans, and are wont to concede the power of the sword to the emperors at their coronation.[1]

This was as much as to say that the imperial authority had its sole origin in the popes, could be enlarged or narrowed at their good pleasure, and that the pope could call each emperor to account for the use of the power entrusted to him. But the highest rung of the ladder was as yet not reached. This was first achieved by Gregory's successor, INNOCENT IV., when the synod of Lyons resulted in the deposition of Frederick; in which act this pope went beyond all his predecessors in the increase of his claims, and the extension of the authority of Rome. It is an error, Innocent declares, in the year 1245, to suppose that Constantine was the first to confer temporal power on the Roman See; rather Christ Himself entrusted to Peter and his successors *both* powers, the sacerdotal and the royal, and the reins of both kingdoms, the earthly

Innocent IV. states the doctrine of papal supremacy in its widest terms.

[1] Ap. RAYNALD., ad a., 1236, 24, p. 481, ed. Rom.

and the heavenly. Constantine, therefore, had merely resigned an unlawfully possessed power into the hands of its legitimate possessor, the Church, and had received it back again from the Church.[1]

Another half century, however, elapsed before theologians were found to reduce this new doctrine to a formal shape, and to furnish it with the usual scholastic, and in such cases very elastic apparatus. Under the influence of circumstances which took place towards the end of the thirteenth century, and of the spirit in which a Martin IV. and a Boniface VIII. ruled, the use which had been *The doctrine as formulated by later theologians;* made of the Donation of Constantine assumed a different form. The Dominican, TOLOMEO OF LUCCA, author of the two last books of the work *De Regimine Principum*, the first two books of which are by Thomas Aquinas, goes beyond[2] his predecessors, and explains the Donation as a formal abdication of Constantine in favour of Silvester;[3]

[1] *Cod. epist. Vatican.*, 4957, 49; *Codex Vindobon. philol.*, 61, f. 70—305, f. 83. In RAUMER, *Geschichte der Hohenstaufen*, IV., 178 (first edition), who quotes the Latin text. The document was not known in the centuries immediately following, though the fact of Innocent IV. having taken up such a position was well known, for ALVARO PELAYO says (*De Planctu Ecclesiæ*, I., 43, about the year 1350), "Collatio autem Constantini potius fuit cessio quam collatio; "sic etiam fertur Innocentius IV. dixisse imperatori Frederico, "quem deposuit."

[2] These last two books were written subsequent to 1298; for the putting to death of Adolf of Nassau, by Albert, is mentioned as an event which had already taken place.

[3] "Primo quidem de Constantino apparet, qui Silvestro in im- "perio cessit."—*De Regimine principum*, 3, 10. *Opuscula Thomæ Aquin.*, Lugd., 1562, p. 232.

and connecting with this other historical circumstances which are either inventions or misconceptions, he thence draws the conclusion, that the power of all temporal princes derives its strength and efficacy solely from the spiritual power of the popes. There was no halting half way; and immediately afterwards, in the contest of Boniface VIII. with Philip of France, the Augustinian monk,[1] AEGIDIUS COLONNA of Rome, whom the pope had nominated to the archbishopric of Bourges, drew the natural conclusions without the slightest disguise in a work which he dedicated to his patron. Towards the middle of the century two theologians of the papal court, AGOSTINO TRIONFO and ALVARO PELAYO, the one an Italian, the other a Spanish minorite, took the same line of argument. This theory, reduced to its simplest terms, runs thus: Christ is Lord of the whole world; at His departure He left this dominion to His representatives, Peter and his successors;

---

[1] If the treatise *De Utraque Potestate* (which is found in GOLDAST, *Monarchia*, II.) were from the pen of Ægidius, he must have professed the very opposite principles in the interest of king Philip. But, seeing that Ægidius, as archbishop of Bourges, is found among those prelates who went to Rome against Philip's will to the council summoned by Boniface, and thereupon was punished with confiscation, one may be quite certain that the writing in question was not composed by him. In his genuine and still unprinted work, the substance of which is given by CHARLES JOURDAIN, *Un ouvrage inédit de Gilles de Rome*, Paris, 1858, Ægidius says bluntly enough, " Patet quod omnia temporalia sunt sub domino Ecclesiæ collocata, " et si non de facto, quoniam multi forte huic juri rebellantur, de " jure tamen et ex debito temporalia summo pontifici sunt subjecta, " a quo jure et a quo debito nullatenus possunt absolvi," p. 13.

And reduced to its simplest terms.

therefore the fulness of all spiritual and temporal power and dominion, the union of all rights and privileges, lies in the hands of the pope. Every monarch, even the most powerful, possesses only so much power and territory as the pope has transferred to him, or finds good to allow him. TRIONFO says without reservation, that if an emperor, like Constantine, has given temporal possessions to Silvester, this is merely a restitution of what had been stolen in an unjust and tyrannical way.[1]

This extreme statement the result of previous objections.

This theory, utterly unknown to the earlier popes and to the whole of Christendom, was invented in the first instance in order to meet the objections to the Donation of Constantine. For there were not wanting persons who declared that Constantine had no power to make such a suicidal Donation, so ruinous to the empire. An emperor could not tear in pieces the empire, for this was in direct contradiction to his office.[2]

The lawyers denied the Donation all validity except that of prescription.

The French advocate, PETER DUBOIS, at Coutances declared, in his opinion about the Bull of

---

[1] *Summa de ecclesia*, 94, 1.
[2] Brought out more in detail by DANTE, for example, in the *De Monarchiâ*, 3, 10; *Opere Minori*, ed. di Fraticelli, Firenze, 1857, II., 460. ["Ergo scindere Imperium, Imperatori non licet. Si ergo "aliquæ dignitates per Constantinum essent alienatæ (ut dicunt) "ab Imperio," &c. Here the sceptical "ut dicunt" shows that Dante doubted the *fact* as well as the rightfulness of the Donation. So also "*Dicunt quidam* adhuc, quod Constantinus Imperator, "mundatus a leprâ intercessione Sylvestri, tunc summi pontificis, "imperii sedem, scilicet Romam, donavit ecclesiæ, cum multis aliis "imperii dignitatibus."]

Boniface VIII. to Philip, that the Donation was from the first legally null and void; all lawyers were unanimous in maintaining this, only the very long prescription conferred on it at the present time a legal validity.[1]

Contemporaneously with him the Dominican, JOHN QUIDORT of Paris, magister of the theological faculty there (died A.D. 1306), in his book *On the Regal and Papal Power*, contended against the Donation of Constantine, for, as all lawyers maintained, the emperor, as semper Augustus, could only enlarge, not diminish the empire; on the contrary, such a mutilation of the empire, of which he was only the administrator, might be set aside by each of his successors as null and void.[2]

From the time that the harmonious relations between the empire and the papacy were destroyed, and one conflict after another between the two powers arose with a sort of inherent necessity, and the transfer of the papacy into French hands made the restoration of due relations impossible (that is to say, from the death of Frederick II. to the death of Lewis the Bavarian, 1250–1346), the Donation of Constantine was perpetually mentioned in the various memorials, opinions, and apologies, which had reference to the contest. The defenders of the imperial cause, appealing to the prevailing

---

[1] Ap. DUPUY, *Histoire du Différend Preuves*, p. 46.
[2] Fratris JOHANNIS DE PARISIIS tract. *de Potestate reg. et pap.*, in SCHARDII *Coll. de Jurisdictione imp.*, p. 208 sq.

view of the civil jurists, usually without circumlocution pronounced the Donation null and void or obsolete.¹ One of the ablest and acutest contenders for the imperial power, the Minorite MARSIGLIO OF PADUA, does not quite know how he stands towards it. "Some say that Constantine conferred the "privilege on the pope," is the expression he uses; but he then goes on to say that those in the papal interest, either because the document was not clear and comprehensive enough, or had become obsolete, or had never been legally valid, had invented this entirely new theory of a universal, spiritual, and temporal power derived immediately from Christ the God-man.² But even this Marsiglio found the Donation of Constantine a welcome weapon against the primacy of the Roman See in general, for from it it was very easy to draw the conclusion that even the ecclesiastical supremacy of the pope over all other churches and bishops rested merely on the grant of the emperor, and therefore on a purely human, perishable, and in such things properly invalid right.³ Marsiglio knew well how to turn this weak spot to good account.

The Donation a very double-edged weapon.

Continued uncertainty as to the extent of the Donation.

In the thirteenth and fourteenth centuries the same amount of uncertainty and arbitrariness as

---

¹ So the author of the inquiry, *Whether the pope had power to enforce an armistice on the Emperor, Henry VII.*, in DOENNIGES, *Acta Henrici vii.*, II., 158.
² *Denfensor pacis*, Heidelberg, 1599, p. 101.
³ l. c., p. 203.

before continued to prevail in the definitions respecting the real extent of the Donation. In the decretal of pope Nicholas III. merely the cession of Rome to the popes by Constantine is mentioned, in accordance with the special object of this document.[1] In the form of oath which the emperor, Henry VII., had to take before his coronation, Clement V. made this monarch swear that he would protect and uphold all the rights which the emperors, and Constantine of course first of all, had granted to the Roman Church, without however going on to state in what these rights consisted.[2] John XXII., in his refutation of Marsiglio of Padua, in the year 1327, merely mentions in passing the fact that Constantine had given up the imperial city to Silvester, quoting the words of the Donation.[3] The oldest, or second oldest commentator on Dante, the compiler of the *Ottimo Commento*, who wrote in the year 1333, contents himself with the indefinite statement that Constantine had given Silvester "all the dignity " of the empire."[4]

The author of the commentary on Dante, which was written in the year 1375, states quite simply that Constantine gave to the pope and the Church

---

[1] In VI. to 1, 6, 17. [2] Clementin, 9, de jur. ej.
[3] Ap. Raynald, a., 1327, 81.
[4] *L'Ottimo Commento della divina Commedia*, Pisa, 1827, 1355. PETER AUREOLI says very much the same (about the year 1316): " Honor imperii translatus est in personam Silvestri et in Rom. " ecclesiam."—*Aurea Scripturæ Elucidatio*, Venetiis, s., a. f. 89.

exactly what the pope possesses to this day;[1] in opposition to which a later commentator, GUINIFORTO DELLI BARGIGI, is convinced that only "the "patrimony in Tuscany, in the neighbourhood of "Rome," is included in the Donation.[2]

RUDOLF or PANDULF COLONNA,[3] canon of Sienna, and probably a Roman by birth (fourteenth century), gives the Donation once more the widest extent of meaning, including "Rome, Italy, and "all western kingdoms."[4] NICOLAS OF CLAMENGE himself says without any hesitation, that Constantine conferred the western empire on the Roman Church, and intended the cardinals to be senators of it.[5]

French theologians try to save France from being included in the Donation.

In France efforts were made to secure the country against the consequences which were drawn, or might be drawn, from the extent of a Donation which embraced the whole of the West.

[1] *Chiose sopra Dante, testo inedito*, Firenze, 1846, p. 161.
[2] *Lo Inferno, col comento di G. d. B.*, pubbl. da G. ZACHERONI, Firenze, 1838, p. 456.
[3] Not Raoul de Coloumelle, canon of Chartres, as the *Histoire littéraire de la France*, XXI., 151, represents him. The *Histoire* itself notices that the author in two manuscripts of his small work is called "Canonicus Senensis," and only in one "Canonicus Carno-"tensis." A Frenchman would have expressed himself differently respecting the "translatio imperii a Francis ad Germanos," and would not have contented himself with saying merely, "Regnum mundi "translatum est ad Germanos vel Teutonicos," p. 297. The whole historical view is taken from the standpoint of a Roman ecclesiastic; and the author gives one pretty clearly to understand that he is a Roman ecclesiastic by noticing that pope Hadrian was by birth "de "regione Viæ latæ," p. 292. Moreover, Radulf has copied Marsilius of Padua, or the latter has copied him, as one can see by comparing them in SCHARDIUS, p. 287 and p. 226.
[4] *De translatione imperii*, in SCHARDIUS, p. 287.
[5] *De annatis non solvendis, Opera*, ed. LYNDIUS, p. 92.

The Parisian theologian, JACOB ALMAIN, contends therefore that Constantine had no power whatever to transfer the empire to the pope without the consent of the people;[1] and in the second place, that the kingdom of Gaul at any rate could not have been included, for the Romans had never been masters of Gaul, and the people of Gaul had never of their own accord voted for submitting to Roman rule. He seems to have had no misgivings as to the extent to which the Celtic population of Gaul had allowed themselves to become Romanized. Almain maintains moreover that it is the common opinion of doctors generally, that as a matter of fact Constantine did not resign the empire.[2]

LUPOLD OF BABENBERG in the fourteenth century, in his treatise *On the Roman Empire*, dedicated to Baldwin, archbishop of Trèves (1307–1354), discusses the Donation very thoroughly while investigating the question whether the king of Rome had to take the oath of a vassal to the Roman See.[3] The discussion with him means nothing less than the decision of the still wider question, whether

<small>Lupold of Babenberg sees the truth, but does not venture to state it.</small>

---

[1] Contradicente populo occidentali." Ap. GERSON, Opp. II., 971, cf. p. 1063.

[2] " Quod resignaverit imperium occidentale, nunquam legitur." It is remarkable how uncertain people were even at this late date (Almain wrote about the year 1510) respecting a fact so unmistakeable. If one considers to what a high degree of historical discernment some writers attained even as early as the twelfth century, one might almost say, that in this direction, and in all that relates to a rational understanding of history, the movement for three whole centuries was a retrogression rather than an advance.

[3] Ap. SCHARD, p. 391.

the pope is really the suzerain of the German empire and possessor of the dominium directum, so that in all countries of the empire all that accrues to the emperor is the dominium utile. Hence we once more meet with the most different opinions as to the validity or nullity of the Donation; whereupon Lupold remarks that all canonists are wont to maintain that the Donation is legally valid and irrevocable. But then the other kingdoms of the West must have stood in the same relation of vassaldom to the pope. Lupold, however, is keen-sighted enough to see through the unhistorical character of the whole fiction. He knows that the emperors ruled over the West just as much after Constantine's time as before it; and he himself had found passages in the ecclesiastical law-books which speak merely of giving up the city of Rome to the pope. In the end, however (belief in the Donation was at that time still so powerful), he does not venture to come to a decision, but prefers to leave the settlement of the matter to higher powers.

The legal question still remains open. From a legal point of view the matter remained just as debatable as ever. It was not, however, easy to explain how Constantine, as elective emperor (and the old Roman emperors were supposed to have been elective like the German ones), could have given away half the empire. In a treatise which, so far as I am aware, has never been printed, and which seems to have been written in the time of Lewis of Bavaria in reference to his contests,[1] the question is discussed, whether in virtue of his election the emperor can forthwith and immediately exercise control over the whole realm, or whether he needs to be empowered by the pope to do so. In consequence of the Donation of Constantine, says the author, the whole jurisdiction of the emperor became dependent on confirmation by the pope; but, on the other hand, it must be admitted that the rights and constituent parts of the realm could not be alienated so arbitrarily, without the consent of the princes, barons, and high officials.[2]

On the other hand the Donation is defended towards the end of the fifteenth century by the Strasburg parish priest, JOHN HUG of Schlettstadt, in his *Wagenfuhr der h. Kirche und des Römischen Reichs*, which he dedicated to cardinal Raymond of Gurk (1493–1505). ACCURSIUS, he says, has declared the gift to be invalid on account of its extravagance, but JOHN TEUTONICUS, the annotator of the *Decretum* (of Gratian), has proved its immutable validity from the Clementines,[3] which have inserted the Donation into the imperial oath.

A new defence of the Donation.

---

[1] *Brevis tractatus de jurisdictione imperii et auctoritate summi Pontificis circa imperium.* Cod. Lat. 5832 in the National Library at Munich, f. 121, ff.

[2] "Sed contra hoc est, quod jura imperii alienari non possunt "quum sint bona republicæ, quæ sine publicis officialibus dispensari "non possunt, ut sunt principes et barones et quorum interest "assistere ministerio imperiali aulæ diversorum apicum," f. 123.

[3] [The *Constitutiones Clementinæ* are that part of the *corpus juris canonici* which contains the decrees of the council of Vienne (A.D. 1311), together with decrees of Clement V.; published in 1313.]

Extension given to the Donation by German law-books.

The German law-books have given the Donation of Constantine a remarkable extension, inasmuch as they maintain that Constantine gave to Silvester the civil or king's bann to the amount of sixty shillings, "in order to compel all those who will "not reform themselves for corporal punishment, to "be compelled to do so by means of fines."[1] This is a specific German invention, utterly unknown to the Romance nations. The sense is as follows: in consequence of the wide and indefinite sphere of the ecclesiastical[2] courts, it became a custom in Germany that the ecclesiastical judges should impose fines, levying them themselves, for various crimes, some of which belonged entirely to the municipal jurisdiction; an abuse which Alexander III. had forbidden as early as the year 1180, but to no purpose. As an authority for this abnormal custom was wanted, and none could be found, the Donation of Constantine—that large and inexhaustible treasury from which political and municipal privileges could be drawn just as they were wanted—was obliged here also to be brought into use.[3]

---

[1] *Sacksenspiegel*, v. HOMEYER, I., 238 (3, 63). *Das Rechtsbuch nach Distinctionen*, edited by ORTLOFF, p. 325 (6, 16). *Schwabenspiegel*, in SENCKENBERG, *Corp. jur. Germ.*, II., 10.

[2] [These ecclesiastical courts (Send-gerichte, synodus) were held by the bishop, or archdeacon, or their substitute (Sendrichter) to try ecclesiastical offences, especially profanation of the Lord's day, and other violations of the decalogue.]

[3] The cardinals, D'Ailly and Zaberella, on behalf of the bishops and their officials, lodged complaints respecting these fiscal gains of the ecclesiastical courts before the council of Constance, and re-

In the ideas of the people and laity generally, the Donation of Constantine had meanwhile acquired another and more comprehensive significance. In the whole of the later Middle Ages we see two diametrically opposite currents prevailing. On the one side the effort to furnish the Church with considerable donations, to create for her a broad foundation of extensive landed property, and to raise the number and condition of clergy living on ecclesiastical endowments; but side by side with this the view which had been making way ever since the twelfth century, that the great possessions and large revenues of the Church were a grievous evil, the sources of nearly all existing abuses, and the causes of a moral deterioration of the clergy.[1] This view gradually assumed a form

Among the laity two opposite views of the Donation prevailed:
1. *That it and all other Church endowments were excellent;*
2. *That the wealth of the Church was a scandal in itself, and disastrous in its effects on the clergy.*

quested that provision might be made against them (ap. V. D. HARDT, Concil. Const., I., p. 8, p. 421, and p. 9, p. 521). But the mischief continued in Germany, and contributed not a little to the general bitterness against the hierarchy and the clergy, as one sees from the Gravamina nationis Germanicæ, c. 64, of the year 1522, not to mention other indications of the same fact.

[1] [We find this expressed in very strong language in some of the political and satirical songs of the thirteenth and following centuries. Such songs took a new tone in England just about that age. The civil commotions of the reign of John, and the weak government of Henry III., afforded every party abundance of material for satire, and plenty of opportunity for giving it free utterance. The clerk with his Latin, the courtier with his Anglo-Norman, and the people with their vigorous old English, all had their word to say. It may be worth while to give a few examples from Mr. WRIGHT's collection of *The Political Songs of England.*

" Roma mundi caput est, sed nil capit mundum ;
Quod pendet a capite totum est inmundum ;
Transit enim vitium primum in secundum,
Et de fundo redolet quod est juxta fundum.

of serious and threatening import to the clerical body, as the notion was developed out of it that originally the clergy had been poor, had lived

> " Roma capit singulos et res singulorum;
> Romanorum curia non est nisi forum.
> Ibi sunt venalia jura senatorum,
> Et solvit contraria copia nummorum."
> " Solam avaritiam Roma novit parca,
> Parcit danti munera, parco non est parca :
> Nummus est pro numine, et pro Marco marca,
> Et est minus celebris ara quam sit arca," &c., &c.

From the *Invectio contra avaritiam* about the time of the interdict.

> " Jacet ordo clericalis
> In respectu laicalis,
> Sponsa Christi fit venalis,
> Generosa generalis;
>   Veneunt altaria,
>   Venit eucharistia,
>   Cum sit nugatoria
> Gratia venalis."

From a *Song against the Bishops*, about 1250.

> " Les contre-estauz abatent li fiz de felonie;
> Lors perit sointe eglise, quant orgoil la mestrie.
> Ceo sustenent li prelaz ki s'i ne peinent mie,
> Pur dreiture sustenir nolent perdre vie."

From a *Song of the Times*, about 1275.

See also *Pierce the Ploughman's Crede* (about 1394) passim, and the pelican's charges against the clergy in the *Complaint of the Ploughman*.]

[Walther von der Vogelweide sings thus on the subject:—

> " Solt ich den pfaffen râten an den trinwen mîn;
> sô spræche ir haut den armen zuo ' sê daz ist dîn,'
> ir zunge sunge unde lieze manegem man daz sîn;
> Gedæhten ouch daz si durch Got ê wâren almnosnære:
> dô gap in êrste geltes teil der künec Constantin.
> Het er gewest daz dâ von übel künftec wære,
> sô het er wol underkomen des rîches swære;
> wan daz si dô wâren kische und übermüete lære."

No. 111, p. 113, Simrock's edition, Bonn, 1870.

His poems abound in anti-papal sentiments.]

solely upon freewill offerings, and had remained poor upon principle, until Constantine by his Donation had put an end to the former state of poverty, especially in Rome, and pope Silvester by his acceptance of it had given an example eagerly followed by the clerical body generally, and had ineradicably implanted in them the passion for acquiring wealth. The view that the wealth of the Church was the great obstacle in the way of all clerical reform gained ground more and more. Sectarianism, which from the middle of the twelfth century onwards assumed numerous and various shapes in Italy, France, and Germany, made common cause with this view, or fostered it and spread it assiduously. It ended in becoming part and parcel of public opinion.

It was precisely this which won for the fabulous Donation of Constantine such universal acceptance, that the fiction so exactly corresponded to the feeling and need of the people at that time. The Middle Ages, with their natural propensity to imagine definite actors, and an act producing effects once for all, in the case of circumstances which really had been gradually and slowly developed, could not account for the fact that the formerly poor Church had gradually become rich, otherwise than by representing this change as having been instantaneous. The Church, which till yesterday had been utterly without property, became suddenly possessed of a superabundance of earthly goods, through the acts of the two Heads, the imperial giver, and the accepting pope. And therewith, said numberless persons, the hitherto closed Pandora-box had been opened for the Church; all the evils from which she was suffering were to be attributed to this source of mischief.[1] Even men, who stood on the heights in their own age, saw the matter thus, and their grief at the infirmities of the Church, the degeneracy of the clergy, and the ceaseless conflict between the spiritual and temporal power, clothed itself in lamentations over Constantine's well-meant, but ill-advised munificence. Thus two contemporaries, whose sentiments agree in many points, DANTE[2]

The fiction of the Donation harmonised admirably with this second view.

---

[1] With what naïveté even ecclesiastics and historians up to the close of the Middle Ages placed themselves quite at the stand-point of the popular view, is shown from the following passage of the monk BERNHARD WITTE (about A.D. 1510) in his *Historia Westphaliæ*, Monast., 1775, p. 61: "Silvestro pontificante ... ecclesiarum " Prælati, qui hactenus in paupertate vixerunt, imo nihil habentes " et omnia possidentes, possessiones habere inceperunt."

[2] Inf., XIX., 115-17:

["Ahi Constantin, di quanto mal fu matre,
Non la tua conversion, ma quella dote,
Che da te prese il primo ricco patre!"

"Ah, Constantine! of how much ill was mother,
Not thy conversion, but that marriage dower,
Which the first wealthy Father took from thee!"
                                        Longfellow's Translation.

DANTE deplores the supposed Donation no less heartily in the *De Monarchiâ*: "O felicem populum! O Ausoniam te gloriosam! si " vel numquam infirmator imperii tui extitisset; vel numquam sua " pia intentio ipsum fefellisset." Lib. II., sub finem.

ARIOSTO places the Donation in the moon, among the things which have been lost or abused on earth:

and OTTOKAR OF HORNECK. The former especially bewails avarice and simony, as the unhallowed fruit of that Donation; but the latter says Constantine added a sword, which they did not know how to wield, to the stole of the priests, and thus broke the strength of the empire.[1]

This view, that the Donation had brought ruin into the Church, assumed in that legend-producing age the form of an actual occurrence. An angel

> " Di varj fiori ad un gran monte passa,
> Ch' ebber già buono odore, or puzzan forte,
> Questo era il dono (se però dir lece)
> Che Constantino al buon Silvestro fece."
> *Orl. Fur.*, c. XXXIV., st. 80.

> " Then passed he to a flowery mountain green,
> Which once smelt sweet, now stinks as odiously;
> This was that gift, if you the truth will have,
> That Constantine to good Silvester gave."
> Milton's Translation. *Prose Works*, I., p. 11, ed. 1753.

From Cary's note on Dante, Inf., XIX., 118.
But perhaps the strongest passage in Dante against the Donation is Par. XX., 55, where Constantine is found in Paradise, *in spite of* the Donation.

> " Lo altro, che segue, con le leggi e meco
> Sotto buona intenzion, che fè mal frutto,
> Per cedere al pastor si fece Greco:
> Ora conosce, come il mal dedutto
> Dal suo bene bene operar non li è nocivo,
> Avvegna che sia il mondo indi distrutto."

> "The next who follows (Constantine), with the laws and me,
> Under the good intent that bore bad fruit
> Became a Greek by ceding to the pastor;
> Now knoweth he how all the ill deduced
> From his good action is not harmful to him,
> Although the world thereby may be destroyed."
> Longfellow's Translation.]

[1] Cap. 118, in PEZ., III., 446.

The angel's lament over the Donation. was said to have cried from heaven, "Woe! woe! "This day hath poison been infused into the Church." The legend is to be found as early as the commencement of the thirteenth[1] century, in WALTHER VON DER WOGELWEIDE. "The angel hath "told us true," says this poet, but he is thinking chiefly of the weakening of the empire, which appears to him to be the evil fruit of the Donation:

> "alle vürsten lebent nû mit êren,
> wan der höhste ist geswachet,
> daz hat der pfaffen wal gemachet."[2]

So, also, the Strasburg chronicler, KÖNIGSHOFEN. "Then was a voice heard over all Rome, which "said, 'This day hath gall and venom flowed into "' holy Christendom,' and know ye that this also "is source and ground of all war between popes[3] "and emperors."

Contemplation of the mischief which the hatred between Lewis the Bavarian and the French popes had created, moved the Minorite JOHN OF

---

[1] [Simrock assigns this poem to A.D. 1198. The one in which the poet talks of having sung for forty years, "von minnen und als "iemen sol," is assigned to the year 1228. This would place his birth about 1168. He took part in the sixth crusade, and probably died soon after his return.]

[2] [That is, "all the princes now live with honours, since the highest (the emperor) is weakened. The election of the clergy has brought about this." No. 5, p. 36, Simrock's edition.]

[3] In the Vienna manuscript, *Hist. Eccles.*, 29, fol. 64 (A.D. thirteenth century), the reason given for the voice of the angel is, "quia (eccle- "sia) major est dignitate, minor religione." The story about the angel is found also in the *Chron. Monast. Mellicensis*, in PEZ, *Scr. Austr.*, I., 182, in the chronicle of THEODORE ENGELHUSEN, in Leibnitz, *Scr. Brunsvic.*, II., 1034.

WINTERTHUR also to complain, that "at this time "one sees plainly enough how truly the angel "spoke, in saying that through that well-meant, but "in its consequences most unhappy, rich dota-"tion and fat present, which Constantine conferred, "poison had flowed into the Church."[1]

Even theologians were not ashamed to appeal to the saying of the angel. JOHN OF PARIS concludes from it that the Donation had displeased[2] God. A hundred years after him DIETRICH VRIE, an Augustinian at Osnabruck, says, that poison certainly at that time had been administered to the Church, but yet only through the *abuse* of the Donation; for wealth in itself was by no means a calamity for the Church.[3] At last this saying of the angel passed into a proverb, common even in the mouth of the lower orders.[4]

<small>Even theologians quote the angel.</small>

At first, however, this angel, who proclaimed the poisoning of the Church, seems to have been a fallen one. For the first who narrates the miracle, GIRALDUS CAMBRENSIS (about the year 1180), (and, as BISHOP PECOCK OF CHICHESTER (1450) assures us, the other chroniclers merely copy Giraldus,) makes the "old enemy" speak

---

[1] Ap. ECCARD, I., 1889.
[2] Ap. SCHARD, *Sylloge*, p. 210.
[3] *Hist. Concil. Const.*, ap. VON DER HARDT, I., 111.
[4] Ab omnibus recitatur, tempore quo Constantinus M. incolpit dotare ecclesiam, audita est vox in aere: "Hodie effusum vene-"num in ecclesia." Jo. MAJOR *de pot. Papæ.* In GERSON's Works, II., 1159.

the words.[1] At any rate, this "evil one" shortly afterwards transformed himself into an angel of light.

The Donation as regarded by the sects of the Middle Ages. The sects of the twelfth and thirteenth centuries, especially the Catharists and Waldenses, proceeded on the principle, that every possession of the Church was in itself objectionable, and that it was damnable for the Church to devote anything more than the mere freewill offerings of the moment, towards supplying means of life to the clergy. The[2] endowment, therefore, of the Church by Constantine was considered by them as a decisive turning-point, involving the ruin of the Church, nay, its utter destruction. Until Silvester, they

---

[1] "The oold enemy made thilk voice in the cir." Pecock's *Repressor*, ed. by CHURCHILL BABINGTON, London, 1860, p. 351. According to PECOCK's statement, the passage is to be found in the *Cosmographia Hiberniæ* of Giraldus. It is not in the printed *Topographia Hiberniæ*; but it is possibly in the still unprinted *Descriptio Mundi* of Giraldus.

[2] [This was the doctrine so widely spread by the Abbot Joachim of Fiore, Dolcino of Novara, and the Fraticelli. The primitive Church had held that poverty was better than riches. That period had come to an end with Silvester. Since his time all popes had been prevaricators and deceivers, except Celestine V. He alone had understood and practised the blessed state of poverty. The Cathari argued that, as Constantine's empire was one of wrong and violence, and he had ceded it to Silvester, the popes since Silvester were successors to an unrighteous kingdom, not to an apostolic Church. This view had its effect also on the various *prophecies* which were circulated in the fourteenth century under the name of Joachim, and others. See a most interesting essay by Dr. DÖLLINGER in Raumer's *Historisches Taschenbuch*, Leipzig, 1871, on *Der Weissagungsglaube und das Prophetenthum in der christlichen Zeit*, pp. 264, 265, 282, 283.]

said, the Church existed; in him it fell, and became extinct by receiving from the hand of Constantine riches and worldly power, until it was once more revived by the " Poor men of Lyons."[1] With the end of its poverty ended the very existence of the Church : property was the poison of which it died. Silvester is, therefore, that mighty, bold, and crafty king prophesied of in Daniel[2] viii. 24, who destroys " the people of the holy ones "—[das Volk der Heiligen;—so the Hebrew, and the *margin* of the English version]. He is also Antichrist, the Man of Sin, and Son of Perdition, of whom S. Paul[3] speaks [2 Thess. ii. 3]. VALDEZ, on the other hand, the founder of the " Poor men " of Lyons," is the Elias, who, according to the words of Christ (Matt. xvii. 11), shall come and restore all things. Later, however, the Waldenses discovered that a church which for eight hundred

<small>Silvester is Antichrist, the destroyer of the Church.</small>

---

[1] RAINER. SACCHONI, in Martene Thesaur. v., 1775, Moneta; *Advers Cathar. et Vald.*, p. 412.

[2] [" And in the latter time of their kingdom, when the transgressors are come to the full, a king of fierce countenance, and understanding dark sentences, shall stand up. And his power shall be mighty, but not by his own power; and he shall destroy wonderfully, and shall prosper, and practise, and shall destroy the mighty and the holy people. And through his policy also he shall cause craft to prosper in his hand; and he shall magnify himself in his heart, and by peace shall destroy many : he shall also stand up against the Prince of princes, but he shall be broken without hand." (Daniel viii. 23-25.) Only by considering Silvester as having become, through the Donation, potentially a Gregory VII., an Innocent III., a Boniface VIII., can we understand how this prophecy could ever have been quoted as referring to him.]

[3] MONETA, IV., 263.

years, from Silvester to Valdez, had entirely vanished, and then had been called into existence again out of nothing, was a nonentity. They maintained, therefore, that their sect or church had not had its first beginning with Valdez, but had already been in existence in the time[1] of Silvester, and that since that pope all the clergy, and those who followed them, were damned.[2] The name Leonenses (i.e. of Lyons) then gave occasion to the invention of a Leo as the supposed founder of the sect. A pious man of this name in the time of Constantine, "disciple and fellow of pope "Silvester," is said to have separated from the now wealthy pope, in order to show his abhorrence of the latter's avarice, and serve the Lord in voluntary[3] poverty.

This notion, that utter poverty of the clergy, and rejection of all property, were among the conditions of the Church's existence, and that, consequently, Constantine and Silvester were the authors of the Church's ruin, was at that time so prevalent, and so much in harmony with the characteristics of the age, that it was always reappearing. The DULCINISTS[4] or APOSTOLIC BRETHREN

[1] PETRUS DE PILICHDORF; *contra Waldenses*, Bibl. Patr. Lugd., xxv., 278.

[2] *De hæresi Paup. de Lugd.*, ap. MARTENE, Thes. v., 1779.

[3] So CONRAD JUSTINGER in Bern, about A.D. 1420, in his chronicle of Bern.

[4] [The followers of DOLCINO OF NOVARA. Clement V. condemned him and others to death. His flesh was torn away from his body with hot pincers, and his limbs then wrenched off, A.D. 1304.]

at the beginning of the fourteenth century, who aspired to realise the primitive Church in its purity, as they conceived it, said that it was Silvester who had reopened the doors of human society and of the Church to Satan.[1] Dolcino himself, in his first letter to Christendom, declared Silvester to be the angel of Pergamus, who "dwells where "Satan's seat is." (Rev. ii. 13.)

The English precursor of Protestantism, WY-CLIF, shared this view. Constantine, he says, foolishly injured himself and the clergy, in burdening the Church so heavily with temporal goods.[2] In the *Trialogus* he represents Antichrist as produced by the Donation of Constantine, and thence deduces the downfall of the Roman empire.[3]

Wyclif of the same opinion.

The days of the Donation of Constantine were, however, numbered. Already, in the year 1443, ÆNEAS SYLVIUS PICCOLOMINI, afterwards pope Pius II., then secretary to Frederick III., had recommended that emperor to summon a fresh council, at which, among other things, the question of the Donation of Constantine, "which caused "perplexity to many souls," should on Frederick's

The fiction exposed. Æneas Sylvius recommends a council to proclaim its unauthenticity, A.D. 1443.

---

[1] "Quando paupertas fuit mutata ab ecclesia per S. Sylvestrum, "tunc sanctitas vitæ fuit subtracta ecclesiæ et diabolus intravit—"in hunc mundum." So the Dulcinist Peter of Lucca, in LIM-"BORCH *hist. inquis.*, p. 360.

[2] THOMAS WALDENSIS, *Doctrin. fidei*, ed. BLANCIOTTI, II., 708, quotes his words from his book *De Papa*.

[3] *Tracts and Treatises*, ed. VAUGHAN, 1845, p. 174.

proposal be finally decided. He himself was well known to be convinced of its unauthenticity, and he notices that neither in the ancient historians nor in *Damasus*, that is, in the Pontifical book, was anything about it to be found. Its unauthenticity, therefore, was to be proclaimed by the council, and Æneas joined with this the *arrière pensée*, that Frederick should again take possession of at least a part of the territory included in the Donation, as belonging to the empire, and thus gain a firm basis in the peninsular for the imperial power, which otherwise would vanish into air.[1]

Three assailants of the Donation; Reginald Pecock, cardinal Cusa, Lorenzo Valla.

Three men appeared almost simultaneously in the middle of the fifteenth century, to prove on historical grounds, that the *fact* of the Donation no less than the document was an invention;—REGINALD PECOCK, bishop of Chichester, cardinal CUSA, and LORENZO VALLA. In contrast to the uncertain vacillation[2] of Cusa, Pecock's exactness of historical investigation, an exactness proportionate to his knowledge of authorities, is very remarkable.[3] In Paris, where scholasticism still

---

[1] *Pentalogus*, in PEZ, Thes. Anecd. IV., p. 3, 679.

[2] The passage out of his *Concordantia Catholica* is printed in BROWN, Fasciculus, I., 157.

[3] *Repressor*, p. 361-67. [Pecock gives eight reasons for maintaining that the Donation is a fiction, most of them tolerably conclusive; e. g. the silence of Damasus, who mentions other small gifts of Constantine; the silence of credible historians; the fact that Constantine bequeathed the very territory in question to his sons, and that Boniface IV. asked the emperor Phocas to give him the Pantheon as a church, A U. 608, &c., &c. By "Damasus" Pecock no doubt means the *Liber Pontificalis* or *Anastasius* (falsely so called),

held the sceptre, criticism had not advanced so far as this fifty years later, as ALMAIN shows. VALLA certainly went much farther than Pecock and Cusa; he undertook to prove that the pope had no right to the possession of Rome, and the States of the Church in particular, that he was "tantum " Vicarius Christi et non etiam Cæsaris." His treatise was rather an artistic, rhetorical production, an eloquent declamation, than a calm historical investigation.[1] He himself considered it as the *chef d'œuvre* of his eloquence. And yet after his treatise had been circulated everywhere, and had caused the greatest excitement, Valla was invited to Rome by Nicolas V., taken into the service of the pope, and received both from Nicolas V. and from Calixtus III., various marks of favour, without any retractation whatever being required of him.

The jurists meanwhile did not allow themselves to be put out of countenance, and held fast to the fiction for about a hundred years longer.[2] ANTONINUS, archbishop of Florence, calls attention to the fact that the passage in Gratian's decretals does not exist in the more ancient manuscripts of the collection, but, at the same time, remarks that the

<small>The canonists, and even some professors of civil law still maintain its validity.</small>

which was usually quoted as a work of pope Damasus in the Middle Ages.]

[1] POGGIALI, *Memorie di Lorenzo Valla*, Piacenza, 1790, p. 119.

[2] "Apud Canonistas nulla ambiguitas est, quin perpetua firmitate " subnixa sit," says Peter of Andlo, *De imperio Romano*, p. 42, in the *Tractatus varii de R. G. imp. regimine*, Norimb., 1657.

legists (professors of civil law) disputed the legal validity of the Donation, while the canonists and theologians upheld it. He himself adopts the idea[1] of a universal dominion of the pope, resting on a divine dispensation, and accordingly sees in the Donation nothing more than a restitution. Meanwhile, defenders of its legal authenticity were not wanting even among the professors of civil law.[2] Above all others BARTOLO must be mentioned here (about 1350), to whom formerly, as Tiraboschi says, almost divine honour was paid. But as he calls attention to the territory in which he and his hearers happen to be, he lets one divine his true meaning.[3] On the other hand, NICOLAS TUDESCHI, who was considered by his contemporaries as the greatest of all canonists, declares that he who denies the Donation lies under the suspicion[4] of heresy. Cardinal P. P. PARISIUS, and the Spanish bishop, ARNOLD ALBERTINUS, declare the same. Whosoever pronounces the Donation to be null and void, says the latter, comes very near to heresy; but whosoever maintains that it never

Its last defenders.

---

[1] The passage out of his *Pars historialis* is found in BROWN, Fascic., I., 159.

[2] The jurists had discovered a passage in proof of the Donation even in the Corpus juris civilis. That is to say, Cod. 5, 27, in a law of the emperor Zeno, they read, "Divi Constantini, qui ... Ro-"manum *minuit* imperium," instead of "*munivit*."

[3] "Videte, *quianos sumus in terris Ecclesiae, idcirco* dico quod illa "donatio valeat." In proœm., ff. n. 14.

[4] *Consil.* 84, n. 2, in cap. per venerabilem, and elsewhere. Compare FRANCISCI BURSATI *Consilia*, Venet., 1572, I., 359.

took place at all is in a still worse case.¹ ANTO-
NIUS,² ROSELLUS, and LUDWIG GOMEZ³ are of the
same opinion; and cardinal HIERONYMUS ALBANO
declares thus much at least, that there exist shame-
less persons who refuse to submit to the "unanimis
" consensus tot ac tantorum Patrum," respecting
the Donation; or, according to the expression of
PETRUS IGNEUS, to the " tota academia Canonis-
" tarum et Legistarum," with the whole host of
theologians to boot.⁴ But after cardinal BARONIUS
had once for all confessed the unauthenticity of
the Donation, all these voices, which had shortly
before been so numerous and so loud, became
dumb.

Since Baronius surrendered it no one has ventured seriously to maintain it.

Only one remark more need be added in conclusion. In consequence of its naturalization
among the Greeks, the Donation in its full extent
found admittance even into Russia, for it exists
in the *Kormczaia Kniga*, the Corpus juris
canonici of the Græco-Slavonic Church, which
was translated from the Greek by a Servian
or Bulgarian, in the thirteenth or fourteenth
century.⁵

[One⁶ further argument may be noticed, not
as being needed, but as being in itself almost

---

¹ *De agnoscendis assert. cath. et hæro quæst.*, 17, n. 14.
² *Tract. de potest. Papæ*, Lugd. s. a., p. 320.
³ In BURSATUS, l. c. 360ᵇ.
⁴ BURSATUS, l. c., quoted all these, and many others.
⁵ Wiener *Jahrbücher der Literatur*, Bd. XXIII., 265.
⁶ *The Testimony of the Catacombs and other Monuments of Christian Art, &c.*, by WHARTON B. MARRIOTT, London, 1870, p. 99.

conclusive. Among the innumerable monuments of Roman art, from the fourth century onwards, some of which have direct reference to Constantine, no reference whatever is made to the Donation. Would it not have been a favourite subject, had it ever been a fact? There appears to be only one representation in mediæval art of the Donation of Constantine. It is a mosaic from the " zophoros," or frieze of the Lateran Basilica. Some of the details of the costumes show it to be *not earlier than the twelfth century*. On one side, " Rex baptizatur " et lepræ sorde lavatur;" on the other " Rex in " scriptura Sylvestro dat sua jura."]

LIBERIUS AND FELIX

It will be necessary first to give the true history of these two men, the sources of which happily flow with all the clearness that could be wished. In this way the origin and tendency of the fable will become more plainly apparent.

The true version of the contest between Liberius and Felix.

The emperor Constantius, under the influence of his eunuchs and certain Arian bishops, wished to force Arianism on the Church and bishops of the West, in that weakened and half ashamed form which the Eusebians had given to it. He, as well as his satellites, made use of all means of seduction, intimidation, and brutal violence, in order to accomplish this object. The Roman bishop, Liberius, had first at Rome, and then at Milan, whither he had been summoned to the imperial court, steadfastly resisted the efforts of Constantius and his eunuch, Eusebius; he was accordingly banished to Berœa, in Thrace, in the year 354. In his place Constantius caused the Roman deacon, Felix, to be consecrated by three Arian bishops (one of whom was the Anomœan Acacius of Cæsarea), in the presence of three eunuchs. Felix had not formally

Banishment of Liberius.

Felix created antipope.

rejected the Nicene Creed, but he held ecclesiastical communion with Arians, which was all that the leaders of that party needed then; for the remainder, viz., the predominance of their doctrine, would gradually follow of itself. In Rome, where Liberius was personally much beloved, the people refused to enter the churches in which Felix showed himself. The whole clergy publicly promised, with an oath, before the congregation that, as long as Liberius lived, they would recognise no other. It ended at last in an insurrection, in which some persons were killed.[1] When Constantius came to Rome two years later, he found the Roman populace still true to Liberius. The Roman ladies besought him earnestly to give them back their bishop, and he granted their request to this extent; that he decreed, that Liberius and Felix (to the latter of whom the greatest number of the clergy had meanwhile joined themselves) should for the future rule the Roman Church in common. But the people assembled in the circus cried out, "One God, one Christ, one bishop." Liberius was, however, not recalled; until in the following year, 357, broken by the sufferings and privations of his exile, pressed with threats, and deprived even of the man who hitherto had been left to him as servant and companion, the deacon Urbicus,

Disturbances in Rome.

---

[1] ATHANAS. *hist. ad monachos*, p. 389. FAUSTINI and MARCELLINI *libell.* præf. SOCRAT., 2, 37; RUFIN, 1, 22; HIERON. *vir. illustr.*, c. 109; *Chron.* ad. a., 354.

he determined to sign a creed which was laid before him, to refuse to hold communion with Athanasius, and in consequence with all decided Nicæans, and thus to enter the Arian court party. He signed the first formula of Sirmio, which was inoffensive in other respects, and left nothing to be desired but the Homoüsion. He went further; he declared himself unable to hold communion with Athanasius, and accordingly entered into communion with the most decided Arians, such as Ursacius, Valens, and Germinius. He courted the favour of the influential protegés of the emperor, the Arian bishops, Epictetus and Auxentius. Later on (in the year 358), he was summoned from Beræa to the imperial court at Sirmio, and, at Constantius' bidding, signed a fresh and still worse formula, which the Arian and Semiarian bishops, just then assembled at a synod in Sirmio, had drawn up. In this formula, with a view to obtaining an express rejection of the Homoüsion, the decisions of the synod at Antioch[1]

Fall of Liberius.

[1] Not merely of the synod held at Antioch in 341, as HEFELE states (*Concilien-Geschichte*, I., 662); for this did not occupy itself either with the case of Paul of Samosata, or with that of Photinus; but also of the synod of 269, which rejected the Homoüsion in the false sense given to it by Paul of Samosata. The object now in view was no longer a mere abstaining from the use of the hated word, but a formal condemnation of it; because, as was represented, under the pretext of the Homoüsion, certain persons (Athanasius and all who held firmly to the Nicene doctrine) wished to set up a sect of their own. SOZOMEN, 4, 15. PHILOSTORGIUS (4, 3), moreover, does not say, as HEFELE represents, that Liberius signed the *second* Sirmian formula. Of the one signed at Berœa he says nothing whatever; but he does mention the one accepted by Liberius

against Paul of Samosata, and the later ones against Photinus and Marcellus of Ancyra, together with one of the formularies of the synod at Antioch, in A.D. 341, were incorporated. Liberius was thus reduced to accepting precisely the position of the Semiarians, now so influential with Constantius. He gave his adhesion to their expression, "substantial likeness," sacrificed the Nicene doctrine, and apprised the eastern Arians of his entry into their communion, and of his separation from Athanasius. It was chiefly on account of this weakness exhibited at Sirmio, under the double influence of the emperor and the bishops, and not on account of what had taken place before at Berœa, that Liberius drew upon himself the reproach of his contemporaries, of being heretical, and an ally of heretics. And, indeed, no other judgment was then possible. He had granted communion to the very worst Arians, such as Epictetus of Centuncellæ and Auxentius of Milan.[1] It was Fortunatianus, bishop of Aquileia, who, according to Jerome, persuaded Liberius to such apostasy.

Liberius fairly called heretical.

Return of Liberius to Rome.

This was the price at which Liberius purchased his return to Rome, where the people joyfully welcomed the bishop, whom they personally loved in spite of his fall. The whole community was,

afterwards at Sirmio, that is the *third*; and of this he says quite correctly, and in agreement with SOZOMEN, that Liberius thereby condemned the Homoüsion and Athanasius.

[1] HILAR. *de syn.*, Opp., II., 464; Frag., 6, II., 680; Sozom., 4, 15. The letters of LIBERIUS in COUSTANT, *Epistolæ Pontiff.*, 442 sqq.

and remained, Catholic. The people of the West had as yet occupied itself but little with the controversies about the consubstantiality of the Son with the Father; they scarcely understood the question at issue or its import. Liberius was therefore able quietly to resume his office without retracting. It had been determined at Sirmio, that Liberius and Felix should preside over the Church of Rome together; for Felix, in consequence of his holding communion with the Arian bishops, was still high in favour at court. At Rome, however, disturbances with wide reaching consequences took place. The clergy were divided, for the majority had broken the oath of fidelity which they had taken to Liberius before his banishment, and had recognised Felix. But the latter was obliged to withdraw from the city, because the people would not tolerate him; and long afterwards when he attempted to get possession of a church on the other side of the Tiber, he was again driven out. He lived eight years from that time without being able to set foot in Rome; but after his death (November 22nd, 365) Liberius pardoned the clergy of his party, and allowed them to resume their position.[1]

Expulsion of Felix.

Nothing is told us of Liberius's own position. He appears not to have retracted what he did at Berœa and Sirmio, and not to have ceased to hold

---

[1] MARCELLINI et FAUSTIN. ad libell. prec. præf. Both these Roman priests were eye-witnesses, and JEROME confirms their statement.

communion with the Arians; otherwise Constantius would not have allowed him to remain long in Rome. The synod of Rimini, however, towards the end of the year 359, and in the year 360, gave him an opportunity of proving his orthodoxy. He rejected the synod, and ordered that those who had taken part in it should be admitted to communion only on condition of retracting; and it was he who, in the year 366, demanded of the Semiarians an adhesion to the Homoüsion, which he had formerly rejected himself, as a sine quâ non of their being recognised by the Church. He might have been led astray at Sirmio, in that the misuse which Paul of Samosata, and Marcellus of Ancyra, and Photinus had made of the Homoüsion was represented to him as a just ground for refraining from using so double-edged a weapon as this word had proved, and for forbidding the employment of it; moreover, they had held up to him the authority of the synod of 269. When he assented to the *substantial likeness* of the Son to the Father, he might (like other otherwise good catholics of that time) have been convinced, that in the Godhead substantial equality and substantial likeness are necessarily equivalent. Thus much may, perhaps, be said in extenuation of his error; but it certainly gives no excuse for his rejection of Athanasius, or for his entering into communion with the leaders of the Arian party. He must however have made good this grievous error even before the synod of Rimini was held (359). Without doubt events since 358 had taught him that that dogmatic word was indeed quite indispensable for the Church; that it, as he says in his epistle to the bishops of the East, in the year 366, was "the sure and impregnable bulwark, against "which all attacks and stratagems of Arianism "shattered."[1]

Liberius, therefore, at no time in his life was actually heretical; but his eagerness to see himself freed from the sufferings of a lonely exile and restored to the bosom of his people, who loved and honoured him, blinded him. He sacrificed the Church to the Arians, he perplexed the consciences of his people in regard to Church matters, and one knows, of course, that Hilary anathematized him. But he remained throughout the rightful bishop of Rome; and his opponent Felix was and remained an illegitimate intruder, in respect to the Arian trouble still more culpable than Liberius. For Felix received violent handling from no one, and obtained and kept his position only by getting himself ordained by Arians, and by ensuring them communion; especially the court bishops, and those who hung about the emperor. Whereas Liberius did not succumb to the ill usage to which he was subjected until after several years of steadfast endurance.

{Evil effects of his fall.}

{Felix more culpable, and without excuse.}

At the death of Liberius, in the year 366, the

[1] Ap. COUSTANT, *Epp. Rom. Pontiff*, p. 460.

Death of Liberius followed by a disputed election;

split which the intrusion of Felix and the secession of many of the clergy to him had called into existence, broke out afresh, this time with bloodshed. A numerous faction of the people, urged on by some of the clergy, wished to decree that none of those, who in violation of their oath, had recognised Felix ten years before, should succeed to the office of bishop. On this ground, Ursinus was set up in opposition to Damasus, who had been elected by a majority of the clergy. A regular civil war

bloodshed;

was the consequence. They fought in the streets and in the churches with such animosity, that, on one occasion,[1] one hundred and thirty-seven dead bodies, mostly from the faction of Ursinus, were found in the Sicinian basilica. Damasus himself could not restrain his own party; and only by the banishment of Ursinus and seven others of this faction, and by the strong measures of the prefect Juvencus, was some sort of order at length restored in the city. The supporters of Ursinus, however, continued their schism and their meetings in the cemeteries of the martyrs, which led to fresh bloodshed and fresh banishment of clergy

And lasting disturbances.

belonging to this faction. Thus passed several years in perpetual disquietude; and thus from that violent act on the part of Constantius there grew so long afterwards the bitter fruit of a disturbance in the Church, which was not completely healed until a whole generation had died out.

[1] AMMIAN. MARCELL., l. 27, 3, 12.

It is very remarkable that the later myth or intentional fiction, which dates from the sixth or seventh century, has metamorphosed this history entirely to the disadvantage of Liberius, and in favour of Felix, who was dubbed an ecclesiastical hero and martyr. And it came to this; that this perjured antipope, consecrated by fanatical Arians, and intruded on the Romans only by the temporal power, was honoured as a saint, and reckoned in the list of the popes as pope Felix II.; while Liberius, even in Rome itself, was represented as a blood-stained tyrant, a heretic, and persecutor of the faithful. *Strange metamorphosis of the facts in the later myth.*

One cannot fail to see that all this was invented with a view to placing the cause of that numerous portion of the Roman clergy, who broke their oath and adhered to Felix in a favourable light, and to represent them as the rightful party, who had withstood heresy and the heretical pope, and had been persecuted on that account. Nevertheless, these fictions must be assigned to a late period, the sixth or seventh century, as it would appear, when only hazy recollections of the events of the fourth century still survived in Rome, and when the story of the Roman baptism of Constantine, with its train of myths, had already disturbed all historic consciousness there, and had thrown into confusion the historical continuity and order of events. There are three documents in which the fictitious history was incorporated, and from which *Object of the fiction to whitewash the party of Felix.* *Not older than the sixth century.*

all later ones have been made; the biographies of Liberius and of Felix in the *Liber Pontificalis*, the *Acts of Felix*, first edited by Mombritius, and the *Acts of Eusebius*.[1]

<small>Memory of Liberius blackened.</small>

These *Acts* have manifestly been invented with a view to branding the memory of Liberius, and representing him in the most glaring way as an heretical apostate and persecutor of the catholic confessors, so that the party of Felix might appear as the oppressed orthodox. Hence the narrator makes pope Damasus condemn Liberius in a synod of twenty-eight bishops and twenty-five priests, immediately after Liberius' death. At the same time, also, this opportunity was seized, in order to give a fresh security against the contradicting testimony of antiquity to the story of the Roman baptism of Constantine,—the pet story of those by whom and for whom the invention was made.

<small>Fable of the Roman baptism of Constantine interwoven with this one.</small>

Hence the biography of Felix begins with a statement, made with affected precision, to the effect, that he had declared the emperor Constantius, son of Constantine, a heretic, who had got himself baptized a second time by Eusebius, bishop of Nicomedia,[2] in the villa Aquila (Achyro) near to Nicomedia.

Here, then, what the father did is transferred to

---

[1] They are to be found in the BALUZE-MANSI Collection, I., 33, and throughout the whole of the Middle Ages were constantly used and copied.

[2] Ap. VIGNOLI, I., 119.

the son, and the intention in Constantine's case to put Rome in the place of Nicomedia, and Silvester in the place of Eusebius, is unmistakeable.

The following narrative was substituted in place of the true one in the two first-mentioned documents, which really hang together.

The fiction as given in the Liber Pontificalis and the Acts of Felix.

When Constantius banished Liberius on account of his defence of the Catholic faith, the Roman clergy elected and consecrated the presbyter[1] Felix as bishop,[2] under the advice and with the consent of Liberius. Felix forthwith holds a council of forty-eight bishops, and finds here that two presbyters,[3] Ursacius and Valens, agree with Constantius, and condemns them. The two persuade Constantius, and with his consent go to Liberius and offer him return from banishment on these terms;—that there should be communion

---

[1] Felix was only a deacon. Rufin., 2, 22; Marcellin. *libell. prec.* præf.

[2] This would only have been possible if Liberius had abdicated at the same time, which he did not do. That one bishop should appoint another co ordinately with himself, or cause himself to be represented by another during his absence, was contrary to ecclesiastical law, especially to one of the Nicene canons. When after all Valerius, bishop of Hippo, did so, Augustine himself, whom he caused to be consecrated with the permission of the primate of Carthage, found that it was "contra morem ecclesiæ," and accordingly gave orders that at every ordination the canons should be read beforehand, in order that such a transgression might not occur again.—POSSID. *vit. Aug.*, c. 8.

[3] Both were bishops, Ursacius of Singidon in Mysia, Valens of Mursa in Pannonia, and had no relations whatever to the Roman Church. The main supporter of Arianism in the Roman territory was Epictetus, bishop of Circumcellæ.

between Arians and orthodox, but that the latter should not be required to be re-baptized.[1] Liberius consents, comes back, and takes up his abode in the cemetery of S. Agnes with the emperor's sister, Constantia.[2] She is urged to gain admittance for him into Rome by intercession with her brother, but declines as a true catholic. Constantius, however, summons Liberius to Rome without the intervention of his sister by the advice of the Arians, gets together a council of heretics, and with its help deposes the catholic Felix from his episcopal[3] office. The very same day a bloody persecution commences, conducted by Constantius and Liberius in concert. The presbyter Eusebius (who distinguishes himself by his courage and catholic zeal, and gathers the people together in his house) reproaches the emperor and Liberius with their crime, declares to the latter that he is no longer in any way the rightful follower of Julius because he had fallen from the faith, and to both, that, in satanic blindness, they have driven out the catholic blameless Felix. Whereupon Constantius, by the advice of Liberius, has him shut up in a deep hole only four foot broad, in which he is found

---

[1] There was no discussion about re-baptism at that time, or for a long time afterwards. The Arians before Eunomius considered catholic baptism to be valid.

[2] A confusion with the sister of Constantine the Great.

[3] All this time, and so long as Liberius was in office there, Constantius was not in Rome. The narrative, however, gives one to understand that he lived there regularly.

dead at the end of seven months. The presbyters, Gregory and Orosius, relations of Eusebius, bury him; upon which the emperor gives orders to shut up Gregory alive in the same vault in which they had placed the corpse of Eusebius. Orosius drags him out from the vault by night half dead; he dies, however, in his arms, whereupon the other, Orosius, records the whole history. Felix, who had reproached the emperor with his re-baptism, is beheaded by the emperor's command. The persecution rages in Rome until the death of Liberius. Constantius publishes an edict that every one who does not join Liberius shall be executed without trial. Clergy and laity are now murdered in the streets and in the churches. At last Liberius dies, and Damasus brands his memory with infamy in a synod.

The description in the *Acts of Eusebius* is considerably more highly coloured than the representation in the Liber Pontificalis, where the circumstances are toned down somewhat; but the object in view, viz., to quash Liberius and make him appear as Constantius' companion in guilt, shines through it all from beginning to end. That the acts of Eusebius were composed in the interest of the antipope Felix, has been already remarked by CAVALCANTI.[1] It appears to me that there was another object joined with this, viz., to place the bloody scenes, which occurred in consequence of

<small>The fiction as given in the Acts of Eusebius.</small>

<small>Its double object.</small>

---

[1] '*Vindiciæ*.' Rom. Pontiff.

the divided election of Ursinus and Damasus, and which may have left behind them a misty recollection even two centuries later in Rome, in a light more favourable to the clergy of the time; and, by this means, the events were ante-dated by two years, and represented as persecutions of the staunch catholic clergy by the two Arians, the pope and the emperor. And they even went so far in their rejection of Liberius and efforts to put Felix in his place, that in the chronological notices of the Liberian basilica, built by that very pope, they passed Liberius over altogether, and placed Felix alone between Julius and Damasus.

The name of Felix interpolated into calendars, liturgies, &c.

Thus, then, Felix was gradually thrust into the lists of the popes, the liturgies, and martyrologies, as rightful pope and a holy martyr; not, however, until a late date, and, as regards the martyrologies, only slowly. Optatus and Augustinus had passed him over in their lists of the bishops of Rome. The twenty-ninth of July was the day which had been dedicated to his memory. But here, when the calendars and martyrologies were examined and compared, the deception became palpably manifest, and showed that the Felix there celebrated was quite a different one; and that not until the eighth century, after the false legends about Felix and Eusebius had been forged, did it occur to people to declare that this Felix was the rival of Liberius. The oldest document as yet known is the Roman calendar, which MARTENE has published in the fifth volume of his *Thesaurus*. He assigns it to the beginning of the fifth century; and rightly, for, with a single exception (Silvester), it contains festivals of martyrs only, and Silvester is the latest of the saints mentioned in it. Hence Damasus, though canonised at an early date, is wanting. Here, then, the twenty-eighth of July was marked as[1] natalis s. Felicis, Simplicii, Faustini, et Beatricis. In all other cases the designation "papa" is added to the names of the popes in this calendar. Several martyrologies, which bear the name of S. Jerome, and,[2] judging from their chief contents, belong to the fifth century (the period before Cassiodorus), agree with this. That of Bede, likewise, without mentioning Rome. Then the *Martyrologium Ottobonianum* of the tenth, and the *Kalendarium Laureshamense*[3] of the end of the ninth century. On the other hand, that of S. Jerome in D'ACHERY separates Felix from the three others which manifestly belong to Rome, and transfers[4] him to Africa. The Vatican calendar itself, of the beginning of the eleventh century,[5] agrees also with this. But how Felix got transferred from Africa to Rome is explained by a martyrology of Auxerre, which falls well into

This interpolation easily detected.

---

[1] So also the *Sacramentarium Gregorianum*. Elsewhere it is always the twenty-ninth.
[2] In MARTENE, *Thes.* III., 1558.
[3] Both in GIORGI's edition of Ado, p. 683, 692.
[4] *Spicileg.*, II., 15, nov. ed.
[5] In GIORGI, p. 699.

the end of the ninth century (the latest of the numerous popes mentioned in it is Zacharias), and is especially rich in Roman material, and accurate in local notices; so that there can be no doubt as to its Roman origin. This is what it says at the twenty-ninth of July :—" Romæ via Aurelia trans-" latio corporis beati Felicis episcopi et martyris " qui iv. idus Novembris martyrio coronatus est. " Eodem die ss. mm. Simplicii, Faustinii et s. Bea-" tricis m. sororis eorum."[1] It appears, therefore, that the bones of the African martyr, Felix, were brought to Rome, and that only on account of this translation, which took place on the twenty-ninth of July, Felix was joined with the Roman martyrs Simplicius, Faustinus, and Beatrix, to whom this day was already dedicated. Thus there are other martyrologies and missals, in which Felix is not found, but only the three others. In the so-called *Sacramentarium* of Gelasius he is wanting also, although Simplicius, Faustinus, and Viatrix (or Beatrix) are celebrated.[2] In the later Gregorian *Sacramentarium*, on the other hand, the day is given as the birthday of the four saints, but in such a way that in the Oratio Felix alone is celebrated, and that as " martyr et pontifex." In the martyrology of the year 826,[3] found at Corbie, as well as in the *Martyrologium Morbacense*, and in

---

[1] In MARTENE, *Coll. ampl.*, VI., 712.
[2] In MURATORI, *Liturgia Romana Vetus*, I., 658; II., 106.
[3] D'ACHERY, *Spicil.*, II., 66.

the *Calendarium Anglicanum*, only Simplicius, Faustinus, and Beatrix are mentioned.[1] Most of them simply mention Felix, without further designation, along with the other three; or, like the Neapolitan of the ninth century, say[2] "Felicis et "Simplicii;" or, "in Africa Felicis," &c., as the calendar of Stablo.

With the eighth century, however, begins, on the other hand, the line of calendars and martyrologies which make Felix a pope, and of course mean one to understand the antipope of A.D. 356. The first is the Roman calendar of the middle of the eighth century, edited by Fronto.[3] Next to this comes the martyrology which Rosweyde was the first to print; which, however, is not a Roman one, as the editor and the Bollandists have stated.[4] It already contains the fable of Felix's martyrdom under Constantius. It is from this source, or from the legends, or from the book of the popes, that Ado has drawn; and the subsequent martyrologists for the most part have copied him. USUARD, NOTKER, RABANUS, WANDELBERT, follow in the same track.

S. EUSEBIUS, celebrated on the fourteenth of

---

[1] The *Calendarium Anglicanum* (of the year 1000) in MARTENE, *Coll. ampl.*, VI., 655. The *Martyrologium Morbacense* in MARTENE, *Thesaur.*, III., 1570.

[2] In MAI. *Coll.*, v., 63.

[3] *Epistolæ et Dissertt. Eccles.*, ed. Veron, 1733, p. 185. Exaratum intra tempora Gregorii II. and III., according to BORGIA, *de Cruce Vaticana*.

[4] See on this point the argument of FRONTO, l. c., p. 187.

August, is found in almost all calendars and martyrologies, with the exception of the oldest, which belongs to the fifth century. This one, however, mentions the church of S. Eusebius as already existing in Rome, because here was a "statio" on the Friday in the fourth week of Lent. In the martyrologies of S. Jerome, and in that of Bede, one reads at the fourteenth of August, "Eusebii tituli conditoris." From which it appears that his festival in the first instance was celebrated only in the church which he had built, thence passed into the Roman calendars, and from them into those of other countries. Nearer notices of him do not exist, and even from the sixth century and further were not to be found. Hence it was all the more easy for the intentional fiction, which aimed at distorting the history of Liberius and Felix, to make use of his name, and transform him into the hero of a tragedy, which should set forth the Arianism and cruelty of Liberius in strong colours.

This fiction, like others, originated in the Liber Pontificalis;

Here, then, as in other cases, it was the *Liber Pontificalis* that created the new tradition, which has influenced chroniclers and the papal biographers. The glaring contradictions of the *Liber Pontificalis*, which resulted from the unthinking interpolations of later hands, were at that time not observed. In the biography of Liberius, which was correctly composed before any one thought of giving Felix a special biographical article, Felix dies peacefully (requievit in pace) on his own estate, on the first of August. On the other hand, in the article respecting him, a few lines farther on, he is beheaded with many clergy and laity, on the eleventh of November. The author of this article, in order that nothing should be wanting for Felix's papal dignity, wished to represent him also as the builder of a church, and so represents him as again building the very "Basilica in viâ Aureliâ," which in the article on Felix the First (A.D. 269–275) had already been mentioned as Felix' work. All the following writers of papal history have therefore naturally followed this account;—PSEUDO-LUITPRAND, ABBO OF FLEURY, the anonymous chronographer in Pez,[1] MARTINUS POLONUS, LEO OF ORVIETO, BERNARD GUIDONIS, AMALRICUS AUGERII. Felix is set forth as the thirty-ninth rightful pope. The revelation of the secret, that Constantius had caused himself to be re-baptized by Eusebius of Nicomedia, costs him his life, and Liberius reigned for five years as an Arian, and by his Arianism caused the martyrdom of many clergy and laity. Nevertheless, all that he did and ordered was declared null and void after his death by Damasus. Bernard Guidonis makes the addition of a martyrdom, which Eusebius is made to endure, because he proclaimed Liberius to be a heretic.[2]

Which contradicts itself.

From that time onwards the theologians accom-

[1] *Thes. Anecd.*, I., p. 313. [2] In MAI, *Spicileg.*, VI., 60.

Theologians accept the fable and make the best of it.

modated themselves to the prevailing view, especially in Rome itself. Who does not know, says the Roman presbyter AUXILIUS, the defender of Formosus, that Liberius gave his assent to the Arian heresy, and that at his instigation the most horrible abominations were practised?[1] And towards the middle of the twelfth century ANSELM, BISHOP OF HAVELBERG, reproaches the Greeks, because Constantius had caused Felix to be put to death for revealing the fact of his second baptism. But he makes excuses for Liberius, who no doubt had allowed much that was heretical, but had nevertheless steadfastly refused to allow himself to be re-baptized.[2]

The ABBOT HUGO OF FLAVIGNY (1090–1102) goes a step farther in his chronicle; he makes Liberius also receive baptism a second time as a thorough[3] Arian. EKKEHARD, in his most influential chronicle,[4] ROMUALD OF SALERNO, the papal historian TOLOMEO OF LUCCA, the *Eulogium* of the monk of Malmesbury, all follow the usual fabulous tradition, that Liberius remained till the day of his death—six, or (according to Tolomeo[5]) eight years—persistently heretical, while Felix is the catholic martyr. Nevertheless, with MARIANUS SCOTUS, GOTTFRIED OF VITERBO, and ROBERT

---

[1] *De ordin.*, I., 25.
[2] *Dialog.*, III., 21, in D'ACHERY, *Specil.*, I., 207.
[3] In PERTZ, X., 301.
[4] PERTZ, VIII., 113.
[5] "Vixit in hoc errore annis octo."—MURATORI, *SS. It.*, XI., p. 833.

ABOLANT, the authority of Jerome is still so powerful, that they narrate how Felix was violently thrust into office by the Arians.

When at last the era of historical criticism and theological investigation came in with the sixteenth century, no small amount of helplessness was exhibited. Hitherto Felix had been regarded as rightful pope, and the time of his pontificate was reckoned at a year and somewhat more. According to this view, Liberius would be deprived of his office by sentence of the church, on account of his lapse into Arianism, and then Felix came in as rightful pope, until at the end of a year he suffered martyrdom. Liberius, however, is said to have survived him by several years, and to have remained an Arian till his death. He could not therefore again become lawful pope after the death of Felix. Nor was the hypothesis of a vacancy of the see for several years either admissible or attempted. On the contrary, an interregnum of thirty-eight days is all that the *Liber Pontificalis* records after the death of Felix. This created a difficulty for the theologians, of which they did not know how to dispose, if Felix was to be retained in his position as pope and saint; and the historians could not deny the irreconcileable contradiction to all contemporary information. Cardinal Baronius had already composed a treatise to show that Felix was neither a saint nor pope. Gregory XIII. had appointed a special congrega-

<small>Difficulties arising when the truth began to be known in the sixteenth century.</small>

tion to decide the question. And then (1582) during some excavations under an altar dedicated to SS. Cosmo and Damian, a body was found with an inscription on stone—" Corpus S. Felicis Papæ et Martyris qui condemnavit Constantium." The stone with the inscription vanished again soon afterwards, and SCHELSTRATE[1] laments that search was made for it in vain. The wording of the inscription in itself would have been quite sufficient to prove it at once to be the clumsy invention of a later age. But Baronius and the congregation thought otherwise; and so Felix kept his place as pope and martyr in the corrected Roman martyrology. Nevertheless, the place was[2] expunged from the subsequent editions of the older Roman breviaries, in which the martyrdom of Eusebius, for merely rebuking the Arianism of Liberius, was related in the words of Ado. Moreover in the Oratio of the breviary the designation of Felix as "pope" was removed. But even such a man as BOSSUET could allow himself, on the strength of documents so palpably forged, to represent Liberius as an obstinate heretic and bloody persecutor of true[3] catholics. Still he contends against Baronius, who had accepted the wholesale persecution and butchery of the catholics in Rome under Liberius as a literal fact.

To complete it all, in the year 1790, a Roman

margin notes: A forged inscription. Baronius, and even Bossuet countenance the fable.

---

[1] *Antiquit. illustr.*, I. [2] See Launoi, *Epist.* 5, p. 41.
[3] *Defens. decl. Gall.*, p. 3, l. 9, c. 33.

ecclesiastic, PAUL ANTON PAOLI,[1] undertook in a lengthy work to prove the legitimacy of Felix, and the authenticity of his sufferings and acts. He has succeeded, he says, in accomplishing the feat, hitherto considered an impossibility, of making *both* the rivals, Liberius and Felix, appear as innocent and guiltless, both of them together, as legitimate popes. All, according to him, rests upon misunderstandings and untrue reports. Athanasius, Hilary, Jerome, all their contemporaries, have been found to be in unintentional and unavoidable error. In Rome men were obliged to believe that the papal chair became vacant through Liberius's guilt, which, however, in reality was not the case, and hence Felix was elected. The Acts of Eusebius are genuine and contemporary. All the awkward statements which they contain are set aside by the convenient and never-failing resource of supposing them to be later interpolations. Moreover, the author has fortunately discovered that Felix lived concealed in the neighbourhood of Rome for thirty-four years after he was driven out of the city; although contemporaneous evidence makes him already dead in the year 365, and, although there was no conceivable reason for his concealment, after the death of Constantius.

The marvellous hypothesis of Paoli.

The whole is a structure of ill-conceived hypo-

---

[1] *Di san Felice Secondo Papa e Martire Dissertazzioni*, Roma, 1790. With a supplement of over 400 pages quarto.

theses and conjectures, which crumbles to dust at the first breath of sober historical investigation.

The case of Felix at last abandoned.
That Felix was never rightful bishop of Rome, but a mere tool of the Arians, foisted upon the people, and successfully rejected by them, has been admitted by all the better ecclesiastical historians, PANVINIUS, LUPUS, HERMANT, TILLEMONT, NATALIS ALEXANDER, FLEURY, BAILLET, COUTANT, CEILLIER. In Rome itself cardinal ORSI[1] has let his own view, which agrees with theirs, shine through, partly by a meaning silence, partly by the appellation "anti-"pope," which he gives to Felix, though he only mentions him once in passing. SACCARELLI[2] has shown, quite decisively and with correct judgment, that it is historically necessary to strike out Felix from the list of Roman bishops. Saccarelli's contemporary, the Augustinian monk BERTI, in one of his treatises on ecclesiastical history, has stated the reasons usually given for and against Felix having a place in the list of the popes in such a way, that he makes one sensible of the weakness of the *former*; and then[3] adds, as if by way of a

---

[1] *Istori. Eccles.*, VI., 201, ed. in 12mo.

[2] *Hist. Eccles.*, V., 334, Rome, 1777.

[3] " Hæret, ut aiunt, in aqua: neque enim tarditate ingenioli mei " percipere possum, quomodo, sedente Liberio, Felix verus Pontifex " sit habendus," etc.—*Historia Eccles. s. Dissertt. hist.*, III., 466, Aug. 1761. This reluctance to speak his meaning openly is easily explained by the fact, that cardinal LAMBERTINI (afterwards pope Benedict XIV.) in his work *De Canoniz. Sanctorum*, 1, 4, p. 2, c. 27, 14, had just maintained, to the no small astonishment of all who were acquainted with ecclesiastical antiquity, "De S. Felicis II. " sanctitate et martyrio nullam amplius superesse dubitationem, sed

joke, that he does not venture to decide. Later on, three other Roman authors, NOVAES, SANGALLO, and PALMA, the two first in their biographies of the popes, the last in his ecclesiastical history, have given up the case¹ of Felix as untenable.²

" disputari ab eruditis duntaxat de qualitate rationeque martyrii." When therefore cardinal BORGIA, in his *Apologia del Pontificato Benedetto X.*, says, " passa quasi per dimostrata a legittimità del ponti-" ficato di S. Felice per quelli che suppongono la caduta di Liberio," he is stating what is manifestly incorrect.

[1] NOVAES, *Elementi della Storia de' Sommi Pontefici*, Roma, 1821, 1, 128; SANGALLO, *Gest. de' Pontef.*, III., 496; PALMA, *Prælectiones Hist. Eccles.*, II., 129.

[2] [In the busts of the popes in the cathedral at Sienna the bust of Pope Joan has been transformed into pope Zacharias. (See p. 30.) Felix, however, retains his place there to this day.]

ANASTASIUS II—HONORIUS I

ANASTASIUS II—HONORIUS I

DANTE sees in hell, in the circle of false teachers and their followers, the cover of a large tomb, with an inscription stating that this tomb contains pope [1] Anastasius,

Strange that Dante should select Anastasius as an instance of an heretical pope.

"Whom out of the right way Photinus drew."

Now, it must always be a matter for astonishment that the great poet, when it occurred to him

---

[1] *Inf.*, XI., 9.

[E quivi per l' orribile soperchio
 Del puzzo, che 'l profondo abisso gitta
 Ci raccostammo dietro ad un coperchio
D'un grand' avello, ov' io vidi una scritta,
 Che diceva : " Anastagio Papa guardo,
 Lo qual trasse Fotino della via dritta "—XI., 4-9.

And there by reason of the horrible
 Excess of stench the deep abyss throws out,
 We drew ourselves aside behind the cover
Of a great tomb, whereon I saw a writing,
 Which said : " Pope Anastasius I hold,
 Whom out of the right way Photinus drew."
                                    Longfellow's Translation.

" The commentators are not agreed concerning the person who is " here mentioned as a follower of the heretical Photinus. By some he " is supposed to have been Anastasius II.; by others, IV.; while a " third set, jealous of the integrity of the papal faith, contend that to represent a pope as suffering the fate of a heretic, should have chosen precisely this one, one of the least known in the Roman list. One would have thought that Liberius or Honorius would have been much more ready to his hand for this purpose, the first especially, who, according to the account which prevailed everywhere in the Middle Ages, ruled at Rome for several years before his death as a notorious Arian, so that, as was supposed, ardent catholics died as martyrs because of him.

<small>This was due to the Decretum of Gratian.</small> It was GRATIAN'S *Decretum* which, directly or indirectly, determined the Florentine poet in his choice. That is to say, Gratian, after the preamble to the Ivonian decretal had inserted a passage from the Pontifical[1] book, in which it is said that

<small>"our poet has confounded him with Anastasius I., emperor of the East. Fazio degli Uberti, like our author, makes him a pope:—

"Anastasio papa in quel tempo era
"Di Fotin vago a mal grado de sui.—*Dittamondo*, II., 14."
            Cary's note in loco.

Those who would save the pope at the expense of the emperor say that Photinus died before the time of pope Anastasius II. Both pope and emperor were called heretical out of respect to the memory of Acacius. But the emperor need not be considered here; Dante probably knew what he meant, and when he says pope, means pope, and not emperor.]

[1] *Decret.*, I., dist. 19, 9. [Gratian's *Decretum* appeared at Bologna, the first school of law in Europe, about 1150. It combined the Isidorian forgeries with those of Deusdedit, Anselm, Gregory of Pavia, and Gratian himself. It displaced all the older collections of canon law, and became the usual manual for canonists and theologians. No book has ever had such influence in the Church, although it teems with errors, both intentional and unintentional. For further particulars, see JANUS, *Der Papst und das Concil.*, III., p. 154-162.]</small>

many persons in Rome separated themselves from the company of pope Anastasius, because he had entered into church communion with the deacon Photinus of Thessalonica, and had intended secretly to bring Acacius again into honour in the church. For which reason God had punished him with sudden death. Throughout the Middle Ages Gratian's *Decretum*[1] was accounted a decisive authority; it did not easily occur to any one to doubt the facts and doctrines stated in it; and hence it comes to pass that the memory of pope Anastasius II. has come down to posterity as that of a man prone to heresy, from whose communion in the Church it was right to withdraw oneself, pope though he was; and only by his sudden death was still greater mischief warded off from the Church. Now what was there to justify this view? *What grounds are there for calling Anastasius a heretic?*

The Byzantine emperors were perpetually finding themselves impelled by the political condition of the empire to endeavour to reconcile the powerful party of the Monophysites to the Church, and thus heal, not merely an ecclesiastical, but also a political disorder, and ward off the grave danger which was threatening the state. With this object, the emperor Zeno, advised by Acacius, patriarch of Constantinople, had published the *Henoticon*

[1] [It became *comparatively* obsolete after Gregory IX. caused the five books of Decretals to be published by Raimond de Pennafort in 1234. It was, in fact, insufficient for the increasing usurpations of the popes.]

(482), which declared the binding authority and dogmatic decisions of the council of Chalcedon, so hateful to all Monophysites, to be an open question. This ended in pope Felix II. calling a synod, and declaring Acacius anathema. Acacius himself certainly remained all the while catholic in his doctrine, but he sacrificed the council of Chalcedon for the sake of peace, and entered into church communion with all Monophysites who had accepted the *Henoticon*. Acacius had almost the whole East on his side, and as Rome broke off from every one who remained in communion with Acacius, a schism in the Church between East and West for thirty-five years was the consequence.

The successors of Acacius were bidden to strike his name off the diptychs as one who had died under excommunication; and the popes Felix and Galasius demanded this as a condition of communion. This, however, the patriarchs dared not do, for fear of a popular commotion; and Rome would not give way, although Galasius himself confessed, that the expectation, that the Orientals would prefer communion with the See of Rome to every other consideration, had proved[1] a delusion.

To heal a schism between the East and the West, The separation had lasted already eleven years, when pope Anastasius ascended the papal throne. He had peace with the Eastern Church more at heart than his two predecessors had had. He did,

---

[1] *Concilia*, ed. Labbé, IV., 1173.

therefore, what Gelasius had refused to do, even at the request of the patriarch Euphemius; he sent two bishops as his legates to Constantinople, still, however, contending that the name of Acacius must no more be mentioned at the altar. In a contemporaneous Roman fragment mention is made of the letter which the pope sent at the time to the emperor. The reader will thence see on what worthless grounds the still continuing schism between the East and the West[1] rested. At this point Photinus arrived in Rome, a man who seems to have been active in ecclesiastical negotiations, and who probably had received a commission from the Orientals to win the pope over to the cause of union. Anastasius admitted him to communion, although from the Roman point of view he belonged to the schismatical party, that is to say, remained in alliance with those who honoured the memory of Acacius. And the pope showed himself[2] ready to give way in the

Anastasius consented to disregard the excommunication of Acacius pronounced by former popes.

[1] In BLANCHINI, Notæ varior. ad Anastas. III., 209.

[2] The expression of the biographer in the Pontifical book "occulte "voluit revocare Acacium," is to be understood of the re-insertion of his name in the diptychs. "Id nonnisi de illius nomine sacris " diptychis restituendo intelligi potest," says VIGNOLI (Liber. Pontif., 1, 171) quite rightly. Cardinal MAI, following in the track of many others (BARONIUS, BELLARMINE, SOMMIER, &c.), says in his note to Bernard Guidonis (Spicil., VI., 98), that the statement in the Pontifical book cannot be true; Anastasius cannot have cherished the intention of securing for the name of Acacius mention in the liturgy, because he, like his predecessors, in the letter which he sent to the emperor immediately after his promotion to the papacy, had demanded that this name should be suppressed. But, in matters of history, it can scarcely be thought possible to build on such weak

question of mentioning Acacius's name at the altar, and thus renounce the haughty bearing which, as exemplified in the conduct of his predecessors, had given such offence to the East. But in Rome, where it was considered a duty and point of honour not to depart from the path of Felix and Gelasius, this excited great displeasure; and it came to a formal separation from Anastasius, for being willing to sacrifice the righteous cause

arguments. Certainly Anastasius *did* do this in the first few weeks of his pontificate, on entering upon the heritage of his predecessors. But what can be more natural than that a peace-loving pope, having become convinced of the impractibility of his own hard requisition, one which shocked the feelings of millions [nearly the whole East remained true to Acacius], should have shown a disposition to renounce a demand, with the surrender of which not a single essential principle of church discipline was surrendered. If it was possible in the case of a man, who for a hundred and thirty years after his death had remained in the enjoyment of church communion and intercession (Theodore of Mopsuestia), at last to expel him, when men became convinced of the fundamental heterodoxy of his writings, it surely was possible, in the case of a bishop, who had always acknowledged catholic dogma, and had only erred in a formal way, and under very extenuating circumstances, to release him after his death from the anathema which had been pronounced on him, when on this act of clemency depended the well-being and peace of the whole Church.

[The anathema against Acacius had been pronounced by Felix in an unusually strong form. It was declared to be irreversible by any power, even by Felix himself: "Nunquamque anathematis vinculis "eruendus."—*Epist. Felic. ad Acacium.* In a subsequent letter to Zeno Felix maintains this inexorable position: "Unde divino judicio "nullatenus potuit, *etiam quum id mallemus*, absolvi."—*Epist.* XI. Writing to Fravitta, who succeeded Acacius in a brief patriarchate of four months, Felix intimates that Acacius is doubtless with Judas in hell. But the anathema was almost a brutum fulmen in the East. Acacius maintained his patriarchate till his death, and the other three patriarchs of Antioch, Alexandria, and Jerusalem remained in communion with him.—MILMAN's *Latin Christianity*, bk. III., c. i.]

of the Roman See, the authority of his predecessors, and the validity of the Chalcedonian decrees for the sake of an insecure peace. The premature and unexpected death of the pope at this position of affairs was regarded by those who had separated from him as a providential deliverance of the Church from very great danger.

The later commentators on Dante—POGGIALI, LOMBARDI, and TOMMASEO—think that Dante, misled by Martinus Polonus, has confused pope Anastasius with the emperor, his contemporary and namesake. This, as one sees, is not the case.[1] PHILALETHES also thinks that, as Acacius had already been dead some time, the whole story rests on an error; that is to say, he supposes that the author of the Pontifical book means one to understand the still-living Acacius, because he makes use of the expression (explained in the note) "to recall" [revocare Acacium]. There is, however, no necessity for this adoption of a glaring anachronism. It is certainly a disfiguring blot in Dante's sublime creation that he has placed an innocent and doctrinally blameless pope, whose desire for peace would have been accounted as a high merit in another age, in hell with the eternally lost heretics. But the error, into which the greatest of Christian poets thus fell, lay not in the historical fact, but in the judgment respecting the fact; and this erroneous judgment Dante shared

Dante's error is lamentable, but he shared it with his generation.

---

[1] *Dante's Divine Comedy*, Dresden, 1839, I., 69.

Anastasius is moreover made to die a horrible death.

with his contemporaries, and with the Middle Ages generally.

In the Pontifical book it is stated, that Anastasius was not able to accomplish his intention with regard to Acacius,[1] because death overtook him as a judgment from heaven. This statement is not sufficient for the chroniclers of the thirteenth and fourteenth centuries. The catastrophe must be more distinctly marked, and the fate which overtook the heretical pope must be such as to excite horror and disgust. They transferred, therefore, the story of the sudden death of Arius to Anastasius. He had gone aside to satisfy a call of nature, and was found afterwards with his intestines out. So MARTINUS POLONUS, AMALRICH AUGERII, BERNARD GUIDONIS.[2] Dante's commentators in the fourteenth century have followed

---

[1] Cardinal MAI also, following in the steps of BELLARMINE, BARONIUS, and NOVAES, maintains that the author of the *Liber Pontificalis* would lead one to suppose that the pope was struck by lightning, and that this was a confusion with the emperor Anastasius, who had met with this kind of death. Entirely without foundation. The Pontifical book does not say one word about lightning. Nothing more than this is conveyed in what it says; that the pope, owing to his opportune, and, as it were, divinely sent death, was prevented from carrying out his ruinous intention. And that the emperor of like name was killed by a flash of lightning is a late fable, unknown to his contemporaries or to the next generation, and at the time when the biography of pope Anastasius was written was not invented. —Conf. TILLEMONT, *Hist. des Empereurs*, VI., 585.

[2] The papal biographer, DU PEYRAT, on the contrary, contents himself with saying, "Anastasius damnatus est et reprobatus."— *Notices et extraits*, VI. [Anastasius, the Librarian (*Patrol.* CXXVIII., 439), says that the pope, in punishment for his error, "nutu divino "percussus est."— ROBERTSON, *Hist. of the Christian Church*, I., p. 527.]

them. According to them Acacius is the associate (compagno) of Photinus, and canon of Thessalonica; but Photinus seduced the pope into denying the divinity of Christ. A great disputation between the pope and the cardinals, bishops, and prelates, who rebuked him for his false doctrine,[1] precedes the catastrophe. The gloss to the *Decretum* makes the pope struck with leprosy.

It was Gratian therefore, mainly, who fixed the judgment of the Middle Ages respecting Anastasius. This pope,[2] he says, is rejected by the Church of Rome. So says also the anonymous writer of Zwetl in his history of the popes. "The "Church[3] rejects him and God smote him." The gloss adds that two popes, Gelasius and Hormisdas, excommunicated him. The fact that Gelasius was Anastasius' *predecessor* was overlooked.[4] But it was now hereby established, as a certain fact, that Anastasius was an heretical pope; and so he was henceforth usually quoted along with Liberius as a second instance of papal heresy. Since Gratian's

Gratian's influence fixed the character of Anastasius as heretical.

---

[1] So the "false Boccaccio," or the *Chiose sopra Dante*, composed in 1375, Florence, 1846, p. 87, and the Latin commentary published by NANNUCCI under the name of PETRUS ALLEGHERIUS, Florent., 1845, p. 137; and then the *Ultimo Commento*, p. 199, which confuses Photinus with the heterodox bishop of the fourth century. So also FRANCESCO DA BUTI, *Commento*, I., 301. Where GRAUL, *Dante's Hölle*, p. 116, found the story that Anastasius denied the divine nature of Christ I do not know.

[2] "Ideo ab Ecclesia Romana repudiatur."—*Distinc.*, 19, c. 8.

[3] Ap. PEZ, *thesaur. Anecd.*, I., p. 3, 351.

[4] [Felix II., A.D. 483   Symmachus, A.D. 498
Gelasius I.   „ 492   Hormisdas   „ 514.]
Anastasius II. „ 496

time theologians were accustomed to appeal to the chapter "Anastasius" in the *Decretum* and to the gloss on it, when they discussed the question of heretical error in a pope, and of the conduct of the Church in such circumstances. The schoolman, ALGER[1] OF LIEGE (about A.D. 1150), must certainly have had other sources than Gratian before him when he asserted that pope Anastasius was condemned along with his Decree, because in it he had declared that the baptisms and ordinations performed by Acacius after the sentence which had passed on him at Rome were valid. In this[2] he contradicted the decisions of his predecessors. Alger here agrees in the main with his contemporary GRATIAN. Gratian has quoted the declaration of Anastasius,—according to which the efficacy of sacraments is not dependent on the character of the dispenser, and, consequently, even the sacraments administered by a bishop who has

---

[1] *Liber de misericordia et justitia*, c. 59. In MARTENE, *thes. Anecd.*, v., 1127.

[2] Alger himself does not mean, as he afterwards explains, that the sacraments administered by Acacius were forthwith null and void. He distinguishes thus: "Quod vera, quamvis non rata pos-"sint esse sacramenta cujuslibet mali sacerdotis, vel hæretici, vel "damnati."—c. 83. But he fancies that Anastasius erroneously declared that the sacraments administered by Acacius were "rata." That is to say, he starts from the principle which certain short-sighted defenders of papal supremacy had already put forth; that a pope who became heretical, immediately, and before even he had in any way made known his heretical opinions, ceased to be pope, and hence all that he subsequently did was null and void. In which case the Church, which, nevertheless, could not possibly do otherwise than recognise him all the while, would find itself in unavoidable error.

lapsed into heresy are valid, and under proper conditions efficacious,—as an instance of a false decision in matters of faith given by a pope, respecting which, the Roman correctors have since contradicted him.[1]

On the other hand, WILLIAM OF SAINT-AMOUR (about A.D. 1245) confuses Anastasius with Liberius. He knows nothing more than that in the time of Hilary, a pope lapsed into heresy, of whom it is recorded "nutu divino fuit percussus;" and he conjectures[2] that this may have been Anastasius II., mentioned by Gratian.

ALVARO PELAYO, who, next to AUGUSTINE OF ANCONA, furthered the aggrandisement of the papal power, with the greatest zeal, beyond all previous bounds, and almost beyond all limits whatever, in his great work on the condition of the Church, makes mention of the judgment[3] which came upon Anastasius, in order to prove his dictum, that an heretical pope must receive a far heavier sentence than any other. OCCAM,[4] also, makes use of the "heretical" Anastasius as an instance to prove, what was his main point, that the Church erred by his recognition. The council of Basle in like manner, with a view to establishing the necessary supremacy of an œcumenical council

Anastasius confused with Liberius.

Occam uses him as an argument.

---

[1] *Decret. distinc.*, 19, c. 7, 8.
[2] *Opera*, ed. Cordes. Constantiæ (Parisiis), 1632, p. 96.
[3] "Divino judicio percussus fuit, nam dum assellaret, intestina "emisit."—*De planctu ecclesiæ*, 2, 10, Venetiis, 1560, II., 38.
[4] *Opus nonaginta dierum.*, Lugd., 1495, f. 124.

over the pope, did not fail to appeal to the fact, that popes who did not obey the Church were treated by her as heathens and publicans, as one reads of Liberius and Anastasius.[1]

He is classed with Liberius as an heretical pope.

"The pope," says DOMENICUS DEI DOMENICI, bishop of Torcello, somewhat later, in a letter addressed to pope Calixtus III. (1455-1458), "the pope by himself alone is not an infallible rule of faith, for some popes have erred in faith, as, for example, Liberius and Anastasius II., and the latter was in consequence punished by God."[2] After him the Belgian JOHN LE MAIRE, also, says (about 1515), Liberius and Anastasius are the two popes of ancient times, who, subsequent to the Donation of Constantine, obtained an infamous reputation in the Church as heretics.[3]

Opposite fate of Honorius.

Whilst Anastasius, most undeservedly, was counted as a heretic, the memory of HONORIUS, on the other hand, was held in honour; and the fact that a general council had pronounced an anathema on this pope for holding heterodox opinions and countenancing heresy, was in the Middle Ages usually ignored. The circumstances were as follows: The Monothelite heresy was a danger-

---

[1] Ap. HARDUIN, VIII., 1327.

[2] *De Cardinalium legit. creat. tract.*, in M. A. DE DOMINIS, *De Republ. eccl.*, Londini, 1617, I., 767 ss.

[3] "In hæresin prolapsus est, et reputatur pro secundo Papa infami post donationem Constantini."—*De Schismatum et Concil. differ.*, Argentor, 1609, p. 594.

ous and unhappy attempt to reunite the Monophysites with the Church by means of a very comprehensive concession, devised and introduced into the Church by certain Oriental prelates; who herein had probably an understanding with the emperor Heraclius, and were acting in accordance with his wishes. The point of difference was this: The council of Chalcedon had declared that the two natures in Christ are united without any confusion or changing of one into the other; there must, therefore, be also a duality of wills, and a human and a divine will be distinguished in Christ. The Monophysites, on their side consistent, made the human will vanish in the presence of the divine, allowing to the Logos alone in Christ the full exercise of the power of volition. The Monothelites, who had formed themselves into a middle party, having for its object the reconciliation of the Monophysites with the Church, on this point agreed with the latter; and thus Cyrus, in Alexandria, brought about a union between the followers of Severus there and the Catholics. Sergius, patriarch of Constantinople, who had an understanding with Cyrus, sought and obtained the assent of pope Honorius against the opposition raised by Sophronius. The manner in which the pope and the two patriarchs of Constantinople and Alexandria held essentially the same view, was this: Honorius had declared, quite in the sense of the other two, that the two decisive texts, in

[margin: Monothelitism an attempted compromise between Monophysitism and the Church.]

which the human and created will is most clearly distinguished from and opposed to the divine will of the Logos, are merely an "economy" in Christ's mode of speaking, that is to say, an accommodation to be taken only in a figurative sense, by means of which Christ merely intended to exhort us to submit our own wills to the divine will. He was compelled therefore, equally with the Orientals, to recognise only a single will in Christ, the divine or theandric, that is, a will having its source in the Logos, and, as it were, merely *flowing through* the human nature—a will in which merely the Logos is the willing power and active principle, while the human nature is purely passive; so that its power of volition is either non-existent, or, at any rate, quiescent. And this he said in so many words: "We recognise," says he, conceding the point to Sergius, but expressing himself with more decision than Sergius, "we recognise one "will in Christ." And thereupon Honorius, like the Monothelites of the East, troubled himself with the notion, that a human will, as belonging to man's sinful nature, must always strive against the Divine; whereas the idea was not far to seek, that the human will, having its root in the sinless nature of Christ, conformed to the divine will, so that a moral unity co-existed with an actual duality of will.

Honorius confessedly a Monothelite.

On the other hand, Honorius, taking the word "energy" (i.e. mode of operation), which had

Honorius's peculiar use of the term "energy."

been used by the Greeks, in a sense altogether different from theirs, gave as his decision, that one ought not to speak either of one or of two energies; for that Christ, by virtue of His one theandric will, showed many modes of operation and activity. Therefore there is unity of will, says Honorius, for it is the Person that wills, and not the natures, and there is multiplicity (not unity, nor duality) of energies or modes of operation. In this way, then, Honorius would have the controversy put down; viz., that it was preposterous to contest about one or two energies in Christ, because neither the one nor the other expression could be used in a rational sense. At the same time, however, it was set forth that all men should be united in the acceptance of a single power of volition. The emperor Constantine stated subsequently in his edict, that Honorius had not only taught false doctrine, but also contradicted himself, merely because he, being used to the oriental terminology, did not understand the sense in which Honorius used the word "energy." Honorius meant by it, *manifestations of activity in the Person*, which are many and various. But the emperor understood by it, *modes of operation in the natures*, of which there must be two, or (according to the Monothelites), on account of the unity of will, only one.

This doctrine of Honorius, so welcome to Sergius and the remaining favourers and supporters of Monothelitism, led to the two imperial edicts, the *Ekthesis* and the *Typus*. It led to them to this extent, that Heraclius was thereby justified in concluding that the Roman See would not oppose such a doctrinal decree as the *Ekthesis*; and the *Typus* of Constans was nothing more than a weaker echo of the *Ekthesis*. The result, however, was different from what had been hoped at Constantinople. The whole East rose up in arms against the new doctrine, and it forthwith became evident that Honorius, with his mode of understanding the question, stood alone in Rome and in the West. For some time efforts were made to excuse Honorius. Pope John IV. (A.D. 640–642) stated in his[1] apology that his predecessor had merely rejected the fond notion of two *mutually opposing* wills; as if, that is to say, Christ had had a will tainted with sin. No doubt the fear, that in admitting the double will one would be irresistibly driven on to accept two mutually opposing wills, was a very considerable element in the declaration of Honorius; only it remains a riddle how a man, who certainly had no Monophysite tendencies, could allow himself to be influenced by so unfounded an apprehension. The excuse

---

[1] MANSI, X., 683. [Severinus, the immediate successor of Honorius, had a brief pontificate of only three months; and appears to have rejected the Ekthesis. John IV. did so in solemn council. Heraclius thereupon wrote to the pope to 'disown the document, saying that he had only published it at the urgent request of Sergius.—ROBERTSON, *Church History*, II., 45.]

which MAXIMUS, appealing to the statement of the papal secretary, brings forward for Honorius is still more forced and untenable. Honorius, he says, only wished to guard against the supposition of two *human* and mutually[1] opposed wills. Manifestly the pope had never thought of any such absurdity. Rather his decision and the cause of his error may be briefly expressed thus: One Willer, therefore one will; for the will is the attribute of the Person, not of the natures.

<small>Some of them absurd.</small>

Honorius had written again to Sergius to the same effect, as well as to Cyrus and Sophronius, and hence it was quite natural that he should come to be regarded as one of the supporters of Monothelitism. The patriarch Pyrrhus [successor of Sergius at Constantinople] had accordingly appealed to him; and, at the Lateran synod in the year 649, the writings of the Monothelites, which claimed for themselves the authority of Honorius, were read out. No one there spoke a word in defence of Honorius. Complete silence was observed respecting him, although the five prelates who were accounted as the originators and main supporters of the false doctrine—Theodore of Pharan, Cyrus of Alexandria, Sergius, Pyrrhus and Paul, patriarchs of Constantinople—were condemned by pope Martin and the synod.

At last came the decisive council of A.D. 680. And here took place what preceding events would

[1] MANSI, X., 687, 691, 739.

Honorius anathematised at the council of A.D. 680.

lead one to expect. Honorius, as a partaker in the Monothelite heresy, was treated in the same way as the other prelates who had already been condemned at Rome, along with them was placed under anathema, and the council insisted upon cursing "the heretic Honorius" by name. He joined himself, it is stated in the decree, in all particulars to Sergius; he spread the heresy of the one will abroad among the people; he deserved to be placed under the same anathema as Sergius, for his dogmatic writings were completely opposed to the doctrine of the apostles and decisions of councils, tending towards the same godlessness as the writings of the most pronounced Monothelites. The emperor Constantine [IV., Pogonatus] in particular, who had taken a[1] very active part at the council, expressed himself to this effect in the letter which he wrote to the pope. And in the edict which was affixed to the great church of the capital, it was said of Honorius that in all points he was[2] to be treated like Sergius and Theodore, as "the companion and associate of "heretics and the sanctioner of heresy." The council[3] itself, after subjecting the writings of

[1] [There were eighteen sessions, lasting from Nov. 7th, 680, to Sept. 16th, 681. The emperor presided in person at the first eleven sessions, and at the eighteenth. In his absence the president's chair was left empty. The number of bishops increased gradually to nearly two hundred.]

[2] MANSI, XI., 697-712. ["Qui fuit cum eis in omnibus cohæreticus "et concurrens et confirmator hæresis."—HARDUIN, III., 1638.]

[3] ["Duas igitur in eo naturales voluntates (φυσικὰ θελήματα), et "duas naturales operationes (φυσικὰς ἐνεργείας), communiter atque

Sergius and Honorius to a careful investigation, declared respecting the two men, " whose godless " doctrine we abominate, whose names we have " deemed it necessary to cast out of the church."

About the intention of the council, to condemn Honorius for actual heresy, and not merely for weakness or negligence or imprudence in his mode of contending against heresy, there cannot therefore exist a doubt. And yet it is certain that he was not heretical in the strict sense of the term; though assuredly it is equally clear that Cyrus, Sergius, Pyrrhus, and Paul were neither more heretical than Honorius, nor less so. The question at issue was one which had not been raised or discussed before, but then for the first time occupied men's minds; a question in which the danger of falling into one of two opposite errors—Nestorianism or Monophysitism—was very imminent. In such cases a certain amount of time and of controversy is always needed, in order that the consciousness of the church may find its bearings and define itself. In the primitive church the erroneous enunciations of individual bishops on questions which had not yet been decided and

<small>No doubt that the council condemned him for actual heresy.</small>

" indivisè procedentes prædicamus; superfluas autem vocum novi-
" tates, et harum adinventores procul ab ecclesiasticis septis abjici-
" mus, et anathemati merito subjicimus; id est, Theodorum Pharani-
" tanum, Sergium et Paulum, Pyrrhum simul et Petrum, qui Con-
" stantinopoleos præsulatum tenuerunt, insuper et Cyrum, qui
" Alexandrinorum sacerdotium gessit, et cum eis Honorium, qui
" fuit Romæ præsul, utpote qui eos in his secutus est."—LABBE, Concil., VI., 1053; HARDUIN, Concil., III., 1422.]

formulated by the Church were treated with gentleness and forbearance, especially if such men had died in communion and peace with the Church. But after the fifth great council, A.D. 553, had set the example in anathematising Theodore of Mopsuestia,—not merely his writings, but himself,— and the popes after some opposition had accepted this, and at last carried it into effect through the whole West, the case was altogether altered. In the synod of 649 [First Lateran] five prelates had been condemned in Rome as Monothelites, among them three who were already dead. One of these was the patriarch of Constantinople, Paul II., who had written to pope Theodore to say that he followed the doctrine of Honorius, and who had thereupon accepted the *Typus* of the emperor Constans. The *Typus*, however, did not go so far as the letter of Honorius; for while this declared expressly for the doctrine of one will, the *Typus* merely commanded silence about the whole question. That the Orientals assembled at the sixth council would not allow the reproach and disgrace of heresy to fall exclusively on the heads of their own patriarchs, but seized the opportunity, not altogether unwillingly, of making the patriarch of old Rome, as he was then called, appear for once among the guilty, was only human nature. And the papal legates, who had just before made a protest respecting a charge of false teaching brought against pope Vigilius, could make neither formal

The papal legates made no protest, but voted for the anathema on Honorius.

nor material objection to the law taking its full course, when the case of Honorius came to be treated; and were therefore obliged to join in voting for his condemnation. And yet the inflexible Monothelites at the council, Macarius, patriarch of Antioch, the monk Stephen, and the two bishops of Nicomedia and Klaneus, had just before declared that they had promulgated no innovation, but merely the doctrine which they had learnt from Honorius and the patriarchs. The assembled Fathers had no alternative, but either to excuse all the six deceased originators and favourers of Monothelitism, or to condemn them all. The Lateran council had rendered the first course impossible; and the Roman legates would probably have protested against a decision which would have compelled the Western Church to make a sentence pronounced by itself in a large synod of no effect. Hence the second course was all that remained.

The reception which the decree would meet with in old Rome might well be watched with anxiety in the new imperial city. A new and hitherto unheard of event had taken place. A pope had been condemned as heretical by an œcumenical council, and the Romans were required to strike out his name, which no one hitherto had thought of aspersing, from the Church's intercessions. Pope Agatho had made an attempt to avoid the threatening blow. With-

Vain attempt of pope Agatho to save Honorius.

out mentioning his predecessor, he had in his letter given utterance to the general assurance, that the Roman See had never swerved from the path of apostolic tradition, never allowed itself to be tainted with heretical innovations. The council answered this with the counter-statement, that they had passed judgment upon the condemned theologians, Honorius included, in accordance with the sentence originally pronounced by Agatho. It was, however, precisely Honorius who had been passed over by Agatho in his letter.

Agatho meanwhile had died at Rome;[1] and the task of speaking out respecting the condemnation of Honorius fell on his successor, Leo II., who had translated the acts of the council from the Greek. Leo saw that both prudence and justice required him to recognise the judgment of the council, that an attempt still to draw a distinction between Honorius and the Oriental bishops had no longer any prospect of success. He therefore sent an acknowledgment to the emperor, containing an express condemnation of Honorius, because[2] "in- "stead of enlightening the Roman Church with "apostolic doctrine, he had surrendered its primi- "tive spotlessness to be defiled by an impious "betrayal of the faith (profana perfidia)." This

Leo II. confirms the anathema.

---

[1] [January, 682, while his legates were still at Constantinople.]
[2] ["Necnon Honorium, qui hanc apostolicam ecclesiam non apos- "tolicæ traditionis doctrina lustravit, sed profana proditione imma- "culatam fidem subvertere conatus est."—HARDUIN, *Concil.*, III., 1475.]

was going almost beyond what was warranted by historical fact. Honorius, as it happened, was the only person in Rome who cherished the doctrine laid down in his letter; nothing is known of any other convert which the Monothelite doctrine had made in Rome. However, in his letter to the Spanish bishops and king Erwig, Leo noticed the transgression of his predecessor in less strong expressions. According to this,[1] Honorius had merely allowed the pure doctrine to be falsified or tainted with error. He had merely been wanting in watchfulness and foresight. In this, however, he altogether contradicted the declaration of Agatho, that all popes had done their duty with regard to false doctrine.

That the circumstance was looked upon in Rome as a mortifying humiliation in the eyes of the Byzantines was natural. Nevertheless, after the decision of the council, no further attempt was made to withdraw the fact from notice, even in the West. On the contrary, as if it was desired to give it the greatest possible publicity, it was inserted in the confession of faith which every newly-elected pope had to sign. Thus it is found in the *Liber Diurnus*,[2] the official book of formulas

No attempt made in Rome to conceal the fact.

---

[1] ["Cum Honorio, qui flammam hæretici dogmatis non, ut decuit apostolicam auctoritatem, incipientem extinxit, sed negligendo confovit."—*Epistola ad Episcopos Hispaniæ.* "Et una cum eis Honorius Romanus, qui immaculatam apostolicæ traditionis regulam quam a prædecessoribus suis suscepit, maculari consentit."—*Epistola ad Erwigium Regem Hispaniæ*, Ap. HARDUIN, *Concil.*, III., 1730, 1735.]

[2] Ed. Garnerii, Paris, 1680, p. 41.

The Liber Diurnus requires every pope to confirm the anathema.

of the Roman Church at that time, intended for the use of the papal curia. The sixth œcumenical council, at which pope Agatho presided in the person of his legates, is here noticed with explicitness of detail. Then follows, after an exposition of the doctrine of two wills, the condemnation of those who opposed the doctrine. Sergius, Pyrrhus, Paul, and Peter, the four patriarchs of Constantinople, together with Honorius, who assented to and promoted (fomentum impendit) their false doctrine, are anathematised together with Theodore and Cyrus.

Marked silence of the Liber Pontificalis.

All the more astonishing is it that the other official work of the Roman Church at that time, the Pontifical book, maintains an unmistakeable and anxiously careful silence respecting all that concerns the part taken by Honorius in the Monothelite controversy and his condemnation. And yet in other respects it contains good and contemporary accounts of this period. First under the popes Theodore and Martin, the appearance of Pyrrhus in Rome, the dispute with Paul about the *Typus*, the Lateran council of A.D. 649, and the tragical end of pope Martin, are all noticed. The biographer of Agatho in this collection evidently had the diary before him, which was kept by the papal legates sent to the council of A.D. 680. These legates, among whom[1] were three bishops, relate

[1] [Abundantius, bishop of Paterneum, John, bishop of Portus, John, bishop of Rhegium, together with the sub-deacon Constantine, the presbyters Theodore and Gregory, and the deacon John.]

that it was they themselves who had challenged the Monothelites at the council to produce the authority of the Apostolic See, to which they appealed.[1] Thereupon the delighted Monothelites laid before the council the letter of pope Vigilius to Mennas. Investigation, however, showed that the passage in point had been interpolated. Not a word about the fact that the Monothelites had above all appealed to Honorius, that the two letters of Honorius, both in Latin and Greek, had been laid before the council, examined, and rejected as heretical. Either the legates have suppressed all this, because they had received very different instructions from Agatho, which they found it impossible to follow at the council, or the compiler of this portion of the Pontifical book, in copying their diary, has omitted all that relates to Honorius. Seeing that the legates produced the acts of the council, and the canons which they themselves had signed, including the condemnation of Honorius, one would rather suppose that the latter alternative was the fact; the more so inasmuch as the compilation, or at any rate the last revision of this part of the Pontifical book, was probably conducted by Anastasius the librarian, who two hundred years after the event, in his letter to the Roman deacon John, took great pains to try and excuse Honorius. The contents of Honorius's letter he did not venture to justify, as later apo-

Either the legates have suppressed the truth,

or, more probably, the compiler of this part of the book has done so.

[1] *Liber Pontificalis*, I., 279, ed. VIGNOLI.

logists[1] of this pope have done; but, says he, we cannot be certain that the secretary did not possibly misunderstand the pope's dictation, or arbitrarily alter the words out of malevolence or caprice. He bethinks himself, however, that this secretary was a very holy man, the abbot John; and now he directs his indignation against the sixth council itself, which, contrary to the command of scripture, had condemned a man who was voiceless and defenceless in his grave;—quite forgetting that the Roman synod of A.D. 649 had done precisely the same in the case of five prelates. The dogmatic decisions of the council were no doubt binding as a rule of faith; but just as the Roman See had rejected the twenty-eighth canon of the council of Chalcedon without detriment to the dogmatic authority of that assembly, so, he thinks, it is possible to reject also the sentence pronounced on Honorius. Did Anastasius not know what Leo II. had done, what stood written in the pope's confession of faith? The only thing in point which he produces is the remark, that no doubt the council condemned Honorius as a heretic, but that, properly speaking, no one could be called a heretic who did not add to his error contentious obstinacy (contentiosa pertinacia).

The silence in the biography of Agatho has nevertheless not prevented the biographer of

Honorius defended at the expense of the council.

---

[1] [For example, the archbishops of Westminster and Baltimore in their recent pastoral letters. The archbishop of Malines also in his controversy with Père Gratry. See Appendix F.]

Leo II., in the very same Pontifical book, from citing the name of Honorius under the head of those who were condemned by the sixth council as Monothelites; and as the lessons for S. Leo's day were taken word for word from this biography, the condemnation of Honorius has been transferred to the older versions of the Roman breviary, no doubt without the following point being observed.

In the East it was natural frequently to recur to the condemnation of Honorius, without, however, exactly calling attention to it as anything extraordinary and astonishing. The patriarchs Tarasius of Constantinople, and Theodore of Jerusalem, mentioned him at the time of the seventh council[1] (A.D. 787) under the head of those who were condemned for Monothelitism; so also the deacon Epiphanius.[2] It occurred to no one to make a difference between him and the other Monothelite leaders who were condemned for heresy. Pope Hadrian II. specially remarked in the letter of his which is appended to the acts of the eighth council, that Honorius was accused and condemned on account of heresy; and moreover, that his condemnation had taken place only in consequence of the Roman See having given its assent.[3]

The anathema on Honorius treated in the East as a matter of course.

It is HINCMAR OF RHEIMS who mentions the

---

[1] [Of Nicæa, which anathematised the Iconoclasts, and restored image-worship.]
[2] *Concilia*, ed. LABBE, VII., 166, 182, 422.
[3] See GARNIER's note to the *Liber Diurnus*, p. 41.

affair of Honorius for the last time in the West, adding the remark, that he must have deserved anathema in his life, otherwise those who sat in judgment upon him would have harmed themselves rather than[1] him. After him the recollection of the circumstance perished in the western churches. Of course, in the notices of the sixth council, as they existed in this or that chronicle, and in the Roman breviary, the name of Honorius, without further explanation, was still read along with the rest who had been condemned by this council. But seeing that all these others were Orientals, that the Monothelite controversy had left no traces behind it in the West, and that none of the historical works in general use in the Middle Ages contained any particulars of the Monothelite question, it occurred to no one any more that in the Honorius thus expelled from communion with the Church was to be understood a pope. Beyond everything else the silence of the Pontifical book decided the point in this direction. Hence it came to pass that not one of the numerous compilers of histories and lists of popes gave even the slightest hint of so remarkable a circumstance, one quite unique in its kind. The PSEUDO-LUITPRAND, ABBO, MARTINUS POLONUS, LEO OF ORVIETO, BERNARD GUIDONIS, GERVASIUS RICCOBALD OF FERRARA, AMALRICH AUGERII—all these writers of

---

[1] In the treatise *De una et non trina Deitate*, cf. CHMEL *Vindiciæ Concil.*, VI., Prague, 1777, p. 137.

histories of the popes are silent. They are able sometimes to relate about him what is somewhat unimportant, such as small liturgical directions; they mention that Leo II., understanding Greek, translated the Acts of the sixth council into Latin. But an event, which in Rome itself had appeared so important that it had been expressly included in the popes' confession of faith, they one and all leave unmentioned, not perhaps of set purpose— only of the compiler of the Pontifical book can one say that he purposely suppressed the proceeding— but openly, because they knew nothing whatever about it, although three œcumenical councils, the sixth, the seventh, and the eighth, had pronounced or confirmed the sentence of anathema on Honorius.

And this was universally the case with the Latin writers from the tenth to the fifteenth century. True that the chronicle of EKKEHARD,[1] that ADO and MARIANUS SCOTUS mention Honorius among those who were condemned by the sixth council, but this name without any further description was, for those times, mere empty sound, conveying no ideas to any one. When, therefore, CARDINAL HUMBERT, in his writing against the Greek Nicetas,[2] inserts a notice of the sixth council, and in this mentions Honorius also as one of those condemned, one may be certain that he

The fact of a pope having been anathematised is thus forgotten.

---
[1] In PERTZ, VIII., 155.
[2] Ap. BARON., Append. ad tom. XI.; *Annal.*, p. 1005, ed. Colon.

had no suspicion of the rank of the person mentioned; otherwise the Byzantines would have been precisely the people in whose minds he would have avoided awakening such a recollection. The oblivion into which the fate of Honorius had fallen is specially astonishing in the letter of pope Leo IX. to Michael Cerularius, patriarch of Constantinople, and to Leo[1] of Achrida, in which all the scandals and heretical errors of their church and its bishops are set before these prelates. The pope confidently contrasts the steadfast orthodoxy of the bishops of Rome with the numerous cases of heresy which had occurred in Constantinople, and calls attention to the way in which the popes, especially in the Monothelite controversies, had continually exercised their judicial office over

Leo IX. shows utter ignorance of it.

---

[1] HARDUIN, III., 931. [Michael Cerularius and Leo, archbishop of Achrida and metropolitan of Bulgaria, provoked the correspondence in 1053, by a letter to the bishop of Trani, in Apulia, warning him against the errors of the Latins. The pope replied from his virtual captivity at Benevento. After quoting the text, "Ego autem "rogavi pro te, ut non deficiat fides tua; et tu aliquando conversus "confirma fratres tuos," the pope proceeds: "Erit ergo quisquam "tantae dementiae, qui orationem illius, cujus velle est posse, audeat "in aliquo vacuam putare? Nonne a sede principis Apostolorum, "Romana videlicet ecclesia, tam per cumdem Petrum quam succes- "sores suos, reprobata et convicta, atque expugnata sunt omnium "haereticorum commenta; et fratrum corda in fide Petri, quae "hactenus nec defecit, nec usque in finem deficiet confirmata?"
 "Praeterimus nominatim replicare nonaginta et eo amplius haereses "ab Orientis partibus, vel ab ipsis Graecis, diverso tempore ex "diverso errore ad corrumpendam virginitatem catholicae ecclesiae "matris emergentes. Dicendum videtur ex parte, quantas Con- "stantinopolitana ecclesia per praesules suos suscitaverit pestes; "quas viriliter expugnavit, protrivit, et suffocavit Romana et Apos- "tolica sedes."]

the patriarchs of Constantinople, and had condemned them; evidently not having the slightest suspicion that Michael and Leo, by quoting the condemnation of Honorius, pronounced at Constantinople and accepted at Rome, could have demolished his whole argument. On the contrary, deceived by the Roman apocryphal documents, he represents to his opponents that Silvester had decided that the First See (that is the Roman) can be judged by none, and that Constantine, together with the whole council of Nicæa, had approved this.[1]

Again, ANSELM OF LUCCA would not have maintained with such confidence that at the eight œcumenical councils which had been held up to that time, it had been proved that the patriarch of Rome was the only one whose faith had never wavered, if he had known that it was precisely at the last three of these eight synods that Honorius had been condemned for heresy.[2] In like manner, RUPER OF DEUTZ would not, as he has done, have contrasted the steadfast orthodoxy of the popes with the heretical aberrations of the patriarchs of Constantinople, if he had not shared the general ignorance respecting the sixth council.[3]

---

[1] [" Illi nempe facitis præjudicium, de qua nec vobis, nec cuilibet " mortalium licet facere judicium; beatissimo et Apostolico Pontifice " Silvestro divinitus decernente, spiritualique ejus filio Constantino " religiosissimo Augusto cum universa synodo Nicæna approbante " ac subscribente, ut *summa sedes a nemine judicetur*."]

[2] *Contra Guibertum Antipapam, Bibl. Patrum Lugd.*, XVIII., 609.

[3] *De divinis Offic.*, 2, 22.

Honorius never quoted in the West as an instance of an heretical pope.

Accordingly, in the West, as often as cases had to be quoted in which popes had erred or become heretical, people appealed to those of Liberius and Anastasius, sometimes also to that of Marcellinus; never to Honorius. This ignorance appears in a very astonishing way under Clement V. At that time there was on the part of the French a pressing desire for a formal anathema on Boniface VIII. The defenders of this pope contended that as being a dead man, who could no longer answer for himself, he was exempt from all human judgment, and therefore even from that of the Roman See. The instance of Honorius would have been very welcome to the agents of the French court; for by means of it they could have proved in the most emphatic way that the church had certainly sat in judgment on a defunct pope, and had condemned him. The fact, however, had long since vanished from the memories of jurists no less than of theologians; and hence in the long controversy and legal discussion the name of Honorius was never mentioned.

Hence it has come to pass that PLATINA has even made Honorius a decided *opponent* of Monothelitism, and he represents Heraclius as banishing Pyrrhus and Cyrus at Honorius's suggestion. But that towards the close of the sixteenth century the learned PANVINIO, whom CIANONI then copied in turn, should allow this to pass unchallenged, is scarcely conceivable.

The fact that Honorius was condemned by the sixth general council was first brought back to the memory of the Western Church by a Greek living in Constantinople, MANUEL KALEKAS, who in the year 1390 wrote a work against the Byzantines for being separated from the West. The papal nuncio ANTON MASSANUS, a Minorite, brought the book from Constantinople to the papal court in 1421; whereupon Martin V. had it translated by the celebrated Camaldulensian abbot, AMBROSE TRAVERSARI. From it cardinal TORQUEMADA,[1] who wrote his *Summa* about the year 1450, first learnt the condemnation of Honorius, which disturbed him greatly; for by no sort of means would it work into his system.[2] Kalekas had made light of the affair in his controversy with the Greeks. He had contented himself with referring to the excuse which Maximus makes for Honorius, without troubling himself with the consideration that the judgment of an œcumenical council must have an authority very different from the evasive answer of a theologian, who knew of no other way of helping his case than to make the secretary answerable for the errors contained in the pope's[3] letter. Now Torquemada was acquainted with the declaration of Hadrian II. from the Acts of

The memory of the West reawakened.

Torquemada finds Honorius's case a great difficulty.

---

[1] QUETIF et ECHARD, *Scriptores O. P.* I., 718.
[2] *Summa de Ecclesia*, 2, 93, ed. Venet., 1560, f., 228. This is the most important work of the Middle Ages on the question of the extent of the papal power.
[3] *Contra Græcorum errores*, Ingolst., 1608, p. 381

the eighth council, to the effect that Honorius had been anathematised for heresy. Nevertheless, he says that we must suppose that the Orientals were misinformed about Honorius, and so had condemned him under [1] a mistake. His sole ground for saying this is, that pope Agatho, in enumerating the monothelite leaders, has not mentioned Honorius among them.

He gives up the council to save Honorius.

This attempt to load an œcumenical council with the charge of a gross error, merely to rescue the honour of one pope, remained, however, on the whole, unobserved, and stood alone at that time. For then, as through the whole of the Middle Ages, the view still prevailed that a pope certainly could apostatise from the faith and become heretical, and in such a case both could and ought to be deposed.

The Honorius question not seriously debated till the sixteenth century.

Not until after the middle of the sixteenth century did any one occupy himself seriously with the question of Honorius. The fact of the condemnation was irreconcileable with the system then developed by BARONIUS, BELLARMINE, and others. Attempts were accordingly made to set it aside.

Various hypotheses.
1. That the acts of the council have been interpolated.

It was pretended, that is to say, that the Acts of the sixth council had been falsified by the Greeks of a later age, and all therein that concerned Honorius had been interpolated by them, in order that the disgrace of so many oriental patriarchs

---

[1] " Creditur quod hoc fecerint Orientales ex mala et falsa sinistra " informatione de præfato Honorio decepti."

being condemned for heresy might be lessened by
the shame of a pope being found in the same pre-
dicament. Then it became necessary to declare
that the letter of Leo II. was also interpolated.
And on this BARONIUS, BELLARMINE, HOSIUS,
BINIUS, DUVAL, and the Jesuits TANNER and
GRETSER determined. But when the *Liber Diurnus*
came to light, the nullity of this attempt was dis-
closed. Another mode of getting out of the
difficulty proved still more untenable; this was to
deny the condemnation of Honorius at the sixth
council, and transfer it to another purely Greek
synod (the quinisext[1] council of A.D. 692 is apparently the one meant), the Acts of which were
then inserted in those of the sixth council. This
was the device resorted to by SYLVIUS, LUPUS, and
the Roman oratorian MARCHESE, who has set forth
this idea in a book of his own.[2]

2. That they are really the acts of another synod.

That the letters of Honorius were forgeries, or
that they had been interpolated, was somewhat
more conceivable; at least the supposition demanded no such immense and elaborate apparatus
of falsification as Baronius and Bellarmine pictured

3. That the letters of Honorius are forgeries.

---

[1] [Called *quinisext*, as being supplementary to the fifth and sixth councils. It is also known as the *Trullan*, from the *Trullus* or vaulted hall, in which it was held. The date of it is doubtful; 686, 691, 692 have all been suggested. Harduin places it as late as 706. The two papal legates signed its 102 canons; but pope Sergius I., to the chagrin of the emperor Justinian II., declined to do so. The council was recognised by the East only, *where its Acts were quoted as those of the sixth council*; and this was the first grave step towards the schism between the East and the West.]

[2] *Clypeus fortium, sive Vindiciæ Honorii Papæ.* Romæ, 1680.

to themselves, or at any rate to their readers. This mode of escape therefore was chosen by GRAVINA and COSTER; STAPLETON also and WIGGERS were inclined[1] towards it.

4. That Honorius was condemned, not for heresy, but for negligence.

Seeing, however, that the letters of Honorius were laid before the council, examined, and condemned *in the presence of the papal legates*, who at any rate must have known their contents, it was found necessary to abandon *this* method of getting out of the difficulty also. Several, therefore, preferred to maintain that Honorius himself had taught what was orthodox, and had only been condemned by the council because he had shown leniency to heresy from an ill-timed love of peace, and had favoured it by rejecting a dogmatic expression which had become indispensable. So DE MARCA, NATALIS ALEXANDER, GARNIER, DU HAMEL, LUPUS, TAMAGNINI, PAGI and many others.

This hypothesis a favourite one in the Jansenist controversy.

This method of defending Honorius became a very favourite one after the outbreak of the Jan-

---

[1] Against endeavours such as these of Bellarmine, Baronius, and others after them,—to set aside well-attested historical facts by throwing suspicion on the witnesses and documents, because they will not square with the system of a particular school or party,—cardinal SFONDRATI has spoken out very strongly on this very question of Honorius. "Quid hoc aliud est, quam contra torrentem "navigare, omnemque historiam ecclesiasticam in dubium vocare? "Sublata vero historia et consequenter traditione usuque Ecclesiæ, "quæ tu arma contra hæreticos satis valida habebis? Male ergo, ut "nobis quidem videtur, Ecclesiæ illi consulunt, qui ut Honorii "causam tueantur, historiam Ecclesiamque exarmant. Ergo si "testibus agenda res est, Honorius Papa hæreticus fuit."—EUGENII LOMBARDI, *Regale Sacerdotium*, p. 721, sq.

senite troubles. It is chiefly owing to the Jansenists that the question of Honorius has become a *quæstio vexata*, in which every effort has been made to confuse and set aside the facts, and with which since 1650 almost every theologian of note has occupied himself. So that within a period of about 130 years one may say that more has been written on this one question of ecclesiastical history than on any other in 1500 years. For the Jansenists it was all-important to invalidate the judgment which the Church had pronounced on the work of Jansen. Accordingly they put forth the theory that the Church both could err and had erred; not, indeed, in the setting forth of doctrine, but in " dogmatic questions of fact," that is to say, in its judgment on a book, or its interpretation of a dogmatic text. They set themselves therefore on the side of Honorius against the council, and readily pursued the course which had already been opened by cardinals TORQUEMADA, BARONIUS, BELLARMINE, DE LAUREA, and AGUIRRE,[1] main-

---

[1] For these writers, foreseeing that the theory of a falsification of the Acts would not hold water, had already taken up the other alternative, that the council had made a mistake in its judgment on the decretals of Honorius.—BENNETTIS (*Privil. Pontif. Vindiciæ*, Rom., 1759, P. II., T. V., p. 389) admits, " Turrecrematæ, Baronio, " Bellarmino ac Spondano locutiones excidisse minus accuratas " ac paulo asperiores." They have simply sacrificed the authority of an œcumenical council, and of a decision accepted by the Papal See itself, to the interests of their own theory. [So also PÈRE GRATRY: " On m'accuse de manquer à l'Église, notre mère, parce " que je dénonce le pernicieux mensonge des décrétales dans les " leçons du Bréviaire romain. Le bréviaire est-il donc l'Église, et " les légendes sont elles donc le bréviaire? Mais, quoi! si l'on

taining that grievous wrong had been done to Honorius and his letters by the judgment of the council. The council, in spite of the care which it bestowed, and although the matter in question was at that time current with every one, had been mistaken in their decision! The opponents of the Jansenists, who would not allow that the Church had condemned a pope as heretical and expelled him from communion, preferred rather to do violence to the clear words of the council, in order to say that Honorius had become subject to the anathema of the council not on account of positive but only of "negative" heresy; that is to say, merely because he had countenanced other heretics and favoured their false [1] doctrine. But FÉNÉLON had already pointed out, that with all the artifices and explanations, by means of which the orthodoxy of Honorius was to be saved, nothing after all was to be gained. For the paramount question must always be this :—Has the Church, represented by a

"manque à l'Église pour vouloir effacer des erreurs dans les leçons du Bréviaire romain, que dire de ceux que veulent effacer des décrets de foi dans les conciles œcuméniques? . . . Oui, je demande ce qu'il faut dire de ceux qui traitent ainsi les décrets des conciles; qui, voyant Honorius, condamné par trois conciles œcuméniques, sans compter vingt papes, répondent tout simplement que ces conciles se sont trompés!"—*Troisième lettre à Monseigneur l'Archevêque de Malines.* Paris, 1870, I., p. 5.]

[1] It is specially the Jesuit GARNIER, who, in his notes to the *Liber Diurnus*, has expended great pains on this point. A whole host of theologians have followed him. At last PALMA (*Prælectiones Hist. Eccles.*, II., 127), whose efforts go beyond everything with this conclusion, asserts that the council certainly invoked an anathema on Honorius, but in the expression of it was not quite in earnest.

full œcumenical council, declared the dogmatic writings of a pope to be heretical, and *thus recognised the fallibility of popes?* If this question must be answered in the affirmative, then it matters very little for the interests of the Roman See whether the synod, in the application of the principle to a particular case (the meaning of the letter of Honorius), has made a mistake or not.[1]

Some Italians of the last century—for example, bishop BARTOLI and the librarian UGHI—once more took refuge in the favourite and most convenient falsification theory, which makes very short work of every stubborn fact. According to BARTOLI,[2] the letters of Honorius are forgeries. At the same time, however, Bartoli adopted the discovery which had already been made by the Augustinian DESIRANT, that besides this the Greeks had forged also the letters of Sergius; so that the doubly-deceived synod had regarded the letter of Honorius also, which agreed with that of Sergius, as heretical. UGHI[3] admitted that the synod openly condemned Honorius for heresy; but thinks that it acted carelessly and without thought in so doing,

---

[1] *Troisième instr. pastor. sur le Cas de Conscience. Œuvres,* éd. le Versailles, XI., 483.

[2] *Apologia pro Honorio I. Rom. Pontif.,* Ausugii, 1750.

[3] " Quæ omnia," he remarks, after quoting the most decisive passages from the acts of the council, " nullo unquam temperamento " emollita . . . manifeste demonstrant, fuisse Honorium non solum-" modo tanquam desidem, sed—tanquam verum hæreticum a synodo " VI. proscriptum."—*De Honorio I. Pontif. Max. Liber,* Bononiæ, 1784, p. 94, cf. p. 98.

because it allowed itself to be deceived by the letter which had been foisted upon Honorius. And, not to adopt any half measures, he declares that the letters of Leo II. are also spurious. The French theologian, CORGNE, likewise has resorted to this lamentable expedient.[1]

<small>6. That the letters of Leo II. also are forgeries.</small>

<small>7. That Honorius was condemned by the Greeks only.</small>

ARSDEKIN and CAVALCANTI thought of another loophole, through which it was possible to escape from the unwelcome conclusion, viz., that it was the Greeks alone who, at the sixth council, pronounced the unjust sentence upon Honorius; the Latins present had not taken part in this mistaken proceeding.

On the other hand, their contemporary, bishop DUPLESSIS D'ARGENTRÉ, maintained that the council had condemned Honorius *as a heretic*, and with justice, for God had allowed him to fall into these errors in his letter to Sergius, in order that popes might learn by his example that freedom from error in the setting forth of doctrine was assured to them only on condition of their taking proper counsel, which he had neglected to do.[2] Cardinal ORSI also has fully recognised the untenableness of the efforts to save the orthodoxy of Honorius, and the openings for attack which were thus exposed by shortsighted theologians. He withdraws, there-

---

[1] *Dissertation critique et théologique sur le Monothélisme.* Paris, 1741, p. 56 sq.

[2] *Collectio judiciorum de novis erroribus.* Paris, 1724, T. I., præf., p. 4. And in his *Variæ Disputationes theol. ad opera.* M. GRANDIN, Paris, 1712, II., 220.

fore, back to the point of view, that Honorius spoke only as a private teacher, neither as pope, nor in the name of the Roman Church, giving a solemn decision after the necessary taking of counsel (*ex cathedrâ*). Cardinal LUZERNE has subjected these tenets to a sharp[1] criticism. One cannot say, he justly remarks, that Honorius gave his opinion on the Monothelite question not as pope, but only as a private teacher. The question was put to him as pope, and he answered as pope, in the same tone and style in which his predecessors, Celestine and Leo, had answered on dogmatic questions. Orsi, however, is quite right on his side, when he argues that Honorius gave his decision without a council and on his own responsibility; without troubling himself about the doctrine held by the churches of the West, which from the first had always believed in a duality of wills; without even giving the Roman Church itself the opportunity of making known its creed as regards this question. If the idea of a decision *ex cathedrâ* be duly expanded, and only those dogmatic announcements be reckoned as *ex cathedrâ* which a pope issues, not in his own name and for himself, but in the name of the Church, *with full consciousness of the doctrine prevailing in the Church, and therefore after previous inquiry or discussion by a council*—then, and only then, can one say that

8. That Honorius spoke, not as pope, but as a private teacher.

Answer to this.

---

[1] *Sur la déclaration du clergé.* Œuvres, Paris, 1855, II., 42, and 190 sq. [On decisions "*ex cathedrâ*," see Appendix E.]

Honorius's judgment was not given[1] *ex cathedrâ*. Neither the Roman Church, nor the Western, nor the greater part of the Eastern Church, has ever been Monothelite. Nevertheless, Honorius issued letters to the Eastern Church, about the Monothelite meaning of which assuredly not a doubt would ever have been raised, but for the fact of the author being pope. Accordingly, the Roman breviary designates him simply as a Monothelite.[2]

The Monothelitism of Honorius would never have been questioned, had he not been pope.

---

[1] [With this interpretation one would readily admit that not only the pope, but every bishop is infallible, when he speaks *ex cathedrâ*.]

[2] HEFELE, in his *Conciliengeschichte*, and in the discussion in the *Tübingen Quartalschrift*, Jahrg., 1857, has treated the question of Honorius with philosophic impartiality, accuracy, and thoroughness. [See also four letters to Monseigneur Deschamps, archbishop of Malines, by A. GRATRY, priest of the Oratory. Paris, 1870.]

POPE GREGORY II AND THE EMPEROR LEO III

POPE GREGORY II AND THE EMPEROR LEO THE ISAURIAN

ACCORDING to later historians, who have been eagerly followed by many theologians, Gregory II. deprived the iconoclast emperor Leo of the kingdom of Italy, and induced the Italians to throw off their allegiance to him, because he attempted to carry his edict against the use of images into effect in Italy as well as in the East. BARONIUS, BELLARMINE, and others have made this supposed fact a main support of their system with regard to the authority of popes over the temporal power. *Gregory II has been represented as heading a revolt against Leo III.*

Of the biographers of popes in the Middle Ages, Martinus Polonus is the only one who, while he makes a confusion by transferring the matter to Gregory III., asserts that the pope, recognising in the emperor Leo an incorrigible iconoclast, induced Rome, Italy, Spain, and the "whole of the West" to throw off their allegiance to the emperor, and forbad all payment of taxes to him. We have here another proof of the incredible ignorance of Martinus Polonus, in representing Spain—Gothic *Martinus Polonus once more the spreader of error.*

and even Saracen Spain—as throwing off their allegiance. And besides that, what we are to understand by the "whole of the West," he himself would have had some difficulty in showing. The other papal biographers, Amalrich, Guidonis, Leo of Orvieto, and others, know nothing of the secession of Italy from the empire. But before Martinus Polonus, SIGEBERT [OF GEMBLOURS], OTTO OF FREYSINGEN, GOTTFRIED OF VITERBO, ALBERT OF STADE, and the so-called LANDULF, the late compiler of the *Historia miscella*, had already accepted the statement that pope Gregory induced the Italians to revolt from Leo. All of these, as well as the Byzantines ZONARAS,[1] CEDRENUS, and GLYKAS, received the statement from one and the same single source. This source is the chronicler THEOPHANES, who wrote the history of this period eighty years after it (he died not earlier than A.D. 819); and his work, in the abbreviated Latin translation of ANASTASIUS BIBLIOTHECARIUS, was used by the above-mentioned Latin chroniclers either directly or indirectly.

Theophanes the source of the statement.

It is altogether futile, therefore, to pile up names of witnesses to this supposed fact (after the manner of BIANCHI[2]), and add to these NAUCLERUS and PLATINA also. All these witnesses resolve themselves into one; and the investigator has merely

---

[1] [ZONARAS and MICHAEL GLYCAS bring their chronicles down to the death of the emperor Alexis I., Comnenus, 1118; CEDRENUS, to 1057.]

[2] *Della Potestà e della Polizia della chiesa.* Rom., 1745, I., 382.

to show (1) that Theophanes[1] is a late authority, very little acquainted with Italian affairs; (2) that the two contemporary Italian witnesses, PAULUS DIACONUS, and the anonymous biographer of Gregory in the Pontifical book, state just the opposite of what Theophanes says; and (3) that ZONARAS, in the twelfth century, and certainly CEDRENUS (both of whom merely copied Theophanes) are here utterly unworthy of consideration. The special object of Zonaras, moreover, is to throw the blame of the loss of its Italian possessions by the Greek empire on the papacy. Accordingly he decorates the erroneous statement of Theophanes with the further statement that Gregory made an alliance with the Franks, who hereupon got possession of Rome, a statement which he thrice repeats. That is, he transfers events, which first took place under Pepin and Charles the Great, to the time of Gregory II. and Charles Martel.

But he is a late authority, contradicted by contemporary witnesses.

The truth of the matter is, then, that, according to the accounts of the two Italian contemporaries, and Gregory's own statements in his letter to Leo, this pope, far from wishing or effecting the

Gregory headed no revolt, but helped to quash one.

---

[1] [THEOPHANES was born about A.D. 750. He was a most zealous advocate of the use of images at the second council of Nicæa in 787. Leo the Armenian made him an object of persecution for his support to the cause of image-worship, imprisoned him for two years, and finally banished him to Samothrace, where he died almost immediately, March 818. His chronicle is a continuation of that of his friend Syncellus, commencing with the accession of Diocletian in 284, and going down to 813.]

overthrow of the Byzantine dominion in Italy, was rather the only, or at any rate the principal, cause of its maintenance. It is true that, when Leo ordered the destruction of pictures and dismantling of churches, the Romans and inhabitants of Eastern[1] Italy, from Venice to Osimo, flung off the Greek yoke, and even wished to elect an emperor of their own. But Gregory strained every nerve to prevent this, and exhorted them unceasingly to maintain their allegiance to the Roman empire of the East.[2] The biographer in the Pontifical book, who, from the fullness, insight, and liveliness exhibited in his narrative, is easily seen to be a contemporary and eye-witness, gives only one circumstance which seems to overpass the line of loyal obedience otherwise observed with great strictness by Gregory, and has given Theophanes an opening for his misrepresentation. The patrician Paul, he says, on becoming exarch, made an attempt on the life of the pope, because he attempted to hinder[3] the imposition of a tax in the province, and would not consent to the plundering of the churches—that is, the carrying off of pictures and of vessels ornamented with figures of saints. Here the point at issue was

---

[1] [The Greek dominions in Italy at this time were:—(1) the exarchate of Ravenna, (2) the duchy of Rome and Naples, (3) the cities on the coast of Liguria, and (4) the provinces in the extreme south of Italy.]

[2] Paul. Diac., *de gestis Longob.*, 6, 49; *Liber Pontif.*, ed. Vignoli, II., 27–36.

[3] "Eo quod censum in provincia possit præpediebat," l. c., p. 23.

hindering the levying of a new impost, in which the pope did no more than set a precedent, which was then followed by others, of refusing to pay a new impost out of the great and numerous patrimonies of the church. But Theophanes and the Greeks[1] after him represent this as an injunction issued to the Italians not to pay any more taxes whatever.

HEFELE, following BOSSUET and MURATORI, has set the events which took place in Italy at that time in their true light, and has shown how devoid of foundation the Greek statement[2] is. It would have been sufficient merely to call attention to this, had not GREGOROVIUS lately revived once more the old view of Bellarmine, and represented the pope as in open revolt against the emperor. "Gregory," he states, "now decided upon open "resistance .... he armed himself, as the Pon-"tifical book says, against the emperor as against "a foe .... The act of open rebellion, at the "head of which the pope boldly placed himself,

Gregorovius has rendered a fresh discussion of the question necessary.

[1] [In this they are followed by GIBBON. "The most effectual and "pleasing measure of rebellion was the withholding the tribute of "Italy, and depriving him of a power which he had recently abused "by the imposition of a new capitation." In a note he adds, "A "*census*, or capitation, says Anastasius (p. 156): a most cruel tax, "unknown to the Saracens themselves, exclaims the zealous Maim-"bourg (*Hist. des Iconoclastes*, l. l.), and Theophanes (p. 344 [tom. "i., p. 361, ed. Bonn]), who talks of Pharaoh's numbering the male "children of Israel. This mode of taxation was familiar to the "Saracens; and, most unluckily for the historian, it was imposed a "few years afterwards in France by his patron Louis XIV."—*Decline and Fall of the Roman Empire*, chap. XLIX., note 38.]

[2] *Conciliengeschichte*, III., 355 ff.

"was perhaps even definitely declared by refusal
"of the tribute from the duchy of Rome,"[1] &c.
But in manifest contradiction to this view, he states
further on, "Gregory could not withdraw himself
"from the tradition of the Roman empire, the seat
"of which was Byzantium; with prudent mode-
"ration he restrained the rebellious Italians, and
"appealed to the legitimate rights of the emperor,
"whom he had no longer much need to fear"
(page 257).

His view inconsistent with itself.

Is it conceivable that so prudent a man as (on Gregorovius's own showing) this pope was, should first have set himself at the head of an open rebellion, and then directly afterwards, without any external compulsion, should again have quashed the rebellion, and come forward as champion of the emperor's rights? For the view that the pope originated and directed the revolt of the Italians, Gregorovius has given no other evidence than his quotation of the words of the Pontifical book, "he "armed himself against the emperor as against a "foe;"[2] but the words which immediately follow,

---

[1] *Geschichte der Stadt Rom.*, II., 255.

[2] [GIBBON quotes the whole passage, but draws the same conclusion as Gregorovius. "Without depending on prayers and miracles, "he boldly armed against the public enemy, and his pastoral letters "admonished the Italians of their danger and their duty." To which he subjoins in the note: "I shall transcribe the important "passage of the *Liber Pontificalis*." "Respiciens ergo pius vir "profanam principis jussionem, jam contra Imperatorem quasi "contra *hostem* se armavit, renuens hæresim ejus, scribens ubique "se cavere Christianos, eo quod orta fuisset impietas talis. *Igitur* "permoti omnes Pentapolenses, atque Venetiarum exercitus contra

and which explain the meaning of this " arming,"
he omits, namely, the words, " in that he rejected
" the emperor's heresy, and sent letters every-
" where, bidding Christians to be on their guard
" against the new form of impiety that had
" appeared." Gregory, therefore, kept himself
rigorously within the sphere of ecclesiastical
matters, declared himself the opponent of the
imperial decree against the use of images, and
charged the faithful not to destroy their images.
But at the same time he exhorted them to show
civil obedience to the imperial power, so much so
that he used all his influence to preserve Ravenna
for the empire, when the Lombards were threatening to seize it; and he placed[1] forces at the
disposal of the imperial governor Eutychius, by
means of which Eutychius was able to put down
the revolt of Tiberius Petavius in Tuscany.

A glance at the position of affairs shows that Gregory,[2] straitened as were the limits within

Difficult position of Gregory II.

" Imperatoris jussionem restiterunt: dicentes se nunquam in ejusdem
" pontificis condescendere necem, sed pro ejus magis defensione
" viriliter decertare " (p. 156), l. c., note 37.]

[1] [This was partly the result of the interference of the Lombard king himself (see next note). It is the more remarkable, inasmuch as Eutychius, the last exarch of Ravenna, had come on an iconoclastic mission from Constantinople; and it was commonly believed of him, as of other imperial emissaries before him, that he meditated the assassination of the pope. It was thanks to Gregory, that Eutychius was not assassinated himself.]

[2] ˊGregory was under the influence of two violent and conflicting feelings, horror of an iconoclastic emperor (an iconoclast in the eyes of an Italian was scarcely a Christian), and horror of a Lombard supremacy. When Ravenna was taken by the Lombards, he

which the difficulties of his surroundings allowed him to act, nevertheless well understood how to maintain the true bearing which prudence and duty alike dictated. The gravest peril, the most pressing and disastrous fate in the eyes of the Romans at that time, and especially of the popes, was to be swallowed up by the Lombards. Gregory shared the general feeling, and he, too, speaks of the "gens nefanda Longobardorum."[1] And this fate, to become the prey of the detested foreigner, was inevitable for Rome and the rest of Byzantine Italy, as soon as the power of Constantinople in the West was broken. That these provinces, if left alone, could not maintain themselves against the overwhelming power of the Lombards, Gregory

organised a league between Venice, the exarch Scholasticus, and Rome; and the forces thus raised recaptured Ravenna while Liutprand was away at Pavia, A.D. 727. Two years later, however, we find Liutprand acting the part of mediator between Gregory and the exarch Eutychius. As regards the question of iconoclasm, it was one fanatic against another. Leo was at least as fanatical in his attack on the use of images, as Gregory in his support of it. And when it is urged in proof of the pope's rebellion that he excommunicated the emperor, we must remember that at that time excommunication of a prince did not necessarily carry with it a release of his subjects from their allegiance; it did not even cut off the prince himself from all spiritual privileges. It merely declared in solemn terms that the pope declined to communicate with him. But "si quis .... imagi-" num sacrarum .... destructor .... extiterit, sit extorris a corpore " D. N. Jesu Christi vel totius ecclesiæ unitate" is strong language.]

[1] [Gregory commences his letter to Ursus, doge of Venice, on the subject of united resistance against the Lombards, in these words: " Quia, peccato faciente, Ravennatum civitas, quæ caput extat " omnium, a *nec dicendâ gente* Longobardorum capta est."—LABBE, *Concil.*, VI., 1447. The Lombards, on their side, had a similar style of abuse. If they wished to express the bitterest contempt for a foe they called him a Roman.]

was well aware.¹ Above all would protection be needed for the Roman See; and at that time the Frankish kingdom alone, under its prince, Charles Martel, could have given this protection. Charles Martel, however, was fully occupied with perpetual wars against the Saxons, Frisians, Saracens, and people of Aquitaine; and, moreover, was on friendly terms with the Lombard king. Thus he was both unable and unwilling to take serious part in Italian affairs. Hence it came to pass that lower Italy, in which the richest possessions of the Roman Chair lay, remained then, and for some time longer, faithful to the Roman emperor in the East. Not a single attempt was made there to revolt from him; and if the influence of the pope had been exerted to bring such a result about, it would certainly have failed. Had Gregory then, as Gregorovius represents, placed himself at the head of a rebellion, he would have entered upon a hopeless undertaking, involving the most ruinous losses to the Roman See.

He knew well that a revolt could not succeed.

¹ [Yet, as Dr. Döllinger remarks in Essay V., "Gregory II. made "an attempt to form a confederation of states, which was to maintain "itself independently of both Greeks and Lombards, the head of it to "be the Roman See," p. 121.]

SILVESTER II

SILVESTER II

A POPE, who was held in great honour by his contemporaries, who was renowned as the most learned scholar and the most enlightened spirit of his time, whose memory remained unsullied for a century after his death, becomes gradually an object of suspicion; the calumnies about him assume larger and larger dimensions, until the papal biographers of the later Middle Ages represent his whole life and pontificate as a series of the most monstrous crimes. According to them, Silvester II. entered into a league with the devil, and exercised his pontifical office in the devil's service and in obedience to his will. *Gradual defamation of the memory of Silvester II. by successive biographers.*

At first writers were content with the timid criticism that Gerbert had devoted himself with far too much zeal to profane sciences, and on that account stood so high in the favour of an emperor with such a thirst for knowledge as Otho III. This is the line taken by the chroniclers Hermann of Reichenau (died A.D. 1054) and Bernold. Hugo of Fleury (A.D. 1109) as yet knows nothing to the *1. That he was too fond of profane arts and sciences.*

discredit of Gerbert; according to him Gerbert attained to such eminence merely by means of his knowledge. But his contemporary HUGO OF FLAVIGNY, whose chronicle ends with the year 1102, goes so far as to state that it was by certain sinister arts (quibusdam præstigiis) that Gerbert contrived to get himself elected archbishop of Ravenna.[1] The chronicler does not appear by this to have intended the interposition of demoniacal agencies; in which case he would certainly have used stronger language. He probably meant court intrigues, by means of which the Frenchman won the favour of the empress Adelaid, who at that time held Ravenna, and of the emperor Otho; so that the latter, evading an open election, simply nominated Gerbert.

2. That his election at Ravenna was due to sinister arts.

Some years later we have SIEGEBERT OF GEMBLOURS (died A.D. 1113) stating that some did not reckon Gerbert among the popes at all, but put in his place a (fictitious) pope Agapitus, because Gerbert had been addicted to the practice of the black art, and had been[2] struck dead by the devil.

3. That he was addicted to magic and the black art.

Siegebert may have had before him the work of CARDINAL BENNO. The main features of the fable appear first in the writings of this calumnious enemy of Gregory VII. Benno, whose work must have been written about the year 1099, asserts that to a certain extent, during the whole of the eleventh century, a school of black magic had

---

[1] PERTZ, X., 367.   [2] BOUQUET, X., 217.

existed in Rome, with a succession of adepts in this art, and he enumerates them in order. The most important personage among them is archbishop Laurentius of Amalfi, who at times gave utterance to prophecies, and also could interpret[1] the notes of birds. Theophylact (Benedict IX.) and the archpriest John Gratian (Gregory VI.) learnt the unholy art from Laurentius, and Hildebrand from John Gratian. But Laurentius himself was the pupil of Gerbert, who was the first to bring the art to Rome. And then Benno relates the story which has since been so often repeated, and which became so popular, that Satan promised his disciple Gerbert that he should not die until he had said mass in Jerusalem. Gerbert accordingly believed himself to be quite safe; for he thought only of the city of Jerusalem, without remembering the Jerusalem church in Rome. The message of death came to him as he was saying mass in this church, and he thereupon caused his tongue and hand to be cut off, by way of expiation.

4. That he sold himself to the devil and died miserably.

Benno certainly did not invent this fable; he found it already existing in Rome. Before him there is no mention of it anywhere,[2] and it evi-

The fable is of Roman origin, invented to explain how a poor man,

---

[1] *Vita et gesta Hildebrandi*, in BROWN, Fascicul., I., 83.

[2] Though DAV. KOELER (*Gerbertus—injuriis tam veterum quam recentiorum scriptorum—liberatur*. Altorf., 1720, p. 33) supposes this, and HOCK (*Gerbert und sein Jahrhundert*, s. 161) considers it as most probable.

The Benedictines in the Bouquet Collection, x., 244, certainly say, "Antesignanos BENNO habuit." I have not been able, however, to discover these predecessors.

dently sprang up nowhere else but in Rome, just like the fable about Pope Joan. A foreigner, with his at that time unheard of and incomprehensible learning, who had acquired very questionable knowledge among those enemies of the faith, the Mahometans in Spain, may well have inspired the Romans with something of awe and horror. At a time in which scientific studies had all but died out in Rome, in which the Roman Chair was under the control of aristocratic factions, and a pope without powerful relations was scarcely able to maintain himself, the populace could not understand how a man like Gerbert, of the very humblest extraction, by mere pre-eminence of intellectual culture, should have raised himself to the highest dignity in Christendom. That could not have come to pass by purely natural means.

Here also, as in the fable of Pope Joan, a verse plays an important part. It is the well-known line—

"Scandit ab R Gerbertus in R, fit postea Papa vigens R."

For it is well known that Gerbert was first archbishop of Rheims, then of Ravenna, and finally became pope of Rome. Originally it was Gerbert himself who was said to have composed the verse, in calm satisfaction after the attainment of the highest dignity.[1] Next the verse was ascribed to him as a prophecy respecting his future destiny,

[1] So HELGALD, in BOUQUET, x., 99.

which was eventually fulfilled. And thus the way was prepared for the next step, which was to make the verse into a prediction or promise of the devil. By this means Gerbert was placed in the power of Satan ; and his wonderful and, at that time, unexampled success must have been the work of the devil, the result of a compact entered into with him. For after the story of Theophilus, which arose in the East in the ninth century, had spread in the West also, and the notion of compacts with the arch enemy (originally quite foreign to the Christian world) had become naturalised, there was nothing to hinder even a pope from being represented as having attained to his dignity by such a compact.

And thus it is stated in ORDERICUS VITALIS, who wrote his chronicle about the year 1141, that Gerbert is said to have studied as a scholar with a demon, and this demon gave utterance to the famous verse. Soon after, however, in WILLIAM GODELL, who wrote some twenty years later, Gerbert has already done formal homage to Satan, in order to attain the fulfilment of his wishes through his power. WILLIAM OF MALMESBURY tells the story in its fully developed form. And now the Dominicans appropriate it; VINCENT OF BEAUVAIS, MARTINUS POLONUS, LEO OF ORVIETO, BERNARD GUIDONIS ; also AMALRICH AUGERII. PETRARCH adheres to them faithfully. In their hands Silvester II. becomes a successor of S. Peter, who

The Dominicans accept and spread the fable.

early in life sold himself to the devil, and by his assistance ascends the papal throne. As pope he has daily and familiar intercourse with Satan, making him his counsellor. But when the entry of a troop of demons into the church warns him of the approach of his end, he publicly confesses his sins before the people, and thereupon has one limb after another hacked off, in order to show penitence for his enormities by means of so agonising a death. Since then the rattling of his bones in the grave is wont to give notice of the approaching death of a pope. On the other hand, DIETRICH VON NIEM (about A.D. 1390) was not far from the truth when he said that the Romans had detested this pope on account of his extraordinary learning, and therefore had accused him of having used magic[1] arts.

<small>The truth recognised in the fourteenth century.</small>

[1] *Privilegia et jura imperii*, in Schardii *Sylloge*, p. 832.

APPENDICES

APPENDIX A.

THE following additional particulars about the fable of Pope Joan, gathered mainly from Baring-Gould's *Curious Myths of the Middle Ages*, the notes to Soames's edition of Mosheim's *Ecclesiastical History*, and the article *Papesse* in Peter Bayle's *Dictionnaire*, will be of interest to those who care to pursue the subject further. Further particulars about the Papess.

It is greatly to the discredit of MOSHEIM that he should write as follows of this monstrous story. "Between *Leo IV.*, who died A.D. 855, and *Benedict III.*, a woman, who concealed her sex, and assumed the name of John, it is said, opened her way to the pontifical throne by her learning and genius, and governed the church for a time. She is commonly called the *Papess Joanna*. During the five subsequent centuries the witnesses to this extraordinary event are without number; nor did any one, prior to the Reformation by Luther, regard the thing as either incredible, or disgraceful to the church. But in the seventeenth century learned men, not only among the Mosheim's discreditable attempt to assign some truth to the fable.

"Roman Catholics, but others also, exerted all the powers of their ingenuity both to invalidate the testimony on which the truth of the story rests, and to confute it by an accurate computation of dates. There are still, however, very learned men who, while they concede that much falsehood is mixed with the truth, maintain that the controversy is not wholly settled. Something must necessarily have taken place at Rome to give rise to this most uniform report of so many ages; but even yet it is not clear what that something was." Book III., part 2, chap. ii., § 4. Tant il est certain que les mêmes choses nous paraissent véritables ou fausses à mesure qu'elles favorisent, ou notre Parti, ou le Parti opposé. One can hardly doubt that it was Protestant prejudice which made Mosheim "*wish* to believe" (as Gibbon says of a dubious story which pleases him) that the myth of Pope Joan might be true. It matters little to Protestants, as Bayle remarks, whether the Papess existed or not; it matters much that they should not give a handle to people to regard them comme des gens opiniâtres, et qui ne veulent jamais démordre des opinions préconçues. Mosheim says, "during the five subsequent centuries the witnesses to this extraordinary event are without number;" he omits to add that they occur in the *last* of the five centuries. For more than 350 years after the death of Leo IV. there is absolute silence about the Papess. Nor is it true that "no

<small>Answer to his statements.</small>

" one prior to Luther's time regarded the thing as
" incredible or disgraceful to the Church." Most
people regarded it as a grievous scandal, and some
doubted the fact. PLATINA, who wrote before
Luther was born, after telling the story, says, " hæc
" quæ dixi, vulgo feruntur, incertis tamen et ob-
" scuris auctoribus; quæ ideo ponere breviter et
" nude institui, ne obstinate et pertinaciter omisisse
" videar, quod fere omnes affirmant."—*Lives of the
Popes*, John VII.

It is almost slaying the dead to argue against the story of Pope Joan; but it is worth while to give a specimen of Bayle's mode of reasoning. Is it conceivable that five centuries hence there will not be a single historian extant of the sixteenth or seventeenth century who mentions the abdication of Charles V., or the assassinations of Henry III. and IV. of France; but that the earliest mention of these great events will be in some " misérable " annaliste" of the nineteenth century? If it should be so, the twenty-fourth century will be very credulous if it believes in these events. To show how impossible it would be for the historians of the ninth century to have suppressed a fact so tremendous as a female pope, who was detected as Pope Joan is supposed to have been detected, Bayle supposes a writer of the eleventh century to narrate as follows:—Charles the Great was very desirous that his successor should be his son; it was therefore a great grief to him that his

Bayle's argument.

A supposed historical parallel.

wife was barren. When at length there were hopes of a child, he was beside himself with joy; but when the child proved to be a girl, he was almost as grieved as before. He determined, therefore, to pass the child off as a boy, and gave it the name of Pepin. Six years later his wife bore him a son; but the parents still felt bound to conceal the sex of the first child, who on Charles's death was crowned as his successor. She reigned for three years without detection. The *dénouement* took place as she was addressing the parliament. The woman-king died in childbirth in the midst of the august assembly; and the nobles, in horror, passed a law which would render such an imposture impossible in future. Imagine half a dozen different accounts of the way in which queen Pepin died, and you have a narrative as like that about Pope Joan " comme deux goutes " d'eau." What amount of credence should we give to this eleventh century writer?

Some writers appear to have believed that the child which the Papess bore was Antichrist! An eminent Dutch minister considers it as immaterial whether its father was a monk or the devil.

The German and French Protestants of the sixteenth century delighted in the story, embellishing it with details of their own, in order to make capital out of it against the papacy. Nor did their fancy exuberate in words only. Some of their accounts are illustrated with woodcuts, which would seem to be more curious and graphic than decent. Mr. Baring-Gould gives a copy of one in which the Papess is strung up to a gibbet over the mouth of hell; rather against the version of the story, which says she was allowed to choose whether she would have the public exposure, or burn for ever in hell.

The *raison d'être* of the myth, as given by Dr. Döllinger in the text, is probably sufficient. Mr. Baring-Gould, however, has little doubt "that " Pope Joan is an impersonation of the great " whore of Revelation, seated on the seven hills, " and is the popular expression of the idea preva- " lent from the twelfth to the sixteenth centuries, " that the mystery of iniquity was somehow " working in the papal court. The scandal of the " antipopes, the utter worldliness and pride of " others, the spiritual fornication with the kings of " the earth, along with the words of Revelation " prophesying the advent of an adulterous woman " who should rule over the imperial city, and her " connexion with Antichrist, crystallized into this " curious myth, much as the floating uncertainty " as to the signification of our Lord's words, " ' There be some standing here which shall not " ' taste of death till they see the kingdom of " ' God,' condensed into the myth of the Wan- " dering Jew."

Mr. Baring-Gould's hypothesis.

He gives the following jingling account of the Papess, which is worth re-quoting. It is a fragment of the rhythmical *Vitæ Pontificum* of Gulielmus Jacobus of Egmonden, preserved in *Wolffii Lectionum Memorabilium centenarii*, XVI.:—

> " Priusquam reconditur Sergius, vocatur
> Ad summam, qui dicitur Johannes, huic addatur
> Anglicus, Moguntia iste procreatur.
> Qui, ut dat sententia, fœminis aptatur
> Sexu: quod sequentia monstrant, breviatur
> Hæc vox; nam prolixius chronica procedunt.
> Ista, de qua brevius dicta minus lædunt.
> Huic erat amasius, ut scriptores credunt.
> Patria relinquitur Moguntia, Græcorum
> Studioso petitur schola. Pòst doctorum
> Hæc doctrix efficitur Romæ legens; horum
> Hæc auditu fungitur loquens. Hinc prostrato
> Summo hæc eligitur; sexu exaltato
> Quandoque negligitur. Fatur quod hæc nato
> Per servum conficitur. Tempore gignendi
> Ad processum equus scanditur, vice flendi,
> Papa cadit, panditur improbis ridendi
> Norma, puer nascitur in vico Clementis,
> Colossæum jungitur. Corpus parentis
> In eodem traditur sepulturæ gentis,
> Faturque scriptoribus, quod Papa præfato,
> Vico senioribus transiens amato
> Congruo ductoribus sequitur negato
> Loco, quo Ecclesia partu denigratur,
> Quamvis inter spacia Pontificum ponatur
> Propter sexum."

Books on the subject of the Papess very numerous.

The literature on the subject is abundant. The arguments of those who maintain the truth of the story are collected and stated by Frederick SPANHEIM in his *Exercit. de Papa Fœmina*. Opp. tom. II., p. 577, and L'ENFANT has given a French translation and better arrangement of them, with additions: *Histoire de la Papesse Jeanne*, La Haye, 1736; two vols. 12mo.

The arguments against the myth are given in

BLONDEL'S famous treatise, *Familier éclairissement de la question, si une femme a été assise au siège papal de Rome*, Amsterdam, 1647-9; in BAYLE'S *Dictionnaire historique et critique*, article *Papesse*. See also *Allatii Confutatio Fabulæ de Johanna Papissa*, Colon., 1645; George ECCARD, *Historia Franciæ Oriental*, tom. II., lib. xxx., § 119; Michael LEQUIEN, *Oriens Christianus*, III., p. 777; Chr. Aug. HENMANN, a Lutheran writer, *Sylloge Diss. Sacrar.*, tom. I., pt. ii., p. 352; J. G. SCHELHORN, *Amœnitates Literar.*, I., p. 146; Jac. BASNAGE, *Histoire de l'Église*, I., p. 408; SCHROECKH, *Kirchengeschichte*, XXII., p. 75-110; J. E. C. SCHMIDT, *Kirchengeschichte*, IV., p. 274-279; A. BOWER'S *Lives of the Popes*, IV., p. 246-260.

APPENDIX B.

<small>The true story of Pope Jutta. Glancia was the daughter of a Thessalian, a clever and studious child. At school she fell in love with Pircius, and eloped with him, dressed in man's clothes.</small>

The story of the Papess, as given in the Tegernsee manuscript in the royal library at Munich (*Cod. lat. Tegerns.*, 781), is as follows :—" Item papa " Jutta, qui non fuit alamannus, sicut mendose " fabulatur chronica martiniana. Glancia puella, " fuit filia ditissimi civis Thessalici, cujus omnis " meditatio æquivoca nota sapientiæ versabatur; " hujus erat intellectus perspicua et ingenium docile, " quam penitus assidua legendi solertia vegetabant; " hæc tempore brevi sibi famam per omnes cir- " cuitus vindicabat ; sed prædicatas laudes rei " veritas excedebat. Erat Pircius in scholis illi " juvenculus coævus. Huic noto discendi capaci- " tatis ingenio, paternis opibus et omni quasi fru- " galitate, consiliis hos ambos, quos ætas æquaverat, " exæquat amor, de jugalitate tractatur, parentes " abnuunt. Crescit inter hos ardor et concupis- " centia, cum diebus sensim pullulat ætas, in oscula " veniunt et amplexus impatientes. Denique lati- " bulum petunt et ardentes junguntur. Ludo " veneris consummato de recessu tractant. Hæc

"inter mulieres, hic inter homines virtutum doti-
"bus ac disciplinarum studiis optant fieri singulares,
"et Athenas ire deliberant inter ipsos. Uterque
"se quot potest opulentiis munit; habitus gestusque
"capit illa viriles et similes animo simul habitus
"mirandos ac spectabiles illos facit. Nulla mora
"properant Athenas, ubi longo tempore student,
"et illa doctior, quidquid est divinæ facultatis, aut
"humanæ disciplinæ vel artium studiosa capescit,
"et ille similiter est omni sapientia gloriosus. Hos
"non Athenæ solum, sed universa Græcia vene-
"ratur. Hi Romam veniunt, in omni facultate
"studium pronunciant, ad hos omnes conveniunt
"tam scholares quam quarumcunque scientiarum
"doctores et quo profundiores accedunt, quas hau-
"riant venas, uberiores inveniunt. Hos omnes et
"omnium facultatum doctores adorant, hos omnes
"cives venerantur et horum mores modestiamque,
"virtutes et sapientiam prædicat omnis Roma, qui
"amplius in omnem terram penetrat sonus eorum.
"Denique functo pontifice mulier nominatione
"omni labio vocatur et voce non impugnata,
"Romanis hortantibus, ad apostolatus apicem pro-
"movetur. Cardinalatur Pircius amasius, vitam
"sagaciter agunt et in eorum gubernatione tota
"lætatur ecclesia. Sed quum status adulteri raro
"radices figunt, vel si germinent, non roborant, et
"si roborent, non perdurant, accidit ergo, quod an-
"tea nunquam, fucata mulier papissa prægnatur et
"insueta tempora partus ignorans ibat ad ecclesiam

The two went to Athens, where they remained as students for a long time. She displayed great ability, and became proficient in all the arts and sciences. He also gained a name for learning. Thence they moved to Rome, where they attracted a large number of scholars. On the death of the pope, Glancia was unanimously elected to succeed. Pircius was made cardinal. After a while Glancia became pregnant, and gave birth to a child on her way to mass, dying on the spot, which the popes now always avoid.

"sancti Johannis Lateranensis cum universo clero "missam solemnem celebratura. Sed inter Colos- "seum et ecclesiam s. Clementis coacta doloribus "cecidit et puerum peperit et pariter expiravit. "Hæc viam papa semper evitat et ante corona- "tionem papa semper manibus virilia palpantibus "exploratur," &c.

"Vide, quos ad gradus virtus et sapientia extollit
Pusillos sic altos in sapientia protexit; sed nihil
Est omnis nostra sagacitas vel industria contra Deum.
Vide carmina, quæ sequuntur.

Disceret ut leges peregrina juvencula plenas
Glancia clara seges mulierum transit Athenas
Cum juvene cupido vir facta, sed ista cupido
Militat in turbis ac doctores docet urbis.
Papa fit et puerum pariens et moritur prope clerum.

Moralitas.

Nil mage grandescit quam doctus jure fruendo,
Nil mage vilescit quam vir sine lege fruendo.

Papa, pater pauperum, perit papissa papellum," &c.

APPENDIX C.

THE story of POPIEL, KING OF POLAND, which is so similar to that of bishop Hatto of Mayence, is thus given by Mr. Baring-Gould :—" Martinus "Gallus, who wrote in 1110, says that king Popiel, "having been driven from his kingdom, was so "tormented by mice, that he fled to an island "whereon was a wooden tower, in which he took "refuge; but the host of mice and rats swam over "and ate him up. The story is told more fully by "Majolus (*Dierum Canic.*, p. 793). When the "Poles murmured at the bad government of the "king, and sought redress, Popiel summoned the "chief murmurers to his palace, where he pre- "tended that he was ill, and then poisoned them. "After this the corpses were flung by his orders "into the lake Gopolo. Then the king held a "banquet of rejoicing at having freed himself "from these troublesome complainers. But during "the feast, by a strange metamorphosis (mira "quadam metamorphosi), an enormous number of "mice issued from the bodies of his poisoned sub-

King Popiel and the mice.

"jects, and rushing on the palace, attacked the
"king and his family. Popiel took refuge within
"a circle of fire, but the mice broke through the
"flaming ring; then he fled with his wife and
"child to a castle in the sea, but was followed by
"the animals and devoured."

<small>The baron of Güttingen and the mice.</small>

He also gives other stories, more or less parallel to that of bishop Hatto; for instance, the one of FREIHERR VON GÜTTINGEN. This baron is said to have possessed three castles between Constance and Arbon, in the canton of Thurgau, namely, Güttingen, Moosburg, and Oberburg. During a grievous famine he collected the poor on his lands together, shut them up in a barn, and burnt them, mocking their shrieks by exclaiming, "Hark how the rats "and mice are squeaking!" Not long after a huge swarm of mice came down upon him. He fled to his castle of Güttingen, which stood in the lake of Constance; but the mice swam after him and devoured him. The castle then sank into the lake, where it may still be seen when the water is clear and the surface unruffled (*Zeitschrift für Deutshe Mythologie*, III., p. 307). Again, there is a mouse-tower at Holzölster, in Austria, with a very similar legend attached, except that here the wicked nobleman locks the poor people up in a dungeon and starves them to death, instead of making a bonfire of them (Vernaleken, *Alpensagen*, p. 328). Another instance is referred to by Dr. Döllinger in the text. The Wörthsee, between Tonning and

Seefeld in Bavaria, is also called the Mouse lake. A COUNT OF SEEFELD once starved all his famishing poor to death in a dungeon during a famine, and laughed at their cries, which he called the squeaking of mice. An island tower was as little use to him as to bishop Hatto or king Popiel, though he took the additional precaution of having his bed swung from the roof by chains. The mice got at him from the ceiling, and picked his bones (*Zeitschrift für Deut. Myth.* I., p. 452). The Mäuseschloss in the Hirschberger lake is another instance of a very similar story. Legends abound in which rats or mice are made instruments of divine vengeance, but they do not always contain the feature of the island tower, which is essential for our present purpose. Sometimes the avenging vermin are toads and frogs instead of rats and mice.

The count of Seefeld and the mice.

The tendency which a story of interest has to attract round itself as evidence circumstances which have no connection with it whatever, is so strikingly illustrated by the famous incident of the so-called "THUNDERING LEGION," that I venture to call attention to it. For the sake of clearness I give the outline of the story. The emperor Marcus Aurelius, in his celebrated war against the Quadri, was reduced to the greatest extremities by a failure of water, just on the very eve of a battle. A large body of Christians in one of the legions fell on their knees, and prayed to heaven for help. A sudden storm followed, which by its thunder and

Analogy from the story of the Thundering Legion.

lightning terrified the barbarians, and by its heavy rain relieved the thirst of the Romans. The truth of the narrative does not concern us; but probably no one who examines the evidence, as collected by Dr. Newman in his *Essays on Miracles* (Essay II., chap. v., section 1), will dissent from his very moderate statement of the result. " On the whole, " then, we may conclude that the facts of this " memorable occurrence are as the early Christian " writers state them; that Christian soldiers did " ask, and did receive, in a great distress, rain for " their own supply, and lightning against their " enemies; whether through miracle or not we " cannot say for certain, but more probably not " through miracle in the philosophical sense of the " word. All we know, and all we need to know " is, that ' He made darkness His secret place, His " ' pavilion round about him, with dark water and " ' thick clouds to cover Him; the Lord thundered " ' out of heaven, and the Highest gave His " ' thunder; hailstones and coals of fire. He sent " ' out His arrows, and scattered them; He sent " ' forth lightnings, and destroyed them.' " Just as the story of Pope Joan fastened on the fact that pontifical processions never passed through the narrow street between the church of S. Clement and the Colisseum, and just as the story of the count of Gleichen made capital out of the big bed and the jewel which the Turkish princess was supposed to have worn in her turban, so this history of the

"Thundering Legion" has incorporated with itself two utterly irrelevant circumstances, and that so completely, that some persons have supposed that by exposing the irrelevancy they have necessarily demolished the story—"as if evidence were the test of truth." CLAUDIUS APOLLINARIS, bishop of Hierapolis, was a contemporary of Marcus Aurelius His statement of this incident in the war against the Quadri is preserved to us by Eusebius (*Hist.* v., 5), and he alleges as evidence that the legion to which these Christian soldiers belonged was thenceforth called the Thundering Legion. TERTULLIAN, writing some five and twenty years later (about A.D. 200), states by way of evidence that the emperor in consequence passed an edict in favour of the Christians (*Apologeticus,* chap. v.; cf. *Ad Scapulam,* chap. iv.). Now there certainly was a Thundering Legion (Legio Fulminatrix), viz., the twelfth; but then it was as old as the time of Augustus. It was one of the nineteen legions levied by him. And as regards Tertullian's argument, there is some evidence that Marcus Aurelius did issue a rescript favouring the Christians, but in the period of his reign which *preceded* the battle. And it is notorious that he persecuted the Christians both before and after that event. Here, then, we have a story, almost certainly true in itself, claiming as evidence circumstances which, however well attested, have nothing whatever to do with it.

<small>Other instances of similar growth of myths.</small>

Instances of strange and unusual objects giving rise to myths might be multiplied almost *ad infinitum*. Thus the story of Arion arose from the figure of a man on a dolphin, which was the customary offering of one saved from shipwreck; the dolphin being a mere emblem of the sea. The story of Horatii and Curiatii seems to be an attempt to explain five barrows. The custom of representing martyrs with the instruments or marks of their sufferings, produced the legend of S. Denys walking with his head under his arm. The allegorical picture of Michael the Archangel conquering the Evil One in the presence of the Church, gave rise to the myth of S. George rescuing Saba from the dragon, &c.

APPENDIX D.

Pope Hadrian's Letter to Henry II., King of England, a.d. 1154.

Adrianus Papa gratum et acceptum habet quod Henricus Rex Angliæ Insulam Hyberniam ingrediatur ut populum illum legibus subdat, ita tamen ut annua Petro solvatur pensio.

Adrianus Episcopus, servus servorum Dei, carissimo in Christo filio illustri Anglorum Regi, salutem et Apostolicam Benedictionem. Laudabiliter satis et fructuose de glorioso nomine propagando in terris et æternæ felicitatis præmio cumulando in cœlis, tua magnificentia cogitat, dum ad dilatandos Ecclesiæ terminos, ad declarandam indoctis et rudibus Populis Christianæ fidei veritatem, et vitiorum plantaria de Agro Dominico extirpanda, sicut Catholicus Princeps, intendis, et ad id convenientius exequendum consilium Apostolicæ sedis exigis et favorem. In quo facto, quanto altiori consilio, et majori discretione procedes, tanto in eo feliciorem progressum te, præstante Domino confidimus habiturum, eo quod ad bonum exitum semper et finem soleant attingere quæ de ardore fidei et religionis amore principium acceperunt.

Sane Hiberniam et omnes Insulas quibus sol justitiæ Christus illuxit, et quæ documenta Fidei Christianæ receperunt, ad jus beati Petri et sacrosanctæ Romanæ Ecclesiæ (quod tua etiam nobilitas recognoscit) non est dubium pertinere, unde tanto in eis libentius plantationem fidei fidelem et germen Deo gratum inserimus, quanto id a nobis interno exadistrictius prospicimus exigendum.

Significasti siquidem nobis, fili in Christo karissime, te Hyberniæ Insulam ad subdendum illum populum legibus, et vitiorum plantaria inde extirpanda, velle intrare, *et de singulis domibus Annuam unius denarii beato Petri velle solvere pensionem*, et jura Ecclesiarum illius terræ illibata et integra conservare; nos itaque, pium et laudabile desiderium tuum favore congruo prosequentes, et petitioni tuæ benignum impendentes assensum, gratum et acceptum habemus, ut, pro dilatandis Ecclesiæ terminis, pro vitiorum restringendo decursu, pro corrigendis moribus et virtutibus inserendis, pro Christianæ Religionis augmento, Insulam illam ingrediaris; et quæ ad honorem Dei et salutem illius spectaverint exequaris; et illius terræ populus honorifice te recipiat; et sicut Dominum veneretur (*jure nimirum Ecclesiarum illibato et integro permanente, et salva beato Petro et sacrosanctæ Romanæ*

Ecclesiæ de singulis domibus annua unius denarii pensione)..

Si ergo, quod concepisti animo, effectu duxeris prosequente complendum, stude gentem illam bonis moribus informare, et agas, tam per te, quam per illos quos ad hoc fide, verbo, et vita idoneos esse perspexeris, ut decoretur ibi Ecclesia, plantetur et crescat Fidei Christianæ Religio, et quæ ad honorem Dei et salutem pertinent animarum taliter ordinentur, ut et a Deo sempiternæ mercedis cumulum consequi merearis, et in terris gloriosum nomen valeas in seculis obtinere.—Rymer's *Fœdera, Conventiones*, &c., I., p. 15.

It is interesting to compare with the claims made by the above document the decision of the recent council of the Vatican.

" Si quis itaque dixerit, Romanum Pontificem
" habere tantummodo officium inspectionis vel di-
" rectionis, non autem *plenam et supremam potestatem*
" *jurisdictionis in universam Ecclesiam*, non solum in
" rebus, quæ ad fidem et mores, *sed etiam iis, quæ ad*
" *disciplinam et regimen Ecclesiæ per totum orbem*
" *diffusæ pertinent*; aut eum habere tantum potiores
" partes, non vero totam plenitudinem hujus su-
" premæ potestatis; aut hanc ejus potestatem non
" esse ordinariam et immediatam sive in omnes ac
" singulas ecclesias, *sive in omnes et singulos pastores*
" *et fideles*; anathema sit."—*Constitutio Dogmatica*
" *Prima de Ecclesia Christi*, cap. iii.

APPENDIX E.

Decisions "ex Cathedrâ."

Difficulty of ascertaining the meaning of "ex cathedrâ."

"Quelles étaient alors les conditions de l'acte *ex cathedrâ*? Qui peut dire ce qu'elles sont aujourd'hui? Connaît-on deux théologiens bien d'accord sur ce point? Nous parlerons des actes *ex cathedrâ* quand nous saurons ce que veut dire le mot *ex cathedrâ*."

Most persons who have endeavoured to discover what the exact meaning of decisions *ex cathedrâ* is, will be inclined to sympathise very heartily with the above words of Père[1] Gratry.

The definition given by the Vatican council is not clear.

Archbishop Manning tells us[2] that the Vatican council has defined the meaning. What the council says is this: "We teach and define that it is a dogma divinely revealed; that the Roman Pontiff, when he speaks *ex cathedrâ*, that is, *when in discharge of the office of Pastor and Doctor of all Christians, by virtue of his supreme Apostolic authority he defines a doctrine regarding faith or*

---

[1] *Troisième lettre à Mgr. Deschamps*, p. 13.
[2] *The Vatican Council and its Definitions*, London, 1870, p. 57.

"morals to be held by the *Universal Church*, by the divine assistance promised to him in blessed Peter, is possessed of that infallibility,"[1] &c.

But some persons have been able to accept the new dogma, that the pope has the Church's infallibility when he speaks *ex cathedrâ*, precisely because neither the nature of the Church's infallibility nor the meaning of *ex cathedrâ* have ever been defined. It would seem, then, that the definition of the Vatican council is itself in need of definition. We must fall back, therefore, on the explanations of the phrase which have been attempted elsewhere.

Those not already committed to a position, with which the meaning of *ex cathedrâ* must at all hazards be made consistent, will probably agree with "JANUS,"[2] that beyond excluding off-hand remarks on dogmatic and ethical questions made by a pope in the course of conversation, the distinction *ex cathedrâ* has no meaning. "When a pope speaks publicly on a point of doctrine, either of his own accord, or in answer to questions addressed to him, he has spoken *ex cathedrâ*,

---

[1] "Docemus et divinitus revelatum dogma esse definimus: Romanum Pontificem, cum ex cathedrâ loquitur, id est, *cum omnium Christianorum Pastoris et Doctoris munere fungens, pro suprema sua Apostolica auctoritate doctrinam de fide vel moribus ab universa Ecclesia tenendam definit*, per assistentiam divinam, ipsi in beato Petro promissam, ea infallibilitate pollere, qua divinus Redemptor Ecclesiam suam in definienda doctrina de fide vel moribus instructam esse voluit," &c. — *Constitutio Dogmatica Prima de Ecclesia Christi*, cap. IV., sub fin.

[2] *Der Papst und das Concil.*, p. 427. English translation, p. 404.

"for he was questioned as pope, and successor of
"other popes, and the mere fact that he has made
"his declaration publicly and in writing makes it
"an *ex cathedrâ* judgment. .... The moment any
"accidental or arbitrary condition is fixed on
"which the *ex cathedrâ* nature of a papal decision
"is to depend, we enter the sphere of the private
"crotchets of theologians. .... Just as if one
"chose to say afterwards of a physician who had
"been consulted, and had given his opinion on a
"disease, that he had formed his diagnosis and
"prescribed his remedies as a private person, and
"not as a physician. .... Thus Orsi maintains
"that Honorius composed the dogmatic letter he
"issued in reply to the Eastern Patriarchs, and
"which was afterwards condemned as heretical by
"the sixth Œcumenical Council, only as 'a private
"'teacher;' but the expression *doctor privatus*, when
"used of a pope, is like talking of wooden iron."

Some have maintained that before a pope speaks *ex cathedrâ* he must have thoroughly discussed the question to be decided, conferring with bishops and theologians. This *appears* to be the present view of bishop HEFELE, judging from his recent most disappointing letter to the clergy of his [1] diocese. But the learned author of the *Concilien-geschichte* does not tell us whether the consulting a synod is an indispensable condition of a definition

---

[1] The words of our Constitution (*Constitutio Dogmatica Prima de Ecclesia Christi*, cap. IV.): "Romani autem Pontifices, prout tempo-

ex cathedrâ, or only a piece of ecclesiastical etiquette. If the latter, the statement is nugatory; if the former, we have the startling paradox that the infallibility of an infallible Head is dependent on consultation with fallible subordinates.

BELLARMINE and his fellow Jesuit, ENDEMON JOHANNES, make it a *sine quâ non* that the pope should address what he defines *ex cathedrâ* to the whole Church. Thus a decree or definition addressed to the Church in France or in Germany would not necessarily be infallible. But surely what is truth for one is truth for all. How can a proposition be an article of faith for France or Germany, if it is not an article of faith for the whole Church?

Others, again, would make it of the essence of an *ex cathedrâ* decision that the document should have been affixed for a certain time to the door of S. Peter's, and in the Campofiore.

" rum et rerum conditio suadebat, nunc convocatis œcumenicis
" conciliis aut explorata Ecclesiæ per orbem dispersæ sententia,
" nunc per synodos particulares, nunc aliis, quæ divina suppeditabat
" providentia, adhibitis auxiliis, &c., contain not only an historical
" notice of what was done formerly, but also imply the rule, in
" accordance with which papal decisions ex cathedrâ will always be
" made."—*Rundschreiben an den hochwürdigen Klerus.* Rottenburg, April 10th, 1871.

But will it suffice if the pope merely consults a synod, and then decrees what he pleases, whether the synod approve or no? Or must at least *some* of the synod agree with him? Or will it be sufficient if he only consults those who are known to agree with him? " This question has become a crucial one since 1713, when Clement " XI. issued his famous Bull *Unigenitus*, which he had drawn up " with the assistance of two cardinals only."—(Janus).

Another necessary condition, according to some, is, that the pope should anathematize those who dispute the decision.

Lastly, the BISHOP OF ST. PÖLTEN maintains[1] that the pope must expressly state that he is defining, in virtue of his office, as supreme teacher in the Church. Hence he would contend that it is still doubtful whether the present pope's *Syllabus* is *ex cathedrâ*, and therefore infallible. Would *Rome* allow that it is doubtful?

In considering these various, and in some cases extraordinary conditions, we can scarcely avoid the conclusion that they are for the most part artificial restrictions, invented for the purpose of excluding certain awkward utterances of popes from being *ex cathedrâ*. Such efforts reach a climax when the view is deliberately put forth, that,[1] as no pope ever has spoken *ex cathedrâ* from

---

[1] *Die falsche und die wahre Unfehlbarkeit der Päpste*, von Dr. Joseph FETZLER, Bischof von St. Pölten, Wien, 1871. The pamphlet contains some strange inconsistencies, as professor Berchtold has already pointed out, e. g.: On p. 34 bishop Fetzler maintains that the well-known brief of Pius IX. *Multiplices inter* (June 10, 1851), in which certain doctrines are condemned as heretical, is not a decision *ex cathedrâ*; and the bishop ridicules professor Schulte for supposing that a definition of an article of faith could be made in condemning a book. On p. 41, however, he tells us, that in theology it is a sure sign (sicheres Kennzeichen) of a dogmatic decision, when any doctrine is declared by the pope to be heretical. The pamphlet in style is perhaps scarcely what one would have expected from a prelate.

[2] *What is the meaning of the late Definition of the Infallibility of the Pope? An Enquiry.* By W. MASKELL, p. 10. Noticed by the dean of Westminster in his recent pamphlet on *the Athanasian Creed*. Dean Stanley justly remarks, "Whether such interpretations "are respectful to the documents which they profess to honour may "well be doubted." (p. 95).

the beginning of time till now, so it is probable that henceforth till the end of time none ever will so speak. And nothing short of this desperate theory can save the Bull of Paul IV.—"*Cum ex Apostolatus officio*," March 15th, 1809 (one of the most terrible ever issued by a pope)—from being *ex cathedrâ*. Every[1] condition, even down to the affixing it on the doors of S. Peter's, is fulfilled. The bishop of St. Pölten attempts to exclude it, because it is not a decision in matters of faith—"keine *Glaubens*entscheidung;" but it is most undeniably a decision in *matters of morals*, and these are claimed as within the sphere of papal infallibility no less than matters of faith.

---

[1] It is perhaps worth while to quote the passages which prove this:—"Cum *ex Apostolatus officio* nobis, meritis licet imparibus, "divinitus credito, cura Dominici gregis nobis immineat *generalis*, "et exinde teneamur pro fideli illius *custodia*, et salubri *directione*, "more Vigilis *Pastoris* assidue vigilare," &c.

"Habita super his cum venerabilibus fratribus nostris S. R. E. "cardinalibus *deliberatione matura*, de eorum consilio, et *unanimi* "*assensu*," &c.

"Hac nostra *in perpetuum valitura* constitutione, ... de *Aposto-* "*licæ potestatis plenitudine* sancimus, statuimus, decernimus et "*definimus*," &c.

"Ut autem præsentes literæ ad omnium quorum interest notitiam "deducantur, volumus eas .... in *Basilicæ Principis Apostolorum* "*de Urbe et Chancellariæ Apostolicæ valvis atque in acie campi Floræ* "per aliquos ex cursoribus nostris publicari et *affigi*," &c.

"Si quis autem hoc attentare præsumpserit, *indignationem omni-* "*potentis Dei*, ac Beatorum Petri et Pauli apostolorum ejus se "noverit *incursurum*"—"hoc" being the infringing or opposing of the Bull. See an able article in the *Allgemeine Zeitung* (Beilage, April 11, 1871), *Die römische Frage, die päpstliche Sittenlehre und die europäische Rechtsordnung.*

APPENDIX F.

THE LATEST DEFENDERS OF HONORIUS.

The apologists for Honorius have overdone their work.

IN order to be convinced how fatal the case of Honorius is to the claims of papal infallibility, one has only to read a few of his apologists. The means resorted to in the vain attempt to overcome the insurmountable difficulty, are *so extraordinary* and *so various*, that one feels that the truth must be on the side which is so fiercely and irrationally assailed. The controversy is one more proof of the simplicity of truth and the multiplicity of error. We are only concerned now with that mode of argument, lately renewed in high quarters, which would demolish the case of Honorius as an instance of papal fallibility, by maintaining that the letters of Honorius are *not* heterodox. This method has at least the advantage of being bold. Three general councils have declared that these letters *are* heterodox, in fact, damnably heretical; and pope after pope has confirmed the decision of these councils. But, in spite of that, three Roman archbishops publicly assure their clergy that the epistles of Honorius are perfectly orthodox. Protestant "private judgment" can scarcely go farther.

A recent pastoral of the ARCHBISHOP OF BALTIMORE contains the following "excellent passage," quoted with approbation by archbishop Manning: "The case of Honorius forms no exception; for "1st, Honorius expressly says in his letters to "Sergius that he meant to define nothing, and he "was condemned precisely because he temporized "and would not define; 2nd, because IN HIS "LETTERS HE CLEARLY TAUGHT THE SOUND CA-"THOLIC DOCTRINE, only enjoining silence as to "the use of certain terms, then new in the Church; "and 3rd, because his letters were not addressed "to a general council of the whole Church, and "were rather private than public and official; at "least they were not published, even in the East, "until several years later." *Bold attempt of the archbishops of Baltimore,*

The ARCHBISHOP OF WESTMINSTER goes even further than his American brother. "I will, "nevertheless, here affirm that the following "points in the case of Honorius can be abundantly "proved from documents:— *of Westminster,*

"(1.) That Honorius *defined no doctrine whatso-*"*ever*. (2.) That he forbade the making of any "new definition. (3.) That his fault was precisely "in this omission[1] of Apostolic authority, for

---

[1] Would the council have solemnly cursed Honorius for mere "omission of Apostolic authority?" And would pope Leo have

"which he was justly censured [i.e. anathematized].
"(4.) That HIS TWO EPISTLES ARE ENTIRELY OR-
"THODOX; though, in the use of language, he
"wrote, *as was usual*, before the condemnation of
"monothelitism, and not as it became necessary
"afterwards. It is an anachronism and an in-
"justice to censure his language used before that
"condemnation, as it might be just to censure it
"after the condemnation had been made;"[1] an
anachronism of which three general councils and
various popes have been guilty. One is not
ashamed of being similarly guilty in company so
respectable.

It is difficult to decide which statement is the most audacious, that the letters of Honorius are entirely orthodox, or that the language for which he was anathematized was usual at the time.

and of Malines. Similarly the ARCHBISHOP OF MALINES maintains of Honorius, that "non seulement il n'a pas enseigné le monothélisme, mais IL A FORMELLEMENT ENSEIGNÉ LE CONTRAIRE."

Summary of the facts. Let us very briefly review the facts.

Of the four oriental patriarchs three had declared for the famous *Nine Articles*, which were an attempt to make peace by means of a doubtful expression.[2]

---

spoken of such omission as a "profana proditio," an attempt to subvert the faith?

[1] *The Vatican Council and its Definitions*: a Pastoral Letter to the Clergy, London, 1870.

[2] Θεανδρικα ἐνεργεια—words capable of an orthodox, but also of a monophysite interpretation. They occur in the seventh and crucial article. The first six are introductory; the last two are anathemas.

The new patriarch of Jerusalem, Sophroniscus, disregarding the promise which he had made as a private theologian, had called a synod and solemnly condemned the *Nine Articles*. Now came the time when Honorius, hitherto quite passive, could keep silence no longer. He was formally asked for his decision. It would seem as if he never clearly understood the question. He gave *four*[1] different answers. (1.) We must confess that Christ had only one will. (Which was heretical.) (2.) We must not say that Christ had two conflicting wills, of which the divine will compelled the human will to act in harmony with it. (Which no one had ever dreamed of saying.) (3.) It would be better not to talk either of one will or of two wills, but to leave such a mere question of language to grammarians. (Which was no answer at all.) (4.) We

---

[1] (1). " Unde et UNAM VOLUNTATEM FATEMUR D. N. JESU CHRISTI, " quia profecto a divinitate assumpta est nostra natura, non culpa " [in] illa profecto, quæ ante peccatum creata est, non quæ post prævaricationem vitiata." (2). " Nam *lex alia in membris*, aut *voluntas diversa* non fuit, vel *contraria* salvatori, quia super legem natus est " humanæ conditionis." (3). " Utrum autem propter opera divinitatis et humanitatis una an geminæ operationes debeant derivatæ dici vel intelligi, ad nos ista pertinere non debent, relinquentes ea grammaticis, qui solent parvulis exquisita derivando " nomina venditare. Nos enim non unam operationem vel duas " dominum Jesum Christum ejusque sanctum Spiritum, sacris literis " percepimus, sed multiformiter cognovimus operatum." Honorii PP., Ep. III., *Ad Sergium Constantinopolitanum Episcopum*. Labbe, *Concil.*, VI., 929, 932. (4). " Auferentes ergo, sicut diximus, scanda" lum novellæ ad inventionis, *non nos oportet unam vel duas opera" tiones definientes prædicare*, sed pro una, quam quidam dicunt, " operatione, oportet nos unum operatorem Christum dominum in " utrisque naturis veridice confiteri; et pro duabus operationibus,

must not talk either of one will or of two wills. The question cannot lawfully be discussed. (Which was a return to the absurd and disastrous policy of Zeno's *Henoticon*; attempting to settle a vexed question by forbidding its discussion).

In the *Ecthesis* the emperor gave this fourth dictum of Honorius the authority of an imperial decree. The *Ecthesis* was received with great favour in the East; and Honorius would no doubt have accepted it. He died, however, before it reached Rome, October, A.D. 638.

"*ablato geminæ operationis vocabulo*, ipsas potius duas naturas, id est, divinitatis et carnis assumptæ, in una persona unigeniti Dei Patris, inconfuse indivise, atque inconvertibiliter nobiscum prædicare propria operantes." "Scribentes etiam communibus fratribus Cyro et Sophronio antistitibus, *ne novæ vocis, id est, unius vel geminæ operationis vocabulo insistere vel immorari videantur*: sed *abrasa hujusmodi novæ vocis appellatione*, unum Christum dominum nobiscum in utrisque naturis divina vel humana prædicent operantem." Honorii PP. Ep. IV., ad eundem. Labbe, *Concil.*, VI., 969. A fresh discussion of the case of Honorius has just appeared in Germany.—*Die Irrlehre des Honorius und das vaticanische Decret*. By A. Ruckgaber, Stuttgart, 1871. The book has been placed on the Index, and the author has submitted to the condemnation.

LONDON:
PRINTED BY WILLIAM CLOWES AND SONS,
STAMFORD STREET AND CHARING CROSS

WORKS

PUBLISHED DURING 1869 AND 1870 BY

Messrs. RIVINGTON,

WATERLOO PLACE, LONDON;

HIGH STREET, OXFORD; TRINITY STREET, CAMBRIDGE

THE ORIGIN AND DEVELOPMENT OF RELIGIOUS BELIEF. By S. BARING-GOULD, M.A., Author of "Curious Myths of the Middle Ages."
    Vol. I. HEATHENISM and MOSAISM. 8vo. 15s.
    Vol. II. CHRISTIANITY. 8vo. 15s.

"*The ability which Mr. Baring-Gould displays in the treatment of a topic which branches out in so many directions, and requires such precise handling, is apparent. His pages abound with the results of large reading and calm reflection. The man of culture, thought, philosophic cast, is mirrored in the entire argument. The book is sound and healthy in tone. It excites the reader's interest, and brightens the path of inquiry opened to his view. The language, too, is appropriate, neat, lucid, often happy, sometimes wonderfully terse and vigorous.*"—ATHENÆUM.

"*Mr. Baring-Gould has undertaken a great and ambitious work. And no one can deny that he possesses some eminent qualifications for this great work. He has a wealth of erudition of the most varied description, especially in those particular regions of mediæval legend and Teutonic mythology which are certain to make large contributions to the purpose he has in hand. It is a contribution to religious thought of very high value.*"—GUARDIAN.

"*Mr. Baring-Gould's work, from the importance of its subject and the lucid force of its expositions, as well as from the closeness of argument and copiousness of illustration with which its comprehensive views are treated, is entitled to attentive study, and will repay the reader by amusement and instruction.*"—MORNING POST.

"*There is very much in the book for High Churchmen to ponder over. This remarkable book teems with striking passages and it is written in a quiet, self-possessed, loving spirit, and our hope is that if any of our readers take up the book to read, they will read it through to the end, since by so doing will they alone be able to enter into the spirit of one who in these times will have much power for good or evil in our Anglican Church.*"—CHURCH REVIEW.

"*The book is a very remarkable one, which very few of our modern divines could have written, and none but those who study it with care and a keen intelligence will be able to understand or appreciate. Within our present limits, we can but glance at its general characteristics, and must still leave the knotty problems in divinity which it leaves unsettled to be discussed and settled by the more lawful judges. . . . But in spite of the magnitude of his subject, its difficulty, grandeur, and importance, we are bound to add that he has managed to deal vigorously and wisely with many of these topics, and again and again opens to the reader new lines of thought of the deepest interest and most profound importance. Mere desultory readers it will do little more than annoy and disappoint; but all who are really in earnest, and love the truth well enough to work hard for it, will here find much worthy of their most careful study.*"—STANDARD.

"*Mr. Baring-Gould's book is interesting, learned, ingenious; bringing contributions to his thesis from most divergent points, he fits them in with masterly completeness and logical consistency.*"—NONCONFORMIST.

A DEVOTIONAL COMMENTARY ON THE GOSPEL
NARRATIVE. By the Rev. ISAAC WILLIAMS, B.D., formerly Fellow of Trinity College, Oxford. A New and uniform Edition. In Eight vols. Crown 8vo. 5s. each.

THOUGHTS ON THE STUDY OF THE HOLY GOSPELS.
Characteristic Differences in the Four Gospels.
Our Lord's Manifestations of Himself.
The Rule of Scriptural Interpretation furnished by our Lord.
Analogies of the Gospel.
Mention of Angels in the Gospels.
Places of our Lord's Abode and Ministry.
Our Lord's Mode of Dealing with His Apostles.
Conclusion.

A HARMONY OF THE FOUR EVANGELISTS.
Our Lord's Nativity.
Our Lord's Ministry—Second Year.
Our Lord's Ministry—Third Year.
The Holy Week.
Our Lord's Passion.
Our Lord's Resurrection.

OUR LORD'S NATIVITY.
The Birth at Bethlehem.
The Baptism in Jordan.
The First Passover.

OUR LORD'S MINISTRY.
SECOND YEAR.
The Second Passover.
Christ with the Twelve.
The Twelve sent forth.

OUR LORD'S MINISTRY.
THIRD YEAR.
Teaching in Galilee.
Teaching at Jerusalem.
Last Journey from Galilee to Jerusalem.

THE HOLY WEEK.
The Approach to Jerusalem.
The Teaching in the Temple.
The Discourse on the Mount of Olives.
The Last Supper.

OUR LORD'S PASSION.
The Hour of Darkness.
The Agony.
The Apprehension.
The Condemnation.
The Day of Sorrows.
The Hall of Judgment.
The Crucifixion.
The Sepulture.

OUR LORD'S RESURRECTION.
The Day of Days.
The Grave Visited.
Christ Appearing.
The Going to Emmaus.
The Forty Days.
The Apostles Assembled.
The Lake in Galilee.
The Mountain in Galilee.
The Return from Galilee.

"*There is not a better companion to be found for the season than the beautiful 'Devotional Commentary on the Gospel Narrative,' by the Rev. Isaac Williams. . . . A rich mine for devotional and theological study.*"—GUARDIAN.

"*So infinite are the depths and so innumerable the beauties of Scripture, and more particularly of the Gospels, that there is some difficulty in describing the manifold excellences of Williams' exquisite Commentary. Deriving its profound appreciation of Scripture from the writings of the early Fathers, it is only what every student knows must be true to say that it extracts a whole wealth of meaning from each sentence, each apparently faint allusion, each word in the text.*"—CHURCH REVIEW.

"*Stands absolutely alone in our English literature; there is, we should say, no chance of its being superseded by any better book of its kind; and its merits are of the very highest order.*"—LITERARY CHURCHMAN.

"*It would be difficult to select a more useful present, at a small cost, than this series would be to a young man on his first entering into Holy Orders, and many, no doubt, will avail themselves of the republication of these useful volumes for this purpose. There is an abundance of sermon material to be drawn from any one of them.*"—CHURCH TIMES.

"*This is, in the truest sense of the word, a 'Devotional Commentary' on the Gospel narrative, opening out everywhere, as it does, the spiritual beauties and blessedness of the Divine message; but it is something more than this, it meets difficulties almost by anticipation, and throws the light of learning over some of the very darkest passages in the New Testament.*"—ROCK.

"*The author has skilfully compared and blended the narratives of the different Gospels, so as to give a synoptical view of the history; and though the commentary is called 'devotional,' it is scholarly and suggestive in other respects. The size of the work, extending, as it does, over eight volumes, may deter purchasers and readers; but each volume is complete in itself, and we recommend students to taste a sample of the author's quality. Some things they may question; but the volumes are really a helpful and valuable addition to our stores.*"—FREEMAN.

"*The high and solemn verities of the Saviour's sufferings and death are treated with great reverence and ability. The thorough devoutness which pervades the book commends it to our heart. There is much to instruct and help the believer in the Christian life, no matter to what section of the Church he may belong.*"—WATCHMAN.

THE GUIDE TO HEAVEN: A Book of Prayers for every Want. (For the Working Classes.) Compiled by a Priest. Edited by the Rev. T. T. CARTER, M.A., Rector of Clewer, Berks. Crown 8vo, limp cloth, 1s.; cloth extra, 1s. 6d.

THE VICTORY OF DIVINE GOODNESS; Including—I. Letters to an Inquirer on Various Doctrines of Scripture; II. Notes on Coleridge's Confessions of an Inquiring Spirit; III. Thoughts on the Nature of the Atonement and of Eternal Judgment. By T. R. BIRKS, M.A., Incumbent of Holy Trinity, Cambridge. Second Edition, with Reply to Recent Strictures. Crown 8vo. 5s.

CONSOLING THOUGHTS IN SICKNESS. Edited by HENRY BAILEY, B.D., Warden of St. Augustine's College, Canterbury. Large type. Fine Edition. Small 8vo. 2s. 6d.
Also, a Cheap Edition, 1s. 6d.; or in paper cover, 1s.

CONSOLATIO; or, Comfort for the Afflicted. Edited by the Rev. C. E. KENNAWAY. With a Preface by SAMUEL WILBERFORCE, D.D., Lord Bishop of Winchester. New Edition. Small 8vo. 3s. 6d.

"*A charming collection from the best writers of passages suitable in seasons of sickness and affliction.*"—CHURCH REVIEW.
"*A very valuable collection of extracts from writers of every school. The volume is an elegant one.*"—CHURCH TIMES.
"*A very useful collection of devotional extracts from the histories of good men of very various schools of thought.*"—JOHN BULL.

"*We are bound to admire the extreme beauty and the warm devotion of the majority of passages here collected to smooth the soul that sorrows, even though penned by men from whom we differ so much in doctrine.*"—ROCK.
"*A work which we feel sure will find a welcome and also prove a soothing guest in the chamber of many an invalid.*"—RECORD.

THE HAPPINESS OF THE BLESSED CONSIDERED as to the Particulars of their State: their Recognition of each other in that State: and its Differences of Degrees. To which are added Musings on the Church and her Services. By RICHARD MANT, D.D., sometime Lord Bishop of Down and Connor. New Edition. Small 8vo. 3s. 6d.

"*A welcome republication of a treatise once highly valued, and which can never lose its value. Many of our readers already know the fulness and discrimination with which the author treats his subject, which must be one of the most delightful topics of meditation to all whose heart is where the only true treasure is, and particularly to those who are entering upon the evening of life.*"—CHURCH REVIEW.
"*The value of this book needs not to be referred to, its standard character having been for many years past established. The edition in which it reappears has evidently been carefully prepared, and will be the means of making it more generally known.*"—BELL'S MESSENGER.

"*All recognise the authority of the command to set the affections on things above, and such works as the one now before us will be found helpful towards this good end. We are, therefore, sincerely glad that Messrs. Rivington have brought out a new edition of Bishop Mant's valuable treatise.*"—RECORD.
"*This beautiful and devotional treatise, which it is impossible to read without feeling a more deepened interest in the eternal blessedness which awaits the true servants of our God, concludes very appropriately with 'Musings on the Church and her Services,' which we cordially recommend to our readers.*"—ROCK.

MATERIALS AND MODELS FOR GREEK AND LATIN PROSE COMPOSITION Selected and arranged by J. Y. SARGENT, M.A., Tutor, late Fellow of Magdalen College, Oxford; and T. F. DALLIN, M.A., Fellow and Tutor of Queen's College, Oxford. Crown 8vo. 7s. 6d.

JOHN WESLEY'S PLACE IN CHURCH HISTORY, determined with the aid of Facts and Documents unknown to, or unnoticed by, his Biographers. By R. DENNY URLIN, M.R.I.A., of the Middle Temple, Barrister-at-Law, etc. With a New and Authentic portrait. Small 8vo. 5s. 6d.

"A book of real and permanent value, written by a man who can think and arrange his thoughts, as well as merely investigate, and who has also a good deal of the historic faculty as well. Moreover, he has the art of saying what he has to say in a few words without any sacrifice of clearness; so that although there is a large amount of information conveyed, and although very considerable reading has gone to its composition, the book is comparatively short, and very easy to read. . . . We should say that Mr. Urlin's book will take its place as a standard book of reference on the Wesley subject."—LITERARY CHURCHMAN.

"We commend to our readers the lucid and interesting chain of argument by which Mr. Urlin makes it plain that the real place of John Wesley in Church History is that of a 'Church Revivalist,' forming and fully carrying out a grand design for the renovation of the English Church of the eighteenth century. . . . The author has allowed himself but a small space for his work, but he has done it most effectively, and in a literary style at once forcible and refined."—EXAMINER.

"Mr. Urlin has brought together all the evidence that he can discover of Wesley's adherence to the doctrine and discipline of the Primitive Church; and out of these materials, some of which were unknown to former biographers, has produced a strongly marked portrait of a High Churchman, and one in which we think modern Wesleyans will have some difficulty in recognizing the features of their founder. . . We freely accord all praise to Mr. Urlin for the spirit and temper which have prompted and controlled his work."—ATHENÆUM.

THE ILIAD OF HOMER, from the Text of Dindorf. With Preface and Notes. By S. H. REYNOLDS, M.A., Fellow and Tutor of Brasenose College, Oxford. Books I. to XII. Crown 8vo. 6s. Forming a Part of the "Catena Classicorum."

"Adopting the usual plan of this series, and giving references to standard works rather than extracts from them, Mr. Reynolds is able to find space for much comment that is purely Homeric, and to show that it is not only a theory but a working principle with him, to make Homer his own interpreter and commentator. 'Ex ipso Homero Homerus optime intelligitur,' is a dictum which no student of Homer would question for a moment; but to acknowledge its truth is one thing, and prove it in practice is another, and the manner in which Mr. Reynolds has effected this will go far to show his capacity for the difficult task he has executed. The notes are by no means overloaded, but seem to us to contain all that they should, in order to carry out the editor's purpose of assisting beginners, while there is much that will prove valuable to advanced students. We heartily commend the book to our readers' notice."—STANDARD.

"Mr. Holmes and Mr. Bigg deserve the gratitude of all scholars for the 'Catena Classicorum,' which is coming out under their superintendence, and which includes such works as the 'Sophocles' of Mr. Jebb, and the 'Persius' of Mr. Pretor. The series supplies so completely a long-felt want, that we can scarcely understand why it is we waited so long for a really good and cheap edition of these classical authors, which we have been obliged to read either in foreign editions, or from English texts with worthless notes, or else from editions like the 'Bibliotheca Classica,' the expense of which is a serious drawback to their general use. The standard set up by the earlier volumes was high, and we can hardly feel surprise if, executed as they are by different hands, some of the succeeding ones should show some falling off in excellence; but so far as we have gone, all, or nearly all, have been good, and some pre-eminently so; and we only hope that the same care and scholarship will be bestowed on the volumes which are yet to come. The present volume we should be disposed to reckon as good. The notes display both scholarship and careful research."—EDUCATIONAL TIMES.

"Mr. Reynolds shows in his short preface how genial scholarship like his can be, and he made to seem. Every note in the book is valuable. His selection is as admirable as his scholarship. At the same time, the notes are so ample that we hope this text-book will displace much of the crude annotation and bad printing which trouble the eye and the mind's eye, in certain editions of the classics from across the Atlantic. The short preface is an extract essence of all Homeric questions and answers."—EDINBURGH EVENING COURANT.

"The new volume of Messrs. Rivington's admirable 'Catena Classicorum' contains the first twelve books of the 'Iliad,' edited by Mr. Reynolds, Fellow and Tutor of Brasenose. The text, which like all the series is printed in a clear bold type, is that of Dindorf, and Mr. Reynolds has added some useful explanatory notes, not too numerous or too abstruse, but well suited for school use."—JOHN BULL.

"We have already more than once expressed a very high opinion of the reprints of classical authors under the title of 'Catena Classicorum' which Messrs. Holmes and Bigg are now issuing. Part I. of Homer's 'Iliad,' comprising the first twelve books, is now before us, and it is sufficient for us to say that it is a most scholar-like and excellent edition that is here presented. The notes are of medium length, neither too long to make the book inconveniently bulky, nor too brief to be useful. . . . Of Mr. Reynolds' Oxford reputation as a philosophical scholar it is needless to speak, and his name is a sufficient guarantee for the soundness and importance of this work."—ENGLISH CHURCHMAN.

RIVINGTON'S MATHEMATICAL SERIES.

MR. HAMBLIN SMITH's Works on ELEMENTARY MATHEMATICS have been so favourably received by many who are engaged in tuition in the University of Cambridge and in Schools, that it is proposed to make them the foundation of a Series to include most of the Mathematical Subjects required in the Cambridge Course.

The following have been already published.

ELEMENTARY ALGEBRA. Part I. By J. HAMBLIN SMITH, M.A., Gonville and Caius College, and Lecturer at St. Peter's College, Cambridge. New Edition. Crown 8vo. 4s. 6d.

EXERCISES ON ALGEBRA. By the same Author. Crown 8vo. 2s. 6d.
(*Copies may be had without the Answers.*)

ELEMENTARY TRIGONOMETRY. Part I. By the same Author. New Edition. Crown 8vo. 4s. 6d.

ELEMENTARY HYDROSTATICS. By the same Author. New Edition. Crown 8vo. 3s.

"*It is evident that Mr. Hamblin Smith is a teacher, and has written to meet the special wants of students. He does not carry the student out of his depth by sudden plunges, but leads him gradually onward, never beyond his depth from any desire to hurry forward. The examples appear to be particularly well arranged, so as to afford a means of steady progress. With such books the judicious teacher will have abundant supply of examples and problems for those who need to have each step ensured by familiarity, and he will be able to allow the more rapid learner to travel onward with ease and swiftness. We can confidently recommend Mr. Hamblin Smith's books. Candidates preparing for Civil Service examinations under the new system of open competition, will find these works to be of great value.*"—CIVIL SERVICE GAZETTE.

ARITHMETIC, THEORETICAL AND PRACTICAL. By W. H. GIRDLESTONE, M.A., of Christ's College, Cambridge, and Principal of the Gloucester Theological College. Second Edition, Revised and Enlarged. Crown 8vo. 6s. 6d.

Also, a School Edition, without the Appendix. Small 8vo. 3s. 6d.

(*Copies may be had without the Answers to the Exercises.*)

"*We may congratulate Mr. Girdlestone on having produced a thoroughly philosophical book on this most useful subject. It appears to be especially suited for older students, who, having been taught imperfectly and irrationally in the earlier part of their school career, desire to go over the whole ground again from the beginning; but in the hands of an intelligent and discriminating teacher, it may also be perfectly adapted to the comprehension of young boys.*"—TIMES.

"*Mr. Girdlestone's Arithmetic is admirably suited to the requirements of higher forms in schools, and for men at the Universities. Mr. Girdlestone shows himself a thorough teacher; processes are lucidly explained, and practical solution of problems well given.*"—GUARDIAN.

"*We must content ourselves with this brief general notice of the work, which we consider one of the highest order of its kind—far, very far superior to those of former days.*"—NAUTICAL MAGAZINE.

"*Mr. Girdlestone's definitions are concise but explicit, and quite plain to modest understandings. So successful a work has rapidly won favour, and the first edition having been exhausted, a second has now been issued, bearing further marks of the author's comprehensive ability. An Appendix contains examination papers of Oxford, Cambridge, Winchester, Eton, &c., and will be found most useful to students preparing for public examinations. This book should rank as a standard one of its class.*"—EXAMINER.

A DOMINICAN ARTIST; a Sketch of the Life of the Rev. Père Besson, of the Order of St. Dominic. By the Author of the "The Tales of Kirkbeck," "The Life of Madame Louise de France," &c. Crown 8vo. 9s.

"*The author of the Life of Père Besson writes with a grace and refinement of devotional feeling peculiarly suited to a subject-matter which suffers beyond most others from any coarseness of touch. It would be difficult to find 'the simplicity and purity of a holy life' more exquisitely illustrated than in Father Besson's career, both before and after his joining the Dominican Order under the auspices of Lacordaire. . . . Certainly we have never come across what could more strictly be termed in the truest sense 'the life of a beautiful soul.' The author has done well in presenting to English readers this singularly graceful biography, in which all who can appreciate genuine simplicity and nobleness of Christian character will find much to admire and little or nothing to condemn.*"—SATURDAY REVIEW.

"*It would indeed have been a deplorable omission had so exquisite a biography been by any neglect lost to English readers, and had a character so perfect in its simple and complete devotion been withheld from our admiration. . . . But we have dwelt too long already on this fascinating book, and must now leave it to our readers.*"—LITERARY CHURCHMAN.

"*A beautiful and most interesting sketch of the late Père Besson, an artist who forsook the easel for the altar.*"—CHURCH TIMES.

"*A book which is as pleasant for reading as it is profitable for meditation.*"—UNION REVIEW.

"*We are indebted to the graceful pen of the translator of Madame Louise de France for another Catholic Life, beautifully written, and full of the spirit of love.*"—TABLET.

"*This tastefully bound volume is a record of the life of Père Besson. From childhood to his premature death in April 1861, at the age of forty-five, he was pre-eminently suited to a life of self-denial, and so full of love and charity, that his saintly character calls forth the warmest admiration, and we feel sure the perusal of it will give pleasure to our readers.*"—CHURCH HERALD.

"*Whatever a reader may think of Père Besson's profession as a monk, no one will doubt his goodness; no one can fail to profit who will patiently read his life, as here written by a friend, whose sole defect is in being slightly unctuous.*"—ATHENÆUM.

"*The life of the Rev. Père Besson, who gave up an artist's career, to which he was devotedly attached, and a mother whose affection for him is not inaptly likened to that of Monica for St. Augustine, must be read in its entirety to be rightly appreciated. And the whole tenour of the book is too devotional, too full of expressions of the most touching dependence on God, to make criticism possible, even if it was called for, which it is not.*"—JOHN BULL.

"*The story of Père Besson's life is one of much interest, and told with simplicity, candour, and good feeling.*"—SPECTATOR.

"*A beautiful book, describing the most saintly and very individual life of one of the companions of Lacordaire.*" — MONTHLY PACKET.

"*We strongly recommend it to our readers. It is a charming biography, that will delight and edify both old and young.*"—WESTMINSTER GAZETTE.

MEMOIR OF THE RIGHT REV. JOHN STRACHAN, D.D., LL.D., First Bishop of Toronto. By A. N. BETHUNE, D.D., D.C.L., his Successor in the See. 8vo. 10s.

"*We have in this volume a most interesting memorial of one of the foremost men in the Colonial Church: the well-told story of a most important period in the annals of Canada. The Canadian Church must always be very dear to Anglicans as a branch of their communion, that more than any other reproduces the special traits of the mother Church. And to Bishop Strachan, the subject of this memoir, it was given to gain and exercise a wide influence over the Church of Upper Canada, and to leave his mark on the ecclesiastical history of the period; so that the story of his life, told gracefully and well by Bishop Bethune as we have it here, will, we hope, engage the warm interest of many of our readers. . . .*

But we have exceeded our limits, and must perforce take leave of the book, warmly recommending it as the life-history of a man of sterling worth, whose lot was cast in busy and stirring times, and the worse side of which makes us think sadly of much that we have had to go through, and of more that seems impending."—LITERARY CHURCHMAN.

"*Written in a simple, straightforward, dignified manner, being wanting just a little in the colouring that might now and then have been given to it. But it is readable, and there is much to interest and profit in the busy, fruitful life of a man like Dr. Strachan.*"—CONTEMPORARY REVIEW.

THE RELIGION, DISCIPLINE, AND RITES OF THE CHURCH OF ENGLAND. By JOHN COSIN, Bishop of Durham. Written at the instance of Edward Hyde, Earl of Clarendon. Now first published in English. By the Rev. FREDERICK MEYRICK, M.A., Rector of Blickling and Erpingham; Prebendary of Lincoln; Examining Chaplain to the Lord Bishop of Lincoln. Small 8vo. 2s.

Messrs. Rivington's Publications

EXAMINATION OF CONSCIENCE UPON SPECIAL SUBJECTS. Translated and Abridged from the French of TRONSON. Forming a Volume of *THE ASCETIC LIBRARY*: A Series of Translations of Spiritual Works for Devotional Reading from Catholic Sources. Edited by the Rev. ORBY SHIPLEY, M.A. Square Crown 8vo. 5s.

"It is a much larger and more elaborate work than is usually devoted to this subject, and arranged on a different plan. The chief virtues and sins have each a section given to them, and the examen is cast in the form of a meditation, with first, second, and third points. The enquiries made of the soul are very searching, and are so framed that self-knowledge, and as a consequence self-condemnation, most necessarily result from the conscientious use of the book. It is especially adapted for those who find a difficulty in using the ordinary manuals, and who are yet aiming at a higher life than common. For Religious Houses it will be found invaluable, more especially, perhaps, to mistresses of novices. It strikes us as a book highly suggestive to those who conduct retreats."—CHURCH TIMES.

"This is volume IV. of the series known as the 'Ascetic Library,' and of all the volumes of the series yet published it strikes us as by far the most useful. . . . Singularly practical and judicious, so that it is difficult to say to what class of persons it will be most useful —those who take it for personal use, those who adopt it as a guide in receiving confessions, or the preacher who uses it as a help in the composition of sermons addressed to the conscience rather than to the intellect. There are some excellent pages on Devotional Reading; while as to the subject of penitence it may give some idea of the method of the book to mention the headings of its successive sections 'Fruits of Penitence,' viz.:—Hatred of Sin,—Self-Abhorrence,—Love of the Cross,—Peace of Heart."—LITERARY CHURCHMAN.

"It is a pleasing sign to see such books as these re-edited for the supply of so great a need. No one but a master of the spiritual life could have compiled a set of reflections so searching and yet so exalting as the book before us. We know of nothing more calculated to lay open to itself the mind of the most spiritual, to reveal the self-deceptions and snares lying in its way, and the subtle forms by which perfunctoriness insinuates itself. The book will be found beyond measure useful to all who desire to know themselves in some degree as God knows them, while to religious and to the clergy it must be an inestimable boon."— CHURCH REVIEW.

"Louis Tronson's self-questionings and meditations range over a wide field—from faith and love to God, down to the demeanour practised in working and rising, conversation, and travelling. We should be far from asserting that his book contains nothing good; on the contrary, much that is excellent in sentiment and devout in expression may be found in it."—RECORD.

INSTRUCTIONS FOR THE USE OF CANDIDATES FOR HOLY ORDERS, And of the Parochial Clergy; with Acts of Parliament relating to the same, and Forms proposed to be used. By CHRISTOPHER HODGSON, M.A., Secretary to the Governors of Queen Anne's Bounty. Ninth Edition, Revised and Enlarged. 8vo. 16s.

THE CHURCH OF GOD AND THE BISHOPS: An Essay suggested by the Convocation of the Vatican Council. By HENRY ST. A. VON LIAÑO. Authorized Translation. Crown 8vo. 4s. 6d.

"Written by a devout Roman Catholic, and is at once thoughtful and reverent. It is a volume which acquires a significancy beyond its literary merit from the position of the writer, and is an index of what is moving in the hearts of men whose attachment to their own Church cannot be doubted."— JOHN BULL.

"The author of this work is a Spanish Catholic of noble family now resident at Munich, where he is well known for his devout and ascetic life, his deep religious convictions, and his zealous attachment to his church, which he believes to be just passing through a peculiarly trying and perilous crisis. It is a brief but excellent summary of the chief bearings of the case against the Church of Rome."—ROCK.

"This book is full of condensed thoughts on the subjects which now most press on the minds of Churchmen. They are delivered with a depth and piety which approaches to the prophetical spirit; and we are told that the private character of the writer corresponds with this description, and that it is acknowledged with reverential deference by those Christians who have the happiness to know him."— CHURCH REVIEW.

THE PRAYER BOOK INTERLEAVED; With Historical Illustrations and Explanatory Notes arranged parallel to the Text. By the Rev. W. M. CAMPION, D.D., Fellow and Tutor of Queen's College, and Rector of St. Botolph's, and the Rev. W. J. BEAMONT, M.A., late Fellow of Trinity College, Cambridge. With a Preface by the LORD BISHOP OF ELY. Fifth Edition. Small 8vo. 7s. 6d.

A PLAIN ACCOUNT OF THE ENGLISH BIBLE. From the Earliest Times of its Translation to the Present Day. By JOHN HENRY BLUNT, M.A., Vicar of Kennington, Oxford; Editor of "The Annotated Book of Common Prayer," &c. Crown 8vo. 3s. 6d.

THE HOLY BIBLE. With Notes and Introductions. By CHR. WORDSWORTH, D.D., Bishop of Lincoln. Volume V. Imperial 8vo. 32s. 6d. Containing Isaiah, 12s. 6d., Jeremiah, Lamentations, and Ezekiel, 21s.

THE CAMBRIDGE PARAGRAPH BIBLE OF THE AUTHORIZED ENGLISH VERSION, with the Text Revised by a Collation of its Early and other Principal Editions, the Use of the Italic Type made uniform, the Marginal References remodelled, and a Critical Introduction prefixed. By the Rev. F. H. SCRIVENER, M.A., Rector of St. Gerrans, Editor of the Greek Testament, Codex Augiensis, &c. Edited for the Syndics of the Cambridge University Press.

Crown 4to.
PART I.—GENESIS TO SOLOMON'S SONG, 15s.
PART II.—APOCRYPHA AND NEW TESTAMENT, 15s.
PART III.—Containing the PROPHETICAL BOOKS, and the CRITICAL INTRODUCTION, 6s. *In the Press.*

"*The Syndics of the University Press deserve great credit for this attempt to supply biblical students and general readers with a copy of the Bible, which presents the arrangement of an unbroken text in paragraphs accommodated to the sense (the numerals, indicating the chapters and verses, being removed to the margin); with the broad distinction between the prose and poetical portions of Scripture duly maintained, and with such passages of the Old Testament as are quoted in the New being marked by the use of open type. . . . After this notice of the nature and objects of the Cambridge Paragraph Bible, it is needless to say one word as to its great value and importance.*"—NOTES AND QUERIES.

"*Mr. Scrivener has carefully collated the text of our modern Bibles with that of the first edition of 1611, restoring the original reading in most places, and marking every place where an obvious correction has been made; he has made the spelling as uniform as possible; revised the punctuation (punctuation as those who cry out for the Bible without note or comment should remember, is a continuous commentary on the text); carried out consistently the plan of marking with italics all words not found in the original, and carefully examined the marginal references. The name of Mr. Scrivener, the learned editor of the 'Codex Augiensis,' guarantees the quality of the work.*"—SPECTATOR.

An edition has also been printed, on *good writing paper*, with one column of print and wide margin to each page for MS. notes.

Parts I. and II. 20s. each. Part III. 10s. *In the Press.*

THE DOCTRINE OF RECONCILIATION TO GOD BY JESUS CHRIST. Seven Lectures, preached during Lent, 1870, with a Prefatory Essay. By W. H. FREMANTLE, M.A., Rector of St. Mary's, Bryanston Square. Small 8vo. 2s.

THE TREASURY OF DEVOTION: A Manual of Prayers for General and Daily Use. Compiled by a Priest. Edited by the Rev. T. T. CARTER, M.A., Rector of Clewer, Berks. Third Edition. 16mo, limp cloth, 2s.; cloth extra, 2s. 6d.

Bound with the Book of Common Prayer, 3s. 6d.

LETTERS FROM ROME ON THE COUNCIL. By QUIRINUS. Reprinted from the "Allgemeine Zeitung." Authorised Translation. Crown 8vo. 12s.

"*The great interest which these communications excited during their periodical publication in the Augsburg paper, not only in Germany, but everywhere throughout the Continent where interest was felt in the proceedings of the Council, is well known, and their reproduction in this country is calculated to open the eyes of Englishmen not a little to the way in which things are managed at Rome under the present system of Curialistic domination. Perhaps the most remarkable thing about the Letters is that they should have been published at all, for, after a few numbers had appeared, the most strenuous efforts were made by the Papal authorities to discover their author, but in vain. We believe that the secret is preserved even now.*"—CHURCH TIMES.

"*Their calm criticism of the proceedings of the Council, their dignified remonstrance against the proceedings of the Roman Curia, and their outspoken fears as to the results which will follow upon the proclamation of the dogma of Infallibility, must have done much to strengthen and consolidate the Opposition (as it is called) in the Council. . . . A word as to the translation. It reads like an English work—the similarity between this and 'Janus' will suggest itself at once.*"—ATHENÆUM.

"*The 'Letters from Rome' are already world-famous. In Italy and in Germany they have created a great sensation. Their revelations, their plainness of speech, the vigour and incisiveness of their style, all combine to make them among the most remarkable productions which this Œcumenical Council has called forth. They are easy and pleasant reading, and are essential for all who wish to know the secrets of this great conspiracy.*"—FREEMAN.

"*It is not much more than a twelvemonth since we noticed at some length the English translation of the remarkable work of 'Janus' on the Pope and the Council, which has since passed rapidly through three editions, and has commanded hardly less attention in this country than in Germany. 'Janus' closed with a sorrowful prediction that, whatever else might be said of the Vatican Synod, it would have no claim to be considered a free assembly, and the volume now before us is one long illustration from beginning to end of the justice of that anticipation. The two books, though evidently emanating from different authorship, have much in common. Both, as we are assured, are 'exclusively the work of Catholics;' both represent the same school of religious thought; both give evidence of deep learning, though there is of course more scope for its direct application in the earlier volume; both are written with consummate ability and unmistakeable earnestness, and in a clear and lucid style; and both, we may add, are admirably translated. The English reader, if he had not referred to the title page, might easily suppose that the Letters were from the pen of a countryman of his own. But it is not in graces of style, still less on any artificial ornament, that the book depends for its grave and permanent interest. It tells a plain unvarnished tale, the more impressive from its severe and terrible simplicity, which intimately concerns the credit and prospects of the Papacy and Roman Catholic hierarchy, and bears indirectly, but not less really, on the future, not only of the vast organization under their rule, but of universal Christendom. . . . Several points of interest we have been compelled to pass over for want of space, but this is the less to be regretted as the 'Letters of Quirinus' are pretty sure by this time to be in the hands of very many of our readers. Whatever may be the final upshot of the conflict evoked by the Vatican Synod in the bosom of the Roman Catholic Church—and it will probably take years before we see the end of it—this collection will retain a permanent value as a faithful record of one of the most remarkable phenomena of the present eventful century, which must inevitably leave its mark for good or for evil, though in a very different way from what its promoters designed, on the future of Christianity and the Christian Church.*"—SATURDAY REVIEW.

"*The history of the Vatican Council will ere long be attempted by many pens, but by whomsoever its proceedings may be narrated, we are firmly convinced that there will not, amid all the diversity of record, be found one to excel this volume in its vividly interesting descriptions of scenes and persons. A record written while events are going on, lacks, of course, the calm deliberate style of the historian, who at his leisure weighs and measures bygone events, and chronicles them all according to the relative importance in which he holds them. But here we have the narrative of events actually being enacted while the writer was employing his pen, he having all the advantage of direct intercourse with the chief actors in the events he is recording.*"—CHURCH HERALD.

A MANUAL OF LOGIC; Or, a Statement and Explanation of the Laws of Formal Thought. By HENRY J. TURRELL, M.A., Oxon. Square crown 8vo. 2s. 6d.

'THE ATHANASIAN CREED,' and its Usage in the English Church: an Investigation as to the Original Object of the Creed and the Growth of prevailing Misconceptions regarding it. A Letter to the Very Reverend W. F. Hook, D.D., F.R.S., Dean of Chichester, from C. A. SWAINSON, D.D., Canon of the Cathedral, and Examining Chaplain to the Lord Bishop of Chichester; Norrisian Professor of Divinity, Cambridge. Crown 8vo. 3s. 6d.

ARISTOPHANIS COMOEDIAE. Edited by W. G. GREEN, M.A., late Fellow of King's College, Cambridge. Classical Lecturer at Queen's College.

THE ACHARNIANS AND THE KNIGHTS.

This Edition of the Archarnians and the Knights is revised and especially adapted for Use in Schools. Crown 8vo. 4s.

"The utmost care has been taken with this edition of the most sarcastic and clever of the old Greek dramatists, facilitating the means of understanding both the text and intention of that biting sarcasm which will never lose either point or interest, and is as well adapted to the present age as it was to the times when first put forward."—BELL'S WEEKLY MESSENGER.

"We should have stated before, perhaps, that there is a thoughtful and intelligent introduction prefixed to this edition of the 'Clouds.' It goes over the old grounds, of course, and deals with the question, 'Was Aristophanes honest in his attack on Socrates and his teaching?' Mr. Green is of the number of those who think he was; but that, withal, he was somewhat narrow and bigoted; 'violently Conservative or a thorough Tory.' He too hastily identified Socrates with what he held to be a dangerous class, the Sophists; and caricatured the man when he wanted to ridicule the class. Mr. Green betrays a secret inclination to palliate this misrepresentation of the greatest of Greek teachers, but he does not allow it to weigh so far with him as to relieve the satirist or comic poet of all blame, although he suggests excuses for it in his distinction between the earlier teaching and the later doctrines of Socrates."—CONTEMPORARY REVIEW.

"Mr. Green has discharged his part of the work with uncommon skill and ability. The notes show a thorough study of the two Plays, an independent judgment in the interpretation of the poet, and a wealth of illustration, from which the Editor draws whenever it is necessary."—MUSEUM.

"Mr. Green presumes the existence of a fair amount of scholarship in all who read Aristophanes, as a study of his works generally succeeds to some considerable knowledge of the tragic poets. The notes he has appended are therefore brief, perhaps a little too brief. We should say the tendency of most modern editors is rather the other way; but Mr. Green no doubt knows the class for which he writes, and has been careful to supply their wants."—SPECTATOR.

"Mr. Green's admirable Introduction to 'The Clouds' of the celebrated comic poet deserves a perusal, as it contains an accurate analysis and many original comments on this remarkable play. The text is prefaced by a table of readings of Dindorf and Meineke, which will be of great service to students who wish to indulge in verbal criticism. The notes are copious and lucid, and the volume will be found useful for school and college purposes, and admirably adapted for private reading."—EXAMINER.

P. TERENTII AFRI COMOEDIAE. Edited by T. L. PAPILLON, M.A., Fellow of New College, Oxford, and late Fellow of Merton. ANDRIA ET EUNUCHUS. Forming a Part of the "Catena Classicorum." Crown 8vo. 4s. 6d.

"An excellent and supremely useful edition of the well-known plays of Terence. It makes no pretension to ordinary critical research, and yet perhaps, within the limits, it is all that could be desired. Its aim being merely 'to assist the ordinary students in the higher forms of schools and at the Universities,' numerous, and upon the whole very scholarly notes and references have been given at the bottom of each page of the text. Perhaps they are a little on the side of excess, seeing that but two of the six extant plays with which Terence is credited are comprised in this moderate sized octavo. We trust that the text of the plays will be edited in a like neat and able manner, and heartily commend the present instalment to the notice of the heads of schools."—WESTMINSTER REVIEW.

"Another volume of the 'Catena Classicorum,' containing the first portion of an edition of Terence, deserves a word of welcome; and though Mr. Papillon's labours cannot claim 'the merit of critical research, or independent collation of MSS.,' they exhibit a fair promise of usefulness as a school and college edition. The footnotes are, in the main, helpful and appropriate."—CONTEMPORARY REVIEW.

"This first instalment of a school edition of Terence gives promise of a renewed vigour in the 'Catena Classicorum' series, to which it belongs. Mr. Papillon is a very competent Latin scholar, trained under Dr. Bradley at Marlborough, and young enough to know what schoolboys need; and we hail as a proof of this his advice to the student of Terence to familiarize himself collaterally with such storehouses of Latin scholarship as Lachmann's or Munro's Lucretius, and Forbiger's or Conington's Virgil. He has himself made reference to these; and, as to grammatical references, limited himself mainly as is the rule with editions in the Catena series to the grammars of Madvig. There is a short but serviceable introduction, dealing with the life, style, and literary merits of Terence. We wish success to this new competitor for the honour of introducing schoolboys to Terence."—ENGLISH CHURCHMAN.

"We have before us another link in that excellent chain of classical authors produced under the general superintendence of Mr. Holmes and Mr. Bigg. Although Mr. Papillon, in his apologetic preface, claims no merit of critical research or independent collation of MSS., we do not think that many readers will complain of the editor's want of industry. We must admit that Mr. Papillon has succeeded admirably in producing a thorough useful and reliable edition of two of Terence's most popular

Messrs. Rivington's Publications

comedies. We find not only an introduction devoted to the life and writings, the style and literary merits, of the great Roman comic poet, but also a complete account, and analysis of each of the plays here printed. . . . Altogether we can pronounce this volume one admirably suited to the wants of students at school and college, and forming a useful introduction to the works of Terence."—EXAMINER.

"Mr. Papillon's 'Terence' strikes us as a thoroughly satisfactory school-book. The notes are all that notes should be. They are clear, and give just the help needed, yet without pandering to laziness. There is often a crispness and raciness about the comments, which is the very thing needed to attract attention to the text, and many of the little construes given are marvels of close-fitting idiomatic rendering. The general critical introduction we have read with a great deal of interest. It gives a singularly clear and vivid view of the character and literary merit attaching to the Terentian writings, and a conspectus of ancient criticisms upon them, which we have not seen done, or at all events not so completely elsewhere."—LITERARY CHURCHMAN.

CLASSICAL EXAMINATION PAPERS. Edited, with Notes and References, by P. J. F. GANTILLON, M.A., sometime Scholar of St. John's College, Cambridge; Classical Master in Cheltenham College. Crown 8vo. 7s. 6d. Or interleaved with writing-paper for Notes, half-bound, 10s. 6d.

"If any of our readers have classical pupils they will find this a most serviceable volume, alike for their own and for their pupils' use. The papers are mostly Cambridge or Oxford scholarship papers, and they are most carefully edited and annotated, so as to make their use as easy and as profitable as possible. The papers chosen are of the very highest order, and we can only say that such a help would have been invaluable to ourselves when engaged in such work as to require it."—LITERARY CHURCHMAN.

"The papers are well selected, and are fairly representative of the principal classical examinations of the present day."—ATHENÆUM.

"All who have had anything to do with examinations, especially as examiners, will recognise the utility of a well-selected and well-edited collection of examination papers. It is a sort of scholastic chart, and marks the rocks and quicksands on which carelessness or ignorance may suffer shipwreck. Mr. Gantillon's book is a judicious collection of papers. His notes convey information in cases where it is not easily accessible, and where if is, mention the sources at which it may be found. In the notes to the philosophical papers, he takes frequent opportunities of stating concisely the opinions of the ancient philosophers, and of referring to the writings of their more modern successors."—SCOTSMAN.

THE AMMERGAU PASSION PLAY. Reprinted by permission from the *Times.* With some Introductory Remarks on the Origin and Development of Miracle Plays, and some Practical Hints for the use of Intending Visitors. By the Rev. MALCOLM MACCOLL, M.A., Chaplain to the Right Hon. Lord Napier, K.T. Second Edition. Crown 8vo. 2s. 6d.

"To those whom the war has deprived of an opportunity to see that most curious relic of former days, this little book will prove highly interesting. . . . It gives a highly interesting sketch of miracle plays in the middle ages, tracing them from a very early period, and also giving much practical information." CHURCH HERALD.

"The Rev. Malcolm MacColl has reprinted from the 'Times' his graphic narrative of the Ammergau Passion Play. It will serve as a pleasant memorial to those who were fortunate enough to be spectators of that drama this year; and also as a useful guide to such as purpose a future visit."—UNION REVIEW.

"Those who were disappointed this year in their intended expedition to the Tyrol, and they are to be numbered by thousands, will do well to procure the Rev. Malcolm MacColl's graphic account."—CHURCH TIMES.

"An extremely able and interesting account of this year's Passion Play. Our readers will not regret buying this little sketch."—LITERARY CHURCHMAN.

"An interesting account of the Passion Play enacted every tenth year at Ober-Ammergau in Bavaria. In this little volume we are furnished with all the particulars in reference to going to, and staying in, the now classical region of Ammergau. In fact, Mr. MacColl gives us a sort of half guide, half history, and a graphic and highly enlightened criticism of the characters and features of the play."—WESTMINSTER REVIEW.

THE COMMENTARIES OF GAIUS: Translated, with Notes, by J. T. ABDY, LL.D., Regius Professor of Laws in the University of Cambridge, and Barrister-at-Law of the Norfolk Circuit, formerly Fellow of Trinity Hall; and BRYAN WALKER, M.A., M.L., Fellow and Lecturer of Corpus Christi College, and Law Lecturer of St. John's College, Cambridge, formerly Law Student of Trinity Hall and Chancellor's Legal Medallist. Crown 8vo. 12s. 6d.

NEW THEOLOGICAL DICTIONARY.

DICTIONARY OF DOCTRINAL AND HISTORICAL THEOLOGY.
By various writers. Edited by the Rev. JOHN HENRY BLUNT, M.A., F.S.A. Editor of the Annotated Book of Common Prayer.

Complete in one volume of 833 *pages, imperial* 8vo (*equal to six* 8vo *volumes of* 400 *pages each*), *and printed in large readable type,* 42s. *or half-bound in morocco,* 52s. 6d.

1. NATURE OF THE WORK. This Dictionary consists of a series of original Essays (alphabetically arranged, and 575 in number) on all the principal subjects connected with the Doctrines of the Christian Church. Some idea of the subjects, and of the length of the articles, may be formed from the following titles of those which occupy the work from page 700 to page 720.

SIGN.	SPINOZISM.	SUFFRAGAN.
SIMONY.	SPIRIT.	SUNDAY.
SIN.	SPIRIT, THE HOLY.	SUPEREROGATION.
SINAITIC CODEX.	SPONSORS.	SUPERNATURAL.
SOCINIANISM.	SUBDEACONS.	SUPERSTITION.
SOLIFIDIANISM.	SUBLAPSARIANISM.	SUPRALAPSARIANISM.
SOUL.	SUBSTANCE.	SUPREMACY, PAPAL.

2. OBJECT OF THE WORK. The writers of all the Essays have endeavoured to make them sufficiently exhaustive to render it unnecessary for the majority of readers to go further for information, and, at the same time, sufficiently suggestive of more recondite sources of Theological study, to help the student in following up his subjects. By means of a Table prefixed to the Dictionary, a regular course of such study may be carried out in its pages.

3. PRINCIPLES OF THE WORK. The Editor and his coadjutors have carefully avoided any party bias, and consequently the work cannot be said to be either "High Church," "Low Church," or "Broad Church." The only bias of the Dictionary is that given by Revelation, History, Logic, and the literary idiosyncracy of each particular contributor. But the Editor has not attempted to assist the circulation of the book by making it colourless on the pretence of impartiality. Errors are freely condemned, and truths are expressed as if they were worth expressing; but he believes that no terms of condemnation which may be used ever transgress the bounds of Christian courtesy.

4. PART OF A SERIES. The Dictionary of Theology is complete in itself, but it is also intended to form part of a Series, entitled, "A Summary of Theology," of which the second volume, "A Dictionary of Sects, Heresies, and Schools of Thought," is in a forward state of preparation for the press.

"Taken as a whole the articles are the work of practised writers, and well informed and solid theologians. . . . We know no book of its size and bulk which supplies the information here given at all; far less which supplies it in an arrangement so accessible, with a completeness of information so thorough, and with an ability in the treatment of profound subjects so great. Dr. Hook's most useful volume is a work of high calibre, but it is the work of a single mind. We have here a wider range of thought from a greater variety of sides. We have here also the work of men who evidently know what they write about, and are somewhat more profound (to say the least), than the writers of the current Dictionaries of Sects and Heresies."—GUARDIAN.

"Mere antiquarianism, however interesting, has little place in it. But for all practical purposes its historical articles are excellent. They are of course, and of necessity, a good deal condensed, yet they are wonderfully complete; see for example such articles as 'Atheism,' 'Cabbala,' 'Calvinism,' 'Canonization,' 'Convocations,' 'Evangelical,' 'Fathers,' 'Infant Baptism,' &c., &c. But the strength of the book lies in the theology proper, and herein more particularly in what one may call the metaphysical side of doctrine: —see the articles on 'Conceptualism,' 'Doubt,' 'Dualism,' 'Election,' 'Eternity,' 'Everlasting Punishment,' 'Fatalism,' and the like. We mention these as characteristic of the book. At the same time other more practical matters are fully dealt with. There are excellent and elaborate papers on such words as 'Eucharist,' 'Confession,' 'Blood,' 'Cross,' 'Antichrist,' to say nothing of the host of minor matters on which it is most convenient to be able to turn to a book which gives you at a glance the pith of a whole library in a column or a page. Thus it will be obvious that it takes a very much wider range than any undertaking of the same kind in our language; and that to those of our clergy who have not the fortune to spend in books, and would not have the leisure to use them if they possessed them, it will be the most serviceable and reliable substitute for a large library we can think of. And in many cases, while keeping strictly within its province as a Dictionary, it contrives to be marvellously suggestive of thought and reflections, which a serious minded man will take with him and ponder over for his own elaboration and future use. As an example of this we may refer to the whole article on Doubt. It is treated of under the successive heads of,—(1) its nature; (2) its origin; 3) the history of the principal periods of Doubt; (4) the consciousness—or actual experience of Doubt, and how to deal with its different phases and kinds; (5) the relations of Doubt to action and to belief. To explain a little we will here quote a paragraph or two, which may not be unacceptable to our readers. . . . The variety of the references given in the course of this article, and at its conclusion, show how carefully the writer has thought out and studied his subject in its various manifestations in many various minds, and illustrate very forcibly how much reading goes to a very small amount of space in anything worth the name of 'Dictionary of Theology.' We trust most sincerely that the book may be largely used. For a present to a clergyman on his ordination, or from a parishioner to his pastor, it would be most appropriate. It may indeed be called 'a box of tools for a working clergyman.'"—LITERARY CHURCHMAN.

"Seldom has an English work of equal magnitude been so permeated with Catholic instincts, and at the same time seldom has a work on theology been kept so free from the drift of rhetorical incrustation. Of course it is not meant that all these remarks apply in their full extent to every article. In a great Dictionary there are compositions, as in a great house there are vessels, of various kinds. Some of these at a future day may be replaced by others more substantial in their build, more proportionate in their outline, and more elaborate in their detail. But admitting all this, the whole remains a home to which the student will constantly recur, sure to find spacious chambers, substantial furniture, and (which is most important) no stinted light."— CHURCH REVIEW.

"The second and final instalment of Mr. Blunt's useful Dictionary, itself but a part of a more comprehensive plan, is now before the public, and fully sustains the mainly favourable impression created by the appearance of the first part. Within the sphere it has marked out for itself, no equally useful book of reference exists in English for the elucidation of theological problems. . . . Entries which display much care, research, and judgment in compilation, and which will make the task of the parish priest who is brought face to face with any of the practical questions which they involve far easier than has been hitherto. The very fact that the utterances are here and there somewhat more guarded and hesitating than quite accords with our judgment, is a gain in so far as it protects the work from the charge of inculcating extreme views, and will thus secure its admission in many places where moderation is accounted the crowning grace.' —CHURCH TIMES.

"The writers who are at work on it are scholars and theologians, and earnest defenders of the Christian faith. They evidently hold fast the fundamental doctrines of Christianity, and have the religious instruction of the rising ministry at heart. Moreover, their scheme is a noble one; it does credit not only to their learning and zeal, but also to their tact and discretion.'—LONDON QUARTERLY REVIEW.

"Infinitely the best book of the kind in the language; and, if not the best conceivable, it is perhaps the best we are ever likely to see within its compass as to size and scope. Accurate and succinct in statement, it may safely be trusted as a handbook as regards facts, while in our judgment, this second part still maintains the character we gave the first, namely, of showing most ability in its way of treating the more abstract and metaphysical side of theological questions. The liturgical articles also in this part deserve especial mention. The book is sure to make its own way by sheer force of usefulness."—LITERARY CHURCHMAN.

"It is not open to doubt that this work, of which the second and concluding part has just been issued, is in every sense a valuable and important one. Mr. Blunt's Dictionary is a most acceptable addition to English theological literature. Its general style is terse and vigorous. Whilst its pages are free from wordiness, there is none of that undue condensation which, under the plea of judicious brevity, veils a mere empty jotting down of familiar statements and mis-statements, at second or, it may be, third hand from existing works. Dean Hook's well-known Dictionary makes the nearest approach to the one now before us, but Mr. Blunt's is decidedly the better of the two."—ENGLISH CHURCHMAN.

"It will be found of admirable service to all students of theology, as advancing and maintaining the Church's views on all subjects as fall within the range of fair argument and inquiry. It is not often that a work of so comprehensive and so profound a nature is marked to the very end by so many signs of wide and careful research, sound criticism, and well-founded and well-expressed belief."— STANDARD.

SERMONS. By HENRY MELVILL, B.D., late Canon of St. Paul's, and Chaplain in Ordinary to the Queen. New Edition. Two vols. Crown 8vo. 5s. each. Sold separately.

"*Messrs. Rivington have published very opportunely, at a time when Churchmen are thinking with satisfaction of the new blood infused into the Chapter of St. Paul's, sermons by Henry Melvill, who in his day was as celebrated as a preacher as is Canon Liddon now. The sermons are not only couched in elegant language, but are replete with matter which the younger clergy would do well to study.*"—JOHN BULL.

"*Henry Melvill's intellect was large, his imagination brilliant, his ardour intense, and his style strong, fervid, and picturesque. Often he seemed to glow with the inspiration of a prophet.*"—AMERICAN QUARTERLY CHURCH REVIEW.

"*It would be easy to quote portions of exceeding beauty and power. It was not, however, the charm of style, nor wealth of words, both which Canon Melvill possessed in so great abundance, that he relied on to win souls; but the power and spirit of Him who said, 'I, if I be lifted up, will draw all men to Me.'*"—RECORD.

"*Every one who can remember the days when Canon Melvill was the preacher of the day, will be glad to see these four-and-twenty of his sermons so nicely reproduced. His Sermons were all the result of real study and genuine reading, with far more theology in them than those of many who make much more profession of theology. There are sermons here which we can personally remember; it has been a pleasure to us to be reminded of them, and we are glad to see them brought before the present generation. We hope that they may be studied, for they deserve it thoroughly.*"—LITERARY CHURCHMAN.

"*Few preachers have had more admirers than the Rev. Henry Melvill, and the new edition of his Sermons, in two volumes, will doubtless find plenty of purchasers. The sermons abound in thought, and the thoughts are couched in English which is at once elegant in construction and easy to read.*"—CHURCH TIMES.

"*The Sermons of Canon Melvill, now republished in two handy volumes, need only to be mentioned to be sure of a hearty welcome. Sound learning, well-weighed words, calm and keen logic, and solemn devoutness, mark the whole series of masterly discourses, which embrace some of the chief doctrines of the Church, and set them forth in clear and Scriptural strength.*"—STANDARD.

A KEY TO THE NARRATIVE OF THE FOUR GOSPELS. By JOHN PILKINGTON NORRIS, M.A., Canon of Bristol, formerly one of Her Majesty's Inspectors of Schools.
(Forming the Fourth Volume of KEYS TO CHRISTIAN KNOWLEDGE.)
Small 8vo. 2s. 6d.

"*This is very much the best book of its kind we have seen. The only fault is its shortness, which prevents its going into the details which would support and illustrate its statements, and which in the process of illustrating them would fix them upon the minds and memories of its readers. It is, however, a great improvement upon any book of its kind we know. It bears all the marks of being the condensed work of a real scholar, and of a divine too. The bulk of the book is taken up with a 'Life of Christ' compiled from the Four Gospels so as to exhibit its steps and stages and salient points. The rest of the book consists of independent chapters on special points.*"—LITERARY CHURCHMAN.

"*This book is no ordinary compendium, no mere 'cram-book'; still less is it an ordinary reading book for schools; but the schoolmaster, the Sunday-school teacher, and the seeker after a comprehensive knowledge of Divine truth will find it worthy of its name. Canon Norris writes simply, reverently, without great display of learning, giving the result of much careful study in a short compass, and adorning the subject by the tenderness and honesty with which he treats it. . . . We hope that this little book will have a very wide circulation and that it will be studied; and we can promise that those who take it up will not readily put it down again.*"—RECORD.

"*This is a golden little volume. Having often to criticise unsparingly volumes published by Messrs. Rivington, and bearing the deep High Church brand, it is the greater satisfaction to be able to commend this book so emphatically. Its design is exceedingly modest. Canon Norris writes primarily to help 'younger students' in studying the Gospels. But this unpretending volume is one which all students may study with advantage. It is an admirable manual for those who take Bible Classes through the Gospels. Closely sifted in style, so that all is clear and weighty; full of unostentatious learning, and pregnant with suggestion; deeply reverent in spirit, and altogether Evangelical in spirit; Canon Norris' book supplies a real want, and ought to be welcomed by all earnest and devout students of the Holy Gospels.*"—LONDON QUARTERLY REVIEW.

THE PRINCIPLES OF THE CATHEDRAL SYSTEM VINDICATED AND FORCED UPON MEMBERS OF CATHEDRAL FOUNDATIONS. Eight Sermons, preached in the Cathedral Church of the Holy and Undivided Trinity of Norwich. By EDWARD MEYRICK GOULBURN, D.D., Dean of Norwich, late Prebendary of St. Paul's, and one of Her Majesty's Chaplains. Crown 8vo. 5s.

Messrs. Rivington's Publications

THE LYRICS OF HORACE. Done into English Rhyme. By THOMAS CHARLES BARING, M.A., late Fellow of Brasenose College, Oxford. Small 4to. 7s.

"*The most jealous regard to the true meaning of the poet, and, in general, a spirited and graceful rendering throughout, claim for this volume, elegant in its accidents of tinted paper, sharply cut type, and ample margin, a high place among the English representations of the Roman lyric poet.*"—RECORD.

THE ILIAD OF HOMER. Translated by J. G. CORDERY, late of Balliol College, Oxford, and now of H.M. Bengal Civil Service. Two vols. 8vo. 16s.

"*A new translation of the Iliad, marked by certainly more than average ability, imparts more than usual interest to the classic element. We believe that few of those who read Mr. Cordery's version will not concur in our opinion that it gives, on the whole, a very fair English copy of the grand Homeric poem, can always be read with pleasure, and contains many passages of great merit. . . . Mr. Cordery's merits seem to be a simplicity which does not, as is too often the case, verge on puerility; faithfulness and care without stiffness, and scholarship without pedantry. His notes, though short, are thoroughly well weighed and well written, and testify to the thought which he has bestowed on every aspect of his task. In conclusion, we repeat that both those who can and those who cannot read the original may turn to Mr. Cordery's version, and be sure of finding in it both pleasure and profit.*"—STANDARD.

"*Mr. Cordery has been very successful in reproducing Homer's terse, vigorous simplicity in readable blank verse.*"—EXAMINER.

"*There is a great masculine vigour in the translation, and now and then, though rarely, a great felicity of expression. That Mr. Cordery's version is always direct may be at once admitted, and in some passages, especially the wrathful passages, this directness attains a very high order of Homeric force. If, however, we compare Mr. Cordery with two of his principal blank verse predecessors, Cowper and the late Lord Derby, we should say he has, on the whole, greatly the advantage of both,—of Cowper (whose Iliad was far inferior to his Odyssey), because he is both closer to his original, and far more vigorous and direct,—of Lord Derby, because Mr Cordery has taken more uniform pains, and not so often merged the rich Homeric detail in the wooden conventionalisms of general phrases. Mr. Cordery's version is by far the best blank verse translation as yet known to us.*"—SPECTATOR.

A PROSE TRANSLATION OF VIRGIL'S ECLOGUES AND GEORGICS. By an Oxford Graduate. Crown 8vo. 2s. 6d.

ESSAYS ON THE PLATONIC ETHICS. By THOMAS MAGUIRE, LL.D. ex S.T.C.D., Professor of Latin, Queen's College, Galway. 8vo. 5s.

THE ELEGIES OF PROPERTIUS. Translated into English Verse. By CHARLES ROBERT MOORE, M.A., late Scholar of Corpus Christi College, Oxford. Small 8vo. 2s. 6d.

HISTORIÆ ANTIQUÆ EPITOME: Founded on the Two First Portions of the Lateinisches Elementarbuch, by Jacobs and Doering. By the Rev. THOMAS KERCHEVER ARNOLD, M.A., formerly Fellow of Trinity College, Cambridge. Eighth Edition. 12mo. 4s.

SACRED ALLEGORIES. Illustrated Edition. By the Rev. W. ADAMS, M.A., late Fellow of Merton College, Oxford.

The SHADOW of the CROSS. Illustrated by BIRKET FOSTER and G. E. HICKS.

The DISTANT HILLS. Illustrated by SAMUEL PALMER.

The OLD MAN'S HOME. Illustrated by J. C. HORSLEY, A.R.A., and BIRKET FOSTER.

The KING'S MESSENGERS. Illustrated by C. W. COPE, R.A.

New Editions, square crown 8vo., 2s. 6d. each.

The Cheap Editions may still be had, 18mo., 1s. each, or 6d. in Paper Covers.

The FOUR ALLEGORIES in one Volume. Presentation Edition. Small 4to. 10s. 6d.

THE SHEPHERD OF HERMAS. Translated into English, with an Introduction and Notes. By CHARLES H. HOOLE, M.A., Senior Student of Christ Church, Oxford. Small 8vo. 4*s.* 6*d.*

"*Mr. Hoole, we think, has acted rightly in translating from the Greek text 'even now not quite complete' as edited by Hilgenfeld. His translation runs fluently enough, and enables any English reader who is curious about the 'Shepherd' to read it through in two or three hours.*"—SATURDAY REVIEW.

"*The 'Shepherd of Hermas,' that singular relic of the sub-apostolic age, and fruitful parent of the long series of Christian allegories which has since appeared, has just been published in a new translation, with an introduction and notes by Mr. Charles H. Hoole, of Christ Church, Oxford. The version is careful and fluent, and the form of the book more convenient than that of any other English edition we know.*"—UNION REVIEW.

"*To our thinking the 'Shepherd of Hermas' is practically one of the most valuable and important of all the early pieces of Christian literature. Of course we do not mean that it is important in the same way that the Ignatian letters are important, or that the elaborate theological writings of Irenæus are important. But for the general reader, for those who are not professional theologians, it has always seemed to us that the 'Shepherd' is exactly the book to open their eyes to the tone of mind and circle of ideas of ordinary Christian folk of the sub-apostolic age, and thereby to clear away the absurd accumulation of prejudices which encrust the mind of the ordinary British Christian of the nineteenth century. For our own part, we can never forget its effect on our own minds, when in the very outset of our acquaintance with Christian antiquity, we came upon it unawares and unguided in an unassisted attempt to read 'The Fathers.' We wish it were placed in all school libraries. Some boys, at least, would be interested in its simple vigour and earnestness, and, at any rate, it would serve to take away that sense of stiffened unreality and separation from common human life and interests which encumbers their notions of Church history. The edition before us has a thoroughly good literary introduction and some good notes. It is a scholarly introduction, and has our warmest recommendation.*"—LITERARY CHURCHMAN.

"*This translation of 'The Shepherd of Hermas' is the first made from the Greek original, as edited by Professor Hilgenfeld. In it Mr. Hoole has given an excellent representation of the original. The version is faithful, reads well, and may therefore be commended to the attention of all who are interested in early patristic literature. The translator has prefixed an introduction of thirty-one pages, and added notes at the close, which are creditable to his learning and judgment.*"—ATHENÆUM.

PRAYERS AND MEDITATIONS FOR THE HOLY COMMUNION. With a Preface by C. J. ELLICOTT, D.D., Lord Bishop of Gloucester and Bristol. With rubrics and borders in red. Royal 32mo., 2*s.* 6*d.*

"*Devout beauty is the special character of this new manual, and it ought to be a favourite. Rarely has it happened to us to meet with so remarkable a combination of thorough practicalness with that almost poetic warmth which is the highest flower of genuine devotion. It deserves to be placed along with the manual edited by Mr. Keble so shortly before his decease, not as superseding it, for the scope of the two is different, but to be taken along with it. Nothing can exceed the beauty and fulness of the devotions before communion in Mr. Keble's book, but we think that in some points the devotions here given after Holy Communion are even superior to it.*"—LITERARY CHURCHMAN.

"*Bishop Ellicott has edited a book of 'Prayers and Meditations for the Holy Communion,' which, among Eucharistic manuals, has its own special characteristic. The Bishop recommends it to the newly confirmed, to the tender-hearted and the devout, as having been compiled by a youthful person, and as being marked by a peculiar 'freshness.' Having looked through the volume, we have pleasure in seconding the recommendations of the good Bishop. We know of no more suitable manual for the newly confirmed, and nothing more likely to engage the sympathies of youthful hearts. There is a union of the deepest spirit of devotion, a rich expression of experimental life, with a due recognition of the objects of faith, such as is not always to be found, but which characterises this manual in an eminent degree.*"—CHURCH REVIEW.

"*The Bishop of Gloucester's imprimatur is attached to 'Prayers and Meditations for the Holy Communion,' intended as a manual for the recently confirmed, nicely printed, and theologically sound.*"—CHURCH TIMES.

"*In freshness and fervour of devotion, few modern manuals of prayer are to be compared with it. Its faults are a too exclusive subjectiveness, and a want of realising the higher Catholic teaching. Thus, the Holy Sacrifice has not its due prominence, the sacrament of Penance is ignored, our full communion with the saints departed is obscured, and the Catholic Church on earth as an outward organisation is put too much in the background. The book, in short, is strictly Anglican, but with a strong tendency to mysticism. For all that, it has a warmth of feeling and a reality of devotion which will endear it to the hearts of many Catholics, and will make it especially a most welcome companion to those among the young who are earnestly striving after the spiritual life.*"—CHURCH HERALD.

"*Among the supply of Eucharistic Manuals, one deserves special attention and commendation. 'Prayers and Meditations' merits the Bishop of Gloucester's epithets of 'warm, devout, and fresh.' And it is thoroughly English Church besides.*"—GUARDIAN.

"*We are by no means surprised that Bishop Ellicott should have been so much struck with this little work, on accidentally seeing it in manuscript, as to urge its publication, and to preface it with his commendation. The devotion which it breathes is truly fervent, and the language attractive, and as proceeding from a young person the work is altogether not a little striking.*"—RECORD.

THE HIDDEN LIFE OF THE SOUL. From the French. By the Author of "A Dominican Artist," "Life of Madame Louise de France," &c. Crown 8vo. 5s.

"'The Hidden Life of the Soul,' by the author of 'A Dominican Artist,' is from the writings of Father Grou, a French refugee priest of 1792, who died at Lulworth. It well deserves the character given it of being 'earnest and sober,' and not 'sensational.'"—GUARDIAN.

"Between fifty and sixty short readings on spiritual subjects, exquisitely expressed, and not merely exquisite in expression, but presenting a rare combination of spiritual depth and of strong practical common sense. We have read carefully a large number of them, for, after reading a few as texts, we could not lay it down without going much further than was sufficient for the mere purpose of reporting on the book. The author was one Père Grou, a native of Calais, born in 1731, who in 1792 found an asylum from the troubles of the French Revolution at Lulworth Castle, known doubtless to many of our readers as the ancestral home of the old Roman Catholic family of Weld, where he died in 1803. There is a wonderful charm about these readings—so calm, so true, so thoroughly Christian. We do not know where they would come amiss. As materials for a consecutive series of meditations for the faithful at a series of early celebrations they would be excellent, or for private reading during Advent or Lent."—LITERARY CHURCHMAN.

"From the French of Jean Nicolas Grou, a pious Priest, whose works teach resignation to the Divine will. He loved, we are told, to inculcate simplicity, freedom from all affectation and unreality, the patience and humility which are too surely grounded in self-knowledge to be surprised at a fall, but withal so allied to confidence in God as to make recovery easy and sure. This is the spirit of the volume which is intended to furnish advice to those who would cultivate a quiet, meek, and childlike spirit."—PUBLIC OPINION.

"The work is by Jean Nicolas Grou, a French Priest, who, driven to England by the first Revolution, found a home with a Roman Catholic family at Lulworth for the ten remaining years of a retired studious, devout life. The work bears internal evidence of being that of a spirit which had been fed on such works as the 'Spiritual Exercises,' the 'Imitation of Christ,' and the 'Devout Life' of St. Francis of Sales, and which has here reproduced them, tested by its own life-experience, and cast in the mould of its own individuality. How much the work, in its present form, may owe to the judicious care of the Editor, we are not aware; but as it is presented to us, it is, while deeply spiritual, yet so earnest and sober in its general tone, so free from doctrinal error or unwholesome sentiment, that we confidently recommend it to English Church people as one of the most valuable of this class of books which we have met with."—CHURCH BUILDER.

THE WITNESS OF ST. JOHN TO CHRIST; being the Boyle Lectures for 1870. With an Appendix on the Authorship and Integrity of St. John's Gospel and the Unity of the Johannine Writings. By the Rev. STANLEY LEATHES, M.A., Minister of St. Philip's, Regent Street, and Professor of Hebrew, King's College, London. 8vo. 10s. 6d.

"Mr. Leathes could scarcely have chosen a more timely theme, for never were the genuineness and authority of the Fourth Gospel more vehemently assailed than now. He is well read on the literature of his subject, and he discusses it with much thoroughness and ability. The book is an appropriate sequel to his former Lectures on the witness of the Old Testament and of St. Paul to Christ, and it well deserves to take its place in the series to which it belongs. Mr. Leathes' book is one of those which we shall keep by us for future reference and help."—LITERARY CHURCHMAN.

"Mr. Stanley Leathes is singularly clear and forcible in his language, and his thoughts and arguments are original and well sustained. The Boyle Lectures for the past three years have placed their authors in the first rank of Biblical critics and expositors."—PUBLIC OPINION.

"The excellence of this volume for popular purposes is—that it dwells largely on what may be called the internal evidence of the gospel itself. Its literary characteristics—which prove that the writer meant it as a history; its spiritual significancy; the inward witness which the belief of its truth creates; its harmony with other acknowledged writings of St. John, are all discussed, and discussed in a way which seems to us conclusive. In an elaborate appendix, the authorship of the gospel and its integrity are discussed though the lecturer is careful to maintain that the substantial truth of which it teaches is largely independent of all such questions. To young men this volume and the companion volume on St. Paul, and the Book of Acts, may be safely commended, as good mental discipline, and as a timely protection against modern 'mistakes.'"—FREEMAN.

A HELP TO CATECHISING. For the Use of Clergymen, Schools, and Private Families. By JAMES BEAVEN, D.D., Professor of Divinity in the University of Toronto. New Edition. 18mo. 2s.

PARISH MUSINGS; OR, DEVOTIONAL POEMS. By JOHN S. B. MONSELL, LL.D., Vicar of Egham, Surrey, and Rural Dean. New Edition. 18mo, limp cloth, 1s. 6d.; or in cover, 1s.

THE STAR OF CHILDHOOD. A First Book of Prayers and Instruction for Children. Compiled by a Priest. Edited by the Rev. T. T. CARTER, M.A., Rector of Clewer, Berks. With Illustrations. Royal 16mo. 2s. 6d.

QUIET MOMENTS: A Four Weeks' Course of Thoughts and Meditations, before Evening Prayer and at Sunset. By LADY CHARLOTTE MARIA PEPYS.

MORNING NOTES OF PRAISE: A Series of Meditations upon the Morning Psalms. By the same Authoress.

New Edition. Small 8vo. 2s. 6d. each. Sold separately.

"*For quiet, calm, genuine devoutness, undisturbed by mannerism or any touch of mere fashion in their way of looking at things or form of expression, these two little volumes stand very high in our regard. And in these days when special fashions in religion are so rife, and force themselves in almost everywhere, it is like getting into harbour after a rough passage to give oneself up for a while to such thoroughly peaceful books as these.*"—LITERARY CHURCHMAN.

"*We can with confidence recommend both these little volumes to our readers as worthy of being ranked among the best of the devotional books of the day. For young persons especially they will be found most valuable, as the teaching contained in each is so thoroughly earnest and so well shows how religion should be brought to bear on the concerns of every day life with its various cares, trials, and temptations.*"—ENGLISH CHURCHMAN.

"*In two very exquisitely bound little volumes Messrs. Rivington republish a couple of companion volumes with which the present generation are scarcely acquainted, but which can never be out of date as expositions of the highest and purest tone of what may be called Church of England piety. . . . We do not know whether we would not prefer putting them into the hands of ordinary Christians—and most Christians fall under this category—than almost anything we know of.*"—CHURCH REVIEW.

"*Lady Charlotte Pepys' style is calculated to attract the class for whom she writes, being lively in expression as well as devout in tone. Both her volumes are, generally speaking, sound in doctrine and wise in their practical suggestions, and may be safely recommended as useful presents to young people. The new edition called for in each case shows that they have already met with some acceptance, to which they are justly entitled.*"—RECORD.

"*Two manuals of devotion which have many merits, but especially that of supplying questions of self-examination of the most searching kind to souls anxious to know their duty to God, and to do it in the daily round of life.*"—ROCK.

THE STORY OF THE GOSPELS. In a single Narrative, combined from the Four Evangelists, showing in a new translation their unity. To which is added a like continuous Narrative in the Original Greek. By the Rev. WILLIAM POUND, M.A., late Fellow of St. John's College, Cambridge, Principal of Appuldurcombe School, Isle of Wight. 2 Vols. 8vo. 36s.

COUNSELS ON HOLINESS OF LIFE. Translated from the Spanish of "The Sinner's Guide," by LUIS DE GRANADA. Forming a Volume of *THE ASCETIC LIBRARY*, a Series of Translations of Spiritual Works for Devotional Reading from Catholic Sources. Edited by the Rev. ORBY SHIPLEY, M.A. Square crown 8vo. 5s.

"*The Dominican friar, whose work is here translated, was one of the most remarkable men of his time, celebrated as a most powerful and popular preacher, as a man of the most devoted and self-denying piety, and of very extensive erudition. It was not we are justly told, 'eloquence and learning alone that gave Fray Luis his great influence. His truly pure and holy example, his zeal for souls, and his perfect devotion to God's service. He inculcated purity by being himself pure, humility by being humble, contempt of the world by refusing honours and dignities, poverty by being himself poor'* . . . *We can speak with confidence of the deep spirit of devotion breathed throughout the general body of the work.*"—ROCK.

"*The book is richly studded with quotations from the Fathers.*"—ENGLISH CHURCHMAN.

"*It is earnest, fervent, and practical; it shows a most intimate knowledge of Holy Scripture, and much skill in its application; and it deals with the great fundamental truths of religion rather than with matters of controversy or private opinion. The life specified is well written and interesting.*"—LITERARY CHURCHMAN.

Messrs. Rivington's Publications

THE DIVINITY OF OUR LORD AND SAVIOUR JESUS CHRIST; being the Bampton Lectures for 1866. By HENRY PARRY LIDDON, D.C.L., Canon of St. Paul's, and Ireland Professor of Exegesis in the University of Oxford. Fourth Edition. Crown 8vo. 5s.

THE PURSUIT OF HOLINESS: a Sequel to "Thoughts on Personal Religion," intended to carry the Reader somewhat farther onward in the Spiritual Life. By EDWARD MEYRICK GOULBURN, D.D., Dean of Norwich, and formerly one of Her Majesty's Chaplains in Ordinary. Second Edition. Small 8vo. 5s.

BIBLE READINGS FOR FAMILY PRAYER. By the Rev. W. H. RIDLEY. M.A., Rector of Hambleden. Crown 8vo.

Old Testament—Genesis and Exodus. 2s.
New Testament, { St. Luke and St. John. 2s.
{ St. Matthew and St. Mark. 2s.
The Four Gospels, in one volume. 3s. 6d.

HOUSEHOLD THEOLOGY: A Handbook of Religious Information respecting the Holy Bible, the Prayer Book, the Church, the Ministry, Divine Worship, the Creeds, &c., &c. By JOHN HENRY BLUNT, M.A. New Edition. Small 8vo. 3s. 6d.

SERMONS FOR CHILDREN; being Thirty-three short Readings, addressed to the Children of S. Margaret's Home, East Grinstead. By the Rev. J. M. NEALE, D.D., late Warden of Sackville College. Second Edition. Small 8vo. 3s. 6d.

DEAN ALFORD'S GREEK TESTAMENT, with English Notes intended for the Upper Forms of Schools and for Pass-men at the Universities. Abridged by BRADLEY H. ALFORD, M.A., Vicar of Leavenheath, Colchester, late Scholar of Trinity College, Cambridge. Crown 8vo. 10s. 6d.

THE NEW TESTAMENT FOR ENGLISH READERS: containing the Authorized Version, with a revised English Text; Marginal References; and a Critical and Explanatory Commentary. By HENRY ALFORD, D.D., Dean of Canterbury. Two volumes, or four parts. 8vo. 54s. 6d.

Separately,
Vol. 1, Part I.—The Three first Gospels. Second Edition. 12s.
Vol. 1, Part II.—St. John and the Acts. Second Edition. 10s. 6d.
Vol. 2, Part I.—The Epistles of St. Paul. Second Edition. 16s.
Vol. 2, Part II.—Hebrews to Revelation. Second Edition. 8vo. 16s.

A MANUAL OF CONFIRMATION, Comprising—1. A General Account of the Ordinance. 2. The Baptismal Vow, and the English Order of Confirmation, with Short Notes, Critical and Devotional. 3. Meditations and Prayers on Passages of Holy Scripture, in connexion with the Ordinance. With a Pastoral Letter instructing Catechumens how to prepare themselves for their first Communion. By EDWARD MEYRICK GOULBURN, D.D. Dean of Norwich. Eighth Edition. Small 8vo. 1s. 6d.

THE CHURCH BUILDER. A Quarterly Journal of Church Extension in England and Wales. Published in connection with The Incorporated Church Building Society. With Illustrations. Volumes for 1869 and 1870. Crown 8vo. 1s. 6d. each.

SELECTIONS FROM MODERN FRENCH AUTHORS. With English Notes. By HENRY VAN LAUN, Master of the French Language and Literature at the Edinburgh Academy. Crown 8vo.

Part I. Honoré de Balzac, 3s. 6d.
Part II. H. A. Taine, 3s. 6d.

"*This selection answers to the requirements expressed by Mr. Lowe in one of his speeches on education, where he recommended that boys should be attracted to the study of French by means of its lighter literature. M. van Laun has executed the task of selection with excellent taste. The episodes he has chosen from the vast 'Human Comedy' are naturally such as do not deal with passions and experiences that are proper to mature age. Even thus limited, he had an overwhelming variety of material to choose from; and his selection gives a fair impression of the terrible power of this wonderful writer, the study of whom is one of the most important means of self-education open to a cultivated man in the nineteenth century.*"—PALL MALL GAZETTE.

"*This is a volume of selections from the works of H. A. Taine, a celebrated contemporary French author. It forms an instalment of a series of selections from modern French authors Messrs. Rivington are now issuing. The print, the extracts, and the notes, are as excellent as in a previous publication of the same kind we lately noticed containing extracts from Balzac. The notes, in particular, evince great care, study, and erudition. The works of Taine, from which lengthy quotations are given, are, 'Histoire de la Littérature Anglaise,' 'Voyage en Italie,' and 'Voyages aux Pyrénées.' These compilations would form first-rate class-books for advanced French students.*"—PUBLIC OPINION.

WALTER KERR HAMILTON: Bishop of Salisbury. A Sketch Reprinted, with Additions and Corrections, from "The Guardian." By H. P. LIDDON, D.C.L., Canon of St. Paul's. 8vo. 2s. 6d.

Or bound with the Sermon "Life in Death," 3s. 6d.

THE MANOR FARM: A TALE. By M. C. PHILLPOTTS, Author of "The Hillford Confirmation." With Illustrations. Small 8vo. 3s. 6d.

"*The Manor Farm, by Miss Phillpotts, author of the 'Hillford Confirmation,' is a pious story, which amongst other things shows the dawning of light in superstitious minds.*"—MORNING POST.

"'*The Manor Farm' relates how, under good influence, a selfish girl became a useful and gentle daughter. The story is a capital illustration of the value of perseverance, and it is a book that will be very useful in parochial reading libraries.*"—JOHN BULL.

"*A prettily got-up and prettily written little book above the average of the class it belongs to.*"—EDINBURGH COURANT.

A PLAIN AND SHORT HISTORY OF ENGLAND FOR CHILDREN: in Letters from a Father to his Son. By GEORGE DAVYS, D.D., formerly Bishop of Peterborough. New Edition. With Twelve Coloured Illustrations. Square Crown 8vo. 3s. 6d.

SKETCHES OF THE RITES AND CUSTOMS OF THE GRECO-RUSSIAN CHURCH. By H. C. ROMANOFF. With an Introductory Notice by the Author of "The Heir of Redclyffe." Second Edition. Crown 8vo. 7s. 6d.

"*The twofold object of this work is 'to present the English with correct descriptions of the ceremonies of the Greco-Russian Church, and at the same time with pictures of domestic life in Russian homes, especially those of the clergy and the middle class of nobles;' and, beyond question, the author's labour has been so far successful that, whilst her Church scenes may be commended as a series of most dramatic and picturesque tableaux, her social sketches enable us to look at certain points beneath the surface of Russian life, and materially enlarge our knowledge of a country concerning which we have still a very great deal to learn.*"—ATHENÆUM.

"*The volume before us is anything but a formal liturgical treatise. It might be more valuable to a few scholars if it were, but it would certainly fail to obtain perusal at the hands of the great majority of those whom the writer, not unreasonably, hopes to attract by the narrative style she has adopted. What she has set before us is a series of brief outlines, which, by their simple effort to clothe the information given in a living garb, reminds us of a once-popular childs' book which we remember a generation ago, called 'Sketches of Human Manners.'*"—CHURCH TIMES.

PAROCHIAL AND PLAIN SERMONS. By JOHN HENRY NEWMAN, B.D., formerly Vicar of St. Mary's, Oxford. Edited by the Rev. W. J. COPELAND, Rector of Farnham, Essex. From the Text of the last Editions published by Messrs. Rivington. In 8 vols. Crown 8vo. 5*s.* each. Sold separately.

SERMONS BEARING UPON SUBJECTS OF THE DAY. By JOHN HENRY NEWMAN, B.D. Edited by the Rev. W. J. COPELAND, Rector of Farnham, Essex. Printed uniformly with the "Parochial and Plain Sermons." With an Index of Dates of all the Sermons. Crown 8vo. 5*s.*

SERMONS PREACHED BEFORE THE UNIVERSITY OF OXFORD. By HENRY PARRY LIDDON, D.C.L., Canon of St. Paul's, and Ireland Professor of Exegesis in the University of Oxford. Third Edition, revised. Crown 8vo. 5*s.*

NEW VOLUMES OF RIVINGTON'S DEVOTIONAL SERIES.

ELEGANTLY PRINTED WITH RED BORDERS, 16mo., 2*s.* 6*d.* each.

THOMAS À KEMPIS, OF THE IMITATION OF CHRIST.
A carefully revised Translation.
Also a Cheap Edition, without the red borders, 1*s.*, or in paper cover, 6*d.*

THE RULE AND EXERCISES OF HOLY LIVING. By JEREMY TAYLOR, D.D., Bishop of Down and Connor, and Dromore.
Also a Cheap Edition, without the red borders, 1*s.*

THE RULE AND EXERCISES OF HOLY DYING. By JEREMY TAYLOR, D.D., Bishop of Down and Connor, and Dromore.
Also a Cheap Edition, without the red borders, 1*s.*
The Holy Living and Holy Dying may be had bound together in One Volume, 5*s.* ; or without the red borders, 2*s.* 6*d.*

A SHORT AND PLAIN INSTRUCTION FOR THE BETTER UNDERSTANDING OF THE LORD'S SUPPER ; to which is annexed the Office of the Holy Communion, with proper Helps and Directions. By THOMAS WILSON, D.D., late Lord Bishop of Sodor and Man. Complete Edition.
Also a Cheap Edition, without the red borders, 1*s.*, or in paper cover, 6*d.*

INTRODUCTION TO THE DEVOUT LIFE. From the French of SAINT FRANCIS of Sales, Bishop and Prince of Geneva. A New Translation.

A PRACTICAL TREATISE CONCERNING EVIL THOUGHTS : wherein their Nature, Origin, and Effect are distinctly considered and explained, with many Useful Rules for restraining and suppressing such Thoughts ; suited to the various conditions of Life, and the several tempers of Mankind, more especially of melancholy Persons. By WILLIAM CHILCOT, M.A.

THE ENGLISH POEMS OF GEORGE HERBERT, together with his Collection of Proverbs, entitled JACULA PRUDENTUM.

CURIOUS MYTHS OF THE MIDDLE AGES. By S. BARING-GOULD, M.A., Author of "Post-Mediæval Preachers," &c. With Illustrations. New Edition. Complete in One Vol. Crown 8vo. 6s.

"These Essays will be found to have something to satisfy most classes of readers; the lovers of legends proper, the curious in popular delusions, the initiated in Darwinian and Monboddoan theories; and if, in the chapters on Tell and Gellert, we are a little struck with the close following of Dasent's track, in his preface to the Norse tales, it must be owned that there are chapters—e.g., those on the Divining Rod, the Man in the Moon, and the Seven Sleepers—which present new matter, and deserve the praise of independent research."—QUARTERLY REVIEW.

"The author, indeed, is sometimes fanciful and overbold in his conclusions; but he conducts us through marvellous ways—ways which he has studied well before he undertook to guide others; and if we do not always acquiesce in his descriptions or arguments, we seldom differ from him without hesitation."—ATHENÆUM.

"We have no space to linger longer about a book which, apart from its didactic pretensions, is an exceedingly amusing and interesting collection of old stories and legends of the middle ages."—PALL MALL GAZETTE.

"That, on his first visit to the varied field of mediæval mythology, Mr. Baring-Gould should have culled as samples of its richness the most brilliant of the flowers that bloomed in it, is scarcely to be wondered at. But it shows how fertile is the soil when he is enabled to cull from it so goodly a second crop as that which he here presents to us. The myths treated of in the present volume vary in interest—they are all curious and well worth reading."—NOTES AND QUERIES.

THE LIFE OF MADAME LOUISE DE FRANCE, daughter of Louis XV. Known also as the Mother Térèse de St. Augustin. By the Author of "Tales of Kirkbeck." Crown 8vo. 6s.

'Such a record of deep, earnest, self-sacrificing piety, beneath the surface of Parisian life, during what we all regard as the worst age of French godlessness, ought to teach us all a lesson of hope and faith, let appearances be what they may. Here, from out of the court and family of Louis XV. there issues this Madame Louise, whose life is set before us as a specimen of as calm and unworldly devotion—of a devotion, too, full of shrewd sense and practical administrative talent—as any we have ever met with."—LITERARY CHURCHMAN.

"On the 15th of July, 1737, Marie Leczinska, the wife of Louis XV., and daughter of the dethroned King of Poland, which Russia helped to despoil and plunder, gave birth to her eighth female child, Louise Marie, known also as the Mother Térèse de St. Augustin. On the death of the Queen, the princess, who had long felt a vocation for a religious life, obtained the consent of her royal father to withdraw from the world. The Carmelite convent of St. Denis was the chosen place of retreat. Here the novitiate was passed, here the final vows were taken, and here, on the death of the Mère Julie, Madame Louise began and terminated her experiences as prioress. The little volume which records the simple incidents of her pious seclusion is designed to edify those members of the Church of England in whom the spirit of religious self-devotion is reviving. The substance of the memoir is taken from a somewhat diffuse 'Life of Madame Louise de France,' compiled by a Carmelite nun, and printed at Autun."—WESTMINSTER REVIEW.

"This 'Life' relates the history of that daughter of Louis XV. who, aided by the example and instructions of a pious mother, lived an uncorrupt life in the midst of a most corrupt court, which she quitted—after longing and waiting for years to do so—to enter the severe order of Mount Carmel, which she adorned by her strict and holy life. We cannot too highly praise the present work, which appears to us to be written in the most excellent good taste. We hope it may find entrance into every religious House in our Communion, and it should be in the library of every young lady."—CHURCH REVIEW.

"The Life of Madame Louise de France, the celebrated daughter of Louis XV., who became a religieuse, and is known in the spiritual world as Mother Térèse de St. Augustin. The substance of the memoir is taken from a diffuse life, compiled by a Carmelite nun, and printed at Autun; and the editor, the author of 'Tales of Kirkbeck,' was prompted to the task by the belief, that 'at the present time, when the spirit of religious self-devotion is so greatly reviving in the Church of England' the records of a princess who quitted a dazzling and profligate court to lead a life of obscure piety will meet with a cordial reception. We may remark, that should the event prove otherwise, it will not be from any fault of workmanship on the part of the editor."—DAILY TELEGRAPH.

"The annals of a cloistered life, under ordinary circumstances, would not probably be considered very edifying by the reading public of the present generation. When, however, such a history presents the novel spectacle of a royal princess of modern times voluntarily renouncing her high position and the splendours of a court existence, for the purpose of enduring the asceticism, poverty, and austerities of a severe monastic rule, the case may well be different."—MORNING POST.

THE PRIEST TO THE ALTAR; or, Aids to the Devout Celebration of Holy Communion; chiefly after the Ancient Use of Sarum. Second Edition. Enlarged, Revised, and Re-arranged with the Secretæ, Post-Communion, &c., appended to the Collects, Epistles, and Gospels, throughout the Year. 8vo. 7s. 6d.

HELP AND COMFORT FOR THE SICK POOR. By the Author of "Sickness; its Trials and Blessings." New Edition. Small 8vo. 1s.

A MANUAL FOR THE SICK; with other Devotions. By LANCELOT ANDREWES, D.D., sometime Lord Bishop of Winchester. Edited with a Preface by H. P. LIDDON, M.A. Large type. With Portrait. 24mo. 2s. 6d.

APOSTOLICAL SUCCESSION IN THE CHURCH OF ENGLAND. By the Rev. ARTHUR W. HADDAN, B.D., Rector of Barton-on-the-Heath, and late Fellow of Trinity College, Oxford. 8vo. 12s.

"Mr. Haddan's estimate of the bearing of his subject, and of its special importance at the present juncture is characteristic, and will well repay attention. . . . Mr. Haddan is strictly argumentative throughout. He abstains with some strictness from everything which would divert either his reader or himself from accurate investigation of his reasoning. But his volume is thoroughly well written, clear and forcible in style, and fair in tone. It cannot but render valuable service in placing the claims of the Church in their true light before the English public."—GUARDIAN.

"Among the many standard theological works devoted to this important subject Mr. Haddan's will hold a high place."—STANDARD.

"We should be glad to see the volume widely circulated and generally read."—JOHN BULL.

"A weighty and valuable treatise, and we hope that the study of its sound and well-reasoned pages will do much to fix the importance, and the full meaning of the doctrine in question, in the minds of Church people. . . . We hope that our extracts will lead our readers to study Mr. Haddan for themselves."—LITERARY CHURCHMAN.

"This is not only a very able and carefully written treatise upon the doctrine of Apostolical Succession, but it is also a calm yet noble vindication of the validity of the Anglican Orders: it well sustains the brilliant reputation which Mr. Haddan left behind him at Oxford, and it supplements his other profound historical researches in ecclesiastical matters. This book will remain for a long time the classic work upon English Orders."—CHURCH REVIEW.

"A very temperate, but a very well reasoned book."—WESTMINSTER REVIEW.

"Mr. Haddan ably sustains his reputation throughout the work. His style is clear, his inferences are reasonable, and the publication is especially well-timed in prospect of the coming Œcumenical Council."—CAMBRIDGE UNIVERSITY GAZETTE.

THE PERFECT MAN; OR, JESUS AN EXAMPLE OF GODLY LIFE. By the Rev. HARRY JONES, M.A., Incumbent of St. Luke's, Berwick Street. Crown 8vo. 3s. 6d.

"Whatever Mr. Harry Jones writes is always well written in point of composition, it is rarely heavy, and generally sensible. Mr. Jones wisely selects practical subjects for his sermons. His mind is eminently practical in cast."—CHURCH TIMES.

"There is a degree of raciness and piquancy about Mr. Harry Jones which it is impossible to resist. Combined with this, however there is a deep earnestness of purpose. This book is decidedly worth reading."—JOHN BULL.

"A volume of excellent sermons."—SPECTATOR.

"Mr. Jones' work is written in a terse and vigorous style, and wherever it deals with what is clearly revealed, abounds in sound, wholesome, practical lessons."—ENGLISH CHURCHMAN.

"Evidently the product of a vigorous mind. It contains many sensible observations."—WATCHMAN.

YESTERDAY, TO-DAY, AND FOR EVER: A Poem in Twelve Books. By E. H. BICKERSTETH, M.A., Vicar of Christ Church, Hampstead. Fifth Edition. Small 8vo. 6s.

"The most simple, the richest, and the most perfect sacred poem which recent days have produced."—MORNING ADVERTISER.

"A poem worth reading, worthy of attentive study; full of noble thoughts, beautiful diction, and high imagination."—STANDARD.

"Mr. Bickersteth writes like a man who cultivates at once reverence and earnestness of thought."—GUARDIAN.

"In these light miscellany days there is a spiritual refreshment in the spectacle of a man girding up the loins of his mind to the task of producing a genuine epic. And it is true poetry. There is a definiteness, a crispness about it, which in these moist, viewy, hazy days, is no less invigorating than novel."—EDINBURGH DAILY REVIEW.

BRIGHSTONE SERMONS. By GEORGE MOBERLY, D.C.L., Bishop of Salisbury. Second Edition. Crown 8vo. 7s. 6d.

A MEMOIR OF THE LATE HENRY HOARE, M.A.

With a Narrative of the Church Movements with which he was connected from 1848 to 1865, and more particularly of the Revival of Convocation. By JAMES BRADBY SWEET, M.A. 8vo. 12*s*.

THE POPE AND THE COUNCIL.

By JANUS. Authorized translation from the German. Second Edition. Crown 8vo. 7*s*. 6*d*.

"*A profound and learned treatise, evidently the work of one of the first theologians of the day, discussing with the scientific fulness and precision proper to German investigation, the great doctrinal questions expected to come before the Council, and especially the proposed dogma of Papal Infallibility. There is probably no work in existence that contains at all, still less within so narrow a compass, so complete a record of the origin and growth of the infallibilist theory, and of all the facts of Church history bearing upon it, and that too in a form so clear and concise as to put the argument within the reach of any reader of ordinary intelligence, while the scrupulous accuracy of the writer, and his constant reference to the original authorities for every statement liable to be disputed, makes the monograph as a whole a perfect storehouse of valuable information for the historical or theological student.*"—SATURDAY REVIEW.

"*Beginning with a sketch of the errors and contradictions of the Popes, and of the position which, as a matter of history, they held in the early Church, the book proceeds to describe the three great forgeries by which the Papal claims were upheld—the Isidorian decretals, the donation of Constantine, and the decretum of Gratian. The last subject ought to be carefully studied by all who wish to understand the frightful tyranny of a complicated system of laws, devised not for the protection of a people, but as instruments for grinding them to subjection. Then, after an historical outline of the general growth of the Papal power in the twelfth and thirteenth centuries, the writers enter upon the peculiarly episcopal and clerical question, pointing out how marvellously every little change worked in one direction, invariably tending to throw the rule of the Church into the power of Rome; and how the growth of new institutions, like the monastic orders and the Inquisition, gradually withdrew the conduct of affairs from the Bishops of the Church in general, and consolidated the Papal influence. For all this, however, unless we could satisfy ourselves with a mere magnified table of contents, the reader must be referred to the book itself, in which he will find the interest sustained without flagging to the end.*"—PALL MALL GAZETTE.

"*In France, in Holland, and in Germany, there has already appeared a multitude of disquisitions on this subject. Among these several are the acknowledged compositions of men of high standing in the Roman Catholic world,—men admittedly entitled to speak with the authority that must attach to established reputation; but not one of them has hitherto produced a work more likely to create a deep impression than the anonymous German publication at the head of this notice. It is not a piece of merely polemical writing, it is a treatise dealing with a large subject in an impressive though partisan manner, a treatise grave in tone, solid in matter, and bristling with forcible and novel illustrations.*"—SPECTATOR.

"*Rumour will, no doubt, be busy with its conjectures as to the name which lurks beneath the nom de plume of 'Janus.' We do not intend to offer any contribution towards the elucidation of the mystery, unless it be as a contribution to say that the book bears internal evidence of being the work of a Catholic, and that there are not many Catholics in Europe who could have written it. Taking it all in all, it is no exaggerated praise to characterize it as the most damaging assault on Ultramontanism that has appeared in modern times. Its learning is copious and complete, yet so admirably arranged that it invariably illustrates without overlaying the argument. The style is clear and simple, and there is no attempt at rhetoric. It is a piece of cool and masterly dissection, all the more terrible for the passionless manner in which the author conducts the operation.*"—TIMES.

SOIMÊME; A Story of a Wilful Life. Small 8vo., 3*s*. 6*d*.

"*There is a very quiet, earnest tone in this story which reconciles the reader to the lesson which it is intended to teach. It is essentially a story of character, and the heroine who is supposed to relate it is presented in a clearly defined and somewhat picturesque manner. . . . To the thoughtful who are passing from youth to riper years 'Soimême' will prove both attractive and useful.*"—PUBLIC OPINION.

"*A pure, good, wholesome little book, styling itself 'The Story of a Wilful Life,' and teaches the old true lesson, that without humility there is no such thing as happiness.*"—DAILY TELEGRAPH.

"*As a sketch of the inner life of a neglected, untutored, and consequently self-willed, almost savage girl, this story has its merits. The writer succeeds fairly with pleasing characters.*"—ATHENÆUM.

"*The story is full of buoyancy and interest, incident being duly intermingled with conversation. Some of the bits of description, as that of the Shropshire lane, are exquisite little idylls. This book is a work of genuine art.*"—CLERICAL JOURNAL.

"*A vein of lofty, moral, and deep religious feeling runs through the whole tale, and the author neither proses nor preaches.*"—STANDARD.

"*A very natural, unaffected, and simple little story for young people—one which they will not only read but enjoy.*"—MORNING HERALD.

"*The author promises to become a valuable accession to the ranks of our popular lady writers. 'Soimême' is a simple life-like story, charmingly told and gracefully written, and, what is better still, its tendencies are excellent. The lessons it teaches are of the highest order.*"—EUROPEAN MAIL.

"*There are many clever little bits of description, and excellent maxims worth remembering. The scenery is all charmingly described.*"—MONTHLY PACKET.

THE FIRST BOOK OF COMMON PRAYER OF EDWARD
VI., and the Ordinal of 1549, together with the Order of the Communion, 1548. Reprinted entire, and Edited by the Rev. HENRY BASKERVILLE WALTON, M.A., late Fellow and Tutor of Merton College. With an Introduction by the Rev. PETER GOLDSMITH MEDD, M.A., Senior Fellow and Tutor of University College, Oxford. Small 8vo. 6s.

"*A volume like this is worth two of Church History. In many respects, indeed, it is the subject of history itself; and with Mr. Medd's introduction and Mr. Walton's editorial work we may be said to have both subject and history thereof. The volume should be in the hands of every member of the Church of England: we may say, it should be in those of every student of Church History.*"—ATHENÆUM.

"*We welcome the seasonable appearance of this work, which indeed supplies a long-felt want, for 'the First Book' has been hitherto accessible to very few. . . . It is especially important at the present time that the principles of the first Reformers should be understood; and no one can look through this edition without gaining some definite information on that point. We commend this new edition of the First Prayer Book, with its introduction to the study of all that are desirous of understanding the principles of those who originated the reform of our public Services.*"—CHURCH NEWS.

"*The more that English Churchmen become acquainted with the Reformed Prayer Book, as our English Divines reformed it, apart from the meddling of foreigners—i.e., the better people became acquainted with 'Edward VI's first book,' the better both for themselves and for the English Church at large. We are therefore delighted to welcome this handy and handsome reprint, with which every pains has been taken to make it as accurate as possible.*'"—LITERARY CHURCHMAN.

"*Mr. Walton deserves the very best thanks of Anglican Churchmen, for putting this most important volume within their reach in so convenient and handsome a form.*"—CHURCH REVIEW.

FEMALE CHARACTERS OF HOLY SCRIPTURE. In a
Series of Sermons. By the Rev. ISAAC WILLIAMS, B.D., formerly Fellow of Trinity College, Oxford. New Edition. Crown 8vo. 5s.

THE CHARACTERS OF THE OLD TESTAMENT. In a Series
of Sermons. By the Rev. ISAAC WILLIAMS, B.D., formerly Fellow of Trinity College, Oxford. New Edition. Crown 8vo., 5s.

"*This is one of the few volumes of published sermons that we have been able to read with real pleasure. They are written with a chastened elegance of language, and pervaded by a spirit of earnest and simple piety. Mr. Williams is evidently what would be called a very High Churchman. Occasionally his peculiar Church views are apparent; but bating a few passages here and there, these sermons will be read with profit by all who profess and call themselves Christians.*'"—CONTEMPORARY REVIEW.

"*This is a new edition of a very popular— and deservedly popular—work on the biography of the Old Testament history. The characters are ably and profitably analysed, and that by the hand of a master of style and thought. . . . The principle of selection has been that of prominence; and partly, too, that of significance in the characters so ably delineated. A more masterly analysis of Scriptural characters we never read, nor any which are more calculated to impress the mind of the reader with feelings of love for what is good, and abhorrence for what is evil.*"—ROCK.

THE WITNESS OF ST. PAUL TO CHRIST: being the Boyle
Lectures for 1869. With an Appendix, on the Credibility of the Acts, in Reply to the Recent Strictures of Dr. Davidson. By the Rev. STANLEY LEATHES, M.A., Professor of Hebrew, King's College, London, and Incumbent of St. Philip's, Regent Street. 8vo. 10s. 6d.

"*It is impossible to follow the writer step by step in his elaborate argument, but we have little doubt that this book will be of great service. There is a learned Appendix on 'The Credibility of the Acts of the Apostles,' which will be very valuable to the theological student. Altogether we think this volume will take a high place among the Boyle Lectures.*"—JOHN BULL.

"*The expectations raised by Mr. Leathes' Boyle Lectures of last year have been amply fulfilled. He has given the Christian world another volume, replete with sound doctrine and solid argument.*"—ENGLISH CHURCHMAN.

"*The above may serve as specimens of the author's style and Christian stand-point; but taken out of the connection they give but a very imperfect idea of the book as one of reasoning conducted in a popular yet conclusive manner. We must refer our readers, therefore, who are interested in the subject— and who, especially at the present day, is not?—to the book itself, for which, as a religious journal, we beg to tender the author our sincere thanks.*"—FREEMAN.

THOUGHTS ON PERSONAL RELIGION; being a Treatise on the Christian Life in its Two Chief Elements, Devotion and Practice. By EDWARD MEYRICK GOULBURN, D.D., Dean of Norwich. New Edition. Small 8vo. 6s. 6d.
    An Edition for Presentation, Two Volumes, small 8vo. 10s. 6d.
    Also a cheap Edition. Small 8vo. 3s. 6d.

DEVOTIONAL COMMENTARY ON THE GOSPEL ACCORDING TO S. MATTHEW. Translated from the French of Pasquier Quesnel. Crown 8vo. 7s. 6d.

"We can hardly give him (Pasquier Quesnel) higher praise than to say that he reminds us in many ways of the author of the 'Imitation.' There is the same knowledge of human nature, shrewdness of observation, intimate acquaintance with the special trials, difficulties, and temptations of the spiritual life, and that fervour and concentration which result from habitual meditation and prayer."—CLERICAL JOURNAL.

"This Commentary is what it purports to be 'devotional.' There is no criticism, no suggestion of difficulties, no groupings of 'various readings.' Its object is to give 'the spiritual sense' of Holy Scripture, and this object is admirably carried out. We are glad to be able to give it our hearty and unqualified approval."—JOHN BULL.

"The want which many devout persons feel for a Commentary on the Scriptures with individual, practical, and devotional application, can hardly be better satisfied than by that of 'Quesnel.'"—CHURCH NEWS.

"This translation is based upon that made by the Non-juror Russell, and it has been especially adapted for the use of members of the English Church in private devotion. It is a very acceptable manual for the religious, and its simple and practical character may be gleaned from the following comment."—ROCK.

"The Comments are brief but pointed, and there is so much to profit the reader by showing him what a depth of spiritual wisdom is treasured up even in the simplest utterances of our Lord, that we are sorry we cannot give the book an unqualified recommendation. Works on the Gospels, suited to the wants of scholars, have been tolerably numerous of late years. Such a book as this, in which considerable intellectual force is blended with devotional feeling, is more rare, and would be welcome were it not that the good in it is marred by the Sacramentarianism which continually obtrudes itself."—ENGLISH INDEPENDENT.

THE HILLFORD CONFIRMATION: A TALE. By M. C. PHILLPOTTS. 18mo. 1s.

THE TREASURY OF DEVOTION: a Manual of Prayers for general and daily use. Compiled by a Priest. Edited by the Rev. T. T. CARTER, Rector of Clewer. 16mo. 2s. 6d.; limp cloth, 2s. Bound with the Book of Common Prayer. 3s. 6d.

A KEY TO THE KNOWLEDGE OF CHURCH HISTORY. (Ancient.) Edited by JOHN HENRY BLUNT, M.A. (Forming the third Volume of KEYS TO CHRISTIAN KNOWLEDGE). Small 8vo. 2s. 6d.

"It offers a short and condensed account of the origin, growth, and condition of the Church in all parts of the world, from A.D. 1 down to the end of the fifteenth century. Mr. Blunt's first object has been conciseness, and this has been admirably carried out, and to students of Church history this feature will readily recommend itself. As an elementary work 'A Key' will be specially valuable, inasmuch as it points out certain definite lines of thought, by which those who enjoy the opportunity may be guided in reading the statements of more elaborate histories. At the same time it is but fair to Mr. Blunt to remark that, for general readers, the little volume contains everything that could be consistently expected in a volume of its character. There are many notes, theological, scriptural,

and historical, and the 'get up' of the book is specially commendable. As a text-book for the higher forms of schools the work will be acceptable to numerous teachers."—PUBLIC OPINION.

"It contains some concise notes on Church History, compressed into a small compass, and we think it is likely to be useful as a book of reference."—JOHN BULL.

"A very terse and reliable collection of the main facts and incidents connected with Church History."—ROCK.

"It will be excellent, either for school or home use, either as a reading or as a reference book, on all the main facts and names and controversies of the first fifteen centuries. It is both well arranged and well written."—LITERARY CHURCHMAN.

Messrs. Rivington's Publications

THE REFORMATION OF THE CHURCH OF ENGLAND: its History, Principles, and Results, A.D. 1514-1547. By JOHN HENRY BLUNT, M.A., Vicar of Kennington, Oxford. Second Edition. 8vo. 16s.

"*The reader will gladly acknowledge the impartiality of treatment and liberality of tone which are conspicuous in every page. It is distinctly a learned book. The author is not a second-hand retailer of facts; he is a painstaking, conscientious student, who derives his knowledge from original sources. We have said that he does not command a brilliant style; but he is by no means a dull writer—on the contrary, he is always readable, sometimes very interesting, and shows considerable skill in the grouping and arrangement of his facts.*"—TIMES.

"*Mr. Blunt gives us, in this volume, an instalment history of the Reformation, in the just proportions of a history, and written carefully from contemporary documents and evidence ... with scholarly knowledge, with an independent judgment, and with careful support given to each statement by quotation of evidence. And Mr. Blunt has given greater effect to his narrative by a skilful division and grouping of his subjects. Undoubtedly, he writes upon very definite views and principles, but those views and principles are not forced upon the facts, but are educed from them as their necessary results. The true account, indeed, of his book is, that it is a sketch of the reign of Henry VIII. in its theological changes, which proves in detail the Church view of those changes. And if that view is the true view, how can a true history do otherwise? The merit of a history is, that it allows facts to evolve views, and does not pervert or conceal facts in order to force upon them preconceived views of its own. And when we characterize Mr. Blunt's volume as stating the Church's case throughout, we conceive it to be an ample justification to say that if he is to relate the facts fairly he could not do otherwise; that he fairly alleges the facts, and the facts prove his case. We hold the book, then, to be a solid and valuable addition to our Church history, just because it does in the main establish the Church case, and bring it ably and clearly before the public, upon unanswerable evidence, impartially and on the whole correctly stated.*"—GUARDIAN.

CATECHETICAL NOTES AND CLASS QUESTIONS, Literal and Mystical; chiefly on the Earlier Books of Holy Scripture. By the late Rev. J. M. NEALE, D.D., Warden of Sackville College, East Grinstead. Crown 8vo. 5s.

"*Unless we are much mistaken this will be one of the most practically useful of the various posthumous works of Dr. Neale, for the publication of which we are indebted to the S. Margaret's Sisters and Dr. Neale's literary executors. Besides 'class notes'—lecture notes as most people would call them—on the earlier books of Holy Scripture, there are some most excellent similar notes on the Sacraments, and then a collection of notes for catechizing children. Throughout these notes are supplemented from other of Dr. Neale's papers, and in particular we would specify an admirable appendix of extracts from Dr. Neale's sermons (chiefly unpublished) bearing upon points touched on in the text.*"—LITERARY CHURCHMAN.

"*The writer's wide acquaintance with Mediæval theology renders his notes on the Old Testament peculiarly valuable.*"—JOHN BULL.

HERBERT TRESHAM. A Tale of the Great Rebellion. By the late Rev. J. M. NEALE, D.D. New Edition. Small 8vo. 3s. 6d.

"*We cordially welcome a new edition of Dr. Neale's 'Herbert Tresham.' The scene is laid in the time of the great civil war, and vivid pictures are drawn of some of the startling events that then disgraced the history of this country. The martyrdom of Archbishop Laud is described in a manner few besides its author could equal, while the narration of the disastrous battle of Naseby, and the disgraceful surrender of Bristol by Prince Rupert, afford proof of the versatility of his genius.*"—CHURCH TIMES.

"*A pleasant Christmas present is Dr. Neale's 'Herbert Tresham.' Such a book is well calculated to correct current views of 17th century history.*"—CHURCH REVIEW.

"*Nothing could be more admirable as a Christmas present.*"—CHURCH NEWS.

THE ANNUAL REGISTER: A Review of Public Events at Home and Abroad, for the Year 1869; being the Seventh Volume of an Improved Series. 8vo. 18s.

⁎⁎* The Volumes for 1863 to 1868 may be had, 18s. each.

"*Well edited, excellent type, good paper, and in all respects admirably got up. Its review of affairs, Home, Colonial, and Foreign, is fair, concise, and complete.*"—MINING QUARTERLY.

"*We are so used at the present day to epitomised books of reference on every variety of subject, that this work, which is an abstract of contemporary history, excites perhaps no great admiration or surprise. It is impossible, however, to glance through its multitudinous contents, so systematically arranged, without deriving some idea of the labour of compilation and authorship involved. The care with which it is compiled and produced reflects the highest credit on the well known firm of publishers.*"—EXAMINER.

"*Solidly valuable, as well as interesting.*"—STANDARD.

"*Comprehensive and well executed.*"—SPECTATOR.

BOOKS FOR THE CLERGY

Blunt's (Rev. J. H.) Directorium Pastorale,
Principles and Practice of Pastoral Work in the Church of England. Crown 8vo. 9s.

Hodgson's (Chr.) Instructions for the Use of
Candidates for Holy Orders, and of the Parochial Clergy, as to Ordination, Licenses, Induction, Pluralities, Residence, &c., &c.; with Acts of Parliament and Forms to be used. 8vo. 16s.

Exton's (Rev. R. B.) Speculum Gregis; or, The
Parochial Minister's Assistant in the Oversight of his Flock. Oblong 12mo. 4s. 6d.

The Priest to the Altar; or, Aids to the De-
vout Celebration of Holy Communion; chiefly after the Ancient Use of Sarum. Second Edition, enlarged, revised, and re-arranged with the Secretæ, Post-Communion, &c., appended to the Collects, Epistles, and Gospels throughout the Year. 8vo. 7s. 6d.

Barrett's (W. A.) Flowers and Festivals; or,
Directions for Floral Decoration of Churches. With Coloured Illustrations. Square Crown 8vo. 5s.

Jones's (Rev. Harry) Priest and Parish. Square Crown 8vo. 6s. 6d.

Nixon's (Bp.) Lectures, Historical, Doctrinal,
and Practical, on the Catechism of the Church of England. 8vo. 18s.

Neale's (Rev. J. M.) Catechetical Notes and
Class Questions, Literal and Mystical; chiefly on the Earlier Books of Holy Scripture. Crown 8vo. 5s.

Wordsworth's (Bishop Charles) Catechesis; or,
Christian Instruction preparatory to Confirmation and First Communion. Small 8vo. 2s.

The Annotated Book of Common Prayer; being
an Historical, Ritual, and Theological Commentary on the Devotional System of the Church of England. Edited by John Henry Blunt, M.A., F.S.A. Imperial 8vo. 36s.

The Prayer Book Interleaved; with Historical
Illustrations and Explanatory Notes arranged parallel to the Text, by W. M. Campion, B.A., Fellow and Tutor of Queens' College, and W. J. Beamont, M.A., Fellow of Trinity College, Cambridge. With a Preface by the Lord Bishop of Ely. Small 8vo. 7s. 6d.

The First Book of Common Prayer of Edward
VI. and the Ordinal of 1549; together with the Order of the Communion, 1548. Reprinted entire, and Edited by the Rev. Henry Baskerville Walton, M.A., late Fellow and Tutor of Merton College. With Introduction by the Rev. Peter Goldsmith Medd, M.A., Senior Fellow and Tutor of University College, Oxford. Small 8vo. 6s.

Liber Precum Publicarum Ecclesiæ Anglicanæ,
à Gulielmo Bright, A.M., et Petro Goldsmith Medd, A.M., Presbyteris, Collegii Universitatis in Acad. Oxon. Sociis, Latine redditus. With all the Rubics in Red. Small 8vo. 6s.

VOLUMES OF SERMONS

Adams's (Rev. W.) Warn- ings of the Holy Week; being a Course of Parochial Lectures for the Week before Easter, and the Easter Festivals. Small 8vo. 4s. 6d.

Body's (Rev. G.) The Life of Justification. A Series of Lectures delivered in Substance at All Saints, Margaret Street, during Lent 1870. Crown 8vo. 4s. 6d.

Goulburn's (Dean) Fare- well Counsels of a Pastor to his Flock, on Topics of the Day. Small 8vo. 4s.

Goulburn's (Dean) Ser- mons preached on Various Occasions during the last Twenty Years. Small 8vo. 6s. 6d.

Harris's (Rev. G.C.) Church Seasons and Present Times: Sermons preached at St. Luke's, Torquay. Small 8vo. 5s.

Heygate's (Rev. W. E.) Care of the Soul; or, Sermons on Points of Christian Prudence. 12mo. 5s. 6d.

Liddon's (Canon) Sermons preached before the University of Oxford. Crown 8vo. 5s.

Moberly's (Bishop) Brigh- stone Sermons. Crown 8vo. 7s. 6d.

Moberly's (Bishop) The Sayings of the Great Forty Days, between the Resurrection and Ascension, regarded as the Outlines of the Kingdom of God: in Five Sermons. Uniform with the Brighstone Sermons. 8vo. 7s. 6d.

Melvill's (Canon) Sermons. Two Vols. Crown 8vo. 5s. each.

Melvill's (Canon) Selection from the Lectures delivered at St. Margaret's, Lothbury, 1850-52. Small 8vo. 6s.

Moore's (Rev. Daniel) Aids to Prayer: a Course of Lectures delivered at Holy Trinity Church, Paddington, on the Sunday Mornings in Lent, 1868. Crown 8vo. 4s. 6d.

Moore's (Rev. Daniel) The Age and the Gospel: Four Sermons preached before the University of Cambridge. Crown 8vo. 5s.

Neale's (Rev. J. M.) Ser- mons to Children: being Short Readings, addressed to the Children of St. Margaret's Home, East Grinstead. Small 8vo. 3s. 6d.

Newman's (J. H.) Paro- chial and Plain Sermons. Edited by the Rev. W. J. Copeland, Rector of Farnham, Essex. 8 vols. Crown 8vo. 5s. each.

Newman's (J. H.) Sermons bearing upon Subjects of the Day. Edited by the Rev. W. J. Copeland, Rector of Farnham, Essex. Crown 8vo. 5s.

Pigou's (Rev. Francis) Faith and Practice; Sermons at St. Philip's, Regent Street. Small 8vo. 6s.

Shipley's (Rev. Orby) Six short Sermons on Sin. Lent Lectures at S. Alban the Martyr, Holborn. Small 8vo. 1s.

Williams's (Rev. Isaac) The Characters of the Old Testament. In a Series of Sermons. Crown 8vo. 5s.

Williams's (Rev. Isaac) Female Characters of Holy Scripture. In a Series of Sermons. Crown 8vo. 5s.

Williams's (Rev. Isaac) The Holy Days throughout the Year. Small 8vo. 5s. 6d.

FAMILY PRAYERS

Goulburn's (Dean) Family Prayers, arranged on the
Liturgical Principle. Large type. Crown 8vo. 3s. 6d. Cheap Edition.
18mo. 1s.

Hook's (Dean) Book of Family Prayer. 18mo. 2s.

Medd's (Rev. P. G.) Household Prayer, from Ancient
and Authorized Sources; with Morning and Evening Readings for a Month.
Small 8vo. 4s. 6d.

Duncombe's (Hon. Augustus) Manual of Family Devotions, arranged from the Book of Common Prayer. Small 8vo. 3s. 6d.

Clerke's (Archdeacon) Daily Devotions; or, Short
Morning and Evening Services for the use of a Churchman's Household.
18mo. 1s.

The Hours of the Passion; with Devotional Forms for
Private and Household use. 12mo. 6s.

Family Prayers from "The Guide to Heaven." For
the Working Classes. Compiled by a Priest. Edited by the Rev. T. T.
Carter, M.A., Rector of Clewer. Crown 8vo. 2d., or cloth limp, 4d.

SACRED POETRY

Lyte's (H. F.) Miscellaneous Poems. Small 8vo. 5s.

Bright's (Canon) Hymns and other Poems. Small 8vo.
4s. 6d.

Monsell's (Rev. Dr.) Parish Musings; or, Devotional
Poems. Small 8vo. 5s. Also a Cheaper Edition, 18mo. Limp cloth,
1s. 6d.; or in cover, 1s.

Mant's (Bishop) Ancient Hymns from the Roman
Breviary. For Domestic Use every Morning and Evening of the Week,
and on the Holy Days of the Church. To which are added, Original
Hymns, principally of Commemoration and Thanksgiving for Christ's Holy
Ordinances. New Edition. Small 8vo. 5s.

Hymns and Poems for the Sick and Suffering; in connection with the Service for the Visitation of the Sick. Edited by the Rev.
T. V. Fosbery, M.A. Small 8vo. 3s. 6d.

Bickersteth's (E. H.) Yesterday, To-day, and For Ever:
a Poem, in Twelve Books. Small 8vo. 6s.

Bickersteth's (E. H.) The Two Brothers, and other
Poems. Small 8vo. 6s.

BOOKS FOR CHURCH SCHOOLS, PAROCHIAL LIBRARIES, Etc.

Bright's (Canon) Faith and Life: Readings for the greater Holy Days, and the Sundays from Advent to Trinity. Compiled from Ancient Writers. Small 8vo. 5s.

Thomas à Kempis, Of the Imitation of Christ. 16mo. 1s.

Staley's (Bishop) Five Years' Church Work in the Kingdom of Hawaii. With Map and Illustrations. Crown 8vo. 5s.

Taylor's (Bishop Jeremy) The Holy Living and The Holy Dying. One Volume. 16mo. 2s. 6d.

James's (Canon) Comment upon the Collects. 12mo. 3s. 6d.

Goulburn's (Dean) Thoughts on Personal Religion. Small 8vo. 6s. 6d.

Goulburn's (Dean) The Pursuit of Holiness: a Sequel to "Thoughts on Personal Religion," intended to carry the Reader somewhat further onward in the Spiritual Life. Small 8vo. 5s.

Goulburn's (Dean) Introduction to the Devotional Study of the Holy Scriptures. Small 8vo. 3s. 6d.

Goulburn's (Dean) The Idle Word: Short Religious Essays upon the Gift of Speech. Small 8vo. 3s.

Goulburn's (Dean) Office of the Holy Communion in the Book of Common Prayer. Small 8vo. 6s.

Blunt's (Rev. J. H.) Household Theology; a Handbook of Religious Information respecting the Holy Bible, the Prayer Book, the Church, the Ministry, Divine Worship, the Creeds, &c., &c.. 18mo. 3s. 6d.

Phillpotts's (M. C.) The Manor Farm: a Tale. Small 8vo. With Illustrations. 3s. 6d.

Phillpotts's (M. C.) The Hillford Confirmation: a Tale. 16mo. 1s.

Adams's (Rev. W.) Sacred Allegories:—The Shadow of the Cross—The Distant Hills—The Old Man's Home—The King's Messengers. With numerous Illustrations. Small 8vo. 5s.

Soimême: a Story of a Wilful Life. Small 8vo. 3s. 6d.

Neale's (Rev. J. M.) Herbert Tresham: a Tale of the Great Rebellion. Small 8vo. 3s. 6d.

Romanoff's (H. C.) Sketches of the Rites and Customs of the Greco-Russian Church. Crown 8vo. 7s. 6d.

Keys to Christian Knowledge. Small 8vo. 2s. 6d. each.
The Book of Common Prayer.
The Holy Bible.
Church History (Ancient).
The Narrative of the Four Gospels.
Christian Doctrine and Practice. (Founded on the Church Catechism.)
The Acts of the Apostles.

Davys's (Bishop) Plain and Short History of England for Children. With Twelve Coloured Illustrations. Square Crown 8vo. 3s. 6d.

Gould's (Rev. S. Baring) Curious Myths of the Middle Ages. With Illustrations. Crown 8vo. 6s.

The Life of Madame Louise De France, Daughter of Louis XV., also known as the Mother Térèse de S. Augustin. Crown 8vo. 6s.

A Dominican Artist: A Sketch of the Life of the Rev. Père Besson, of the Order of St. Dominic. Crown 8vo. 9s.

Trelawny's (Rev. C. T. Collins) Perranzabuloe, the Lost Church Found. Crown 8vo. 3s. 6d.

CATENA CLASSICORUM

A Series of Classical Authors,

EDITED BY MEMBERS OF BOTH UNIVERSITIES UNDER THE DIRECTION OF

THE REV. ARTHUR HOLMES, M.A.
SENIOR FELLOW OF CLARE COLLEGE, CAMBRIDGE, AND PREACHER AT THE CHAPEL ROYAL, WHITEHALL,

AND THE REV. CHARLES BIGG, M.A.
LATE SENIOR STUDENT AND TUTOR OF CHRIST CHURCH, OXFORD, SECOND CLASSICAL MASTER OF CHELTENHAM COLLEGE.

Crown 8vo.

The following Parts have been already published:—

SOPHOCLIS TRAGOEDIAE, edited by R. C. JEBB, M.A., Fellow and Assistant Tutor of Trinity College, Cambridge, and Public Orator of the University.
    The Electra. 3s. 6d.
    The Ajax. 3s. 6d.

JUVENALIS SATIRAE, edited by G. A. SIMCOX, M.A., Fellow and Classical Lecturer of Queen's College, Oxford.
    Thirteen Satires. 3s. 6d.

THUCYDIDIS HISTORIA, edited by CHARLES BIGG, M.A., late Senior Student and Tutor of Christ Church, Oxford; Second Classical Master of Cheltenham College.
    Books I. and II. 6s.

DEMOSTHENIS ORATIONES PUBLICAE, edited by G. H. HESLOP, M.A., late Fellow and Assistant Tutor of Queen's College, Oxford; Head Master of St. Bees.
    The Olynthiacs. 3s.
    The Philippics. 2s. 6d.

ARISTOPHANIS COMOEDIAE, edited by W. C. GREEN, M.A., late Fellow of King's College, Cambridge; Assistant Master at Rugby School.
    The Acharnians and the Knights. 4s.
    The Clouds. 3s. 6d.
    The Wasps. 3s. 6d.

ISOCRATIS ORATIONES, edited by JOHN EDWIN SANDYS, B.A., Fellow and Tutor of St. John's College, Cambridge.
    Ad Demonicum et Panegyricus. 4s. 6d.

PERSII SATIRARUM LIBER, edited by A. PRETOR, M.A., of Trinity College, Cambridge; Classical Lecturer of Trinity Hall. 3s. 6d.

HOMERI ILIAS, edited by S. H. REYNOLDS, M.A., Fellow and Tutor of Brasenose College, Oxford.
    Books I. to XII. 6s.

TERENTII COMOEDIAE, edited by T. L. PAPILLON, M.A., Fellow of New College, Oxford, and late Fellow of Merton.
    Andria et Eunuchus. 4s. 6d.

www.ingramcontent.com/pod-product-compliance
Lightning Source LLC
Chambersburg PA
CBHW030424300426
44112CB00009B/837